Education Policy and Power-Sharing in Post-Conflict Societies

Giuditta Fontana

Education Policy and Power-Sharing in Post-Conflict Societies

Lebanon, Northern Ireland, and Macedonia

Giuditta Fontana
University of Birmingham
Birmingham, UK

ISBN 978-3-319-81038-6   ISBN 978-3-319-31426-6 (eBook)
DOI 10.1007/978-3-319-31426-6

© The Editor(s) (if applicable) and The Author(s) 2017
Softcover reprint of the hardcover 1st edition 2016
This work is subject to copyright. All rights are solely and exclusively licensed by the Publisher, whether the whole or part of the material is concerned, specifically the rights of translation, reprinting, reuse of illustrations, recitation, broadcasting, reproduction on microfilms or in any other physical way, and transmission or information storage and retrieval, electronic adaptation, computer software, or by similar or dissimilar methodology now known or hereafter developed.
The use of general descriptive names, registered names, trademarks, service marks, etc. in this publication does not imply, even in the absence of a specific statement, that such names are exempt from the relevant protective laws and regulations and therefore free for general use. The publisher, the authors and the editors are safe to assume that the advice and information in this book are believed to be true and accurate at the date of publication. Neither the publisher nor the authors or the editors give a warranty, express or implied, with respect to the material contained herein or for any errors or omissions that may have been made.

Cover illustration: © Jason Lindsey / Alamy Stock Photo

Printed on acid-free paper

This Palgrave Macmillan imprint is published by Springer Nature
The registered company is Springer International Publishing AG Switzerland

Acknowledgements

I am glad to be finally able to thank some of those who helped and supported me during the research for this book. First, I express my gratitude to my two academic mentors, Professor Michael Kerr and Professor Rory Miller, who pushed me towards increasingly ambitious projects and gave me infinite opportunities to learn from them. The valuable comments and advice of my PhD examiners, Professor Brendan O'Leary and Dr Germ Janmaat, also made it possible for me to turn my doctoral thesis into this book.

The financial contribution of King's College London School of Arts and Humanities, the Council for British Research in the Levant and the Sir Richard Stapley Educational Trust allowed me to spend extensive periods in Lebanon, Northern Ireland and Macedonia. There, I am deeply grateful to all my interviewees, who answered my questions, replied to all my follow-up emails and phone calls, gave me access to their writings and contacts, and often became precious intercultural interpreters.

Countless friends and colleagues have helped me and supported me during the research for this book. Some hosted me during my nomadic years, others read parts of my work, helped me with translations and suggested further sources. They all patiently listened to my intricate and evolving arguments and conclusions. I hope they enjoy the final product.

Finally, this work would not exist without my parents, Lanfranco and Marianna, who taught me that it is worth fighting for the things you love. Last but not least, I thank my husband Alessandro, the best *compagno di viaggio* I could hope for, and Leonardo, who is adding spice to my life and work.

Contents

1 **Introduction** — 1
  1.1 Hypotheses — 3
  1.2 Lebanon, Northern Ireland and Macedonia — 4
    1.2.1 Demography — 4
    1.2.2 The Three Conflicts — 9
    1.2.3 Peace Agreements: Consociations and Education Reforms — 10
  1.3 Methods — 12
  1.4 Chapter Structure — 13
  1.5 Contribution to Knowledge — 17

2 **Power-Sharing and Education Policy in Deeply Divided Societies** — 23
  2.1 Individual and Ethnic Identities — 24
    2.1.1 Social Identity Theory — 25
  2.2 Deeply Divided Societies and Violent Conflict — 27
    2.2.1 Identity-Based Conflict in Deeply Divided Societies — 28
    2.2.2 Group Identities and Violent Conflict — 29
  2.3 Conflict Resolution and Consociation — 30
    2.3.1 Establishment and Resilience of Consociations — 33
    2.3.2 Complex Consociations — 35
    2.3.3 The Consociational Paradox and Its Critiques — 36

viii CONTENTS

    2.4 Why Education?   39
        2.4.1 Schooling as Socialisation into a Myth-Symbol Complex   41
        2.4.2 Education as Socialisation into a Political Order   42
        2.4.3 Schools and Identity-Based Conflict   43
        2.4.4 From War to Peace   44
    2.5 Conclusion   48

3 Compulsory Education in Lebanon, Northern Ireland and Macedonia   61
    3.1 Lebanon   62
        3.1.1 French Mandate (1920–1943)   62
        3.1.2 National Pact (1943–1958)   65
        3.1.3 Compromises (1958–1974)   69
        3.1.4 Civil War (1975–1989)   72
        3.1.5 The Taif Agreement and Beyond (1990–Present)   74
    3.2 Northern Ireland   77
        3.2.1 Northern Ireland (1920–1947)   78
        3.2.2 Limited Reform (1947–1968)   81
        3.2.3 Troubles (1968–1998)   82
        3.2.4 The Belfast Agreement and Beyond (1998–Present)   86
    3.3 Macedonia   89
        3.3.1 As Part of Yugoslavia (1918–1989)   90
        3.3.2 Independent Macedonia (1991–2000)   98
        3.3.3 The Ohrid Agreement and Beyond (2001–Present)   102
    3.4 Conclusion   105

4 Reforming History Education   123
    4.1 History Education in Deeply Divided Societies: Theoretical Debates   124
    4.2 Lebanon   127
        4.2.1 Mission Impossible   128
        4.2.2 A State Secret   129
        4.2.3 Political Disagreement Versus Historical Events   132
        4.2.4 Fragmented Pasts   134
    4.3 Northern Ireland   136
        4.3.1 The 2005 Curriculum and Its Weaknesses   137
        4.3.2 An Escapable Connection?   139

	4.4	Macedonia	140
		4.4.1 A Proportional Curriculum	141
		4.4.2 We Are Not Touching History	144
	4.5	Conclusion	146
5	**Formulating Citizenship Education**		159
	5.1	Citizenship Education in Deeply Divided Societies: Theoretical Debates	160
	5.2	Lebanon	162
		5.2.1 Citizenship and Civic Education	163
		5.2.2 The Weaknesses of a Nationalist Civic Education	164
		5.2.3 Moral Preaching	167
	5.3	Northern Ireland	168
		5.3.1 Elusive Bird: EMU	169
		5.3.2 Formulating and Implementing Personal Development and Mutual Understanding and Local and Global Citizenship	170
		5.3.3 Still 'Patchy': The Limits of Personal Development and Mutual Understanding and Local and Global Citizenship	173
		5.3.4 Transformative, Not Prescriptive	175
	5.4	Macedonia	175
		5.4.1 Lost in the Curriculum: Civic Education	176
		5.4.2 The Strategy for Integrated Education	178
		5.4.3 Towards a Civic Culture	179
	5.5	Conclusion	180
6	**Languages of Instruction**		193
	6.1	Teaching Languages in Deeply Divided Societies: Theoretical Debates	194
	6.2	Lebanon	197
		6.2.1 Enrichment Bilingual Education	199
		6.2.2 Old and New Cleavages in Language Policy	201
		6.2.3 'Practicality Won over Principle'	202
	6.3	Northern Ireland	202
		6.3.1 Irish-Language Education: Not in the Cold Anymore	203
		6.3.2 Ulster-Scots: Cashing in the Cheque	206
		6.3.3 Parity of Languages	207

	6.4 Macedonia	207
	6.4.1 The Unintended Consequences of Increasing Access	208
	6.4.2 Corrective Measures	213
	6.4.3 Walking the Line	216
	6.5 Conclusion	217
7	**Inter-group Contact and Separation in Schools**	227
	7.1 Separate and Common Schools in Deeply Divided Societies: Theoretical Debates	228
	7.2 Lebanon	232
	7.2.1 Private versus Public?	233
	7.2.2 Sterilised Jars?	236
	7.2.3 A Communal Backyard	238
	7.3 Northern Ireland	238
	7.3.1 Facilitate and Encourage Integrated Education	241
	7.3.2 A Sterile Debate?	244
	7.3.3 Sharing	248
	7.3.4 Change in the Air?	251
	7.3.5 Less Divided but Not Less Diverse	253
	7.4 Macedonia	254
	7.4.1 Devolving Education	254
	7.4.2 Separating Education	256
	7.4.3 The Strategy for Integrated Education	259
	7.4.4 Permanent Coexistence	263
	7.5 Conclusion	264
8	**Conclusion: Separate to Unite**	279
	Bibliography	285
	Index	311

List of Figures

Fig. 1.1	Lebanese population by sect according to the 1932 census	5
Fig. 1.2	Northern Ireland's population by religious affiliation according to the 2011 census	7
Fig. 1.3	Northern Ireland's population by national identity according to the 2011 census	7
Fig. 1.4	Macedonia's population by ethnic affiliation according to the 2002 census	8
Fig. 1.5	Macedonia's population by religious affiliation according to the 2002 census	9
Fig. 6.1	Lebanese schools by language of instruction in 2010	200
Fig. 6.2	Number of primary and secondary school students in Irish-medium education between 2001 and 2013	204
Fig. 6.3	Percentage students by language of instruction in primary and lower secondary schools in Macedonia between 2000 and 2012	209
Fig. 6.4	Percentage students by language of instruction in upper secondary education in Macedonia between 2000 and 2012	210
Fig. 7.1	Distribution of schools by foundation year in Lebanon	233
Fig. 7.2	Lebanese schools by type in 2010	234
Fig. 7.3	Percentage students by type of school in Lebanon in 2010	235
Fig. 7.4	Primary school pupils by school type in Northern Ireland in 2012–2013	239
Fig. 7.5	Post-primary students by school type in Northern Ireland in 2012–2013	240
Fig. 7.6	Religion of primary school pupils by school type in Northern Ireland in 2012–2013	241

Fig. 7.7	Religion of secondary school students by school type in Northern Ireland in 2012–2013	242
Fig. 7.8	Number of students in integrated schools in Northern Ireland between 1981 and 2012	244
Fig. 7.9	Pupil enrolments by primary school type in Northern Ireland between 2000 and 2012	247
Fig. 7.10	Students by ethnic belonging and language of instruction in primary and lower secondary schools in Macedonia in 2011–2012	260

CHAPTER 1

Introduction

This study explores the political function of education in three deeply divided societies that experienced violent identity-based conflict: Lebanon, Northern Ireland and the Former Yugoslav Republic of Macedonia (hereafter, Macedonia). By examining debates over education reform, it investigates the contribution of compulsory schooling to the regulation of identity-based conflicts through consociational power-sharing.

An academic and policy consensus is emerging that consociational power-sharing is the most acceptable and effective constitutional mechanism for managing violent conflict in deeply divided societies. Consociations are characterised by group cleavages and elite decision-making by consensus and by four key constitutional provisions: executive power-sharing (or parity in executive participation), veto rights for community representatives, proportionality in elections or appointments, and communal autonomy.[1]

In Lebanon, Northern Ireland and Macedonia, three peace agreements (in 1989, 1998 and 2001, respectively) restructured or established consociations to regulate conflicts between hostile religious, national and ethnic groups. Lebanon's Document of National Accord (hereafter the Taif Agreement), Northern Ireland's Agreement Reached in the Multiparty Negotiations (hereafter the Belfast Agreement) and Macedonia's Framework Agreement (hereafter the Ohrid Agreement) also mapped extensive reforms of formal education. Schools, previously accused of contributing to mutual hostility by socialising children into separate worlds, were portrayed as instruments for peace-building. In the new consociations, schooling would further 'national belonging' and 'fusion',[2] develop a 'culture of tolerance'[3] and promote 'the peaceful and harmonious development of society'.[4]

What educational reforms were promoted and with what results in the following decades? What narratives of identity and belonging came to dominate the manifest and hidden curricula? Once the dust settled, did the three agreements, and the new patterns of power they institutionalised, fundamentally alter the political function of education in Lebanon, Northern Ireland and Macedonia? Ultimately, did consociations provide a political context conducive to the transformation of these religious, national and ethnic conflicts?

To address these questions, this study looks at reforms of the history, citizenship and language curricula and at attempts to promote inter-group contact in schools after the Taif, Belfast and Ohrid Agreements. It examines the dialectical relationship between education reforms, consociational principles and inter-group power hierarchies, to identify constraints and opportunities in compulsory schooling reform. Finally, it traces the political function of education in Lebanon, Northern Ireland and Macedonia to evaluate whether consociations, effective in ending violence, also offer an opportunity to promote the long-term resolution of ethnic, religious and national conflicts.

This work argues that despite a flurry of rhetoric in the immediate aftermath of the three peace agreements, education reforms consolidated rather than altered the political function of education in these three societies. Before and during the violent conflicts, schools helped socialise children into the separate and mutually exclusive identities associated with different ethnic, religious and national groups. After the peace agreements, schools continued to defy the maxim that 'in the field of public education, the doctrine of "separate but equal" has no place'.[5] To this day, compulsory education in the three consociations often conveys separate narratives of belonging through the curricula and frequently furthers the separation of children of different backgrounds into different schools. On the one hand, this sustains the integrity of ethnic, religious and national groups upon which a stable consociation rests, thereby contributing to short-term political and elite stability. On the other hand, in this educational landscape, external pressures and internal political crises frequently translate into politicised zero-sum debates over education and into the reproduction of mutually exclusive narratives of identity.

This study adds to the fields of comparative politics and comparative education. The long-standing debate over the scope for long-term conflict regulation through consociational power-sharing has generally overlooked non-political institutions, but McCrudden and O'Leary's work on domestic and international judiciaries signals a new interest in the contribution of such institutions to consociational stability and legitimacy.[6] Despite recognising that schools contribute to the sanctioning of collective identity, the comparative politics literature has stopped short of comparing education policy across multiple consociations. Through a comparison of the curricula and structures of compulsory education in Lebanon, Northern Ireland and Macedonia, this work shows that the narratives and values promoted by schools can help stabilise and legitimise consociations but can also accelerate a relapse into conflict.

Just as consociational research has overlooked the role of non-political institutions, research on education in post-conflict and divided societies has not confronted the relationship between constitutional arrangements and education policy.[7] In doing so, this study identifies a typology of consociational education systems, characterised by the tension between the protection of equally legitimate group identities and the promotion of overarching narratives. It also shows that consociational politics places crucial constraints on the design and implementation of education reforms.

1.1 Hypotheses

This study compares reforms of the curricula of history, citizenship education and languages as well as of the structure of education systems after peace agreements in Lebanon (1989), Northern Ireland (1998) and Macedonia (2001), to investigate the political function of formal education in consociations. It tests three hypotheses.

The first hypothesis is that education systems help reproduce the founding values and narratives of power-sharing, thereby contributing to the stability of consociational government. This analysis aims to highlight the extent to which the priorities and values underpinning education reform converge in the three consociations, and proposes a typology of consociational education systems. It also aims to show that the existing literature has underestimated the contribution of non-political institutions to the legitimacy and stability of consociational power-sharing.

The second hypothesis is that the success of specific education reforms depends on their compatibility with the values and hierarchies sustaining the political system. This comparison shows that reform initiatives are considerably constrained by consociational education systems and that they are successfully implemented and mainstreamed only when, alongside fostering overarching plural identities, they promote group equality. This explains the failure of efforts to integrate and homogenise the curricula and structures of schooling in the three societies, and initiates a debate on the most appropriate approaches to the design of education reforms in consociations.

The third hypothesis is that consociation per se is not incompatible with long-term conflict resolution. This study proposes that consociational governments can employ education to facilitate mutual knowledge and understanding and to help establish or re-establish peaceful, harmonious and interdependent relationships among the different communities in plural societies (reconciliation). A prime example is Northern Ireland's *shared education* initiatives.[8] Yet, it also finds that in periods of political instability, schools often convey mutually exclusive and hostile narratives of identity, hindering rather than furthering peace processes.

1.2 Lebanon, Northern Ireland and Macedonia

The most different systems design method of comparative research was employed to select Lebanon, Northern Ireland and Macedonia as the three case studies. This method is ideally suited to the aims of the present research: to generate novel hypotheses in a previously unexplored field and to discern patterns among few case studies. Lebanon, Northern Ireland and Macedonia are similar in two important respects: they experienced violent conflicts among religious, national and ethnic communities and established consociational power-sharing to regulate these conflicts. Still, a comparison of education policies across these three consociations is particularly interesting because of the similarities and differences in their demographic structure, their violent conflicts and their peace agreements.

1.2.1 Demography

Lebanon, Northern Ireland and Macedonia are heterogeneous societies and comprise several communities, which may be ' "peoples", "national groups", cultural groups, ethnic, religious or language groups'.[9] The three societies differ in the degree of diversity in their populations, in the most (politically) relevant markers of identity and group membership, and in

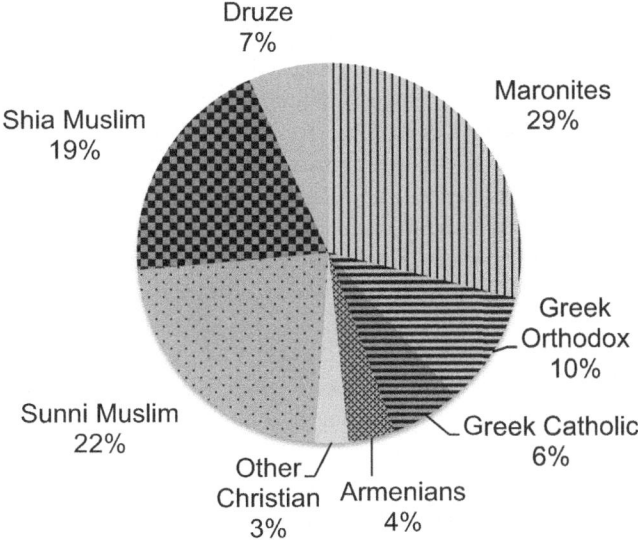

Fig. 1.1 Lebanese population by sect according to the 1932 census (Lebanese 1932 census, qtd. in Imad Salamey, *The government and politics of Lebanon* (London: Routledge, 2014): 25)

the political impact of demography. Moreover, Chap. 3, tracing the history of education in Lebanon, Northern Ireland and Macedonia, confirms that the most politically salient marker of identity in each society 'is the one that is perceived as being important from the point of view of the allocation of government resources'.[10]

Thus, religious affiliation emerged as the primary marker of communal belonging in Lebanon, where 18 official religious sects coexist. Religious sects in Lebanon largely determine 'identity, social position and political power', so they are functionally similar to ethnic, national and racial groups elsewhere.[11] Chapter 3 explains that religious belonging has also been historically associated with diverging national outlooks, political ideologies and foreign affiliations, and has competed with important integrative factors, such as the overwhelming prevalence of the Arabic language as a mother tongue. The last official census was conducted in 1932 and, as Fig. 1.1 shows, found a slight majority of Christians (Maronites, Greek Orthodox, Greek Catholics, Armenians and Other Christians) over Muslims (Sunni, Shia and Druze).

The confessional political system of independent Lebanon overestimated the Christian population and assigned parliamentary seats according to a ratio of six Christians for every five Muslims. The posts of president, prime minister and speaker of the parliament were allocated to individuals belonging to the three largest religious sects: a Maronite, a Sunni and a Shia, respectively. Due to the destabilising political impact of demographic change, no census has been conducted since 1932, and successive waves of refugees have been marginalised in economic life and excluded from political participation. Thus, Sawsan and Khawaja present the substantial Palestinian refugee population as Lebanon's 'unrecognised sect', a group lacking political representation despite its considerable demographic weight.[12]

The constitutional reforms agreed after the 1975–1989 civil war acknowledge demographic change and a new balance of power among local communities: they assign equal numbers of parliamentary seats to Christians and Muslims as well as to the Sunni and Shia. In fact, electoral results suggest that the Christian Maronites may only account for 19 % of the total Lebanese population, the Sunni Muslims for only 21 % and the Shia Muslims for over 34 %.[13]

Thus, the distribution of parliamentary seats does not reflect the relative demographic strength of Lebanon's communities: it grants Christians a political influence disproportionate to their demographic weight and lessens the political relevance of Shia Muslims, thereby fuelling the Sunni-Shia resentments which, since 2005, have 'replaced the civil war's Muslim-Christian divide'.[14]

Similarly, Connolly and Maginn point to the 'apparently contradictory fact that you can be a "Protestant" or a "Catholic" in Northern Ireland while also being an agnostic or an atheist'.[15] As Chap. 3 explains, the political saliency of religious identities in Northern Ireland is due to their coincidence with national belonging and with aspirations for the constitutional future. Northern Ireland is less religiously diverse than Lebanon, with only two major Christian denominations: Protestants account for about 42 % and Catholics for about 40 % of the population (Fig. 1.2).

Chapter 3 explains that Catholics historically viewed themselves as Irish and called for a united and independent Ireland, while Protestants privileged British nationality and sought to preserve the union of Northern Ireland with Great Britain. In fact, the 2011 census questions this dichotomy: as Fig. 1.3 shows, in 2011, 40 % of the population viewed themselves as British, 21 % as Northern Irish and only 25 % as Irish. This confirms

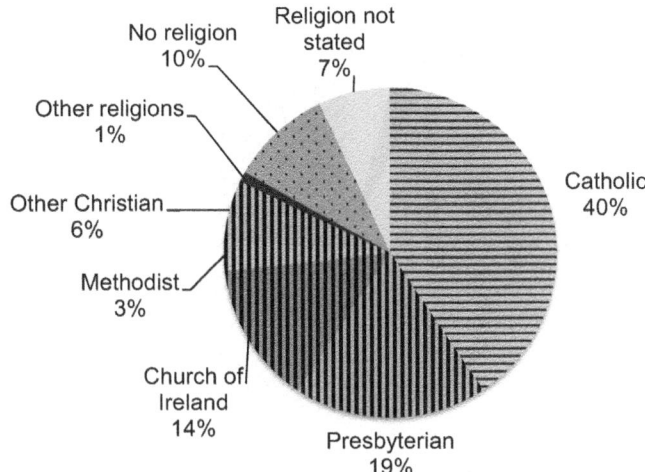

Fig. 1.2 Northern Ireland's population by religious affiliation according to the 2011 census ('Religion – full detail_QS218NI' Northern Ireland statistics & research agency, *Census 2011*, http://www.ninis2.nisra.gov.uk/public/Theme.aspx?themeNumber=136&themeName=Census%202011)

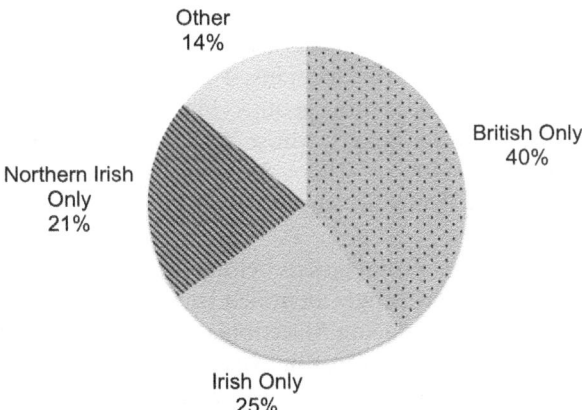

Fig. 1.3 Northern Ireland's population by national identity according to the 2011 census ('National Identity - Full Detail_QS205NI' Northern Ireland Statistics & Research Agency, Census 2011, http://www.ninis2.nisra.gov.uk/public/Theme.aspx?themeNumber=136&themeName=Census%202011)

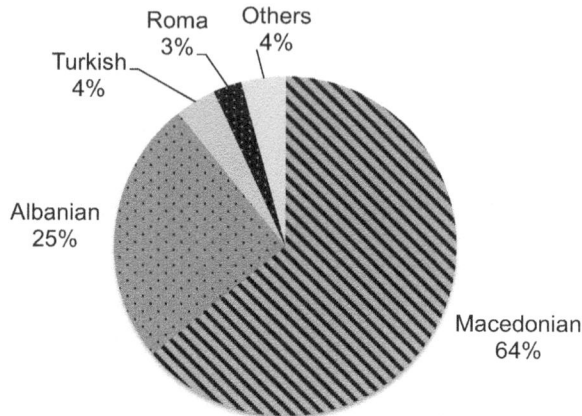

Fig. 1.4 Macedonia's population by ethnic affiliation according to the 2002 census (State Statistical Office, *Census of population, households and dwellings 2002. Book X: Total population according to ethnic affiliation, mother tongue and religion* (Skopje: State Statistical Office, 2002): 62)

that a considerable number of Catholics do not hold an exclusively Irish national identity.

Macedonia is diverse in terms of its ethnic belonging and mother tongue. In 2002, ethnic Macedonians accounted for only 64 % of the population, with a further 25 % of Albanians, 4 % of Turks, 3 % of Romas and smaller percentages of other ethnic groups (Fig. 1.4). Ethnic Macedonians speak the Macedonian language, whose genesis was inextricably linked to the creation of a state, as Chap. 3 shows. The mother tongues of Albanians, Turks and Roma are the Albanian, Turkish and Romani languages, respectively.

Ethnicity also overlaps with religious belonging, and since the late 1990s, political discourse has increasingly identified Islam with being Albanian and Orthodox Christianity with being Macedonian. As Fig. 1.5 shows, in 2001 the majority of Macedonia's population was Orthodox Christian or Muslim (primarily Sunni). As in Lebanon, no census could be conducted since 2002 because of the politicisation of demographic figures.

A comparison of the demographic structures of Lebanon, Northern Ireland and Macedonia confirms that they are three deeply divided societies: among their indigenous populations, demographic and identity cleavages coincide, local communities claim separate descent and often

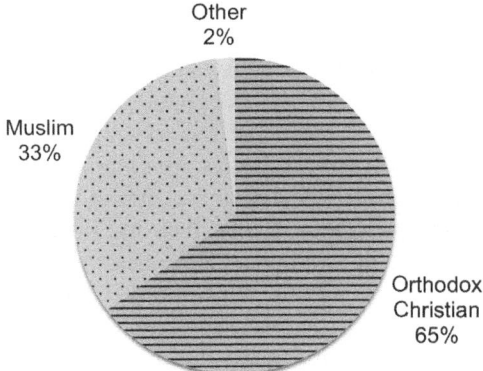

Fig. 1.5 Macedonia's population by religious affiliation according to the 2002 census (ibid., 334)

'coexist in parallel rather than live together'.[16] While the existence of deep communal fractures is not sufficient 'for the aggregation of interests',[17] in the three societies, 'most political parties mobilise along ethno-national lines'.[18] However, in all three societies multiple political parties compete for the votes of members of each ethnic, confessional and national community. Moreover, overarching interests and cross-cutting political cleavages exist in all three societies. Most apparently, Hanf found that most Lebanese hold a desire for peaceful coexistence and a perception of collective interests above those of different communities.[19]

1.2.2 The Three Conflicts

McCrudden and O'Leary reflect that 'one person's "national" conflict may be another's "ethnic" conflict and in conflicts of these kinds, there may indeed be a "meta-conflict" – that is, a conflict about what the conflict is about'.[20] This is certainly the case for the three, deeply different conflicts in Lebanon, Northern Ireland and Macedonia.

Chapter 3 explains in more detail the origins and course of the Lebanese civil war, the Northern Irish Troubles and the 2001 ethnic conflict in Macedonia. The Lebanese civil war claimed between 100,000 and 140,000 lives in its 15 years of fighting (1975–1989).[21] The Troubles, lasting three decades (1968–1998), claimed 3,488 lives.[22] In contrast, the ethnic conflict in Macedonia lasted about seven months (February–

August 2001) and involved mainly paramilitaries and state security forces. The conflict led to 150–200 deaths and 650 wounded and about 7 % of the population of Macedonia was displaced during this period.[23]

The three conflicts differed in their scale and duration, in the number of competing groups involved and in the relationship between these groups and the institutions of each state. But they are comparable as identity-based conflicts that set local religious, national and ethnic groups in competition for recognition and influence over the borders and institutions of contested states. This is why formal education was at the heart of each violent conflict: for decades, schools legitimised and reproduced the prevailing power hierarchies and identity-forming narratives, as Chap. 3 shows.

Finally, the three conflicts impacted the majority of the population in Lebanon, Northern Ireland and Macedonia either directly or indirectly, by furthering residential and social separation, and increasing cultural polarisation. Lebanon differs from Northern Ireland and Macedonia, in that, as Hanf argues, 'the Lebanese had an independent state but they became a nation only [in the 1980s] when the state was in mortal danger'.[24] The embryonic 'territorial' Lebanese identity born out of the civil war may explain the resilience of the state and society when faced with the powerful centrifugal pressures unleashed by the Syrian withdrawal in 2005, the Arab Spring in 2011 and the Syrian civil war.

1.2.3 Peace Agreements: Consociations and Education Reforms

The Taif, Belfast and Ohrid Agreements re-established or established consociational power-sharing to regulate the violent conflicts in Lebanon, Northern Ireland and Macedonia. Evoking the 1943 Lebanese National Pact, the 1973 Sunningdale Agreement and the 1974 Yugoslav Constitution, these peace agreements established the four core features of consociations: executive power-sharing, communal autonomy, proportional representation and mutual veto rights. Through these institutions, all three agreements attempted to 'recognise the cleavages explicitly and turn them into constructive elements of stable democracy'.[25]

Chapter 2 explores theoretical and policy debates over the structure and long-term impact of consociations in more detail. The consociations established in Lebanon, Northern Ireland and Macedonia differ in their degree of liberalism. Macedonia closely approximates an ideal liberal consociation, which 'rewards whatever salient political identities emerge in democratic elections'.[26] In contrast, Lebanon approximates a corporate consociation because it accommodates communities according to predetermined, ascriptive identities (religious in this case) and assumes the permanence and internal homogeneity of groups.[27] The variance of case studies along the liberal-corporate spectrum makes the findings of this research more widely applicable.

The three consociations are similar, in that they are 'complex consociations' which rely on 'at least one other conflict-regulating strategy or principle [beyond consociational power-sharing] in their design'.[28] As Chaps. 2 and 3 show, the Ohrid and Belfast Agreements map territorial autonomy and decentralisation, while the Taif Agreement envisages measures for transition to majoritarian democracy and social integration, most evidently through education reform.

The fact that the peace agreements in question present education reforms as instruments for long-term peace-building and reconciliation, illustrates that schools were perceived as having contributed to violent conflict in Lebanon, Northern Ireland and Macedonia. The Taif Agreement calls for the protection of private institutions, the extension of state control over all schools, the reform of national curricula and the production of unified textbooks for history and civic education.[29] These provisions aimed to encourage 'feelings of unity among citizens and the development of notions of solidarity and fraternity' as well as to 'consolidate the process of national cohesion'.[30]

In contrast, the Belfast Agreement does not provide details for future education reforms, only calling for the promotion of the Irish language and 'initiatives to facilitate and encourage integrated education'.[31] This work confirms that, as McGarry and O'Leary suggest, this is largely because even prior to 1998, Northern Ireland's education system conformed to 'consociational' principles: it allowed choice between Catholic maintained, state controlled (mainly Protestant) and integrated schools, all of which received equal funding.[32]

Finally, the Albanian insurgency during the 2001 conflict in Macedonia demanded expansion of mother tongue education and state funding for the Albanian-language Tetovo University. Accordingly, the Ohrid Agreement granted official funding to universities teaching in languages spoken by at least 20 % of the population (the Macedonian and Albanian languages). It also guaranteed the rights to compulsory education in the mother tongue and to learning the official state language (Macedonian).[33]

In sum, the Taif, Belfast and Ohrid Agreements present education reform as a tool for long-term peace-building through amendments of the history education and civic education curricula (in Lebanon), changes in the languages of instruction (in Northern Ireland and Macedonia) and promotion of contact between children of different backgrounds in schools (in Lebanon and Northern Ireland). This suggests that education reform may be a mechanism complementary to constitutional reforms in post-conflict complex consociations. This study analyses the four education reforms mapped in the peace agreements (history education, citizenship education, languages and the structure of the education system) to discern common and diverging approaches to schools in consociations.

1.3 Methods

This work investigates the political function of education in consociations through primarily qualitative methods. The analysis is based on over 75 semi-structured interviews carried out in the course of research visits to Lebanon, Northern Ireland and Macedonia. The interviewees were key politicians, policymakers, representatives of monitoring agencies and educational practitioners from a variety of ethnic, national and religious backgrounds and representing different political opinions. Most interviewees, in the course of their career, had worked in (or consulted for) the main centres of educational policymaking, including the local education ministries. The interview questions focused on the benefits and shortcomings of initiatives for the reform of history education, citizenship education, the language of instruction and the structure of the education system since the Taif, Belfast and Ohrid Agreements. More broadly, the interviews explored the intended and unintended sociopolitical consequences of education reforms, with particular reference to their impact on peace-building and reconciliation. Qualitative analysis also relied on curricular and textbook material, government papers, official reports, case-specific literature, newspaper articles and a variety of other primary and secondary sources.

Quantitative methods were used to compare and evaluate statistical data and surveys. Government and international databases were employed to collect data on school enrolments, on the implementation of education reforms and on the ethnic, national and religious composition of the school population in Lebanon, Northern Ireland and Macedonia. Finally, surveys carried out by national and international organisations (such as the United Nations Development Programme [UNDP] and the Organization for Security and Co-operation in Europe [OSCE]) provided estimates of public support for specific reforms and of the long-term sociopolitical impact of certain education initiatives.

There is considerable agreement that schools are one of the few 'institution[s] that society can formally, intentionally and extensively use to achieve the mission of peace education'[34] or employ to reproduce the practices and narratives at the heart of conflict. To highlight the educational priorities of successive consociational governments in Lebanon, Northern Ireland and Macedonia, this work looks only at schools that adopt the official curriculum and/or receive some form of state subsidy. These institutions are most receptive to reform initiatives and, as Chap. 3 shows, they represent the overwhelming majority of schools in the three societies.

This analysis focuses on compulsory schooling because most children experience it during the most sensitive years for their socialisation into group values and identity (around 12 years of age).[35] About 97 % of Lebanese children attend primary education and 76 % attend secondary school[36]; about 95 % of children in Macedonia attend the compulsory, nine-year primary school[37]; and about 99 % of children in Northern Ireland attend compulsory education.[38]

Finally, decision-making regarding curricular content and the basic structures of compulsory education is centralised in Beirut, Belfast and Skopje and this greatly facilitates comparative analysis of education reform.[39] Indeed, this work frequently treats Northern Ireland as a separate state for analytical purposes: despite being part of the UK, policymakers, even during direct rule, had considerable autonomy in the design of reforms, and education was regulated by separate legislation.

1.4 Chapter Structure

This introduction explains the rationale for this study, presents its hypotheses and introduces the three case studies: Lebanon, Northern Ireland and Macedonia. It also summarises the research methods, chapter structure and theoretical contribution to the fields of conflict regulation and education studies.

Chapter 2 provides an overview of the academic literature on conflict regulation through consociational power-sharing and on the relationship between formal education and violent ethnic, religious and national conflicts. It aims to situate this study in the context of the most relevant academic and policy debates.

Chapter 3 traces the history of education as an instrument for the building of nation-states and for the reproduction of communal identities in Lebanon and Northern Ireland since 1920, and in Macedonia since 1918. It proposes that, before and during the three conflicts, school curricula and structures contributed to perpetuating the narratives, values and practices that fed inter-group animosity. The Taif, Belfast and Ohrid Agreements did not fundamentally alter the political function of education and the political priorities for education reform. Actually, the four aspects of schooling they tackled (history education, civic education, languages and contact between pupils of different backgrounds) reflect both the most politically salient markers of group identity and the dominant perceptions of the roots of violent conflict.

Chaps 4, 5, 6 and 7 focus on history education, civic education, languages and the promotion of contact between children of different backgrounds in compulsory schools. They first provide brief reviews of the literature and then analyse comparatively the debates over reform of each aspect of education in consociational Lebanon, Northern Ireland and Macedonia. Chapter 4 focuses on reform of history education and finds that debates in the three societies reflect tensions between the two ideal functions of history: to promote unity among the diverse citizenry and/or to reflect, acknowledge and value the historical narratives of each religious, ethnic and national community. Tracing debates over reform of the history curricula in the three consociations, Chap. 4 suggests that the founding principles and practices of the political system impact on the contents of history education. In Lebanon, the involvement of politicians representing each community in the process of curriculum drafting set the stage for the failure of efforts to frame a unified, homogeneous and nationalistic history textbook. In Macedonia, the founding principle of proportionality seeped into the curriculum: information about the history of each ethnic community is proportional to its demographic weight. Finally, the Northern Ireland history curriculum focuses on historical skills rather than narratives, thus attempting to decouple history and national identity. In all three cases, the teaching of history in schools appears to reflect, and in some perspectives further, continuing communal monopolies over narratives of the past.[40]

Similarly, lack of consensus about national identity and the legitimacy of the state problematises the definition of citizenship in the three societies. Chapter 5 explores reforms of citizenship education after the three peace agreements and argues that, similar to history education, the citizenship education curricula are torn between the ambition to legitimise communal diversity and the desire to foster allegiance to the state. In Northern Ireland, a flexible curriculum aims to stimulate, through debate and critical thinking, the formulation of consensual notions of citizenship. In contrast, in Lebanon and Macedonia, the curricula promote overarching 'national' identities and teach majoritarian democracy. Thus, the contents of education clash with the reality of consociational politics and with the political saliency of ethnic and religious identities. The chapter proposes that schools contribute to inter-group tensions and mistrust of state institutions when they convey values and principles incongruent with the dominant practices of wider politics and society.

Chapter 6 draws attention to a further constraint to education reform in consociations: the need to ensure their symmetrical impact on all the major communities. It does so by tracing initiatives to reform the language(s) of instruction in the three education systems. In Lebanon, the end of the civil war brought a consensus on the benefits of multilingual education. In contrast, in Northern Ireland, language is being politically constructed as a further marker of identity, coinciding with salient national and religious cleavages: Irish-medium schools are instrumental to this process. Similarly, in Macedonia the expansion of mother tongue education led to the physical separation of children belonging to different communities into different schools. State initiatives to introduce the Macedonian language from the first grade aimed to reverse the trend of declining proficiency in the state language among children of Albanian, Turkish and Serbian backgrounds. These initiatives were bitterly opposed, and denounced as attempts to assimilate children into ethnic Macedonian culture.

This echoes debates over the reform of the very structure of education systems in Lebanon, Northern Ireland and Macedonia, examined in Chap. 7. The Taif and Belfast Agreements called for more opportunities for contact among children belonging to different socio-economic, religious, ethnic and national backgrounds. Similar to Macedonia's 2010 Strategy for Integrated Education, they implicitly endorsed the 'contact hypothesis', which states that inter-group contact furthers tolerance, reduces fear and promotes reconciliation in post-conflict societies. In fact, Chap. 7 proposes that the three consociations ultimately generated or entrenched consociational education systems, which rely on a plurality of separate institutions catering to different communities rather than on common, mixed schools. Separate schools subsidised by the state may help individual social mobility, demonstrate group influence over state institutions, and even legitimise the state among formerly marginalised communities when they are endowed with equal resources. Separate schools also reproduce the basic building blocks of the political system (the different religious, ethnic, national and political communities), thereby furthering the stability and legitimacy of consociational governments. Yet, Chap. 7 warns that the physical separation of children can further prejudice political extremism and fear of members of different communities. Thus, separate schools can hinder reconciliation. Finally, it points out that separate schools are rarely equal, despite the allocation of ostensibly equal resources. Most institutions are deeply different and provide different long-term opportunities: this may foster feelings of relative deprivation among the members of disadvantaged communities and destabilise peace processes. Chapter 7 also argues that 'consociational education systems' are not incompatible with initiatives for mixed education, which may contribute to the emergence of syncretistic identities and to the consolidation of peace. To succeed, initiatives for inter-group contact need to promote both group equality and relationship building, to hold broad institutional support, to be tailored to the specific sociopolitical context and to impact symmetrically on the communities involved.

This study concludes first, that the political function of education in consociations is remarkably similar to that of education during conflicts: it socialises children into different group identities and political allegiances through the curricula and separate schools. 'Consociational education systems' reproduce group boundaries and consolidate the different political communities, thus legitimising consociational government and facilitating its operation.

Second, the priorities for education reform in Lebanon, Northern Ireland and Macedonia converge after the establishment of consociational power-sharing. Consociational education systems come to reflect the tension between two political principles: the fostering of group equality and the encouragement of overarching plural identities. They do so both through the curricula for 'national subjects' and through the structure of the education system.

Third, education reform cannot change society but it can make schools flexible enough to accommodate and even encourage social change if and when it occurs. In the three consociations, education reforms succeeded when they promoted values congruent with those of the political system and when they impacted similarly on all the main communities.

This suggests that the imposition of unified narratives of identity and the top-down integration of schools may be inadequate and even counterproductive in deeply divided societies.

Finally, this study concludes that consociation per se is not incompatible with initiatives for conflict transformation. Consociation provides the political and social stability essential for the formulation, promotion and implementation of initiatives for peace-building in the education system. In turn, education can be employed as a complementary mechanism to further the long-term resolution of violent inter-group conflicts. Yet, the cases of Lebanon and Macedonia show that when they are internally unstable or subject to negative external pressures, consociations allow for curricula which convey mutually exclusive narratives of identity and for the physical separation of children belonging to different communities. This contributes to the long-term vulnerability of the system and the potential for relapse into violent conflict.

1.5   CONTRIBUTION TO KNOWLEDGE

This study aims to contribute to the academic debate on conflict regulation through consociational power-sharing. It looks at how formal education furthers the stability and legitimacy of consociations, thus redressing past consociational focus on 'political (executive and legislative) issues'.[41] By examining the curricula and structures of education systems, it adds an internal factor to the list of variables facilitating the persistence of consociations and their re-establishment after conflicts: the coherence between state values and the values conveyed by schools.

This work also elaborates on the education system as an instrument for conflict transformation and long-term reconciliation in deeply divided societies. Advocates of consociation admit that communities tend to further separate after the establishment of power-sharing, but argue that the stability and legitimacy provided by consociation may facilitate conflict resolution and the emergence of overarching identities.[42] Critics point out that conflict resolution is not an endogenous outcome of constitutional reforms, but should be consciously pursued through, for example, initiatives for social integration.[43] Recent conceptualisations of the practice of 'complex consociation' bridge these two positions and propose mechanisms to encourage long-term conflict resolution within a consociational framework.[44] Yet they overlook the potential contribution of non-political institutions, such as schools, to stability and long-term conflict management. This is surprising, as consociational agreements, such as the Taif, Belfast and Ohrid Agreements, often present education as an instrument for long-term peace-building. Accordingly, education reforms can facilitate the transition from a conflict to a post-conflict society. This study opens a debate on the most effective approaches to education reform in post-conflict consociations.

As far as the specific literature on education for peace is concerned, this is the first study of the reform of structures and curricula in the compulsory education systems of three consociations. It finds that political and constitutional structures influence formal education: consociations generate consociational education systems, which reflect the tension between pluralism and parity of esteem at the heart of power-sharing. This study proposes that successful initiatives for education reform generally acknowledge and accommodate both the fostering of group equality and the promotion of overarching allegiances. Thus, it provides valuable insights on the factors constraining the formulation and implementation of education reforms in these three societies, and in deeply divided societies more generally.

NOTES

1. Brendan O'Leary, 'Debating Consociational Politics: Normative and Explanatory Arguments,' in S. Noel (ed.), *From Power Sharing to Democracy* (Quebec: McGill University Press, 2005): 35; Michael Kerr, *Imposing Power-Sharing: Conflict and Coexistence in Northern Ireland and Lebanon* (Dublin: Irish Academic Press, 2005): 31; Arend Lijphart, *Democracy in Plural Societies* (London: Yale University Press, 1977): 5.
2. Part III, Section F, Art.5, *Taif Agreement*.
3. Rights, Safeguards and Equality of Opportunity, Reconciliation and Victims of Violence, Art.13, *Belfast Agreement*.
4. Preamble, *Ohrid Agreement*.
5. Chief Justice Warren, qtd. in Luther A. Huston, 'High Court Bans School Segregation. 9-to-0 Decision Grants Time to Comply' *New York Times*, 18/05/1954.
6. John McGarry and Brendan O'Leary, 'Power Shared after the Deaths of Thousands,' in Rupert Taylor (ed.), *Consociational Theory: McGarry and O'Leary and the Northern Ireland Conflict* (London: Routledge, 2009): 25; Christopher McCrudden and Brendan O'Leary, *Courts and Consociations. Human Rights Versus Power-Sharing* (Oxford: Oxford University Press, 2013).

7. Marc Howard Ross, 'Peace Education and Political Science,' in Gavriel Salomon and Edward Cairns (eds.), *Handbook on Peace Education* (New York: Psychology Press, 2009), 121.
8. See Chap. 7.
9. Theodor Hanf, *Coexistence in Wartime Lebanon. Decline of a State and Rise of a Nation* (London: IB Tauris, 1994): 21.
10. Frances Stewart, *Religion Versus Ethnicity as a Source of Mobilisation: Are There Differences?*, Microcon Research Working Paper 18 (Brighton: MICROCON, 2009): 44.
11. Abdulrahim Sawsan and Marwan Khawaja, 'The Cost of Being Palestinian in Lebanon,' *Journal of Ethnic and Migration Studies* 37, no. 1 (2011): 153.
12. This is despite the religious and political differences among Palestinians in Lebanon. Sawsan and Khawaja, 'The Cost of Being Palestinian,' 155.
13. The figure is based on electoral results, Muhammad Faour, 'Religion, Demography, and Politics', 912; A competing estimate, based on the number of registered voters by religious sect, is provided in Imad Salamey and Rhys Payne, 'Parliamentary Consociationalism in Lebanon: Equal Citizenry vs Quotated Confessionalism', *The Journal of Legislative Studies* 14, no.4 (2008): 457.
14. Are Knudsen and Michael Kerr, 'Introduction. The Cedar Revolution and Beyond' in Are Knudsen and Michael Kerr (eds.), *Lebanon after the Cedar Revolution*, (London: Hurst, 2013): 5.
15. Paul Connolly and Paul Maginn, *Sectarianism, Children and Community Relations in Northern Ireland* (Coleraine: University of Ulster, 1999): 7.
16. International Crisis Group, *Macedonia: Make or Break* (Brussels: International Crisis Group, 2004): 4.
17. Theodor Hanf, 'The Sacred Marker. Religion, Communalism and Nationalism,' in Theodor Hanf (ed.), *Dealing with Difference. Religion, Ethnicity and Politics: Comparing Cases and Concepts* (Baden-Baden: Nomos, 1999): 386.
18. John Nagle and Mary-Alice Clancy, *Shared Society or Benign Apartheid? Understanding Peace-Building in Divided Societies* (London: Palgrave, 2010): 7.
19. Hanf, *Coexistence*, 34.
20. McCrudden and O'Leary, *Courts and Consociations*, 127.
21. Samir Makdisi and Richard Sadaka, 'The Lebanese Civil War,' paper presented at the *Yale-World Bank Workshop on 'Case Studies on the Economics and Politics of Civil War*,' April 13–14, 2002, Yale University, 2003, 23; Knudsen and Kerr, 'Introduction', in Knudsen and Kerr (eds.), *Lebanon after the Cedar Revolution*, 39.
22. Between 14/07/1969 and 31/12/1998 according to Malcolm Sutton, 'An Index of Deaths from the Conflict in Ireland', *CAIN Web Service*

http://cain.ulst.ac.uk/sutton/tables/Status_Summary.html (accessed 20/02/2014).
23. Sasho Ripiloski, *Conflict in Macedonia. Exploring a Paradox in the Former Yugoslavia* (London: First Forum Press, 2011): 100–101.
24. Hanf, *Coexistence*, 642.
25. Andrew Finlay, *Governing Ethnic Conflict. Consociation, Identity and the Price of Peace* (London: Routledge, 2010): 60.
26. Stefan Wolff, 'Liberal Consociationalism in Theory and Practice: Power Sharing and Territorial Self-Governance,' *Unpublished Research Paper*, 2011, http://www.stefanwolff.com/files/LibConTalkPaper.pdf: 4; Brendan O'Leary, 'Foreword: The Realism of Power-Sharing,' in Kerr, *Imposing Power-Sharing*, xxv.
27. Wolff, 'Liberal Consociationalism', 4; O'Leary, 'Foreword,' in Kerr, *Imposing Power-Sharing*, xxv. The Taif Agreement envisaged 'abolishing political sectarianism' but this provision was never implemented.
28. O'Leary, 'Debating Consociational Politics', in Noel, (ed.), *From Power Sharing*, 34–35; see also Stefan Wolff and Karl Cordell, 'Power Sharing,' in Karl Cordell and Stefan Wolff (eds.), *Routledge Handbook of Ethnic Conflict*, (London: Routledge, 2010): 307.
29. Part III, Section F, *Taif Agreement*.
30. International Bureau of Education, *World Data on Education, Sixth Edition* (Geneva: UNESCO, 2007): 34, 32.
31. Rights, Safeguards and Equality of Opportunity, Economic, Social and Cultural Issues, Art.4, and Reconciliation and Victims of Violence, Art.13, *Belfast Agreement*; The St Andrews Agreement adds the promotion of the Ulster Scots vernacular, *Northern Ireland (St Andrews Agreement) Act 2006*, (22/11/2006) http://www.legislation.gov.uk/ukpga/2006/53/contents/enacted: 16.
32. John McGarry and Brendan O'Leary, 'Consociational Theory, Northern Ireland's Conflict, and Its Agreement Part 2. What Critics of Consociation Can Learn from Northern Ireland,' *Government and Opposition* 41, no. 2 (2006): 275; Arend Lijphart, 'The Framework Document on Northern Ireland and the Theory of Power-Sharing,' *Government and Opposition* 31, no. 3 (1996): 272.
33. Art.6.2, *Ohrid Agreement*.
34. Daniel Bar-Tal, 'Peace Education in Societies Involved in Intractable Conflict. Goals, Conditions and Directions.,' in Salomon and Cairns (eds.), *Handbook on Peace Education*, 24.
35. George Eaton Simpson and J. Milton Yinger, *Racial and Cultural Minorities: An Analysis of Prejudice and Discrimination* (New York; London: Plenum, 1985): 157; Louis Oppenheimer, 'Contributions of Developmental Psychology to Peace Education,' in Salomon and Cairns

(eds.), *Handbook on Peace Education*, 106–107; Connolly and Maginn, *Sectarianism*, 15. Marc Hooge, Britt Wilkenfeld, 'The Stability of Political Attitudes and Behaviors across Adolescence and Early Adulthood: A Comparison of Survey Data on Adolescents and Young Adults in Eight Countries' *Journal of Youth and Adolescence*, 37 (2008).
36. United Nations International Children's Emergency Fund, *At a Glance: Lebanon*, http://www.unicef.org/infobycountry/lebanon_statistics.html
37. 'The Former Yugoslav Republic of Macedonia', in International Bureau of Education, *World Data on Education, Seventh Edition 2010/2011* (Geneva: UNESCO, 2011): 14.
38. Data produced by an officer in the Statistics and Research Branch, Department of Education Northern Ireland and provided through personal correspondence with the author (22/05/2014).
39. Macedonia is currently implementing limited administrative decentralisation, devolving implementation of central decisions to municipalities, as explained in Chap. 7.
40. Alison Kitson, 'History Teaching and Reconciliation in Northern Ireland,' in Elizabeth A. Cole, *Teaching the Violent Past. History Education and Reconciliation*, (Plymouth: Rowman and Littlefield Publishers, 2007): 124.
41. John McGarry and Brendan O'Leary, *The Northern Ireland Conflict. Consociational Engagements* (Oxford: Oxford University Press, 2004): 13.
42. Lijphart, *Democracy*, 88; McGarry and O'Leary, 'Consociational Theory, Northern Ireland's Conflict, and Its Agreement Part 2,' 256.
43. John McGarry, 'Introduction: The Comparable Northern Ireland,' in John McGarry (ed), *Northern Ireland and the Divided World. Post-Agreement Northern Ireland in Comparative Perspective* (London: Routledge, 2001): 17; Rupert Taylor, 'Northern Ireland: Consociation or Social Transformation?,' in McGarry (ed), *Northern Ireland and the Divided World*, 38; McGarry and O'Leary, 'Consociational Theory, Northern Ireland's Conflict, and Its Agreement Part 2,' 251.
44. Wolff and Cordell, 'Power Sharing,' 307.

CHAPTER 2

Power-Sharing and Education Policy in Deeply Divided Societies

This study investigates the political function of compulsory education in deeply divided societies and its relationship to consociational political systems. It does so by comparing debates over education reforms after peace agreements in Lebanon (1989), Northern Ireland (1998) and Macedonia (2001). Before looking at the three case studies, it is necessary to outline the theoretical rationale for this research.

This chapter examines first the theoretical approaches to the study of individual and group identities in deeply divided societies emerging from violent conflicts. Second, it explores current debates on conflict regulation: it considers consociational approaches to the management of ethnic, national and religious conflicts and refers to specific features of Lebanon, Northern Ireland and Macedonia to illustrate the benefits and shortcomings of consociation. Finally, it introduces the debate over the social and political functions of education and over the contributions of schools to war and peace.

This chapter situates the study in its appropriate theoretical context and demonstrates that the comparative analysis of education policy in consociations can contribute both to theories of conflict regulation and to theories of peace education.

© The Editor(s) (if applicable) and The Author(s) 2017
G. Fontana, *Education Policy and Power-Sharing in Post-Conflict Societies*, DOI 10.1007/978-3-319-31426-6_2

2.1 Individual and Ethnic Identities

While ethnicity may appear as an ascriptive characteristic acquired at birth by every individual, many of its constitutive elements are voluntaristic, and individuals have some choice in their degree of identification with ethnic groups.[1] Smith argues that ethnic groups are characterised by a common name, myth of common ancestry, elements of a common culture (such as religion or language), shared historical memories (often informed by religious myths), link to a territory or homeland and a sense of solidarity.[2] As Chap. 3 explains, local religious, national and linguistic communities in Lebanon, Northern Ireland and Macedonia meet Smith's criteria and can be considered ethnic groups. When ethnic groups demand sovereignty over a territory, as in the case of certain communities in Northern Ireland and Macedonia, they can be considered ethnonational.[3]

According to Smith, the sum of accepted historical narratives (a common past generally linked to a homeland), markers of identity (both physical and immaterial features) and exemplary heroes and enemies (or stereotypes) constitutes a 'myth-symbol complex'.[4] Myth-symbol complexes endow ethnic groups with 'an aura of primordiality, of being a natural entity, of having always been there'.[5] In fact, the markers and boundaries between communities in deeply divided societies are socially constructed and reproduced in a context where individual identities are 'multiple, nested and overlapping'.[6] Yet, Chap. 3 shows that markers of identity and community boundaries are 'deeply constructed', making their change slow and painful.[7]

The construction, reproduction and evolution of group identities occur in an inter-group context, where identity markers are expected to identify 'a particular community as distinctive and bounded'.[8] Markers of identity often maximise the perceived difference between communities in a plural society: Lambkin notes that had race been chosen as a 'badge' of identity in Northern Ireland, it would have eroded the boundary between the Unionist and Nationalist communities.[9] Similarly, the Arabic language mitigates more politically salient religious cleavages in Lebanon. Indeed, Hughes suggests that the very existence of ethnic groups 'is possible only if there are ways of telling who belongs to the group and who does not, and if a person learns early, deeply, and usually irrevocably to what group [he or she] belongs'.[10] In other words, identity markers and group boundaries are salient, and can become politically relevant only if community members and non-members are aware of their distinctiveness.

Moreover, politically salient markers and narratives of belonging are born out of the interaction between groups and the institutions of a state. Stewart argues that during violent conflicts, communities mobilise on the basis of the identity 'that is perceived as being important from the point of view of the allocation of government resources'.[11] Brubaker also introduces the distinction between 'state-formed' nationalisms and 'counter-state' nationalisms,[12] particularly relevant to deeply divided societies, where group identities are often framed in alignment or opposition to the state (as Chap. 3 shows).

Finally, the saliency of specific markers of identity depends on the political regime: in democratic contexts, the voluntaristic aspects of ethnonational belonging, such as a sense of solidarity or a shared history, assume particular significance.[13] Indeed, group identities that are 'experienced and understood as something deep and natural' tend to be 'learn[ed] over time and grounded in and shaped by a person's experience'.[14] But how do individuals learn and internalise group identities? Why are collective identities so resilient? Social identity theory offers some answers to these questions.

2.1.1 Social Identity Theory

Refuting a monolayered view of individual identity, social identity theory views identification as an individual process of construction and reconstruction of the self, and places the most significant sources of collective identity in categories which may appear as ascriptive, such as ethnicity, gender or nationality. It confirms that a minimal group identity can be provided through common characteristics apparent to outsiders, that set the group apart from an 'other'.[15] Nonetheless, collective identification is strongest when members of a group are aware of their similarities, and define themselves on this basis (e.g., through a common name, as in 'Macedonians').

Identification with a group and internalisation of group identity impacts on individual cognitive processes. Tajfel and Turner argue that identification with groups provides individuals with an instrument to maximise self-esteem, and demonstrate that once a particular group identity (or social identity) has been internalised, individuals compare themselves with 'others' so as to fare favourably.[16] Thus, they tend to favour fellow group members by, at a minimal level, discriminating against 'others', and to overestimate their commonalities with fellow group members, viewing non-members as maximally different.[17] This process of categorisation can culminate in depersonalisation and total identification of the self, and/or the other, with groups.[18]

Moreover, every individual unconsciously selects perceptual evidence in light of past experiences to make sense of the present. Evidence is then categorised into 'explanatory clusters': psychological 'shortcuts' essential to understanding the past, participating in collective life and responding to change.[19] Stereotypes are a kind of explanatory cluster: they represent an abstract exemplary group member and produce expectations about the collective and individual behaviours of communities and their members.[20] Explanatory clusters and stereotypes are intrinsic to human cognition and impact on how information is selected and perceived: individuals tend to reject evidence deviating or contradicting their preconceptions thereby producing and reproducing stereotypes.[21]

Viewed through the prism of social identity, stereotypes have important consequences for inter-group relations. Far from being fixed, stereotypes tend to reflect the state of inter-group relations: worsening inter-group relations will result in negative stereotypes of the other and emphasise inter-group differences.[22] Thus, the state of inter-group relations can affect the contents and saliency of some aspects of group identity and vice versa.

In sum, cognitive psychology and social identity theory draw a connection between the fate of groups and the self-esteem of their members, and argue that the contents and saliency of group identity evolves alongside inter-group relations. This explains why, in the context of a politically salient Unionist-Nationalist dichotomy in Northern Ireland, various Protestant denominations have downplayed their differences and endorsed an overarching Protestant identity whose minimal function is differentiation with Catholics/Nationalists. Similarly, differences among Christian sects in Lebanon are concealed by the adoption of a 'Christian' identity, maximally different from the (similarly heterogeneous) 'Muslim' group.

Social psychology also proposes that individuals perceive themselves and others along a continuum, from uniqueness to full identification with group stereotypes, according to four factors. First, perceptions of vulnerability in the face of a threat or inter-group competition harden group boundaries and lead to increasing identification with fellow group members.[23]

Second, the permeability of group boundaries influences levels of identification: impermeable boundaries and immediate ability to identify group members (such as through obvious physical differences) help internalise identities.²⁴ This partly explains the frequency of religious cleavages in intractable conflicts: religious groups have hard boundaries and encourage endogamy so that 'a separate ethnic group can emerge in a relatively short time'.²⁵

Third, the stability and legitimacy of hierarchical patterns in society influences the intensity of individual identification with groups. Where group hierarchy appears legitimate, members of low-status groups may regard discrimination as unavoidable, consent to it, and attempt to join the more prestigious, higher-status group.²⁶ Similarly, where a hierarchical pattern appears stable, members of low-status groups are discouraged from undertaking collective action against sociopolitical discrimination.

Finally, the saliency of a particular identity at a particular time determines the intensity of individual identification with the group. As Tajfel puts it, 'groups (and intergroup relations) come to life when their potential designations as such have acquired a psychological and behavioural reality'.²⁷ In other words, the relevance of communities depends on whether certain identity markers are politically, economically and socially salient at a particular time. The interdependence of inter-group relations, group identity and individual self-esteem has important sociopolitical consequences in deeply divided societies.

2.2 Deeply Divided Societies and Violent Conflict

Paradigms of modernisation hold that states, through economic development and processes of nation-state building can impose on their citizens a homogeneous mass culture and common allegiance to the state. Primordial ascriptive allegiances to religious, ethnic or linguistic groups would gradually disappear, alongside the distinctive myth-symbol complexes of local communities. Nowhere has this proven more illusory than in divided or plural societies.

Indeed, despite efforts at nation-state building (further explored in Chap. 3), societies such as Lebanon, Northern Ireland and Macedonia remain divided by segmental cleavages into distinctive religious, linguistic, ethnic and national communities. This is partly due to their similar historical origins: the three jurisdictions emerged from processes of decolonisation and the redistribution of imperial territories into 'nation-states'.²⁸ Chapter 3 explains that in the new political units, some communities had no allegiance to the state: the nationalisms of Muslims in

Lebanon, Nationalists in Northern Ireland and Albanians in the territory of present-day Macedonia emerged as further societal cleavages 'by providing a loyalty to a "nation" that [was] not coeterminous with the state'.[29] Moreover, controversies over the legitimacy of the state and its boundaries were amplified by the geographical positions of the three societies, situated on 'ethnic frontiers', in unstable regions at the margins of withdrawing empires.[30] Inter-communal cleavages were nurtured and exploited by external powers with irredentist claims, such as the Republic of Ireland.

Deeply divided societies are characterised by weak public allegiance to the state among a significant portion of their population and by strong loyalty to 'primordial' communities or ethnic groups.[31] The number of cleavages, and the extent to which these crosscut or coincide determines how divided a society is: deeply divided societies typically possess multiple and overlapping cleavages. Here, members of different communities often lead separate and parallel lives, and political divisions frequently coincide with salient social fractures. In this context, 'the act of voting' may become simply 'a duty or means of expressing substantive [communal] loyalties'.[32] Yet deep and overlapping cleavages do not necessarily lead to violent inter-communal conflict.

2.2.1   *Identity-Based Conflict in Deeply Divided Societies*

Ethnic conflicts emerge when 'the goals of at least one conflict party are defined in … ethnic terms' and 'the primary fault line of confrontation is one of ethnic distinctions'.[33] Thus the Lebanese civil war, Northern Irish Troubles and 2001 conflict in Macedonia are ethnic conflicts, which involved communities in violent struggles over the identity and very existence of the state, the extent of power to be exercised centrally and 'whether there should be one or more central governments'.[34]

The relationship between ethnonational cleavages, other social, political and economic divisions, and the political system can facilitate the outbreak of violent conflict. Where societal cleavages coincide, they reinforce each other, and make violent conflict more likely.[35] In pre-conflict Lebanon, Northern Ireland and Macedonia, religion, ethnonational identity, political allegiances and attitudes to the state overlapped, exacerbating intergroup tensions.

Moreover, when the legitimacy of a state is founded on narratives of common ethnic descent, and political order is premised on the ethno-cultural homogeneity of the citizenry, diversity can appear as a threat to popular sovereignty and be openly suppressed.[36] This makes violent conflict more likely. For example, in the 1990s, the founding narratives and state-building policies promoted by the newly independent Macedonian state emphasised the congruence of the state with the ethnic Macedonian nation. These policies nurtured ethnic Albanian feelings of collective exclusion and fear of assimilation, which ultimately motivated the 2001 insurgency.

Finally, the outbreak of violent conflict also depends on contextual and logistical factors. Hanf argues that inter-group tensions increase with urbanisation, when their members 'start competing' for resources.[37] A history of hostile inter-group relations, support for violence by public authorities or communal elites and a catalysing event encourage descent into war.[38] The existence of logistical opportunities, such as support from external actors, inaccessible terrain, financial resources, potential leaders and media outlets make armed conflict more likely.[39] In this perspective, ethnicity is a tool for collective political mobilisation in the context of material grievances and opportunities for violent action.

2.2.2 *Group Identities and Violent Conflict*

The 'psychocultural' approach to ethnic conflict suggests that, far from being simply a label, ethnonational identity may be an independent factor in the outbreak and persistence of violent conflicts.[40] As explained, social psychology proposes that individuals identify most strongly with groups when salient group identities are threatened, group stereotypes are endorsed by group members, 'others' are depersonalised, group boundaries are impermeable and hierarchical patterns are deemed illegitimate and unstable.[41] The same four variables also facilitate inter-group conflict.

Thus, an analysis of markers of identity can shed light on the state of inter-group relations in a society. This is because group leaders and 'ethnic entrepreneurs' may help reformulate group identities, but the scope for the reinterpretation of identity markers, boundaries and stereotypes is in turn constrained by a community's myth-symbol complex.[42] Myth-symbol complexes, or more simply, communal 'cultures', are conveyed through formal and informal social institutions (the family, media, schools and sociocultural organisations) long before the outbreak of violent conflicts. Thus, the mobilisation of group identities for conflict follows a long process of social construction, institutionalisation and internalisation of identities.[43]

In turn, violent conflict hardens group boundaries and mutually exclusive identities and this hampers their inclusive reformulation. Ross proposes that when 'exclusive identity claims [are] concretised as mutually exclusive claims to control a territory' or the institutions of a state, 'material resource distribution will not settle the conflict'.[44] This effectively means that the 'psychological components' of conflict, such as threatened group identities, 'contribute to a continuation of the conflict even after the initial, objective causes have become irrelevant'.[45] For example, Taush et al. argue that in Northern Ireland mounting calls for the protection of 'symbols of cultural expression' reflect a latent conflict, which continues despite decreasing socio-economic disparity.[46] This suggests that the myth-symbol complex, or 'culture' of communities engaged in violent conflict is an independent factor hindering the demobilisation of identities after the signing of peace agreements. Thus, beyond a redistribution of resources, conflict resolution may require 'mutual acknowledgement and transforming the narrative about what is contested into an inclusive one'.[47]

Chapter 3 shows that, before and during conflict, the contents and structures of compulsory education in Lebanon, Northern Ireland and Macedonia embodied, conveyed and reproduced both the power hierarchies among communities and their mutually exclusive myth-symbol complexes. Social psychology suggests that for long-term reconciliation to occur, both the power hierarchies and the myth-symbol complexes conveyed by schools need to change. This work sheds light on the process of reformulation of the curricula and structures of formal education, and examines how unequal power relations and conflictual identities affected reforms. It also highlights which factors constrained the inclusive reinterpretation of core narratives and identities in plural societies emerging from conflict.

2.3   Conflict Resolution and Consociation

Historically, most states have responded coercively to diversity and to identity-based conflicts on their territory, through the elimination, assimilation, oppression or subjugation of cultural and ethnic communities. Despite this, research into the regulation of violent identity-based conflicts has largely focused on the benefits and shortcomings of non-coercive responses to inter-group tensions. Conflict regulation research and practice has focused on five main approaches: assimilation/integration, partition, autonomy, democratisation and consociation.[48]

This work only focuses on the latter because, as Nagle and Clancy put it in their critique of consociation, from Bosnia and Herzegovina to Northern Ireland, from Macedonia to Iraq and Lebanon, 'consociationalism is promoted as the only show in town'.[49] In fact, increasing numbers of conflict settlements include elements of consociational power-sharing, such as provisions for communal autonomy or mutual veto rights. This is largely because such safeguards are often instrumental to achieving ceasefires. Indeed, O'Leary summarises that if the priority is 'limitation, mitigation and containment of conflict without necessarily solving it',[50] it is often necessary to 'give [consociational] power-sharing a chance'.[51]

Consociational power-sharing challenges J.S. Mill's maxim that 'free institutions are next to impossible in a country made up of different nationalities' where 'the united public opinion necessary to the working of representative government cannot exist'.[52] According to O'Leary, a political consociation is a 'state or region within which two or more cultural or ethnic or national communities peaceably coexist, with none being institutionally superior to the others, and in which the relevant communities cooperate politically through self-government and shared government'.[53]

The constitutional structure of consociations was first analysed by Lijphart, who focused on plural societies characterised by ethnic, religious, cultural and linguistic cleavages (such as Lebanon).[54] McGarry and O'Leary refined consociational theory and advocated its application to societies deeply divided along national lines (such as Northern Ireland and Macedonia).

According to Lijphart, 'consociational democracies' are characterised by the presence of segmental cleavages and by consensus decision-making rather than competition among segmental elites. They have four characteristics. First, consociations operate through executive power-sharing. Executive power-sharing was initially interpreted as 'a grand coalition' of the leaders of all communities: in 'unanimous' consociations (such as Lebanon), the executive includes representatives of all the indigenous communities.[55] McGarry and O'Leary reformulated the principle of executive power-sharing as 'meaningful cross-community executive power-sharing' founded on the principle of 'joint consent'. In such 'concurrent consociations' the executive includes representatives of the majority of each segment, and in 'weak consociations' executive coalitions may include partners entrusted with a minority of communal votes.[56] The constitutional structures of Northern Ireland and Macedonia favour meaningful rather than unanimous executives.

Second, consociations prescribe mutual vetoes or concurrent majority rules to protect the interests of all communities in a society. For example, the Lebanese cabinet is required to adopt resolutions on 'major issues' by consent or with a majority of two-thirds of its members.[57] For certain laws, the Macedonian parliament requires a concurrent overall majority and a majority among the representatives 'claiming to belong to the communities not in the majority in the population of Macedonia'.[58] In Northern Ireland, 'key decisions' are taken by parallel consent or weighted majority of the Unionist and Nationalist representatives.[59]

Third, Lijphart argues that consociations require proportional electoral systems, political representation, civil service appointments and management of funding. Proportionality is an important legitimating principle in Lebanon, Northern Ireland and Macedonia, but the three consociations vary in their electoral systems and mechanisms for cabinet allocation. Since the Taif Agreement, Lebanon has allocated parliamentary seats according the principle of Muslim-Christian parity: the cabinet is a grand coalition of representatives of the religious sects, with the positions of president, prime minister and speaker of the parliament reserved for members of the Maronite, Sunni and Shia communities. Lebanese 'confessionalism'[60] approximates an ideal type of 'corporate consociation', which accommodates communities according to ascriptive identities, such as religion or ethnicity, and assumes the permanence and internal homogeneity of groups.[61] Corporate consociations are inherently fragile because they struggle to adapt to changing demographics: they create resentments both among excluded groups and among the communities participating in what is an inherently unequal sharing of government positions.[62] Thus, 'major problems' such as the redistribution of power and executive positions 'must wait for major upheavals'.[63] In other words, communities can renegotiate their relative power and influence upon state institutions only during violent conflicts.

In contrast, liberal consociation 'rewards whatever salient political identities emerge in democratic elections'.[64] It aims to flexibly and proportionally accommodate self-determined identities. Macedonia is an almost ideal example of liberal consociation: it relies on a proportional electoral system and provides guarantees for communities accounting for over 20 % of the total population (the ethnic Albanians and ethnic Macedonians).

The fourth characteristic of consociations is the institutionalisation of segmental autonomy or self-government. According to Lijphart, consociations can promote communal autonomy through three mechanisms.

First, federal arrangements can ensure that state boundaries approximate linguistic boundaries (as in Switzerland). Second, separate 'personal status laws' can regulate the conduct of members of religious or cultural communities, as is the case in Lebanon. Third, communities can be granted the right to 'establish and administer their own autonomous schools, fully supported by public funds'.[65]

Educational autonomy appears integral to consociation as conceptualised by Lijphart. He reiterates that 'a solution that has worked well ... is to provide educational autonomy by giving equal state financial support to all schools, public and private, as long as basic educational standards are met'.[66] Similarly, he advocates the establishment of cultural councils for each community in plural societies, charged with 'the administration of schools for those who wish to receive an education according to the group's linguistic and cultural traditions'.[67] Finally, looking at Northern Ireland, he argues that '"segregated schools" if they are under the community's own control and are "separate *and* equal" in terms of government financial support' contribute to cultural autonomy.[68] Elsewhere, in an attempt to mitigate the sharp edges of autonomy, he admits that 'voluntary self-segregation' is a likely outcome of separate schools, but argues that this 'is acceptable as long as the option of multicultural and multiethnic education is also made available and provided that all schools are treated equally'.[69]

Thus, consociations, as conceptualised by Lijphart and refined by McGarry and O'Leary, manage politicised ethnic identities by recognising them explicitly and turning communities into the pillars supporting a stable representative democracy.[70] Schooling and formal education are repeatedly mentioned as integral to the consociational institutions, but consociational theory has not analysed explicitly or extensively the educational arrangements of deeply divided societies. The present study aims to fill this gap by comparing education policy in consociational Lebanon, Northern Ireland and Macedonia.

2.3.1 *Establishment and Resilience of Consociations*

This study hypothesises that the values and narratives conveyed through formal education can contribute to the stability of consociational power-sharing. This contribution has been overlooked in the literature about the factors facilitating the establishment and maintenance of consociations.

Lijphart argues that at a social level, a multiple balance of power between more than two groups, the isolation of communities and the presence of certain cross-cutting cleavages (such as socio-economic equality) further consociational stability.[71] Chapter 1 has explained that members of different communities in Lebanon, Northern Ireland and Macedonia often lead separate and parallel lives.

At the political level, Lijphart argues that prior traditions of elite accommodation, a multiparty system with moderate representation of all segments and a small population size, providing for a small government workload, facilitate the success of consociational arrangements.[72] The three societies have a small population size: 4,424,888 people in Lebanon,[73] 1,811,000 people in Northern Ireland,[74] and 2,022,547 people in Macedonia.[75] Chapter 3 also explains that the three societies have multiparty systems, with most communities represented by more than one political party. Finally, Lebanon has a prior tradition of elite accommodation, explored in Chap. 3: the National Pact of 1943–1975. McGarry and O'Leary add a further element to the political factors aiding consociational arrangements: the existence of elites determined to cooperate, free to negotiate and able to muster popular support for power-sharing.[76]

Moreover, Lijphart argues that overarching threats (such as external threats perceived as such by all segments in a small country) or overarching loyalties (e.g., to the state or a monarchy) can help maintain consociations. In the case of Macedonia, ambition to join the European Union (EU) emerged as a significant cross-cutting cleavage after independence. In the case of Lebanon, since the civil war, it has been 'populated overwhelmingly by people who see themselves as Lebanese'.[77]

Finally, Kerr demonstrated that external pressures were 'the defining political factor in the success, implementation, maintenance and failure of consociation' in Lebanon and Northern Ireland.[78] This is also the case for Macedonia, where the USA and EU were instrumental in mediating and drafting the Ohrid Agreement and in enforcing its implementation.

In sum, with the possible exception of communal isolation, none of the key factors examined in the literature concern the contribution of non-political institutions (such as schools) to the establishment and maintenance of stable consociations. Yet, as part and parcel of arrangements for communal autonomy and equality, schools deserve scholarly attention.

2.3.2 Complex Consociations

Recent consociational research has widened its scope to reflect the practice of conflict management and regulation, in particular 'complex power-sharing' or 'complex consociation'.[79] According to O'Leary, complex consociations combine the four constitutional and political institutions outlined earlier with 'policies, institutions, and constitutional arrangements that address an antagonistic self-determination dispute, incorporate peace processes, involve elements of at least one other major domestic conflict-regulating strategy and … enlist external or international powers in the making, implementation and maintenance of the settlement'.[80]

Complex power-sharing approximates closely the reality of peace agreements: beyond constitutional engineering, the Taif, Belfast and Ohrid Agreements include mechanisms regulating the involvement of external actors, policies aimed at social integration, prescriptions for police restructuring and education reform.

In their complementary mechanisms, the three peace agreements reflect closely the negotiators' perceptions of the underlying causes of conflict. For example, the Belfast Agreement is a settlement between national communities, and includes complementary trans-state arrangements (the North–South Ministerial Council and British–Irish Inter-Governmental Conference). Complementary mechanisms regulating external involvement had a more detrimental effect in Lebanon, where continuing Syrian occupation stunted political development and the implementation of the consociational peace agreement. The Ohrid Agreement recognises the role of the EU, OSCE and the USA in guaranteeing its implementation, but does not postulate any trans-state institutions, emphasising conflict regulation within Macedonia's impermeable borders.

The Ohrid Agreement provides for territorial decentralisation as a complementary mechanism for conflict management, and recommends decentralisation of the administration of some services at a municipal level. Chapter 7 highlights its (limited) impact on schooling. Northern Ireland (when powers are devolved) approaches a 'federacy' with the UK.[81] In contrast, Lebanon's provisions for territorial devolution have never been implemented and the state remains centralised.[82]

The Taif Agreement combines rigid corporate consociational institutions with integrationist approaches to conflict resolution, embodied first and foremost in its extensive provisions for education reform. In fact, as Chap. 1 mentioned, the agreements of Lebanon, Northern Ireland and

Macedonia present schools as instruments to promote reconciliation. This shows that, despite being overlooked in the literature, education reform is an integral part of complex consociational arrangements and of transition out of conflict in deeply divided societies.

2.3.3   The Consociational Paradox and Its Critiques

The Prussian General von Clausewitz famously argued that 'war is the continuation of politics by other means'. Miall suggests that consociation is 'Clausewitz in reverse': the continuation of a military conflict by political means.[83] Indeed, in contrast to coercive approaches, to assimilation and to partition, consociations do not explicitly seek conflict resolution in the short- to medium term. O'Leary confirms that accommodation of conflictual identities comes at the expense of a shared political vision, and that 'consociation is a politics with a shared vision of catastrophe'.[84]

This does not mean that consociational arrangements should be conceived of as temporary: McCrudden and O'Leary point out that 'time-limiting' them would undermine their major function, the provision of security and stability.[85] Consociationalists argue that a stable political framework and institutions allow the expression and negotiation of the differences and group needs at the heart of ethnonational conflicts. They suggest that this, in the long term, may decrease the political saliency of ethnic and national identities and lay the foundations for peaceful democratisation.[86]

Here lies the 'consociational paradox': McGarry argues that 'the institutional accommodation of rival groups and an extensive period of cooperation between them is more likely to transform identities in the long run than any of the integrationist options'.[87]

Yet, the most fundamental criticism of consociational theory is precisely that it lacks 'clarity from its adherents as to how it helps society move from conflict management to transformation'.[88] In particular, critics argue that consociationalists are unclear as to how ethnic parties would evolve into parties with cross-communal appeal and how identity-based politics would transform into a democratic political system. Consociations are criticised for their 'elitism': accordingly, power-sharing executives are insulated from effective opposition and elites are unaccountable to their passive and deferential public.[89] They are also criticised for being inherently unstable. If they found their raison d'être upon societal fractures, then they will necessarily reduce politics to bargaining for communal rights. The resulting entrenchment and further politicisation of ethnonational fractures can favour the exploitation of mutual fears by elites and descent into violent conflict.[90]

Political critics of consociation suggest centripetalism as an alternative method of constitutional and political engineering. Centripetalists 'place a premium on promoting cross-ethnic electoral and party systems that make politicians reliant on the votes of different ethnic communities to gain election'.[91] Yet, centripetalism generally encounters the resistance of local minority communities because it does not entrench their group rights. Moreover, polarisation of voting patterns along communal lines largely predates the establishment of consociations.[92]

In fact, the ideal typology of liberal consociation responds directly to most political critiques. Yet its practical implementations generally fall short of rewarding 'whatever salient political identities emerge in democratic elections'.[93] For example, the arrangements for self-designation of elected members of the Northern Ireland Assembly as 'Nationalist', 'Unionist' or 'other' allows for the emergence of 'others'. Still, 'others' are penalised during cross-community voting procedures, which protect primarily the interests of Nationalists and Unionists.

A further criticism of consociation is particularly relevant to the present analysis of education in deeply divided societies. Critics argue that consociational theory fails to account for social change and for the evolution of the saliency and content of conflictual identities. They maintain that consociationalists accept uncritically 'the primacy and permanency of ethnicity' and emphasise primordial and fixed ascriptive identities.[94] Finlay claims that consociational research takes ethnicity for granted and does not explain the mechanisms whereby it is acquired and able to evolve: thus the institutions, practices and narratives of power-sharing would constrain 'the space for other ways of being and other forms of politics'.[95]

In particular, critics of consociation argue that power-sharing rests 'on precisely the division it is supposed to solve'.[96] Finlay maintains that the peace process in Northern Ireland reflects the 'assumption that [each community] ... [has] a special 'cultural heritage'... which demands expression and recognition here, now and in perpetuity'.[97] What Shirlow and Coulter polemically call 'the "two tribes" model advanced within the Belfast agreement' would contribute to casting societal divisions in 'marble'.[98] Through a comparison of education reform in consociational Lebanon, Northern Ireland and Macedonia, this study aims to analyse the identity-forming narratives conveyed through schools and to highlight the extent to which they help entrench and reproduce mutually exclusive communities.

Moreover, Finlay argues that 'communal segregation increases following the signing of the peace agreement'.[99] Recent data from Northern Ireland raise some doubts: in 2001, over 50 % of electoral wards were single identity (with 80 % or more of their population from one community) but this proportion declined to 37 % in 2011. Yet, the same census data also show that most mixed neighbourhoods are 'self-segregating at street level'.[100] Surveys carried out by Hanf in Lebanon show that more people desired to live 'among people with a similar background' in 2006 than during the civil war (in 1987).[101] Beydoun explains this process as the 'generalised confessionalisation [of Lebanon] since the war', encompassing (among other phenomena) the increasing influence of religious authorities, the declining numbers of mixed residential areas, and the proliferation of community-affiliated exclusive institutions and services.[102] Finally, in Macedonia, a 2008 United Nations Development Programme (UNDP) survey highlighted that ethnic Albanians and ethnic Macedonians have only limited 'interactions with people from other ethnic groups': only 37 % of ethnic Macedonians work with people of different backgrounds and only 64 % of ethnic Albanians have friends of other ethnic backgrounds. The UNDP also reported sharp and increasing residential separation in Macedonia.[103] Observing these data, critics of consociation in Northern Ireland, Lebanon and Macedonia question whether power-sharing can ultimately further reconciliation and conflict resolution.

In fact, Lijphart warns that consociations make societies 'more thoroughly plural' in the short term.[104] Yet, he views societal pillarisation as positive: decreasing opportunities for contact limit 'the chances of ever-present potential antagonisms to erupt into actual hostility'.[105] The proliferation of segmental rather than cross-communal networks would promote the internal cohesion of each community, furthering elite legitimacy and ability to compromise.[106]

In contrast, the 'contact hypothesis' maintains that reconciliation requires contact between members of different communities. To test the hypothesis, Hewstone et al. surveyed 811 adults in mixed and separated residential areas of Belfast over time. They found that positive and sustained inter-communal contact (even when superficial or indirect) promotes better inter-group relations by reducing mutual fear and anxiety and improving mutual knowledge and self-disclosure.[107] Varshney similarly proposes that inter-communal civic networks in Indian cities make them more resilient to external and internal tensions and shocks, and prevent descent into 'endemic and ghastly' inter-group violence.[108]

Actually, consociation and inter-group contact are not mutually exclusive. The emergence of complex power-sharing provides an opportunity to promote contact within consociations and perhaps end the long-standing, sterile debate between 'consociationalists' and 'integrationists'. Integrationists propose social transformation as an *alternative* to power-sharing, positing that tackling civil rights, discrimination and socio-economic inequalities would in itself further reconciliation.[109] They call for policies encouraging integration, economic convergence and participatory democracy to further overarching loyalties and cross-cutting cleavages.[110]

Ethnic and nationalist categories may have been superimposed on an unjust social order, but social psychology explains that social identities change more slowly than material interests. This is why policies aimed at social transformation have failed to gain substantive support in deeply divided societies: here, integration often appears as a means to repress group rights or assimilate communities. Yet specific measures aimed at reconciliation and social integration can be implemented in the context of complex approaches to consociational design: as Chap. 7 shows, *shared education* in Northern Ireland is a prime example.

It remains to be explored whether complex power-sharing provides the political context and stable conditions in which social transformation can be pursued. The constraints consociation places upon specific peace-building initiatives also need to be explained. This study argues that valuable evidence can be provided by a group of institutions overlooked in consociational research: non-political institutions, especially those that reflect and reproduce core identity-forming narratives. Indeed, the Taif, Belfast and Ohrid Agreements explicitly place non-political institutions (such as police forces and education) at the centre of transition from a conflict to a post-conflict society.

2.4 Why Education?

Formal education is a particularly interesting non-political institution because, through curricula, structures and daily practices, schools produce, convey and reproduce key identity-forming narratives. Thus, they contribute to defining and redefining individual and collective identities, as well as the boundaries between communities in deeply divided societies.

Cognitive approaches to learning propose that 'learners cannot understand reasons until they have already acquired a view … in order to be critical you must first be indoctrinated'.[111] Individuals are indoctrinated into the explanatory clusters, stereotypes and myth-symbol complexes of communities they belong to through a process of socialisation, 'a process of learning through which an individual is prepared, with varying degrees of success, to meet the requirements laid down by other members of society for his behaviour'.[112] Mass education systems were introduced in parallel to the extension of franchise in the nineteenth and early twentieth centuries, and they responded to the needs of democratising 'nation-states' and of industrialising European economies.[113] The educational models developed in Britain, France and other European powers were later 'diffused by their respective colonial and/or ideological systems'.[114] Thus, mass compulsory schooling emerged as an instrument of socialisation into the values, assumptions and patterns of behaviour underpinning collective life in a society.

Eckstein highlights that political systems are stable only if the 'authority pattern [of governments] is congruent with the other authority patterns of the society of which it is part'.[115] In newly created democracies, elected governments depended on the acceptance of a 'fictive image' of cultural homogeneity within their borders and on collective support for their values and practices.[116] Thus, schools were entrusted with transmitting a common, sanctioned myth-symbol complex to all citizens. This included a standardised culture through a common language and official version of the past, common rituals and practices, and markers of belonging and identity. Socialisation of children into the values and culture laid out by previous generations would help assimilate the necessarily diverse citizenry and blend 'ethnic differences'. It would also transmit stereotypes of different others (individuals not belonging to the nation-citizenry), sustain sociopolitical stability and create 'the united public opinion necessary to the working of representative government'.[117] As Green summarises, mass education systems 'tried to create the civic identity and national consciousness which would bind each [citizen] to the state and reconcile each [citizen] to the other'.[118]

In sum, mass education systems reflect and reproduce the myth-symbol complex (or culture) of states, their internal patterns of authority, and the narratives and principles upon which the political system is founded. These three functions of mass schooling are particularly problematic in deeply divided societies, where the culture of some communities does not coincide with that of the state, where authority patterns are perceived as unjust and where the legitimacy of political institutions is contested.

2.4.1 Schooling as Socialisation into a Myth-Symbol Complex

Bourdieu, in his analysis of class differences in France, views the state as the spokesperson of dominant classes and as the primary agency laying down the essential features of citizens and 'others'.[119] He argues that the process of education approximates the imposition of an arbitrary culture (the myth-symbol complex of a dominant social class, or of an ethnic group) by an arbitrary power (the state) for the purpose of perpetuating the social order and hierarchical pattern among (class or ethnic) groups. When social change occurs and hierarchical patterns among communities change, the contents and structures of schooling follow. The more dependent education systems are on the state, the slower they are in responding to social change. In this perspective, education reform is an expression of 'conflict and competition between social class, ethnic, religious and gender groups'.[120] Thus, negotiation over the contents and structures of compulsory education is an amplified debate over the fundamental identity (or identities) of a society.

Moreover, Bourdieu claims that the practices and contents of schooling reflect a 'legitimate culture', which is the expression of the values and interests of dominant groups. He maintains that the more arbitrary the power distribution in society, the further 'legitimate culture' is from the myth-symbol complex of some communities.[121] Thus, rigid and illegitimate intergroup hierarchies would create and reproduce a gap between arbitrary (or state) 'legitimate' education and the culture of some communities.

Application of Bourdieu's analysis to ethnic and national communities in deeply divided societies explains the continuing existence, alongside the state education system, of schools associated with specific communities. Through schools, states attempt to socialise its citizens into a dominant myth-symbol complex. Yet, community schools may emerge as instruments of collective resistance to socialisation and assimilation. As Chap. 3 shows, community schools in Lebanon, Northern Ireland and Macedonia emerged as valuable 'means of preserving group identity through generations'.[122] Indeed, recent research in Northern Ireland confirms that individual identification with communities and expression of stereotypes increase markedly in the first years of primary school.[123] This suggests that compulsory education remains a tool to transmit 'a set of predispositions towards certain cultural events and symbols and a deep sense of belonging to one community in opposition to the other' or to the state.[124]

2.4.2 Education as Socialisation into a Political Order

Beyond expressing a particular culture and reproducing certain power hierarchies, compulsory schools affect individual political attitudes. Easton argues that the survival of democratic political systems depends 'upon the success of a society in producing children most of whom acquire positive feelings about it'.[125] He finds that, in the USA, children come to 'idealise' or 'hostilise' the political system by becoming aware of an external authority superior to the family and by personalising key institutions. He refrains from drawing direct connections between adult political attitudes and children's feelings, but he proposes that by age 11, children have generally developed marked support or hostility towards the US political system.[126]

Success in conveying diffused support for the political system depends first upon the stability of the political system. Second, it depends on the triangular relationship between the state, the 'gatekeepers who could regulate the flow of support to the authorities', and the citizens.[127] In a deeply divided society, such as Lebanon, Northern Ireland or Macedonia, the elites and institutions associated with local religious, ethnic and national communities act as gatekeepers, mediating the interactions between the state and its citizens. The state's ability to bypass gatekeepers and nurture diffused support for the political system depends on its relationship with gatekeepers and on the cohesiveness of communities: the more cohesive the community, the harder it is for the state to bypass it.

In this respect, Easton offers an important contribution to analysis of the constraints to political socialisation in deeply divided societies. Chapter 3 substantiates Easton's findings and shows that the success of states in imposing a myth-symbol complex, and furthering positive feelings about the political system, depend on their relationship with the local ethnic communities. When local communities are not cohesive or when states have a positive relationship with communal elites (or gatekeepers), states can succeed in conveying a culture and widespread support for the political system. In contrast, when states have an antagonistic relationship with some local cohesive communities (such as during violent identity-based conflicts), states will attempt to shape 'good loyal citizens' and face the resistance of some communities, which attempt to form 'good disloyal citizens'.[128] The process of political socialisation into hostility or support for the political system also occurs through formal education.

2.4.3   Schools and Identity-Based Conflict

Bourdieau and Easton argue that education has a key nation-building function: it transmits core myth-symbol complexes (or cultures), furthers children's internalisation of communal identities and contributes to the development of support (or hostility) towards the sociopolitical system. The contents and practices of formal education can also contribute to instability within a state, and even to the outbreak and continuation of violent conflict among its population, because they reflect and reproduce socio-economic hierarchies and political allegiances. In deeply divided societies, hierarchies, allegiances and identities often coincide with communal cleavages: this amplifies the economic, political and symbolic impact of education reforms on certain groups.

Education policy can reproduce socio-economic inequality by restricting access to schooling and providing unequal educational opportunities to members of different communities.[129] This can cause violent rebellions against the state, such as the 2001 ethnic conflict in Macedonia. Thus, education reforms after conflicts tend to focus on expanding access to compulsory schooling and assess progress through quantitative rather than qualitative indicators.[130] These policies overlook the fact that higher average levels of education are not correlated to improved social harmony: social cohesion depends on how equally education levels are distributed.[131] Moreover, the quality of education is as important as access to school: perceptions of differential quality and of unequal long-term returns to schooling between members of different communities can motivate violent uprisings.[132]

Politically, Brown sees education as a tool for inclusion or exclusion. Through its contents, practices and structures, education may promote and convey inclusive overarching narratives of identity, but it may also reproduce exclusivist militant discourses.[133] Above all, as Easton proposes, schooling may promote either support for or opposition to the political system and the state itself. Hanf highlights that schools will succeed in assimilating a diverse population only if 'the assimilating group [is] willing to accept members of other groups and the latter [is] willing to sacrifice at least certain aspects of their identity'.[134] Thus, strong and hostile 'gatekeepers' may undermine state efforts to convey diffused support for the political order, erode attempts at conveying a culture or myth-symbol complex, and question the legitimacy of authorities. This would contribute to the perpetuation of inter-group conflict. Indeed, Chap. 3 shows that in Lebanon, Northern Ireland and Macedonia, education policy emerged as an arena for conflict between the state and ethnic communities, and among different communities, becoming enmeshed in the wider 'ideological battleground' over state identity and legitimacy.[135]

Symbolically, the contents and structures of education express whether a state recognises the myth-symbol complexes of all of its communities. Attempts to shape a culturally homogeneous society through schools imply the exclusion of the myth-symbol complexes of certain communities from the curricula and daily practices of schools: this may further intergroup conflicts. Conversely, state failure to impose a sanctioned culture on children through common institutions, may lead to the emergence of separate schools, which become further markers of group membership.[136]

Psychologically, Bar-Tal demonstrates that schools are instrumental in reproducing the 'collective orientation of fear ... hatred and anger as well as guilt or pride' functional to coping with intractable conflicts.[137] He argues that during a conflict, compulsory education is 'directed to strengthen the rationale for the continuation of conflict, to develop delegitimisation of the rival, and to reinforce patriotism in order to secure and maintain mobilisation for the conflict, participation in it, and even the readiness to die for the collective'.[138] In turn, the culture, attitudes and practices that help individuals and communities cope with protracted violent conflicts also hinder peace processes.

In sum, schools can provide a motivating factor for rebellion but their structures and contents can also indirectly motivate the escalation (or perpetuation) of identity-based conflicts. Dupuy points out that education is generally addressed in peace agreements when it is perceived to have contributed to violent conflict.[139] This suggests that the negotiators of the Taif, Belfast and Ohrid Agreements viewed schools as contributors to the three violent conflicts in Lebanon, Northern Ireland and Macedonia. By comparing education policy in these deeply divided societies, this study aims to highlight the contributions of schools to violent identity-based conflicts before offering insights on how education reform can foster reconciliation.

2.4.4 *From War to Peace*

Bar-Tal clearly expresses the dilemmas intrinsic to education reforms after violent inter-group conflicts. He argues that 'after decades of indoctrination in which schoolchildren in societies engaged in intractable conflict were socialised for participation in such conflict ... educational systems alone cannot redirect the society to change its ethos and culture'.[140]

Continuing arguments over precisely how schools perpetuate inter-group conflicts further complicate the formulation of education reforms. Tony Gallagher, examining Northern Ireland, highlights three contending perspectives. In the first perspective, 'separate schools enhanced religious divisions by providing different curriculums that heightened inter-group antagonisms'. In the second perspective, 'the mere fact of separation, allied with the hidden curriculum of separate schools, encouraged religious differences'. In contrast, the third perspective held that 'the issue of separate schools was largely irrelevant as the main basis for violent conflict lay in the unjust relationship of domination and subordination between the majority and minority communities'.[141]

The latter perspective holds that the remediation of unjust inter-group hierarchies solves conflicts in deeply divided societies. Redressing inequalities is a necessary step towards conflict resolution, but this chapter has also shown that schools help socialise children into communal identities, myth-symbol complexes and attitudes to the political system. These three elements are 'psychological components' of violent conflicts: they may 'contribute to a continuation of the conflict even after the initial, objective causes have become irrelevant'.[142] Thus, the redistribution of material resources and political power alone do not solve inter-group tensions in the long term. This suggests that schools are independent actors in the reproduction and perpetuation of inter-group conflicts in deeply divided societies: when unreformed, they may continue to convey the narratives and identities that sustained violent conflict.

The other two theoretical perspectives hold that curricular contents, or the structures of schooling, perpetuate the narratives and hierarchies underpinning inter-group conflict. They advocate different priorities for education reform after violent conflicts: changes to manifest curriculum (the explicit contents of education) or reforms of the daily practices and structures of schools (the hidden curriculum). The Taif, Belfast and Ohrid Agreements prescribe both reforms to the manifest and hidden curricula, confirming that in practice schools contribute to inter-group conflict both 'structurally (through separate schooling) and functionally (through curricula and teaching and learning processes that emphasise the development of separate national identities)'.[143]

The National Subjects
There is considerable agreement that the contents of curricula embody 'legitimate' knowledge, convey particular myth-symbol complexes and further allegiance or opposition to political institutions. The available literature points to 'national subjects' as areas of learning deemed crucial to

the construction of nations and nation-states: language, history, geography, religious education and civic education are the prime instruments for divulgation of specific myth-symbol complexes.[144]

As Chap. 1 mentioned, the Taif, Belfast and Ohrid Agreements emphasise reform of the curricula of national subjects: the Taif Agreement focuses on producing unified curricula and textbooks for history and citizenship education; the Belfast Agreement promotes the Irish language; and the Ohrid Agreement addresses the linguistic demands of ethnic Albanians by granting funding to universities teaching in the language of at least 20 % of the population, guaranteeing mother tongue primary and secondary education, and reaffirming the right of all children to learn the Macedonian language.

Thus, an evaluation of the political function of formal education in consociational Lebanon, Northern Ireland and Macedonia requires comparative analysis of debates over the national subjects: Chaps. 4, 5 and 6 look at history education, citizenship education and language policies in the three societies. This work shows that the contents of each national subject emerge from lengthy, and at times brutal negotiations between states and their communities, and among representatives of different communities. Negotiations over the contents and lexicon of curricula can 'become cultural and ideological battlegrounds' and reflect the state of inter-communal relations.[145] As debates over history education in Lebanon highlight, this is also the case for teaching materials, particularly textbooks, whose existence 'implies that an agreed knowledge base has been determined'.[146]

In fact, Davies finds that reform of curricula and textbooks after violent conflicts concentrates either on sanitisation (elimination of controversial contents) or sensitisation (rewording of controversial contents).[147] In a third approach, curricula and textbooks may be reformulated to 'incorporate [a plurality of] group specific epistemological and ontological values and views'.[148] Even when they reflect a consensus regarding the past and visions for the future, a unified curriculum can be problematic when it does not speak equally to members of different communities. Conversely, the promotion of different curricula reflecting the cultures and allegiances of different communities may deepen inter-communal distance and mistrust. Finally, multiperspective curricula are often controversial in post-conflict societies because they imply granting legitimacy to 'a tradition aiming at some form of dismemberment of the state'.[149] Thus, debates and decisions over curricula in consociational Lebanon, Northern Ireland and Macedonia reflect the dilemmas incurred when attempting to construct 'states that reflect and incorporate the diversity of their citizens and yet have an overarching set of values, ideals and goals to which all citizens are committed'.[150]

The Structure of Schooling
Smith argues that states can shape the basic structure of the education system in three ways. They can promote 'conformity to a single set of dominant values (assimilation)' through a system of mandatory, state-sponsored, standard institutions; they can permit 'the development of identity-based institutions (separate development)', legitimising the authority of communities upon their children; and they can 'encourage shared institutions (integration)', by promoting, alongside other institutions, common schools.[151]

The relationship between separate institutions and the development of differentiated identities is more ambiguous than that between curricular contents and exclusive identities, especially after a violent conflict. In particular, the literature distinguishes between the impact of separate schools and of segregated schools. Separate schools may be requested and voluntarily chosen by members of a particular community who 'have access to an appropriate form of education for their young people'. In contrast, segregated schools are imposed legally as part of a wider system of institutionalised discrimination in which 'the state decides on the appropriate form, with or without the consent' of communities.[152]

Equally funded and legitimate parallel institutions may succeed in accommodating different cultures and allegiances in deeply divided societies.[153] 'Communitarians' also argue that 'wider cultural tolerance' is rooted in specific communal values and is best promoted in separate schools, while 'culturalists' argue that shared schools cannot ensure the fair and equal representation of all communities and group identities.[154] The promotion and equal funding of a plurality of separate schools resonates with Lijphart when he observes that 'the voluntary self-segregation that [autonomous communal] schools entail is acceptable as long as the option of multicultural and multiethnic education is also made available and provided that all schools are treated equally'.[155] Yet, Chap. 3 shows that the distinction between imposition and demand for separate schools is ambiguous in deeply divided societies, where communities often create separate institutions as a response to institutionalised discrimination and socio-economic exclusion.

Moreover, Gallagher contends that 'whether schooling systems are segregated or separate, there is evidence that such systems can have a detrimental impact on social cohesion'.[156] Separate schools may exacerbate inter-group conflicts by reinforcing socio-economic cleavages, harden group boundaries by socialising children into opposing myth-symbol complexes, or 'initiate pupils into conflict' by validating group differences and furthering mutual ignorance and suspicion.[157] Conversely, mixed schools which do not deal with diversity and the roots of conflict, and which do not promote cooperation between children from different backgrounds, may exacerbate inter-group hostility.[158]

Chapter 7 considers in more depth the theoretical debate over whether separate schools further or hinder conflict resolution, and goes on to compare initiatives to promote inter-group contact through schools in consociational Lebanon, Northern Ireland and Macedonia. In fact, Davies argues that unlike curricula, the structure of the education system tends to go unchallenged in the aftermath of violent conflicts.[159] This is the case for Macedonia, whose Ohrid Agreement does not mention structural reforms to schooling. In contrast, the Taif Agreement calls for expansion in state education provision and envisages the establishment of state control over private schools. Similarly, the Belfast Agreement calls for promotion of integrated education to further a 'culture of tolerance at all levels of society'. Chapter 7 comparatively traces these initiatives to determine whether political consociations affect the structure of education systems, and generate 'consociational' education systems.

2.5 Conclusion

The influence of schooling on the adoption of ethnic and political identities is often deemed secondary to the influence of families and peers.[160] The socio-economic context and proximity to violence also affect the salience of ethnic identities: Connolly and Healey found that children who grow up in deprived areas in Belfast start identifying with a community and express ethnic prejudices earlier.[161] Magill et al. add that children's attitudes are affected by their parents' relationship to the conflict.[162] In Northern Ireland, individual characteristics were also found to impact on the salience of certain conflictual identifications: in particular 'masculine sub-cultures' impacted on the socialisation process of boys.[163] In Lebanon, the UNDP found that religious background impacted on political preferences and actions but socio-economic background impacted on civic attitudes and social values.[164]

Despite its obvious limits, formal education influences the individual process of identification with groups and the development of positive or negative attitudes to political systems and states. Connolly and Maginn argue that in Northern Ireland, children as young as three years old can identify and express prejudice against 'others', but add that 'the more that children are able to acquire attitudes that run counter to the general ethnocentric biases that they have learnt and continue to maintain, the more their overall levels of prejudice reduce'.[165] Indeed, the state and its ethnic communities insist on controlling schooling precisely because of their 'conviction that social attitudes are significantly affected in schools'.[166]

Moreover, in contrast to the family and peer groups, the hidden and manifest curriculum of schools can be reformed centrally, and 'what is taught in schools, how it is taught and how education is financed and delivered are all policy areas in which government decisions have both an early and lasting impact, for better or for worse'.[167] Camargo Abello reflects that 'while the formal education system responds in part to the structure of the society in which it functions, it does, at the same time, have the capacity to construct alternatives for that society'.[168] If 'education systems do not cause wars',[169] some aspects of formal education (such as differential access, unequal opportunities and legitimation of exclusive conflictual identities) certainly contribute to the outbreak and perpetuation of violent conflicts. Conversely, reforms in the curricula and structures of schooling may contribute to social cohesion, loosely understood as 'the property by which whole societies, and the individuals within them, are bound together through the action of specific attitudes, behaviours, rules and institutions which rely on consensus rather than pure coercion'.[170] By fostering social cohesion, education may contribute directly to the sustainability of peace processes.

Davies proposes first that educational choices made during peace negotiations or in their immediate aftermath, however casual, tend to solidify. Second, she argues that the trajectory of education reforms in post-conflict societies 'depends on who is in charge after conflict'.[171] In other words, education policy depends on the post-war political system and on its ideological rationale. Bourdieu and Easton suggest that the contents, practices and structures of compulsory education are instrumental in reproducing the hierarchies and principles underpinning sociopolitical systems. It is therefore reasonable to expect that, in consociations, education reform would be harnessed to reflect and reproduce the founding principles of power-sharing.

This work is the first comparative research on the contents and structures of education in societies whose political system is based on consociational power-sharing. It aims to contribute to the theory and practice of conflict regulation through complex consociation. It also intends to determine the political function of schools in Lebanon, Northern Ireland and Macedonia, and to evaluate the extent to which they can be employed to aid transition out of violent conflict. Before focusing on key debates over education reform in consociational Lebanon, Northern Ireland and Macedonia, it provides an historical overview of the establishment and development of each education system.

Notes

1. Stuart J. Kaufman, 'Ethnicity as a Generator of Conflict,' in Cordell and Wolff (eds.), *Routledge Handbook of Ethnic Conflict*, 91; Tony Gallagher, *Education*, 15.
2. Kaufman, 'Ethnicity', in Cordell and Wolff (eds.), *Routledge Handbook of Ethnic Conflict*, 92.
3. Michael Kerr, *Imposing Power-Sharing*, 18; Arend Lijphart, 'The Northern Ireland Problem: Cases, Theories, and Solutions,' *British Journal of Political Science* 5, no. 1 (1975): 87–88; Joseph Ruane and Jennifer Todd, 'Ethnicity and Religion,' in Cordell and Wolff (eds.), *Routledge Handbook of Ethnic Conflict*, 70.
4. Anthony D. Smith, *The Ethnic Origins of Nations* (Oxford: Blackwell, 1999): 58.
5. Theodor Hanf, 'The Sacred Marker,' in Hanf (ed.), *Dealing with Difference*, 387.
6. Will Kymlicka, 'Foreword,' in James A. Banks, *Diversity and Citizenship Education. Global Perspectives* (Jossey-Bass, 2007): xiv.
7. John Nagle and Mary-Alice Clancy, *Shared Society or Benign Apartheid?*, 5.
8. Gallagher, *Education*, 16.
9. B.K. Lambkin, *Opposite Religions Still? Interpreting Northern Ireland after the Conflict* (Aldershot: Avebury, 1996): 17.
10. Qtd in Paul Connolly and Julie Healy, *Children and the Conflict in Northern Ireland: The Experiences and Perspectives of 3–11 Years Olds* (Belfast: OFMDFM Research Branch 2004): 14.
11. Frances Stewart, *Religion Versus Ethnicity*, 44.
12. Colin Clark, 'The Nation-State,' in Cordell and Wolff (eds.), *Routledge Handbook of Ethnic Conflict*, 51–52.
13. Michael H. Hogg, Deborah J. Terry, and Catherine M. White, 'A Tale of Two Theories: A Critical Comparison of Identity Theory with Social Identity Theory,' *Social Psychology Quarterly* 58, no. 4 (1995).

14. Connolly and Healy, *Children*, 13–14.
15. Leonie Huddy, 'From Social to Political Identity: A Critical Examination of Social Identity Theory ' *Political Psychology* 22, no. 1 (2001): 141.
16. John C. Turner, 'Towards a Cognitive Redefinition of the Social Group' in Henri Tajfel (ed.), *Social Identity and Intergroup Relations*, Cambridge: Cambridge University Press, 2010: 33–36.
17. Mark Rubin and Miles Hewstone, 'Social Identity, System Justification, and Social Dominance: Commentary on Reicher, Jost et al., and Sidanius Et al.,' *Political Psychology* 25, no. 6 (2004): 824, 832.
18. Hogg et al., 'A Tale of Two Theories,' 260.
19. Gallagher, *Education*, 23–24.
20. Ibid., 24–25; Huddy, 'From Social to Political Identity,' 133. Hogg et al., 'A Tale of Two Theories,' 261.
21. Gallagher, *Education*, 24–25; International Bureau of Education, *Différenciation Intergroupes En Milieu Scolaire. Discussion Métodologique Et Analyse Comparative Dans Dix Pays* (Geneva: UNESCO, 1995), 8.
22. Ibid., 12.
23. Lynn Davies, *Education and Conflict: Complexity and Chaos* (London: Routledge, 2004): 77, 136; Huddy, 'From Social to Political Identity,' 136; Penelope Oakes, 'Psychological Groups and Political Psychology: A Response to Huddy's 'Critical Examination of Social Identity Theory',' *Political Psychology* 23, no. 4 (2002): 818.
24. Leonie Huddy, 'Contrasting Theoretical Approaches to Intergroup Relations,' *Political Psychology* 25, no. 6 (2004): 956; Huddy, 'From Social to Political Identity,' 142.
25. Hanf, 'The Sacred Marker,' Hanf, *Dealing with Difference*, 387.
26. Rubin and Hewstone, 'Social Identity,' 826 and Shana Levin et al., 'Ethnic Identity, Legitimising Ideologies, and Social Status: A Matter of Ideological Asymmetry,' *Political Psychology* 19, no. 2 (1998): 374, 400. See also: Claire McGlynn et al., 'Moving out of Conflict: The Contribution of Integrated Schools in Northern Ireland to Identity, Attitudes, Forgiveness and Reconciliation,' *Journal of Peace Education* 1, no. 2 (2004): 148.
27. Henri Tajfel, 'Instrumentality, Identity and Social Comparisons', in Henri Tajfel (ed.), *Social Identity and Intergroup Relations*, Cambridge: Cambridge University Press, 2010: 485; Gallagher, *Education*, 29–30.
28. Lijphart, 'The Northern Ireland Problem,' 88; Jennifer Jackson-Preece, 'Origins of Nations,' in Cordell and Wolff (eds.), *Routledge Handbook of Ethnic Conflict*, 16.
29. Lijphart, *Democracy*, 82.
30. John McGarry, 'Introduction,' in McGarry (ed), *Northern Ireland and the Divided World*, 19.

31. Lijphart, *Democracy*, 168.
32. Richard Rose's view on Northern Ireland in 1971, qtd. in Ed Cairns and Tara Cairns, 'Children and Conflict: A Psychological Perspective,' in Seamus Dunn (ed.), *Facets of the Conflict in Northern Ireland* (London: St Martin's Press, 1995): 105.
33. Karl Cordell and Stefan Wolff, 'The Study of Ethnic Conflict,' in Cordell and Wolff (eds.), *Routledge Handbook of Ethnic Conflict*, 4.
34. John McGarry and Brendan O'Leary, 'Consociational Theory, Northern Ireland's Conflict, and Its Agreement. Part 1: What Consociationalists Can Learn from Northern Ireland,' *Government and Opposition* 44, no. 1 (2006): 55.
35. McGarry, 'Introduction,' in McGarry (ed), *Northern Ireland and the Divided World*, 14.
36. Jackson-Preece, 'Origins of Nations,' in Cordell and Wolff (eds.), *Routledge Handbook of Ethnic Conflict*, 23.
37. Hanf, 'The Sacred Marker,' in Hanf, *Dealing with Difference*, 387.
38. Kaufman, 'Ethnicity,' in Cordell and Wolff (eds.), *Routledge Handbook of Ethnic Conflict*, 241.
39. Zoltan Barany, 'Ethnic Mobilisation in the Postcommunist Context,' in Zoltan Barany and Robert G. Moser (eds.), *Ethnic Politics after Communism* (London: Cornell University Press, 2005): 80.
40. Kaufman, 'Ethnicity,' in Cordell and Wolff (eds.), *Routledge Handbook of Ethnic Conflict*, 91, 98.
41. Oakes, 'Psychological Groups and Political Psychology,' 815.
42. Huddy, 'From Social to Political Identity,' 143–145; Kaufman, 'Ethnicity,' in Cordell and Wolff (eds.), *Routledge Handbook of Ethnic Conflict*, 93; Smith, *The Ethnic Origins of Nations*, 58; International Bureau of Education, *Différenciation Intergroupes En Milieu Scolaire. Discussion Métodologique*, 10.
43. Kaufman, 'Ethnicity,' in Cordell and Wolff (eds.), *Routledge Handbook of Ethnic Conflict*, 93.
44. Ross, 'Peace Education,' in Salomon and Cairns (eds.), *Handbook on Peace Education*, 123.
45. Nicole Taush, Katharina Schmidt, and Miles Hewstone, 'The Social Psychology of Intergroup Relations,' in Salomon and Cairns (eds.), *Handbook on Peace Education*, 75.
46. Ibid., 79.
47. Ibid.
48. Cordell and Wolff (eds.), *Routledge Handbook of Ethnic Conflict*.
49. Nagle and Clancy, *Shared Society or Benign Apartheid?*, 64.
50. Asaf Siniver, 'Managing and Settling Ethnic Conflict,' in in Cordell and Wolff (eds.), *Routledge Handbook of Ethnic Conflict*, 187.

51. O'Leary, 'Debating Partition,' in Cordell and Wolff (eds.), *Routledge Handbook of Ethnic Conflict*, 153.
52. Qtd. in Jackson-Preece, 'Origins of Nations,' in Cordell and Wolff (eds.), *Routledge Handbook of Ethnic Conflict*, 20.
53. Brendan O'Leary, qtd. in Kerr, *Imposing Power-Sharing*, 26.
54. Lijphart, *Democracy*.
55. Ibid., 25.
56. McGarry and O'Leary, 'Consociational Theory, Northern Ireland's Conflict, and its Agreement. Part 1,' 62–63.
57. Part II, Section D, Art.6, *Taif Agreement*.
58. Art. 5.1, *Ohrid Agreement*.
59. Strand One. Democratic Institutions in Northern Ireland, Safeguards, Art.5d, *Belfast Agreement*.
60. Meaning the "sectarian power-sharing formulae," Mohammad F. Mattar, 'Is Lebanese Confessionalism to Blame?,' in Choueiri (ed.), *Breaking the Cycle*, 49.
61. John McGarry and Brendan O'Leary, 'Iraq's Constitution of 2005: Liberal Consociation as Political Prescription,' *International Journal of Constitutional Law* 5, no. 4 (2007): 675.
62. Ibid., 691; Knudsen and Kerr, 'Introduction,' in Knudsen and Kerr (eds.), *Lebanon after the Cedar Revolution*, 40.
63. Ahmad Beydoun, 'A Note on Confessionalism,' in Theodor Hanf and Nawaf Salam (eds.), *Lebanon in Limbo. Postwar Society and State in an Uncertain Regional Environment* (Baden-Baden: Nomos, 2003): 81.
64. McGarry and O'Leary, 'Iraq's Constitution of 2005,' 675.
65. Arend Lijphart, *Thinking About Democracy. Power Sharing and Majority Rule in Theory and Practice* (London: Routledge, 2008): 46.
66. Ibid., 84.
67. Ibid., 70.
68. Arend Lijphart, 'The Framework Document', 272.
69. Lijphart, *Thinking About Democracy*, 70.
70. Lijphart, *Democracy*, 45; Benjamin Reilly, 'Centripetalism,' in Cordell and Wolff (eds.), *Routledge Handbook of Ethnic Conflict*, 297; Finlay, *Governing Ethnic Conflict*, 8.
71. Lijphart, *Democracy*, 54, 66–67; Kerr, *Imposing Power-Sharing*, 27.
72. Lijphart, *Democracy*, 54, 66–67; Kerr, *Imposing Power-Sharing*, 27.
73. World Bank estimate for 2012 reported on: The World Bank, *Population (Total)*, http://data.worldbank.org/indicator/SP.POP.TOTL
74. Russell, Raymond, *Census 2011: Key Statistics at Northern Ireland and LGD Level* (Belfast: Northern Ireland Assembly Research and Information Service, 2013): 3.
75. State Statistical Office, *MakStat Database*, http://makstat.stat.gov.mk/pxweb2007bazi/Dialog/Saveshow.asp

76. Kerr, *Imposing Power-Sharing*, 28; McGarry, 'Introduction,' in McGarry (ed), *Northern Ireland and the Divided World*, 15.
77. Michael Kerr, 'The Philosophy of Lebanese Power-Sharing,' in Choueiri (ed.), *Breaking the Cycle*, 252.
78. Kerr, *Imposing Power-Sharing*, 29.
79. Stefan Wolff and Karl Cordell, 'Power Sharing,' in Cordell and Wolff (eds.), *Routledge Handbook of Ethnic Conflict*, 307.
80. Brendan O'Leary, 'Debating Consociational Politics,' in Noel (ed.), *From Power Sharing*, 35.
81. John McGarry and Brendan O'Leary, 'Territorial Approaches to Ethnic Conflict Settlement,' in in Cordell and Wolff (eds.), *Routledge Handbook of Ethnic Conflict*, 254.
82. Michael Kerr and Amal Hamdan, 'Lebanon: The Hybridity of a Confessional State,' in John Loughlin, John Kincaid and Wilfried Swenden (eds.), *Routledge Handbook on Regionalism and Federalism* (London: Routledge, 2013): 499–509.
83. Miall et.al. qtd. in Harvey Cox, 'Keeping Going: Beyond Good Friday,' in Marianne Elliott (ed.), *The Long Road to Peace in Northern Ireland* (Liverpool: Liverpool University Press, 2007): 159.
84. O'Leary, 'Foreword,' in Kerr, *Imposing Power-Sharing*, xxii.
85. McCrudden and O'Leary, *Courts and Consociations*, 10.
86. Rupert Taylor, 'Northern Ireland: Consociation or Social Transformation?,' in McGarry (ed), *Northern Ireland and the Divided World*, 38.
87. John McGarry, 'Northern Ireland, Civic Nationalism and the Good Friday Agreement,' in McGarry (ed), *Northern Ireland and the Divided World*, 124; Lijphart, *Democracy*, 124, 2.
88. Nagle and Clancy, *Shared Society or Benign Apartheid?*, 45.
89. Rupert Taylor, 'The Belfast Agreement and the Politics of Consociationalism: A Critique,' *The Political Quarterly* 77, no. 2 (2006): 219; Lijphart, *Democracy*, 49; McGarry, 'Introduction,' in McGarry (ed), *Northern Ireland and the Divided World*, 18.
90. Taylor, 'The Belfast Agreement,' 218–220; Joseph Marko, 'Human Rights and Ethnopolitics,' in Cordell and Wolff (eds.), *Routledge Handbook of Ethnic Conflict* (London: Routledge, 2010): 241.
91. Benjamin Reilly, 'Centripetalism: Cooperation, Accommodation and Integration', in Stefan Wolff and Christalla Yakinthou (eds.), *Conflict Management in Divided Societies. Theories and Practice* (London: Routledge, 2012): 57; Donald L. Horowitz, 'The Northern Ireland Agreement: Clear Consociational, and Risky,' in McGarry (ed), *Northern Ireland and the Divided World*.

92. Jonathan Tonge and Jocelyn Evans, 'Party Members and the Good Friday Agreement in Northern Ireland,' *Irish Political Studies* 17, no. 2 (2002), 71.
93. Stefan Wolff, 'Liberal Consociationalism', 4; O'Leary, 'Foreword,' in Kerr, *Imposing Power-Sharing*, xxv.
94. McGarry and O'Leary, 'Consociational Theory, Northern Ireland's Conflict, and Its Agreement. Part 1,' 46; Taylor, 'The Belfast Agreement,' 220; John McGarry and Brendan O'Leary, 'Consociational Theory, Northern Ireland's Conflict, and Its Agreement Part 2', 270–271.
95. Finlay, *Governing Ethnic Conflict*, 25, 36.
96. McGarry and O'Leary, 'Consociational Theory, Northern Ireland's Conflict, and Its Agreement Part 2,' 270–271.
97. Finlay, *Governing Ethnic Conflict*, 33.
98. Peter Shirlow and Colin Coulter, 'Enduring Problems: The Belfast Agreement and a Disagreed Belfast,' in Elliott (ed.), *The Long Road to Peace in Northern Ireland*, 208; Wilford, qtd. in McGarry and O'Leary, 'Consociational Theory, Northern Ireland's Conflict, and Its Agreement. Part 1,' 46.
99. Finlay, *Governing Ethnic Conflict*, 6.
100. Paul Nolan, *Northern Ireland Peace Monitoring Report Number Three* (Belfast: Community Relations Council, 2014): 115. Others argue that residential segregation is increasing: Jonathan Tonge, *The New Northern Irish Politics?* (New York: Palgrave, 2004): 190; Claire Mitchell, 'Religious Change and Persistence,' in Colin Coulter and Michael Murray, *Northern Ireland after the Troubles, a Society in Transition* (Manchester: Manchester University Press, 2008): 142; Northern Ireland Council for Integrated Education, *A Shared Future: Policy and Strategic Framework for Good Relations in Northern Ireland. Promoting Shared Education* (Belfast: NICIE, 2005): 12.
101. 55 % in 1987 and 59 % in 2006. Theodor Hanf, *E Pluribus Unum? Lebanese Opinions and Attitudes on Coexistence* (Byblos: UNESCO, 2007): 18; Economic and Social Commission for Western Asia, *Unpacking the Dynamics of Communal Tensions: A Focus Group Analysis of Perceptions among Youth in Lebanon* (New York: United Nations, 2009): 18.
102. Beydoun, 'A Note,' Hanf and Salam (eds.), *Lebanon in Limbo*, 78–80.
103. United Nations Development Programme, *People Centered Analysis Report* (Skopje: UNDP, 2008): 60–61.
104. Lijphart, *Democracy*, 42.
105. Ibid., 88.
106. Lijphart, *Thinking About Democracy*, 35.
107. A 20 % improvement in indicators linked to tolerance. Miles Hewstone et al., *Can Contact Promote Better Relations? Evidence from Mixed and Segregated Areas of Belfast* (Belfast: OFMDFMNI, 2008): 9.

108. Ashutosh Varshney, *Ethnic Conflict and Civic Life: Hindus and Muslims in India* (London: Yale University Press, 2003): 9.
109. Gary K. Peatling, *The Failure of the Northern Ireland Peace Process* (Dublin: Irish Academic Press, 2004): 45.
110. McGarry, 'Introduction,' in McGarry (ed), *Northern Ireland and the Divided World*, 17; Taylor, 'Northern Ireland,' 38; McGarry and O'Leary, 'Consociational Theory, Northern Ireland's Conflict, and Its Agreement Part 2,' 251.
111. Robert Young, 'Liberalism, Postmodernism, Critical Theory and Politics,' in Richard Smith and Philip Wexler (eds.), *After Postmodernism: Education, Politics and Identity* (London: The Falmer Press, 1995): 13.
112. David Easton, *Children in the Political System* (New York: McGraw-Hill Book Company, 1969): 10.
113. Gallagher, *Education*, 139–141; Andy Green and John Preston, 'Education and Social Cohesion: Recentering the Debate,' *Peabody Journal of Education* 76, no. 3/4 (2001): 250; Green, *Education, Globalisation and the Nation State* (London: Macmillan, 1997), 131, 133.
114. William C. Cummings, 'How Educational Systems Form and Reform,' in Joseph Zajda and Macleans A. Geo-JaJa (eds.), *The Politics of Education Reforms* (Springer, 2010): 22.
115. Easton, *Children*, 34.
116. Gallagher, *Education*, 65, 139; Easton, *Children*, 4.
117. Qtd. in Jackson-Preece, 'Origins of Nations,' in Cordell and Wolff (eds.), *Routledge Handbook of Ethnic Conflict*, 20; Cummings, 'How Educational Systems Form and Reform,' in Zajda and Geo-JaJa (eds.), *The Politics of Education Reforms*, 30; Gallagher, *Education*, 35, 141; Easton, *Children*, 27.
118. Green, *Education*, 134.
119. Pierre Bourdieu and Jean-Claude Passeron, *Reproduction in Education, Society and Culture* (London: Sage, 1990).
120. Haim Gaziel, 'Why Educational Reforms Fail: The Emergence and Failure of an Educational Reform. A Case Study from Israel.,' in Joseph Zajda (ed.), *Globalisation, Ideology and Education Policy Reforms* (Springer, 2010): 51.
121. Bourdieu and Passeron, *Reproduction in Education*, 9, 18, 41.
122. Amy Gutmann, 'Unity and Diversity in Democratic Multicultural Education,' in Banks (ed.), *Diversity and Citizenship Education*, 86.
123. Paul Connolly, Alan Smith, and Berni Kelly, *Too Young to Notice? The Cultural and Political Awareness of 3–6 Years Olds in Northern Ireland* (Belfast: Northern Ireland Community Relations Council, 2002).
124. Connolly and Healy, *Children*, 15, 104.
125. Easton, *Children*, 5.

126. Ibid., 389–390, 394.
127. Ibid., 410–412.
128. Michael Kerr, 'Nations Apart. Mutually Exclusive Identity Forming Narratives in Northern Ireland's Education System,' in Theodor Hanf (ed.), *The Political Function of Education in Deeply Divided Countries* (Baden-Baden: Nomos, 2011), 32.
129. Theodor Hanf, 'What Case Studies Can Teach Us,' in Hanf (ed.), *The Political Function of Education*, 335; Graham K. Brown, 'The Influence of Education on Violent Conflict and Peace: Inequality, Opportunity and the Management of Diversity,' *Prospects* 41, no. 2 (2011): 196; Marina Camargo Abello, 'Are the Seeds of Violence Sown in Schools?,' *Prospects* XXVII, no. 3 (1997): 450.
130. Alan Smith, 'Education in the Twenty-First Century: Conflict, Reconstruction and Reconciliation,' *Compare* 35, no. 4 (2005): 377.
131. Andy Green, P. Preston, and R. Sabates, *Education, Equality and Social Cohesion: A Distributional Model* (London: Institute of Education, 2003): iii, v; Andy Green, John Preston, and Germen Janmaat, *Education, Equality and Social Cohesion. A Comparative Analysis.* (London: Palgrave, 2006): 180.
132. Camargo Abello, 'Are the Seeds of Violence Sown in Schools?,' 450; Brown, 'The Influence of Education on Violent Conflict and Peace,' 196; United Nations Educational Scientific and Cultural Organisation, *Education for All Global Monitoring Report 2011. The Hidden Crisis: Armed Conflict and Education* (Paris: UNESCO, 2011): 162.
133. Brown, 'The Influence of Education on Violent Conflict and Peace,' 202, 192.
134. Hanf, 'What Case Studies Can Teach Us,' in Hanf (ed.), *The Political Function of Education*, 334.
135. Davies, *Education*, 44.
136. Davies, *Education*, 44, 76; Green, *Education*, 183; Brown, 'The Influence of Education on Violent Conflict and Peace,' 196, 202.
137. Daniel Bar-Tal, 'Peace Education in Societies Involved in Intractable Conflict. Goals, Conditions and Directions.,' in Salomon and Cairns (eds.), *Handbook on Peace Education*, 22; Daniel Bar-Tal, 'Why Does Fear Override Hope in Societies Engulfed by Intractable Conflict, as It Does in the Israeli Society?,' *Political Psychology* 22, no. 3 (2001): 619.
138. Bar-Tal, 'Peace Education,' 36.
139. Kendra E. Dupuy, 'Education in Peace Agreements, 1989–2005,' *Conflict resolution quarterly* 26, no. 2 (2008): 161.
140. Bar-Tal, 'Peace Education,' 36.
141. Tony Gallagher, 'Balancing Difference and the Common Good: Lessons from a Post-Conflict Society,' *Compare* 35, no. 4 (2005): 434.

142. Taush et al., 'The Social Psychology of Intergroup Relations,' in Salomon and Cairns (eds.), *Handbook on Peace Education*, 75.
143. Alan Smith, *The Influence of Education on Conflict and Peace Building. Background Paper Prepared for the Education for All Global Monitoring Report 2011* (Paris: UNESCO, 2010): 8.
144. Smith, 'Education in the Twenty-First Century,' 380–381; Sarah Graham-Brown, 'The Role of the Curriculum,' in Minority Rights Group International, *Education Rights and Minorities* (London: Manchester Free Press, 1994).
145. Smith, 'Education in the Twenty-First Century,' 381.
146. Laurie Shepherd Johnson, 'Moving from Piecemeal to Systemic Approaches to Peace Education in Divided Societies: Comparative Efforts in Northern Ireland and Cyprus,' in Zvi Bekerman and Claire McGlynn (eds.), *Addressing Ethnic Conflict through Peace Education* (London: Palgrave, 2007): 28.
147. Davies, *Education*, 176.
148. Dupuy, 'Education,' 160.
149. Qtd. in Ken Wylie, 'Citizenship, Identity and Social Inclusion,' *European Journal of Education* 39, no. 2 (2004): 242.
150. James A. Banks, 'Preface,' in Banks (ed.), *Diversity and Citizenship Education*, xix.
151. Smith, 'Education in the Twenty-First Century,' 379.
152. Crispin Jones, 'State Education and Minority Rights,' in Minority Rights Group International, *Education Rights and Minorities*, 8.
153. Gallagher, *Education*, 149–150; Hanf, 'What Case Studies Can Teach Us,' in Hanf (ed.), *The Political Function of Education*, 335.
154. Gallagher, *Education*, 151.
155. Lijphart, *Thinking About Democracy*, 70.
156. Qtd. in Smith, *The Influence of Education on Conflict and Peace Building*, 10.
157. Gallagher, *Education*, 125; Brown, 'The Influence of Education on Violent Conflict and Peace,' 192; Lambkin, *Opposite Religions Still?*, 195.
158. Gallagher, *Education*, 26; Tony Gallagher, 'Desegregation and Resegregation: The Legacy of Brown Versus Board of Education, 1954,' in Bekerman and McGlynn (eds.), *Addressing Ethnic Conflict*, 17.
159. Davies, *Education*, 109.
160. McGlynn et al., 'Moving out of Conflict,' 153; Byron G. Massialas, 'Some Propositions About the Role of School in the Formation of Political Behaviour and Political Attitudes of Students: Cross-National Perspectives,' *Comparative Education Review* 19, no. 1 (1975): 172; Shirley Ewart and Dirk Schubotz, *Voices Behind the Statistics. Young People's Views of Sectarianism in Northern Ireland* (Belfast: National Children's Bureau, 2004): 7, 15.

161. Connolly and Healy, *Children*, i.
162. Claire Magill, Alan Smith, and Brandon Hamber, *The Role of Education in Reconciliation. The Perspectives of Children and Young People in Bosnia Herzegovina and Northern Ireland* (Londonderry: INCORE, 2009): 1.
163. Connolly et al., *Too Young to Notice?*, 46.
164. United Nations Development Programme, *Education and Citizenship. Analysis of Survey Results of 9th Grade Students in Lebanon* (Beirut: UNDP, 2008): 29.
165. Paul Connolly and Paul Maginn, *Sectarianism*, 34.
166. John P. Darby, 'Divisiveness of Education in Northern Ireland,' *Equity & Excellence in Education* 12, no. 1 (1974): 10.
167. United Nations Educational Scientific and Cultural Organisation, *Education for All*, 160.
168. Camargo Abello, 'Are the Seeds of Violence Sown in Schools?,' 452.
169. United Nations Educational Scientific and Cultural Organisation, *Education for All*, 131.
170. Andy Green, Germ Janmaat, and Christine Han, *Regimes of Social Cohesion* (London: Centre for Learning and Life Chances in Knowledge Economies and Societies, 2009): 19.
171. Davies, *Education*, 168.

CHAPTER 3

Compulsory Education in Lebanon, Northern Ireland and Macedonia

This chapter provides a historical and political background to the analysis of education reform in consociations. It traces the evolution of education systems in Lebanon, Northern Ireland and Macedonia, and summarises wider efforts to build nation-states before the establishment of the current consociations in 1989, 1998 and 2001, respectively. It also considers the Taif, Belfast and Ohrid Agreements and subsequent political developments in the three societies. A concluding section explains the political function of compulsory education during identity-based conflicts.

Education systems in Lebanon, Northern Ireland and Macedonia emerged in the context of inter-communal conflicts within contested states. As the territorial realities of controversial partitions crystallised, markers of identity evolved to reflect and frame political conflicts, and communal belonging came to be conflated with specific political attitudes and national aspirations. Markers of identity and belonging, myths of the past and loyalty (or opposition) to the state were at the core of the three conflicts. Schools, as sites of definition, legitimation and reproduction of language, ideology and historical narratives, emerged as symbolic (and at times physical) 'battlegrounds for the hearts and minds of the next generation'.[1]

3.1 Lebanon

In what is the territory of present-day Lebanon, the Ottoman *millet* system entrenched religion as a primary component of collective political identity, while the 1864 *Reglement* provided for proportional representation of religious communities in the administrative council of the *mutassarrifyya* of Mount Lebanon.[2] The 1740 Franco-Ottoman treaty (Capitulations) established the precedent of foreign patronage over a religious community, granting the French the right to intervene in Ottoman affairs to defend Christians.[3] European influence paved the way for the introduction of romantic notions of nationalism, which postulated the coincidence of nation and state.[4] This context generated political practices characterised by a tribalism overwritten by religious differences.[5] It contributed to construct some sects, or confessional communities as '*quasi*-nations'.[6] Before independence, and increasingly under the constraining parameters of the new independent state, the 18 sects treasured their histories and markers of identity and projected them upon the Lebanese state. Thus, Lebanon's nation-state building experience is defined by the dialectical, interdependent and often antagonistic relationship between the state and its communities.

The following analysis traces education policy in four formative periods of Lebanon's modern history: the French Mandate of 1920–1943, the establishment of independent Lebanon in 1943–1958, the consolidation of a corporate consociation between 1958 and 1974, and the civil war of 1975–1989. It then highlights the main education reforms in the Taif Agreement and provides an overview of key political developments since 1990.

It shows that debates over primary education between 1920 and 1989 mirrored wider tensions between a weak state attempting to impose an overarching narrative of collective identity and strong religious communities determined to protect and project their group identities and narratives. This created 'the educational landscape, or shall we say archipelago, that is the Lebanese educational system'.[7]

3.1.1 *French Mandate (1920–1943)*

Having secured a 'Mandate for Syria and Lebanon' in the aftermath of World War I, French authorities defined the two new state entities and their borders. To ensure the economic and strategic viability of the newly created Greater Lebanon, they annexed the four provinces of Beirut, the North, the South and the Bekaa (inhabited by large Sunni and Shia communities) to the *mutasarrifiyya* of Mount Lebanon (populated primarily by Christians and Druze).[8] Most Christians accepted the new borders, but from the early 1920s Sunni Muslims contested them and 'made it abundantly clear that Greater Lebanon, as a national entity separate and distinct from Arab Syria, was meaningless to them, and in the long term unacceptable'.[9] In protest, they boycotted the 1921 census and their notables demanded the right of self-determination and unification with the rest of Ottoman Syria.[10]

The Mandatory authorities also set out to build new state institutions in Greater Lebanon: Hanf argues that 'the Jacobin ideas of many French administrators' crumbled before the concerted opposition of local leaders, determined to protect 'the fundamental rights of the communities'.[11] Rapidly, the French authorities came to view inter-communal cooperation as the key to stability. This meant that from birth, Lebanon's institutions were liberal and democratic but not secular.[12] Thus, the 1926 constitution institutionalised a political system founded on the sharing of power between the elites of the different religious communities.[13] The 1936 Franco-Lebanese treaty, paving the way for independence, further entrenched communal representation in government.[14] The confessional political system allowed considerable autonomy in decision-making for the French High Commissioner. Successive French representatives juggled Maronite ambitions to dominate the new institutions and Muslim pan-Arab sympathies, while encouraging the emergence of new political and economic elites to replace traditional religious figures.[15]

The Mandate also entrusted France with developing public education in Lebanon.[16] As early as 1920, a Division of Education (becoming the Ministry of Public Education in 1926) was established to enforce central control over the education system, and to revive state schools.[17] The French authorities attempted to use curricula and textbooks to encourage allegiance to the new state and promote peaceful coexistence among citizens belonging to different communities. They warned that 'a divided country will never be strong'[18] and behaving 'as a colonial rather than as a mandatory power' diffused primarily French culture.[19] French replaced Turkish as the official language taught in official schools, and the teaching of French became mandatory in all schools. Beyond strengthening Lebanese cultural affiliation to France, this policy aimed to weaken 'one of the major bonds of the nationalist movement, the Arabic language'.[20]

Similarly, the 1925 national curricula guidelines warned that 'differences among religious groups have caused a lot of bloodshed in the past'[21] and attempted to submerge communal differences by conveying a Christian and philo-European narrative of Lebanese identity. Geography and history devoted a disproportionate amount of time to Europe and France, and most curricula emphasised Lebanese particularism, contrasting it with the history and identity of the Arab Middle East.[22]

In fact, different identities, informed by different interpretations of the past, thrived in Greater Lebanon, as exemplified by incensed debates over history textbooks for state primary schools in the 1930s. In 1935, two Sunni scholars composed the *History of Syria and Lebanon*, a textbook reflecting a Syrian nationalist outlook and refuting Lebanese particularism.[23] As a response, the 1937 *History of Lebanon* relied on a Maronite interpretation of Lebanon's past, emphasising the Phoenician rather than Arab ancestry of the Lebanese population, focusing on Lebanese specificity and downplaying or ignoring the Arab affiliations of parts of the population and their cultural and historic connection with Ottoman Syria.[24] Only the vocal protests of representatives of the Muslim communities ensured that the *History of Lebanon* was never adopted as an official state school textbook.[25]

The articulation of legitimate, overarching founding myths for a Lebanese state was arduous in and of itself, but ambitions to convey allegiance to the state through schools also faced insurmountable structural obstacles. The 1869 Ottoman Special Education Law had introduced public state schools in the *mutasarrifiyya* of Mount Lebanon, but in 1918, most schools in Lebanon were foreign and private.[26] Indeed, before the Mandate, education was provided mainly by missionary organisations, often sponsored by foreign powers that aimed, through schooling, to gain a foothold in the Levant. Thus, French missionaries educated mainly Maronite children while British and American missionaries focused on the education of Muslim children.[27] Ottoman state schools accounted for just over 20 % of the schools in Greater Lebanon, and their operation was suspended in 1918 (after the Ottoman defeat in World War I).[28]

In the 1920s the Mandatory authorities attempted to revive the state sector and succeeded in increasing the number of state schools from 91 in 1924 to 183 in 1941. Still, public schools came to cater for only 16 % of school children in 1941, while private schools affiliated to local religious communities accommodated 52 % of children.[29] This is because the French High Commissioner came to rely on representatives of the religious communities in expanding primary education: as early as January 1919, he offered generous subsidies to communities wishing to reopen or found private schools.[30] Article 8 of the Mandate and Article 10 of the 1926 Constitution also established that 'there shall be no violation of the right of religious communities to have their own schools'.[31] Far from violating communal rights to private schools, the state started providing them with regular financial aid from 1928.[32]

In Greater Lebanon, the divide between private and public school came to coincide with socio-economic and communal cleavages. State schools were expected to 'remedy regional disparities' and cater for the underprivileged, so from the 1920s their pupils were predominantly Muslim.[33] Moreover, the limited reach of state schools explains partially the failure to socialise the population into overarching identities and to promote allegiance to the state during the Mandate. Through subsidised private primary schools, religious communities continued to convey diverging and exclusive conceptions of identity, rooted in different interpretations of the past and projecting different visions for Lebanon's future.[34]

The Mandate was a formative period for the Lebanese state and for its education system. The French authorities envisaged a liberal state whose schools shaped homogeneous Francophile Lebanese citizens, a vision hampered by the necessity to accommodate the local confessional communities. Since the 1920s, the institutionalisation of a confessional political system intertwined the fate of the Lebanese state with that of its religious communities. The structure of the Lebanese education system mirrored this mutual interdependence: by the 1940s, schools were divided into private and public and further fragmented into institutions affiliated to specific communities. Alongside the state, each community retained different narratives of Lebanon's past and visions for its future and set out to convey them to children in private schools, whose activities were subsidised by the state.

3.1.2 *National Pact (1943–1958)*

Independence within the borders of Greater Lebanon was 'the second choice of all parties, and all Lebanon could get in 1943'.[35] The National Pact, an agreement between the Maronite and Sunni elites at the eve of independence, aimed to pave the way for independence from France by reconciling the two main political and national aspirations of Lebanon's communities.[36] Lebanese nationalists advocated an independent Lebanese nation-state, pointing at the sociopolitical exceptionality of Mount Lebanon and its tradition of mountain refuge for persecuted minorities.[37] According to Lebanese nationalists, 'the Lebanese remained Lebanese, regardless of the extent to which the outside world might choose to classify them as Arabs, because their language happened to be Arabic'.[38]

In contrast, Arab nationalists maintained that the French-sponsored Greater Lebanon could not exist as a 'nation-state separate and distinct from Syria'.[39] On the one hand, Syrian nationalists called for the incorporation of Lebanese territory into a secular Syrian state encompassing the whole of Ottoman Syria. On the other hand, pan-Arabists aimed to establish (in their view re-establish) a strong Arab state encompassing the whole Eastern Mediterranean.[40] Choueiri summarises that through the 1943 National Pact, the Maronite community, the foremost advocate of Lebanese nationalism, recognised 'the Arab character of Lebanon', while the Sunni community, sidelining its support for Arab nationalism, accepted Lebanese independence from other Arab states.[41] Thus, the independent Lebanese state was born through a 'double negation' of national aspirations.[42]

The National Pact, initially a political expedient to achieve unity in the struggle against imperial France, would evolve into the backbone of Lebanon's stability and very existence.[43] A state rooted in the National Pact 'was not meant to express unity but to reconcile differences',[44] but the continuing ideological and political clash between Lebanese and Arab nationalisms ultimately 'impede[d] the normal development of the state and [kept] its political legitimacy and ultimate viability continuously in question'.[45]

Lebanon emerged in the 1940s as a corporate consociation: its executive operated as a grand coalition of communal representatives and a fixed number of parliamentary seats were allocated to each sect. Lebanon's corporate consociation helped insulate central institutions from intercommunal tensions, thereby ensuring their survival and stability even when tensions appeared between the weak central state and a decentralised political system based on mutually exclusive religious communities.[46] Yet, by assigning parliamentary seats according to the six Christians to five Muslims ratio, the Lebanese corporate consociation created inflexible structures with limited room for reform in response to changing sociopolitical circumstances. The National Pact established the parameters for future political struggles: Lebanon's sects would attempt to project their narratives of identity upon state institutions and to project their aspirations upon Lebanon's borders.⁴⁷ In particular, the ideological clash between Lebanese and Arab nationalism permeated Lebanese political struggles, setting the Maronite vision of Lebanon as 'the last line of communal defence' in a majority Muslim Middle East in opposition to the Sunni frustration with a state repressing their pan-Arab aspirations.⁴⁸

Moreover, Lebanon's corporate consociation entrenched confessionalism as the basis for state legitimacy, thereby helping to cement inter-communal boundaries and to construct the collective political consciousness of communities that, in 1943, 'were not equally confessional, or even confessionalist'.⁴⁹ The political system was superimposed on existing local clientelistic networks, and local patrons often reinvented themselves as political representatives.⁵⁰ However, the corporate consociation also entrenched extensive non-territorial autonomy for local confessional communities, and confessionalism emerged as the 'unequally accepted and diversely interpreted contract … that stipulates the preservation of a minimal public space [for sects]'.⁵¹ Thus, Salibi summarises that, since the independence of the Lebanese state, its citizens have been given two identities—one national and one communal or confessional: schools were one of the instruments employed to transmit these 'hyphenated' identities to children.⁵²

One of the architects of the National Pact reflected that 'perhaps it is true that not all our countrymen are Lebanese in their hearts, but sensible policies can ensure that they are Lebanese in their minds'.⁵³ Thus, the first Lebanese government identified education policy as a nation-building priority and attempted to shape schools contributing to the development of a common, overarching Lebanese sense of identity.⁵⁴ In 1943, the government declared its ambition that 'our schools should graduate a generation unified in aims and national feelings', and its successor presented schools as 'the best soil to cultivate virtues and tolerance'.⁵⁵ Similarly, in 1946, the government wondered 'how desirable it would be if on the national soil we unified school programmes to create a spiritual homogeneity among the citizens of the state'.⁵⁶ Three reforms exemplify state efforts to employ schools as instruments of integration.

First, in 1946 Arabic became compulsory in all Lebanese schools, and new curricula required the teaching of all subjects in Arabic, while English was introduced as a foreign language alongside French.⁵⁷ Immediately, an argument emerged between bilingualists and monolingualists: advocates of Arabic monolingualism in schools were predominantly Muslim. In contrast, bilingualists were predominantly Christian and viewed (French-

Arab) bilingualism both as an economic advantage in the labour market, and, more importantly, as a reflection of 'a double heritage, the Arab and the Western'.[58] As Chap. 6 explains, the debate over the language of instruction in state schools, as an expression of wider disputes over the identity and allegiance of the Lebanese, would continue until the end of the civil war.

Second, in 1946 the government introduced new curricula: they aimed to convey, through geography, history, literature and citizenship education, uniform sociopolitical attitudes, pride for a common past and an overarching vision for the future.[59] The new curricula included more material on Lebanon and the Middle East than their predecessors and presented the National Pact as the founding myth of a Lebanon 'united for a day, united forever'.[60]

Third, the state immediately identified private schools as its adversaries: in 1946 it reported to the United Nations Educational, Scientific and Cultural Organization (UNESCO) that students 'who speak the same language and even belong to the same family find themselves at the end of their studies with a conception of various vital problems wholly dependent on the school they attended'.[61] From 1946, private institutions were required to implement the national curriculum as a step towards the establishment of state control over the narratives and values transmitted in private schools.[62]

However, with the deterioration in regional security due to the beginning of the Arab-Israeli conflict in 1948, education reform receded in importance. While ostensibly supporting state schools, Lebanese governments increased funding for private establishments.[63] In 1956 a new class of schools was created: private free schools, which were fully subsidised by the government and offered free private education to underprivileged children. Enrolment in state schools declined as financial aid encouraged religious communities to open new schools that, the government noted, 'absorb[ed] a good number of the pupils who frequented official schools'.[64]

Moreover, a pivotal decree in March 1950 tempered previous emphasis on establishing state authority over private education. It reaffirmed that all schools were to adopt the national curriculum, but allowed private schools to choose different textbooks, pedagogies and supplementary subjects. It stated that only books on the history and geography of Lebanon required ministerial approval and only Lebanese students were to be taught in Arabic.[65] Ultimately, the decree appeared to sanction communal prerogatives over the education of children.[66] Rather than facing a sharp break from the Mandate era, private schools in independent Lebanon continued to convey different narratives of identity and founding myths of the nation to children from different confessional backgrounds.[67]

Abouchedid and Nasser trace the ambiguities of early Lebanese education policies to the political system and argue that 'perplexed by the politics of consociationalism, the Ministry of Education failed to express or even to maintain a consistent education policy'.[68] More accurately, education policy expressed an underlying clash between 'Muslims calling for cultural homogeneity' and 'Christians championing cultural heterogeneity'.[69] This mirrored fundamental tensions at the heart of Lebanon's power-sharing: below the surface of inclusive nationalism, simmered the divergent markers of identity, visions for the state and foreign policy orientation of different confessional communities.

In a regional environment polarised between pan-Arab nationalism (championed by Egyptian President Gamal Abdel Nasser) and the Baghdad pact (a pro-Western, anti-Communist organisation formed by Turkey, Iraq, the UK, Pakistan and Iran in 1955), the domestic conflict over foreign policy orientation strained Lebanon's institutions and led to the 1958 civil war.

3.1.3 *Compromises (1958–1974)*

The 1958 war can be best interpreted as the breakdown of a rigid corporate consociational political system, inadequate 'to channel political and socio-economic changes'.[70] In particular, the war embodied the emergence of a Sunni challenge to the political predominance of the Maronite community and 'ownership' of the executive Presidency.[71] Rather than settling the ambiguities at the heart of Lebanon's nation-state building project, the 1958 civil war institutionalised the 'sanctity of the [National] Pact'.[72] In its aftermath, President Fouad Chehab embarked on extensive reforms and called for the 'building of a new society'.[73] He encouraged the fine-tuning of Lebanese political and non-political institutions to ensure equilibrium among the different sects: his 'object was not the creation of a secular state, but to ensure that all communities got their share of the cake'.[74]

This approach permeated education policy. Some had seen the 1958 civil war as proof that the state had failed in furthering social cohesion through education.[75] After 1958, the government set out to expand schooling and partly succeeded in reducing regional disparities over the following decade. State schools increased from 184 in 1941 to 1487 in 1980: the majority were located in the South, the Bekaa and the North, and over 60 % of state school students were Muslim.[76]

Despite popular calls to improve the quality of state schools and increase government funding for public education, successive governments relied heavily on private schools to extend the reach of primary education.[77] Private institutions expanded their educational provision and the number of Christian community schools increased from 451 in 1920 to 548 in 1977. The previously underdeveloped Muslim educational provision increased sevenfold over the same period, from 41 community schools in 1920 to 300 in 1977.[78]

Moreover, in 1959, the state transferred powers of inspection to the regional level and specified that, while state schools should be inspected, private schools would only be 'supervised'.[79] Private schools remained free to promote 'their own divergent views of national identity and sense of civic loyalty'.[80] Once again, the divergence in values and narratives was most apparent when looking at textbooks for the national subjects, particularly history. Christian primary schools largely used textbooks that glorified a pre-Arab Lebanese past, while the newly politically conscious Shia community produced *The Enlightening History*, which focused on the anti-colonial struggles of the 'Arab nation'.[81]

Finally, the government revised the national curricula in 1968. In an attempt to sidestep the increasingly salient issue of Lebanese and Arab identities, the new curricula avoided references to the 'Lebanese nation', 'Lebanese identity' and other thorny social, political and civic issues.[82] In the early 1970s, the state also eliminated exams for citizenship education and most schools stopped teaching it. In its place, the government introduced one hour per week of religious education in all schools in 1973: the new subject was taught by clergymen chosen by religious authorities but paid by the state.[83]

Palestinian refugees emerged in this period as significant political actors and, as most other local political actors, relied partly on schools to convey identities and political allegiances to children. About 100,000 Palestinians settled in Lebanon after the 1948 Arab-Israeli war and a further 200,000–500,000 arrived in the aftermath of the 1967 Six-Day War and of the 1970 ousting of the Palestinian Liberation Organisation (PLO) from Jordan.[84] Palestinians resided in refugee camps and were marginalised from Lebanese society, politics and economy through an array of legal measures that prevented them from 'participating in government, working in more than 70 professions, accessing health and unemployment benefits, building and owning their own homes, travelling freely within Lebanon and obtaining a passport'.[85] Palestinian children attended schools managed by the United Nations Relief and Works Agency for Palestine Refugees in the Near East (UNRWA). These schools followed the Lebanese national curriculum but their hidden curriculum conveyed a vision of Lebanon as a pawn in the Arab struggle against the state of Israel and as 'Palestine's surrogate battlefield'.[86] Despite its official neutrality, the Lebanese state suffered the consequences of the PLO increasing military presence on its territory. The 1969 Cairo Agreement between the PLO and the Lebanese Army transferred de facto sovereignty over Palestinian refugee camps to the PLO and committed Lebanon to tolerance towards the PLO's military actions against Israel. Thus, from 1969, the PLO could act as 'a state within the state'. In return, the Cairo agreement bound the PLO 'not to interfere in Lebanese affairs'.[87]

'Lebanese affairs' were once again strained along familiar lines of identity, belonging and political allegiance. Lebanese nationalism 'deteriorated into a group ideology' associated with the Christian right, while Arab nationalism had an appeal 'almost exclusively among the Muslim masses'.[88] Moreover, Hanf notes that the early 1970s witnessed increasing social conflicts, which 'were not conflicts between communities but between social and economic groups and interests'.[89] However, socio-economic fractures often coincided with confessional and national cleavages: Muslims (particularly Shia) were overrepresented in the lowest socio-economic group and among the least educated.[90] Thus, the Shia Movement of the Dispossessed (Amal) exemplifies the coincidence of communal and socio-economic interests: by founding new schools and orphanages, the movement exploited 'the political potential of social assistance as a means of outflanking the traditional elites and entering the political arena'.[91]

Adding to these overlapping socio-economic, confessional and national cleavages was the perception, particularly among Christians, that 'the state could not guarantee the safety of its citizens' against the Palestinian insurgency.[92] The weakness of the central state was an intrinsic and valued aspect of communal autonomy in a corporate consociation, but in the 1970s it also 'created insecurity, forcing factions to establish their own independent power structures and to look for support beyond Lebanon's borders'.[93] One after the other, Lebanon's communities created militias.

Hanf aptly summarises the main perspectives explaining Lebanese descent into civil war in the early 1970s:

> One thesis is that the sham conflict of the traditional political class could no longer conceal the fundamental economic contradictions in the country: it is regarded as a conflict between rich and poor. Another thesis holds that the conflict is one between a Lebanese nationalism mainly supported by Christians and an Arab nationalism with largely Muslim support: a conflict of identity. A third thesis treats it primarily as a conflict between the concept of a traditionalist, "confessional" state and that of a modern, secular and politically integrated state: a conflict between pre-modern and modern politics.[94]

In fact, in the mid-1970s the positions of rival factions were 'a lump sum': Muslim communities proposed 'a package of domestic, pan-Arab and Palestinian politics' and challenged the Christian emphasis on sovereignty and stability.[95] Through schools and the media, communal actors disseminated divergent and hostile narratives: mutually exclusive identity markers and political allegiances both reflected and framed deepening communal polarisation, and inter-communal differences evolved into 'confessional labels and fighting banners'.[96]

3.1.4   Civil War (1975–1989)

In the 15 years of civil war, the impact of fighting, the population movements, the hollowing of state authority, the cantonisation of Lebanese territory, the re-emergence of communities as the primary provider of services to citizens, and the communal *quasi*-monopoly over education, further undermined the state education system.

During the war, militia leaders channelled state financial resources to areas under their control and instituted '*para*-statal systems' complete with autonomous education systems.[97] Harik argues that the social institutions filling the gap of a retiring state 'were also set to work on projects that specifically reinforced primordial communal attachments'.[98] Indeed, in South Lebanon, Amal opened over 33 state schools and Hizbollah employed Iranian funding to build and operate new theological schools.[99] The new schools, beyond adding 'legitimacy to new elites', had an important political and military function: they provided rewards for the families of the fallen and strengthened the social fabric so as to 'keep residents on the land'.[100] Moreover, Harik suggests that social institutions created by the rival militias in 'their' territories 'were made to illustrate deliberate models of the new republic that the planners hoped would arise in the aftermath of the civil war'.[101] Schools reflected the narratives, identities, political ideologies and visions of the different confessional communities: thus, the communalism 'of a Maronite [was] projected as Lebanese nationalism, of the Sunni Muslim it [was] Arab Nationalism..., of the Shiite [sic] egalitarianism'.[102]

Diverging outlooks were conveyed through, for example, the new contents of certain national subjects, such as history. Indeed, the history curriculum emerged as a further ideological battleground in the midst of a war that, to more than one communal leader, was about the establishment of the 'real' history of Lebanon.[103] In the areas under the control of the Progressive Socialist Party (PSP), new history books portrayed the Lebanese Republic as the creation of cunning Christian elites at the expense of other sects, and civic education classes conveyed socialist principles. Sunni and Maronite schools generally continued to formally teach history according to the state curriculum, but in practice their textbooks avoided discussing the origins of Lebanon's ethno-religious communities, thus presenting them as mutually exclusive, immemorial and stable. In particular, the history books portrayed the socio-economic development of each community as a parallel process, taking place in different geographical locations: this conveyed an image of innate Maronite orientation towards Europe and Sunni orientation towards the Arab world.[104] Thus, the history curricula reproduced the ideological building blocks of Lebanese nationalism and pan-Arabism on which the National Pact and the very existence of independent Lebanon had been founded.

Finally, in the territories controlled by militias, schools were employed as military recruitment grounds. Teachers persuaded children that their survival, and that of their family and community, was at stake and encouraged them to join local militias.[105]

Ironically, in 1981 the government initiated an attempt at comprehensive education reform.[106] The ambition to create through schools 'a democratic being' and to further 'respect of the other – individual and collective' was not accorded political priority and was quickly sidelined in the context of civil war.[107] In fact, the positions of religious and communal representatives over education are remarkably consistent with their positions in previous decades. Before and during the war, the representatives of Christian schools advocated 'cultural pluralism', meant as the provision of equal state funding to religious schools and the promotion of an education furthering mutual recognition, respect and coexistence. Cultural pluralism would teach Christians 'that Muslims are not carbon copies of them and vice versa'.[108] In contrast, Muslim educational councils consistently called for better state education, for state supervision of private schools and for the 'unification of textbooks and instruction' so as 'to strengthen national unity and Lebanon's identity, and its Arab relationships'.[109] Interestingly, and perhaps reflecting Christian weakness at the end of the war, the Muslim position would, almost unaltered, appear in the Taif Agreement.

3.1.5 *The Taif Agreement and Beyond (1990–Present)*

The *Document of National Accord*, known as the Taif Agreement, was approved by the Lebanese National Assembly in 1989 and ratified in August 1990. It attempted to settle controversies over Lebanon's identity, borders and very existence, establishing that 'Lebanon is a sovereign, free, and independent country and a final homeland for all its citizens' and that 'Lebanon is Arab in belonging and identity'.[110]

The agreement reflects the reality of Syrian and Israeli occupation of Lebanese territory in 1989. It enshrines a 'special relationship' between Lebanon and Syria, further entrenched in the May 1991 Lebanon-Syria Treaty of Cooperation.[111] The 'special relationship' was manifested most clearly in the continuing Syrian military occupation of the Lebanese territory and intrusion in Lebanese domestic politics. Under occupation, the selective implementation of Taif's provisions became 'a potent lever of Syrian power over Lebanon'.[112] In contrast, Taif advocates taking 'all the steps necessary to liberate all Lebanese territories from the Israeli occupation': this allowed Hizbollah alone among the Lebanese militias to retain its arms and continue military resistance in the South.[113]

Domestically, the agreement re-established a consociation in Lebanon. This reflected the 'political culture of coexistence and compromise' nurtured by the National Pact and expressed by most Lebanese citizens throughout the 15 years of war.[114] As mentioned, Taif assigned equal numbers of parliamentary seats to Christians and Muslims, and reaffirmed the customary assignment of the positions of president, prime minister and speaker of the chamber of deputies to a Maronite, Sunni and Shia, respectively. In the post-war constitutional 'fine-tuning', presidential powers were reduced to the advantage of the speaker and, more substantially, of the prime minister.[115]

Hudson argues that Taif was based on a 'consociationalism-plus' model.[116] Indeed, the agreement envisages the establishment of a complex consociation rather than a return to corporate practices. This is most evident in its prescriptions for the phased abolition of political sectarianism, which were never implemented under Syrian occupation.[117] Thus, the Lebanese political system relapsed into familiar corporate consociational patterns and into rigid structures unable to adapt to socio-demographic and strategic changes. Under the Syrian aegis, the agreement was not implemented and the 'troika' of the president, prime minister and speaker of the parliament came to dominate the political system, overshadowing both the cabinet and the deputies in decision-making.[118] Successive governments between 1992 and 2005 redefined the function of the state as 'to make the economy "competitive"… but … play only a minimal role in income distribution and welfare provision'.[119] This view of the function of the state would also influence education policy.

The complex consociation established in Taif also relied on education reform as a complementary mechanism to further long-term stability. The Taif Agreement calls for the expansion of state elementary school provision, protection of private institutions, establishment of state control over private schools, reform of national curricula and production of unified textbooks for history and civic education.[120] It establishes an explicit link between education policy and sustainable peace in Lebanon, echoing two recurring themes in the history of Lebanon's education system: state attempts to establish control over private schools and state designs to promote overarching narratives and allegiances through the curricula. Finally, the education reforms mapped in Taif reflect long-standing Muslim educational priorities in calling for 'the re-socialisation of children along national unitary lines'.[121]

Chapters 4, 5 and 7 explain debates over the reforms mapped out in Taif: the drafting of a unified history curriculum and textbook, the framing of a common citizenship education curriculum and textbook, and the redressing of the dichotomy between public and private schools. They show that successive Lebanese governments reiterated rhetorical commitments to producing common curricula to convey 'feelings of unity among citizens and the developments of notions of solidarity and fraternity' and to establish state control over private institutions.[122] Yet, the pluralist principles underpinning Lebanon's corporate consociation also legitimise the thriving of parallel schools and of competing identities and allegiances.

Indeed, in the early 1990s, the civil war appeared to have solved the fundamental debate over identity, teaching 'the Lebanese that they [were] a nation and that they want[ed] to remain a nation'.[123] It also appeared to have settled the long-standing struggles over borders, establishing that an independent Lebanese state should exist.[124] Yet, the momentous changes of 2000–2005 revived clashes over the intertwined issues of communities' relative power in the state and of Lebanon's alignments in the regional state system. In 2000, Israel withdrew from South Lebanon, and its conflict with Hizbollah reduced to inter-border skirmishes over the contested territories of Shebaa, Ghajar and Kfar Shuba. This, combined with the UN Security Council Resolution 1559 of 2004 delegitimised Hizbollah's military presence in Lebanon in the eyes of the majority of the Sunni and Maronite communities.

Moreover, the assassination of ex-Prime Minister Rafic Hariri in 2005, and the subsequent Syrian military withdrawal from the Lebanese territory, triggered the polarisation of Lebanese politics into rival blocs: the pro-Syrian, pro-Iranian 8 March coalition, and the pro-Western 14 March coalition. Knudsen and Kerr observe that from 2005 'this two-bloc system has left Lebanon ungovernable'.[125] Indeed, the March 8 and March 14 coalitions hold fundamentally different perspectives on the 1990–2005 period, rely on rival external sponsors and express conflicting aspirations for the reform of Lebanon's corporate consociation.[126] They are headed by the Shia party Hizbollah and the Sunni Future party respectively, confirming that the most politically salient cleavage in post-2005 Lebanon is not between Christians and Muslims, but between Sunni Muslim and Shia Muslims. Indeed, representatives of the Maronite community sit on both sides of the political divide. The Sunni-Shia cleavage solidified in 2008 when Hizbollah, protesting against government attempts to dismantle its telecommunications network, turned its weapons against fellow Lebanese citizens and occupied central Beirut.[127] The 2011 Arab Spring, the civil war in Syria, the influx of over a million registered Syrian refugees and the employment of Lebanese territory as a base for military operations both against and in support of the Syrian regime added fuel to the fire, and brought Lebanon back to the brink of war.

This section has shown that since its creation, the Lebanese state has existed in a complex, dialectical and interdependent relationship with its communities and that state institutions have evolved into arenas for clashes of identity and political allegiance, periodically tearing up the fabric of society. The same tensions have also permeated the education system: efforts to reform curricula and state schools in the 1940s exemplify the state's drive to impose itself as a legitimate and hegemonic actor. However, the founding principles of Lebanon's consociation also legitimised communal control over certain private schools. From the late 1950s, and increasingly during the civil war, the legitimacy of a state built on the principle of religious and communal pluralism came to depend on the extent to which each confessional community was included in state institutions and narratives. This affected education policy: pluralism, initially viewed as the provision of mixed common plural schools, came to be understood as the provision of financial support for a plurality of communal institutions conveying diverging narratives of identity.

The history of Lebanon's education system provides an important clue as to the political function of education in consociations: before and throughout the civil war, schools remained the primary 'means of preserving and reproducing group identity' in Lebanon.[128] Chapters 4, 5, 6 and 7 trace reforms of history education, citizenship education, the languages of instruction and the fragmented structure of the education system after the Taif Agreement to determine in which ways the manifest and hidden curricula helped or hindered consociational politics.

3.2 Northern Ireland

The Government of Ireland Act of 1920 established a devolved parliament in Stormont (Belfast), under the ultimate authority of the British Parliament, for six of the nine counties of the province of Ulster, severing what would become Northern Ireland (under continuing British sovereignty) from the emerging sovereign Irish Free State in the South. In contrast to Lebanon, the borders of Northern Ireland were dictated by demography: it was 'the largest area [of the Irish isle] which could be comfortably held with a majority in favour of the union with Britain'.[129] Here, societal cleavages crystallised in parallel to the solidification of the border in the 1920s and early 1930s, and religious denomination emerged as the primary marker of identity. To their respective counterparts, Catholic came to mean (Irish) Nationalist and disloyal to the Stormont parliament, while Protestant came to mean (British) Unionist and loyal to Stormont. As Akenson puts it, the hostile reciprocal perceptions of Catholics as 'traitors' and Protestants as 'oppressors', became 'self-fulfilling predictions'.[130]

At the time of partition, schools in Northern Ireland (like schools in Ottoman Lebanon) were largely under the control of local churches.

The Irish Education Act of 1831 had established non-denominational, free elementary education in Ireland under the premise that 'admitting children of all persuasions should not interfere with the particular tenets of any [religious denomination]'.[131] Yet, clerical campaigns succeeded in bringing most schools under the control of the Protestant or Catholic clergies, and schools evolved into denominational establishments 'that served their own faith communities'.[132] Thus, by the late 1800s, Ireland had a dual and unequal education system separated along denominational lines. Separate schools protected and reproduced the Protestant distinctive identity within a majority Catholic Irish isle, and provided Catholic children with 'a Catholic education, on Catholic principles, with Catholic masters and the use of Catholic books'.[133]

This section considers education policies at the establishment of Northern Ireland (1920–1946), under Unionist political hegemony (1947–1967) and during the Troubles (1968–1998), before briefly introducing the Belfast Agreement and subsequent educational reforms. Reflecting on the complexity of Northern Ireland's education system, Bell asserted that 'if you were starting from a blank sheet of paper this is not what you would start from, everybody is in agreement with that'.[134] This historical analysis of the political function of education in Northern Ireland shows that the complex structure of the education system is due to the fact that different education sectors became further markers of identity. Before and during the conflict, the Protestant/Unionist community and the Catholic/Nationalist community employed 'their' schools to reinforce religious and national cleavages and convey allegiance or opposition to the British state.

3.2.1 *Northern Ireland (1920–1947)*

Institutions in Northern Ireland were established under enormous sociopolitical pressures, and the education system is no exception. Unionists were determined to preserve their political dominance and control over the administration to ensure continued union with Great Britain. They maintained that Catholics were intrinsically disloyal to the state, but also feared Westminster's indifference in the destiny of Northern Ireland. In contrast, the Nationalist minority questioned the institutions and the very existence of Northern Ireland as separate from the Irish Free State: they initially boycotted local institutions in the conviction that partition was reversible.[135]

Kerr argues that in the early 1920s, 'the government's core objective was to dispel the notion that partition might be a temporary expedient prior to the unification of Ireland'.[136] The creation of the first Northern Ireland Ministry of Education in 1921 provided an ideal opportunity to pursue this objective through the curricula and structures of compulsory schooling. A committee, supervised by the Unionist Robert Lynn, was tasked with investigating the local education system: its recommendations would form the backbones of the 1923 Education Act (Northern Ireland). The 1923 Act established the basic architecture for Northern Ireland's complex education system. It created three school sectors: controlled schools, fully funded and managed by the state; maintained schools, partially funded and including limited state representation on the management board; and voluntary schools, privately funded and independently managed.[137] The first Northern Ireland government hoped that financial incentives and flexible management structures would persuade the local clergies to transfer schools to state management. This would effectively establish the control of the secular state over an education system previously dominated by local churches.[138]

The government's approach to state building also permeated curricular choices. Severing a further bond with the Irish Free State, Irish-language education was rapidly dismissed as a 'purely sentimental thing'.[139] Moreover, religious instruction was prohibited in state-controlled schools. This is because Northern Ireland's policymakers viewed religious denomination as the most divisive marker of identity in the province: Minister of Education Lord Londonderry hoped that a non-denominational state education system would attract pupils from both the Unionist/Protestant and the Nationalist/Catholic communities and contribute to integration when 'union is so essential to the well-being of the province'.[140] Clerical marginalisation in education was also expected to bring about 'a process of incremental integration' and to foster allegiance to Northern Ireland.[141]

Darby ironically observes that 'with rare ecumenical spirit, all the churches opposed the [1923 Education] Act'.[142] The Act was passed with no input from the Nationalist community: in their campaign against the very existence of the state, the Catholic clergy and laity refused to recognise the Ministry of Education, appealed to Dublin for school funding and boycotted the Lynn committee.[143] Hereafter, the Catholic clergy refused to transfer its schools to state management, ostensibly fearing Protestant proselytism, but most probably concerned with the loyalty to the new state presumably fostered by controlled schools.[144] Similarly, the

Protestant clergy resisted pressures to transfer its schools to state management, claiming it would turn them into non-denominational 'godless [state] schools'.[145] The United Education Committee called for Bible instruction in schools and for 'Protestant teachers to teach Protestant children'.[146]

Northern Ireland Prime Minister James Craig was painfully aware of the need to close Unionist ranks before the 1925 general election and the final deliberations of the Irish Boundary Commission. He agreed to amend the 1923 Education Act to permit 'simple Bible instruction' and to allow controlled schools to appoint teachers on the basis of their religious denomination. Rapidly, the Protestant clergy started transferring schools to state management but Unionist campaigns continued. They complained about the Catholic refusal to transfer schools to state management and demanded the presence of school owners (the Protestant clergy) on the five Education and Library Boards (ELBs), which managed state-controlled schools.[147]

By 1930, the Protestant and Catholic clergies had eroded governmental resolve to establish a unified, non-denominational education system in Northern Ireland. With the 1930 Education Act, the new Unionist government legitimised and enshrined the reality of separate schools catering for children of different backgrounds. As the Prime Minister concluded, with the new Act 'it will be absolutely certain that in no circumstances whatever will Protestant children ever be in any way interfered with by Roman Catholics, any more than Protestants wish to interfere with Roman Catholic children'.[148]

The Protestant clergy accepted full state funding but, in transferring schools to state management, retained the right to impart Bible instruction in state schools and to sit on school boards.[149] Thus, with the 1930 Act, the government effectively acquiesced in the gradual transformation of non-denominational state schools into de facto Protestant institutions.[150] For its part, by 1930 the Catholic clergy had realised that Dublin would not financially support Catholic schools in the north and accepted the 50 % funding being offered by the state to voluntary schools. The clergy retained direct control of Catholic schools but started lobbying Stormont for full financial support. Hereafter, while turning a blind eye to Protestant clerical influence on controlled schools, successive governments would increase funding to Catholic schools.[151]

The trajectory of Northern Ireland's education policy appears parallel to that of Lebanon. In both cases, new governments set out to create an education system that socialised children into overarching identities and allegiance to the state. In both cases, local confessional and national communities succeeded in shifting political priorities away from challenging children's physical and emotional separation in schools, and towards fostering the equality of separate schools through, for example, financial support for private (or voluntary) establishments.

3.2.2 Limited Reform (1947–1968)

After World War II, local legislation reinforced the dual and unequal structure of schooling, entrenching two 'self-encapsulated' educational sectors that were ostensibly 'demarcated on religious lines', but also reproduced the national aspirations of the Unionist and Nationalist communities.[152]

The 1947 Education Act established the basic structure of Northern Ireland's education cycles, introducing primary education up to age eleven, followed by a test determining each pupil's academic ability (known as the 11-plus) and admission to either grammar or secondary school depending on the test results. The Act introduced mandatory Bible instruction and daily acts of worship in the controlled sector, thereby wiping out the last traces of Londonderry's plan for an inclusive, non-denominational state education system.[153] Hereafter, Protestant schools were swiftly transferred to state management. The 1947 Education Act also provided 65 % funding for voluntary schools that accepted two state representatives on their boards, and this increased to 80 % in 1968.[154] Thus, the 1947 Act ensured the survival and thriving of a Catholic maintained education sector outside state control. The 1947 Education Act and the 1968 Education Act therefore cemented the separate and parallel structures of Northern Ireland's education system: in 1967, over 99 % of pupils in state-controlled schools were Protestant and 99 % of pupils in maintained schools were Catholic.[155]

Beyond separating children at a very young age, different school sectors socialised pupils into deeply divergent narratives and allegiances associated with the Protestant/Unionist and Catholic/Nationalist community. No national curriculum existed, so teachers 'had almost complete autonomy to decide what was taught to students between the ages of 4 and 14'.[156] Catholic maintained schools argued that 'the only agreed syllabus for Catholics is the catechism of their Church' but in fact complemented it with good doses of Irish nationalism, adopting textbooks produced in Dublin, teaching Irish history and the Irish language.[157] In contrast, state-controlled schools adopted books produced in the UK and taught history from an English perspective.[158] Thus, the contents of schooling reflected the coincidence of denominational, national and political cleavages in Northern Ireland: children were taught not only different religious denominations but also different narratives, which sustained the identity and national aspirations of Unionists and Nationalists. Beyond fostering children's identification with a community, schools in Northern Ireland also helped 'determine whether a child would be loyal or disloyal to the state'.[159]

However, the 1947 Act did not placate clerical dissent. The Protestant clergy had succeeded in bending the state education system into de facto Protestant schools, but now 'considered it unfair that the Catholics could opt to stay outside the state system and still benefit from public money'.[160] In contrast, the Catholic hierarchy continued to demand full state funding for their schools. Northern Ireland's Catholics continued to experience systematic socio-economic and political discrimination, exemplified by occupational figures: in 1971, 16 % of Protestant men held managerial positions compared with only 9 % of Catholic men, while 16 % of Protestant men were unskilled or unemployed compared with as much as 31 % of Catholic men.[161] In this context, Catholic schools were the main instrument for the social mobility of Northern Ireland's minority and 'the importance of separate Catholic schools was not only ideological or cultural, but, in a very real sense, material'.[162]

In fact, by expanding access to education for all citizens, the 1947 Act had armed a 'time bomb': a new generation of Catholics 'educated beyond the capacity or the willingness of society to find suitable work for them'.[163] This new generation did not refuse to engage with Stormont: they accepted partition as a reality to be dealt with and realised that the Irish government would not act upon its irredentist claim to the north. In their campaigns, they adopted the language of human rights and appealed for 'British rights for British citizens'. In the Unionist camp, Prime Minister Terence O'Neill was attempting to reformulate Unionism and 'build bridges' with the Catholic/Nationalist community.[164] Still, the Unionist majority in the Stormont parliament only agreed to electoral reforms amending the local franchise to grant 'one-man one-vote' in April 1969. By that time, the Troubles had already started.

3.2.3 Troubles (1968–1998)

Obershall concisely summarises that 'the Troubles had three major clusters of collective violence': the first, starting in 1968, was followed by the 1973 British peace initiative at Sunningdale; the second, starting with opposition to the Sunningdale Agreement and power-sharing executive, was followed by the 1985 Anglo-Irish Agreement; the third, marked by Republican and Loyalist violence, ended with the Belfast Agreement on 10 April 1998.[165]

Having established direct rule over Northern Ireland in 1972, London attempted to pacify the province through an ambiguous balancing of sticks (counterinsurgency and military interventions) and carrots (social policies promoting the social inclusion and equality of the Catholic community). During direct rule, the education system emerged as the primary 'institutional scapegoat for the conflict'.[166] Rather than the product of primordial religious differences, the fragmented education system was now seen as an independent factor contributing to inter-communal strife. Research indicated that 'at best, prejudices are not diminished by education and, at worst, they are in fact strengthened'.[167] Thus, British officials called on Northern Ireland's schools to promote understanding and harmony between the Unionist/Protestant and Nationalist/Catholic communities through their curricula and by encouraging contact between children from different backgrounds.[168]

The most ambitious attempt to employ schools for peace-building occurred during the short 1974 power-sharing executive. In April 1974, Northern Ireland Education Minister Basil McIvor called for the Assembly to create a new class of schools, 'shared schools', which would involve both the Protestant and the Catholic clergies in their management.[169] McIvor argued that 'the mixing of school children would contribute to the reduction of community tension in Northern Ireland' and envisaged that all controlled and Catholic maintained schools could, over the long term, evolve into 'shared schools'.[170] Despite initial resistance, the power-sharing executive committed to support the establishment of shared schools. Chadwick argues that 'the 1974 decision showed that a Northern Ireland government, in which both Catholics and Protestants participated, could act to allow for shared schools'.[171] Certainly, the Protestant clergy appeared 'prepared to give at least a guarded welcome to the idea of shared schools', mainly because mixed education could undermine Catholic control over some schools.[172] Still, the Catholic hierarchy was opposed outright.[173] This opposition did not escalate only because the fate of 'shared schools' was intertwined with the destiny of the power-sharing government: when the power-sharing executive collapsed in May 1974, the plan for mixed schools was sidelined.

Subsequent governments endorsed the ambition to create mixed schools but recognised that 'integration will be best served by leaving it to develop … quietly, without publicity and certainly without overt pressure from Government'.[174] The 1978 Education Act stated that future policy 'should not create or perpetuate barriers against integrated education' and provided mechanisms for transformation of controlled and maintained schools to shared establishments.[175] Despite giving a powerful signal of intent, and laying the ground for the establishment of a third educational sector, the 1978 Act failed to create momentum for integration of the existing schools: no school transferred to mixed status.[176] The first integrated school, Lagan College, was created in 1981 by an independent parent-led civil society organisation: *All Children Together*.[177] In the 1980s and 1990s, the expanding network of integrated schools impacted upon the educational discourse in Northern Ireland, making it difficult to express open political opposition to the mixed education of children belonging to Catholic/Nationalist and Protestant/Unionist backgrounds.[178] The success of integrated education also confirmed that initiatives for inter-communal mixing could thrive when independent from clerical and political pressures.[179]

For its part, the Department of Education of Northern Ireland (DENI) started providing resources and material to facilitate joint activities among pupils from state-controlled and Catholic maintained schools. It also introduced the voluntary cross-curricular theme of *Education for Mutual Understanding* (EMU) whose aims and contents are explained in Chap. 5.[180] In a 1982 circular, it clarified that DENI 'is not questioning the right to insist on forms of education in schools which amount to segregation' but qualified this 'right' as being 'coupled to an inescapable duty to ensure that effective measures are taken to ensure that children do not grow up in ignorance, fear or even hatred of those from whom they are educationally segregated'.[181] Still, the Catholic clergy remained suspicious, and maintained that 'short of banning religion altogether, there is no greater injury that could be done to Catholicism than by interference with the character and identity of our schools'.[182] National identity, religion, community and school remained one and the same: only by attending Catholic maintained schools could children become part of the religious (and national) community.

State 'intrusion' in schools culminated with the 1989 Education Reform Order (ERO), which aimed to standardise the educational experience of all children in Northern Ireland. First, the 1989 ERO introduced a statutory curriculum to be implemented in all state-funded schools, which provided core contents for history education and institutionalised EMU as a compulsory cross-curricular theme.[183] The introduction of a statutory curriculum opened a debate about the status of religious education, leading to the joint formulation of a core religious education curriculum by representatives of the Catholic Church and of three Protestant Churches (Church of Ireland, Presbyterian and Methodist). This was a symbolically important step towards dialogue and reconciliation.[184] Yet, it was also a limited step: to this day, it is unclear whether it is even possible to speak of a common religious education curriculum in Northern Ireland due to the flexibility of the religious education syllabus. Two, deeply different approaches to religious education persist in the Catholic maintained and state-controlled sectors, confirming that religious denomination remains a fundamental and impermeable marker of communal identity in Northern Ireland, and that schools remain an instrument for reproducing and conveying it.[185]

Second, the 1989 ERO expanded funding for the activities that brought together children from controlled and Catholic maintained schools and institutionalised them under the rubric of *Inter-School Contact Schemes*.[186] Echoing arguments voiced in the 1920s, the Catholic maintained sector opposed both EMU and inter-school activities because they might offer opportunities for proselytism.[187] It also argued that EMU and inter-school contact could 'undermine the traditions of the society', thereby implying that separate schooling was instrumental to the integrity and thriving of two supposedly mutually exclusive cultures in Northern Ireland.[188] Finally, the 1989 ERO placed a statutory requirement on DENI 'to encourage and facilitate the development of integrated education': to this end, the government provided full funding for integrated schools.[189] Both the state-controlled and the Catholic maintained sectors raised cries of 'social engineering'.[190]

These protests were temporarily silenced by the 1993 ERO, which established full state funding for all schools that adopted the statutory curriculum and accepted state representatives on their governing boards. The 1993 ERO responded to London's increasing political emphasis on parental choice in education, but also reflected Northern Irish concerns. In the late 1980s, research had found that the standard of education in Catholic maintained schools was lower than in state schools. Policymakers were deeply aware that schooling exacerbates violent identity-based conflicts when different religious, national or ethnic groups have access to education of differing quality. To redress this imbalance, the state started funding Catholic maintained schools on a par with state-controlled and integrated schools.[191] For its part, the Catholic Church modified the schools' management structures and created a Council for Catholic Maintained Schools (CCMS).[192]

In 1995, Smith observed that Northern Ireland's education system was 'a genuinely segregated system ... but in almost all the publicly measurable ways few obvious differences could be found'.[193] Indeed, state-controlled, integrated and Catholic maintained schools followed the same curriculum, participated to the same inter-school activities and were funded by the same state agencies. Yet, they remained managed by separate bodies, and catered to different sections of Northern Ireland's population: as such, most schools remained markers of identity and belonging.

3.2.4 The Belfast Agreement and Beyond (1998–Present)

The *Agreement* finalised in Belfast on 10 April 1998 was presented to the electorate and approved in two joint referendums in Northern Ireland and the Republic of Ireland in May 1998. Like the Taif Agreement, the Belfast Agreement provided for the establishment of a complex consociation as a mechanism to regulate the Troubles. However, Northern Ireland's consociation differs from its Lebanese counterpart in being more liberal: rather than assigning a fixed proportion of parliamentary seats and cabinet positions to each community, it 'rewards whatever salient political identities emerge in democratic elections' but still provides strong institutional checks and balances to protect the interests and identities of Unionists and Nationalists.[194] Despite its flexibility, Northern Ireland's consociation had a delayed start: the Assembly was suspended between 11 February and 30 May 2000, on 10 August 2001, on 22 September 2001 and from 14 October 2002. The Assembly was restored only on 7 May 2007, after the 2006 St Andrews Agreement paved the way for the Democratic Unionist Party's (DUP) acceptance of power-sharing with Sinn Féin.[195]

Northern Ireland's consociation is complex because it provides for devolution (under current British sovereignty) and a possible future transfer of the territory to Irish sovereignty (subject to majority opinion in a referendum). Therefore, the Belfast Agreement differs from Taif's focus on unalterable borders. This is because the Belfast Agreement is foremost a settlement between Northern Ireland's national communities, the Irish Nationalists and the British Unionists.[196] Since 1998, Northern Ireland's political institutions have been largely premised on the assumption that citizens identify with one of two 'traditions': the Protestant/Unionist tradition and the Catholic/Nationalist tradition are accorded 'parity of esteem'.[197] Thus, a local politician confirms that 'the agreement is based on the institutionalised assumption of two communities, separate but equal, and living in peaceful coexistence'.[198]

In contrast to the extensive provisions of the Taif Agreement, the Belfast Agreement maps only two education reforms. McGarry and O'Leary argue that this is because Northern Ireland's education system, allowing for choice between equally funded Catholic maintained (de facto Protestant) state-controlled, and integrated sectors, already conformed to 'liberal consociational' principles.[199] However, the Lebanese education system also reflected the consociational principle of communal autonomy at the end of the civil war. It was because of the insistence of Muslims that the Taif Agreement provided for extensive education reforms to promote social integration and nation-state building through schools. This suggests that the reforms mapped in the Belfast and Taif Agreements did not just reflect the necessities of the newly established consociational political systems: rather, they responded to the idiosyncrasies and political priorities of those political parties and communities that participated in conflict and entered into peace.

Indeed, reflecting the newly entrenched inclusion of Nationalists in state institutions, the Belfast Agreement required the state to 'place a statutory duty on the Department of Education to encourage and facilitate Irish-medium education'.[200] It also called for 'the promotion of a culture of tolerance at every level of society, including initiatives to facilitate and encourage integrated education'.[201] These two reforms exemplify the dual function of education in the Belfast Agreement: on the one hand, schooling is expected to protect and reproduce the mutually exclusive markers and narratives of identity of Northern Ireland's confessional, national and political communities. On the other hand, education is expected to provide opportunities for mixing and to encourage mutual understanding among children of different backgrounds. Chapters 4, 5 and 6 show that this tension seeped into debates over the curricula for history education, citizenship education and languages. Chapter 7 discusses how this dual political function of education impacted on reforms of the overall education system.

Controversy over education policy was one of the first tests faced by Northern Ireland's power-sharing executive. The appointment of Martin

McGuinness, a former Irish Republican Army leader, as Minister of Education in the first power-sharing executive, led to walkouts in schools and protests against 'placing... children's development in the hands of a person with connections to paramilitaries'.[202]

McGuinness' outspoken opposition to academic selection at age 11 also proved contentious. As mentioned previously, since 1947 children had only been admitted to the prestigious grammar schools on the basis of a state-run test taken at the age of 11 (the '11-plus'). Opponents of academic selection at age 11 argue that it perpetuates social stratification and leaves working-class pupils behind.[203] Supporters of the 11-plus test see grammar schools as an instrument for social mobility, as part of the heritage and tradition of Northern Ireland and as key to academic excellence.[204] The debate over the 11-plus test turned into a heated political battle because of the polarisation of Nationalist parties and Unionist parties into different camps: the former opposed academic selection while the latter supported it. A day before the suspension of the Northern Ireland Assembly in 2002, McGuinness announced the elimination of the state-run 11-plus test. The decision to eliminate it was only finalised by the British minister responsible for education after a widespread consultation in 2004, and the last state-run 11-plus test took place as late as 2008. Yet, the controversial decision to abolish academic selection remained associated with the contentious figure of McGuinness.[205]

In Unionist eyes, the abolition of the 11-plus embodied Nationalist political assertiveness, but also 'the ineffectual nature of Unionist political representatives'.[206] The quality gap between grammar and non-grammar secondary schools in the state-controlled sector remained much larger than in the Catholic maintained sector, so the abolition of academic selection was perceived as hitting the Protestant/Unionist community disproportionately. The abolition of the 11-plus, combined with three key interlocking structural reforms proposed after the Belfast Agreement (the Entitlement Framework, Area Planning and the Education and Skills Authority discussed in Chap. 7), led to 'a sense of loss within the Protestant community of its schools while the Catholic sector remains largely intact'.[207] Once again, the education system was at the forefront of communal perceptions of relative disadvantage that could destabilise the peace process. Indeed, by late 2012, Unionist perceptions of the negative returns of peace led to violent and protracted protests in Belfast.

Before the Belfast Agreement, Northern Ireland's education policies were largely premised on the assumption that 'religion is the bedrock reality upon which the political, social, and constitutional structure of Northern Ireland rests'.[208] Thus, efforts to establish mixed schools focused on neutralising religion by making schools non-denominational (in the 1920s), proposing the involvement of the Catholic and Protestant clergies in management (in 1974) or presenting them as pan-Christian (as integrated schools). Similarly, the introduction of a core curriculum for religious education was hailed as a momentous step on the path to reconciliation. The limited impact of these initiatives suggests that religion, far from a 'bedrock reality', was collectively constructed as an impermeable communal boundary in the context of a clash of competing nationalisms. The 'seemingly irresistible demand for segregated schooling' derived from the political function of schools as agents of socialisation into mutually exclusive 'clusters' of religious, national, socio-economic and communal cleavages.[209] The Protestant/Unionist community and the Catholic/Nationalist community employed their respective schools to convey diverging narratives of identity and attitudes to the state, thus preserving their internal cohesion and external political alignment.

Before and during the Troubles, successive governments came to accept the maxim that 'good fences make good neighbours' and gradually accorded parity of funding and 'esteem' to all educational sectors. Contrary to Taif, the Belfast Agreement did not challenge the existence of parallel and separate school sectors but endowed education with the dual function of preserving communal identities while promoting mutual understanding and tolerance. Chapters 4, 5, 6 and 7 examines education reforms since 1998 to determine the principles guiding education policy in consociational Northern Ireland.

First, though, an analysis of the development of education in Macedonia sheds further light on the political function of schools in deeply divided societies.

3.3 Macedonia

Macedonia embodies the paradigm of a contested state. Its borders emerged from the partition of the territory of historic Macedonia, previously under Ottoman control, among Bulgaria, Serbia and Greece during the First Balkan War (1913). The state was first constructed under the aegis of Socialist Yugoslavia, which constituted Macedonia as a republic and engaged in extensive nation-building. The Macedonian republic only became independent because of the collapse of Yugoslavia.

This section considers the evolving political function of schooling alongside the development of Macedonia from a Serbian province (1918–1944), to a founding republic in socialist Yugoslavia (1945–1974 and 1974–1991), to an independent nation-state between 1991 and 2001. Finally, it summarises the Ohrid Agreement of 2001, which established a liberal consociation in Macedonia. It shows that in the Macedonian territory, successive states attempted to employ education to convey a collective, overarching identity to their diverse population. The curricula and the structure of the education system in the territory of present-day Macedonia mirrored the founding narratives and principles underpinning each state building project: schools evolved from an instrument of Serbian cultural assimilation in 1918–1944, to a vehicle for conveying Marxism in 1945–1991, to a tool for constructing an independent nation-state between 1991 and 2001.

3.3.1 As Part of Yugoslavia (1918–1989)

Lampe shows that the history of the Yugoslav state was characterised by two distinct nation-building projects: the monarchical state (1918–1944) enforced Serbian dominance over the government and its cultural apparatus,[210] while the Communist regime (1945–1989) articulated collective identity through a distinctive interpretation of Marxist doctrine, accommodating the diversity of the local population.[211] Both the monarchy and the communist regime attempted to strike a balance between the demands and ambitions of Yugoslavia's many ethnic, linguistic and religious groups.[212] In this context, schools were employed both as instruments for nation-state building and as tools to nurture the linguistic and cultural specificities of the different local communities.

At the establishment of Yugoslavia in 1918, the educational infrastructure in the territory of present-day Macedonia was almost non-existent. As in Lebanon, in the historic territory of Ottoman Macedonia most schools were affiliated to religious establishments or neighbouring states (particularly Serbia, Bulgaria and Greece that hoped to gain a strategic foothold in Macedonia).[213] When Serbia annexed present-day Macedonia in 1913, the Serbian military authorities started employing schools in 'new Serbia' to assimilate their subjects and impose allegiance to Belgrade.[214]

A Serbian Province (1918–1944)
The Kingdom of Serbs, Croats and Slovenes emerged from the ashes of the Austro-Hungarian and Ottoman empires in 1918, and was renamed

the Kingdom of Yugoslavia in 1929. At the 1919 Paris Peace Conference, Serbian representatives consistently refused to acknowledge the existence of non-Serbian people in present-day Macedonia and Kosovo.[215] Indeed, the monarchical nation-state building project excluded both the ethnic Macedonian and the ethnic Albanian populations of Yugoslavia.

Education policy from the late 1920s exemplifies the marginalisation of ethnic Macedonians and ethnic Albanians in the new state. The Yugoslav state expanded access to schooling: in 1939 about 51 % of children were enrolled in primary schools, compared with about 27 % before World War I.[216] Yet education policy and management were centralised in Belgrade, and Serbo-Croatian was imposed as the only language of instruction. Moreover, in an attempt to convey allegiance to the new state, new textbooks glorified the Yugoslav monarchy and promoted the image of Yugoslavs as a single people belonging to three 'tribes': the Serbs, the Croats and the Slovenes.[217] Serbian history dominated the new narratives of the past while idealised portrayals of the tripartite Yugoslav nation 'contradicted the reality of an unsolved national question'.[218] In fact, local elites resisted Belgrade's directions and continued distributing pre-war textbooks for over a decade. In Croatia, textbooks emphasised multinational coexistence within the Habsburg empire, while in Serbia (including the territories of present-day Kosovo and Macedonia) they completely ignored the multi-ethnic nature of the state. In most schools, the uniform textbooks distributed by Belgrade were introduced only in 1937.[219]

In 'new Serbia' (present-day Macedonia) schooling remained an instrument for the assimilation of the local population into the 'official culture' of Serbian officers, teachers and colonists: use of the Macedonian and Bulgarian languages was forbidden in 1918 and traditional cultural expressions were suppressed.[220] Despite a common resentment against Serbian political and cultural dominance of the Kingdom of Yugoslavia, the population in 'new Serbia' was torn between Bulgarian and Macedonian collective identities.[221] Even the members of the main Macedonian nationalist parties were split between advocates of Macedonian independence and champions of unity with the Bulgarian nation.[222] The ethnic Albanian population of 'new Serbia' was equally marginalised: they were considered 'Albanian-speaking Serbs', and use of the Albanian language was forbidden.[223] From the mid-1920s, the Yugoslav authorities also encouraged ethnic Albanians to declare themselves Turks and to migrate to Turkey.[224] This did not placate Albanian demands for self-determination: armed resistance against Serbian rule in Kosovo and Western Macedonia continued into the 1920s and Islamic schools became 'underground centres of nationalist education and anti-government activities'.[225]

The collapse and partition of the Yugoslav state along ethnonational lines during World War II is testament to Belgrade's failure to formulate and convey an overarching identity to the citizens of Yugoslavia. The war also allowed the expression of underlying clashes of competing nationalisms encouraged by foreign powers in the territory of Macedonia. Italian occupiers nurtured Albanian nationalism, allowing the inhabitants of Kosovo and Western Macedonia to use the Albanian language in administration, schooling and even university education.[226] The Kingdom of Bulgaria occupied most of present-day Macedonia and the majority of the local ethnic Macedonian elites transferred their allegiances to Bulgaria. As part of their resistance to Italian, German and Bulgarian occupation, Yugoslav partisans created an Anti-Fascist Assembly of Macedonia, which purported to represent the interests of ethnic Macedonians and competed with Bulgarian authorities for popular allegiance. This culminated in the Anti-Fascist Assembly of Macedonia proclaiming the creation of a Macedonian Republic as the nation-state of ethnic Macedonians in 1944.[227] Nurturing ethnic Macedonian nationalism not only helped the partisan struggle against Italian and Bulgarian occupation of the Macedonian territory, but also reflected the long-standing position of the Yugoslav Communist Party, which since the 1920s had held that Macedonians constituted a distinct nation with a right to self-determination.[228] In fact, ethnic Macedonians lacked many of the attributes of distinct ethnonational groups in the 1940s: the daunting task of constructing a Macedonian nation would fall on the shoulders of the new Communist regime and its schools.

The People's Republic of Macedonia (1945–1973)

The Federal People's Republic of Yugoslavia was proclaimed in November 1945: it would embody a communist alternative to the Soviet Union and it would tirelessly search for a formula to promote the 'brotherhood and unity' of its ethnolinguistic communities.[229] In contrast to the monarchy, the new communist regime recognised the existence of most ethnolinguistic communities on the federal territory, but established a firm hierarchy among three kinds of groups.[230] Slovenes, Serbs, Croats, Montenegrins, Bosniaks (or Muslims) and Macedonians were 'constituent nations' and formed the largest proportion of the population in the constituent republics of Slovenia, Serbia, Croatia, Montenegro, Bosnia-Herzegovina and

Macedonia respectively. Despite being part of Serbia, the provinces of Kosovo and Vojvodina were also endowed with extensive territorial autonomy because of their distinctive demography: an Albanian majority in the former and over 26 ethnic groups in the latter. Territorial autonomy did not apply to the second and third categories of ethnolinguistic communities, 'national minorities' (communities which possessed 'homelands' outside Yugoslavia as in the case of Turks and Albanians) and 'ethnic groups' (communities deemed simply as a distinct ethnic group like the Vlachs). Still, both national minorities and ethnic groups were granted extensive cultural and linguistic rights in federal Yugoslavia.[231]

The communist regime also established an explicit link between schooling and the thriving of Yugoslav 'democracy'. Höpken reflects that 'highly fragmented societies need a kind of 'universal ethics' to develop an integrative capacity'.[232] Yugoslavia's universal integrative doctrine was Marxism, tainted with an overarching nationalism that accommodated the distinctiveness of constituent nations. The education system was employed to convey this doctrine so as to 'bring into being the new socialist man', as the government declared in 1952.[233] Beyond expanding access to education and making primary school compulsory and free, the state promoted curricula designed to 'provide [Marxist] political training'.[234] The national subjects were reformulated through Marxist prisms: geography divided the world into 'bourgeois republics' and 'socialist democracies' while historical periodisation followed Marxist determinism and the progression of societies from slavery, to serfdom, capitalism and ultimately socialism.[235] The history curricula were also employed to convey a 'supra-nationalism' founded on the struggle for freedom and statehood during World War II.[236] Official narratives of World War II as a war of national liberation reflected the experience of the communist partisan resistance, but sidelined the collective memories of other ethnolinguistic groups, such as that of ethnic Albanians under Italian occupation.[237]

While promoting Marxism and emphasising the common historical experience of Yugoslav citizens, the state had to walk a fine line between encouraging allegiance to the federal state and recognising its multinational, multireligious and multilingual citizenry. Indeed, as early as 1946 the federal state declared that Yugoslavia's schools could succeed in promoting democracy only if they protected the linguistic rights of all recognised ethnolinguistic communities in Yugoslavia.[238] Thus, successive governments expanded instruction in the languages of the ethnolinguistic communities in primary school.[239] Moreover, the federal state granted considerable autonomy in education policy to its constituent republics, allowing them to frame policies 'in conformity with [*their own*] national culture, traditions, and level of development'.[240] The republics exploited their educational autonomy to the point that, in 1956, the prominent politician Edvard Kardelj worried that textbooks produced in the republics could provide 'nourishment for nationalism' rather than promote Marxism.[241]

The Republic of Macedonia was an exception to such worries: here, the federal state pursued a deliberate 'policy of ethnogenesis' motivated by its strategic and political interests.[242] Nation-building in Macedonia aimed to solidify Yugoslavia's southern border, to tie Macedonian identity to the federal state and to 'counter and discredit' Greece's and Bulgaria's 'negation of [a Macedonian national] identity' and their irredentist claims over the Macedonian territory.[243] In fact, in the immediate aftermath of World War II, Yugoslav President Josip Broz Tito had hoped to constitute a Balkan union of socialist republics, including Yugoslavia, Albania, Bulgaria and Greece. Yet following Yugoslavia's dispute with the Soviet Union in 1948, 'overnight Belgrade became the staunch defender of the [territorial] status quo in the Balkans'.[244]

The federal state employed both religion and language to cement an exclusive ethnic Macedonian identity within the borders of the Republic of Macedonia. In 1958, the communist federal state supported the creation of a Macedonian Autocephalous Orthodox Church, separate from the Serbian Orthodox Church. As Phillips observes, the Macedonian Orthodox Church 'was the only Christian church ever to have been set up by a Communist party in an atheist state'.[245] In fact, by creating a national church for Macedonia, the federal state aimed to strengthen Macedonian collective identity as distinct from the identity of its Christian Orthodox neighbours: Serbia, Bulgaria and Greece. To this day, the existence of the Macedonian Orthodox Church remains controversial and its independence is not recognised by other Orthodox Churches.[246]

Moreover, even before its official codification, completed only in 1953, the Macedonian language was adopted as the official language of the Republic of Macedonia and as a federal language.[247] The standard Macedonian language emerged as a further 'instrument for reducing Bulgarian cultural influences' in the Republic of Macedonia: the language was deliberately codified so as to maximise its differences with the Bulgarian and Serbo-Croat languages.[248] Schools in the Republic of Macedonia were employed to teach the new standard Macedonian language to the local population. In this, they faced enormous practical challenges: no textbooks in the Macedonian language existed and most teachers did not speak the newly codified standard language. Moreover, over 67 % of the population of Macedonia was illiterate after World War II. The state succeeded in reducing illiteracy levels to under 36 % by 1953 and to about 18 % by 1971.[249]

The expansion of access to education impacted on Yugoslavia's national minorities and ethnic groups, which were granted the right to mother tongue education. By 1952, there were 25,645 pupils enrolled in Albanian-language classes in the Republic of Macedonia, and by 1972 this had expanded to 54,801 pupils.[250] Similarly, Turks were allowed to use their alphabet and mother tongue in elementary school teaching.[251] The expansion of mother tongue education resulted in the proliferation of separate schools catering for children from uniform ethnolinguistic backgrounds. Belgrade, worried that this would further 'the isolation of national minorities', encouraged the merging of schools teaching in several languages and the opening of minority-language sections in Macedonian or Serbo-Croatian language schools.[252] In this, the Yugoslav regime differs from governments in Lebanon and Northern Ireland, which accommodated demands for the respect of different communities by funding a plurality of separate institutions rather than plural mixed schools.

Despite attempts to encourage contact between members of different communities in Yugoslavia's political and non-political institutions, ethnic Albanians remained alienated from the ideologies and narratives underpinning Yugoslavia's state building project. As a non-Slavic people, they were excluded by the pan-Slav ideal at the core of the federal state.[253] This alienation was exacerbated by the memory of World War II: during the war, Albanian nationalists fought against Tito's partisans to protect the Italian-sponsored administrative unit of 'Greater Albania' (including Kosovo and Western Macedonia).[254] Greater Albania was dismembered at the end of the war but the brief attempt to establish a Balkan union, encompassing Yugoslavia and Albania, rekindled hopes of a 'permanent solution to the Kosovo [and Western Macedonia] question'.[255] When Yugoslavia's relationship with the USSR (and Albania) deteriorated and Belgrade was expelled from the Communist Information Bureau in 1948, ethnic Albanians became prime targets in the state-led 'hunt for pro-Moscow elements' within communist Yugoslavia.[256] Hereafter, Belgrade limited Albanian cultural expressions: it promoted measures against history teachers, the display of flags and the celebration of national holidays.[257]

By 1968, large-scale demonstrations for Albanian ethnolinguistic rights erupted in both Kosovo and Macedonia: demonstrators demanded an Albanian-language university and recognition of Kosovo as a seventh constituent republic in Yugoslavia's federation.[258] As a result of the demonstrations, the University of Pristina was established in 1969: ethnic Albanians in federal Yugoslavia now had access to mother tongue instruction at every level of the education system.

Decentralisation to Dissolution (1974–1990)
The 1974 Yugoslav constitution fine-tuned the relationship between the federal state and the six constituent republics, redistributing some powers to the local level. Comisso argues that the new constitution made Yugoslavia a quasi-consociational state by establishing the equal representation of constituent nations in federal decision-making and a grand-coalition executive body, devolving decision-making to the republics, entrenching isolated communal elites and legitimising highly autonomous ethnic communities.[259] The 1974 constitution also increased the prerogatives of the provinces of Kosovo and Vojvodina and, without severing their territory from the Republic of Serbia, granted them 'practically the same rights as the federal republics'.[260]

The new constitution did not impact on the political function of education in Yugoslavia. Schools were still expected to convey unifying overarching narratives of identity and ideological orientation and to accommodate the legitimate cultural expressions of ethnolinguistic communities. Thus, the 1974 constitution re-emphasised that 'all education is to be Marxist' and the federal state reiterated the right to mother tongue education for nationalities and ethnic groups.[261] Yet the six republics were entrusted with most policy-making powers over education, including responsibilities for textbook and curriculum design.[262] This entrenched disparities between the different republics in terms of access and quality of education: overall primary school enrolment had increased from 65 % in 1953 to 95 % in 1988 in Yugoslavia. Still, in 1988 only 0.8 % of Slovenia's population was illiterate while the figure was as high as 10.9 % in Macedonia.[263] Devolution of decision-making in education also led to divergences in the contents of curricula. According to Höpken, most textbooks throughout Yugoslavia emphasised 'self-managed socialism' and 'brotherhood and unity', but these ideological catchphrases only provided children with 'codes necessary for behaving in conformity with the existing political system' rather than furthering their allegiance, and diffused support for the state.[264]

The principle of proportionality underpinning Yugoslavia's political system affected curricula in another fundamental way. From 1974, history curricula and textbooks in the republics applied 'proportional considerations' to Yugoslav history and the history of local ethnolinguistic communities. As Höpken summarises, 'the party simply applied to education the same kind of superficial quotas it had implemented'.[265] This suggests that plural states may transpose the expedients facilitating the operation of politics directly into their education systems.

Education policy in Macedonia differed from priorities in the other Yugoslav constituent republics because of its emphasis on building a cohesive ethnic Macedonian identity while also promoting allegiance to the federal state. Contrary to other republics, in Macedonia textbooks and curricula explicitly focused on the national question, and the 'national history' of the Republic of Macedonia was emphasised at the expense of Yugoslav history.[266]

Moreover, in the 1980s, ethnic Macedonian elites started employing the education system to integrate (or in ethnic Albanian eyes assimilate) the ethnic Albanian minority.[267] In 1981, ethnic Albanians in Kosovo had called for the establishment of an Albanian-majority republic in Yugoslavia and unrest had spilled over into the Tetovo region in North-Western Macedonia. Ethnic Macedonian elites feared the creation of a seventh republic in Yugoslavia: harbouring secessionist aims, the new republic could have revived Bulgarian, Greek and Serbian claims to Macedonian territory.[268] Therefore, Macedonian authorities supported Serbia's hard line in Kosovo and harshly suppressed manifestations of Albanian nationalism in Macedonia. New legislation prohibited assigning children certain 'nationalist' Albanian names, banned some Albanian nationalist songs, replaced Albanian toponyms with Macedonian ones, and unsuccessfully attempted to slow the demographic growth of Albanians by limiting welfare benefits for families with more than two children.[269]

In this context, schools had two functions. First, they were employed to assimilate individual ethnic Albanians. New curricula increased the amount of Macedonian instruction in Albanian-language schools, Albanian-language textbooks were rewritten to further emphasise Macedonian identity and laws established the very high figure of 30 as the minimum number of pupils required to open Albanian-language classes.[270] As a result, Phillips reports that between 1981 and 1989, the number of students in Albanian-language secondary schools was halved.[271] Albanian teachers who refused to comply with the new curricula were removed from their positions.[272] Second, education entrenched the collective sociopolitical exclusion of the ethnic Albanian community. Most of the Albanian elite had attended the Albanian-language University of Pristina, but authorities in the Republic of Serbia closed the university in 1990. This effectively deprived ethnic Albanians (who could attend primary and secondary school in the Albanian language throughout Yugoslavia) of access to university and motivated mounting calls for the creation of an Albanian-language university in Macedonia. In the following decades, the issue of tertiary education in Albanian would emerge as a recurring theme in the relationship between ethnic Albanians and the independent Macedonian state.

Throughout federal Yugoslavia, by the 1990s, the end of the Cold War added to the economic problems and increasing ideological uncertainty following Tito's death in 1980, and eroded the legitimacy of Marxism as an overarching integrative doctrine.[273] Debates over the relative powers of the federal state and of the constituent republics, strained relationships between Serbia, Slovenia and Croatia. In Yugoslavia, as in Lebanon and Northern Ireland, the conflict between different ethnolinguistic communities over distribution of power, national aspirations and legitimate narratives of identity in a contested state, sharpened inter-communal boundaries. Ethnonationalist sentiments emerged as channels to convey local grievances to Belgrade, and new local elites appealed to revisionist ethnocentric narratives of the past.[274] In Yugoslavia, 'as the political climate of hostility worsened, categories of identity were reduced to stereotypes and prejudices',[275] and when Slovenia and Croatia amended their constitutions to introduce the right to secede from the Yugoslav Federation in 1991, the die was cast for the bloody dissolution of the federal state.

3.3.2   Independent Macedonia (1991–2000)

Ripiloski observes perceptively that 'statehood was effectively imposed on Macedonia by Yugoslavia's collapse'.[276] Macedonia's elites were painfully aware of the serious economic, strategic and ideological consequences independence would bring. Even in the midst of Yugoslavia's break-up, most of the ethnic Macedonian politicians held on to the ideal of a future federation with Serbia, and even the independence referendum of September 1991 allowed for Macedonia's 'right to join a future union of sovereign states of Yugoslavia'.[277] The peaceful withdrawal of the Yugoslav army from Macedonian territory left the newly independent Republic helpless. The Yugoslav army had secured Macedonia's contested borders and the nation-building policies promoted by the Yugoslav federal state had largely shaped the distinctive linguistic and religious attributes of ethnic Macedonians.[278] Now 'the Bulgarians asserted that Macedonia was part of great Bulgaria and the Greeks swore that it was a sacred part of Greece. The Serbs insisted that it was Southern Serbia and the Albanians that much of Macedonia was part of greater Albania'.[279] Debates with Greece over Macedonia's official name delayed the new state's diplomatic recognition, admission to the United Nations and access to international funding to sustain its weak economy. Fears of a Serbian invasion, the disastrous economic consequences of diplomatic isolation, the possible internal rebellion of ethnic Albanians, and spillovers of disorders from Kosovo all threatened the integrity and existence of the new state.[280] Insecurity in its immediate neighbourhood heightened the elites' fear of partition of the Macedonian territory between Albania, Bulgaria, Serbia and Greece.

In the context of strategic instability and threats to the integrity of an independent state, the new constitution redefined Macedonia as 'a nation-state of [the] Macedonian people', constructing ethnicity as a fundamental pillar of citizenship.[281] This reflected the intimate relationship between the state and the ethnic Macedonian community: as Rossos observes, to ethnic Macedonians, their 'survival as a people and nation, and that of their language and culture, depend[ed] on the continuing existence of their state'.[282] Thus, ethnic Macedonian nationalism grew 'not so much from pride, but from desperation to survive'.[283] Certain markers of identity and belonging assumed increasing political significance: the new constitution established Macedonian as the sole official language and recognised a special status for the Macedonian Orthodox Church, reaffirming the special function of language and religion in marking the boundaries of the ethnic Macedonian community.[284]

Government efforts to emphasise the congruence between state and ethnic community also influenced education policy. The curricula were immediately reformed to 'remove [Marxist] ideology'.[285] This reformulation resulted in increasing focus on Macedonian ethno-religious attributes and symbols. Moreover, the national subjects presented the natural boundaries of the state as stretching to encompass all the territories inhabited by ethnic Macedonians. Thus, geography and history were employed to show that most of the Macedonian '"national" territory [was] under foreign occupation by neighbouring states'.[286] Furthermore, despite constitutional guarantees, successive governments failed to uphold the right to mother tongue instruction for children belonging to the Albanian, Turkish and Serbian communities. From 1995, all schoolteachers were required to be Macedonian citizens and to pass a Macedonian language test: this put teachers belonging to ethnolinguistic minorities in a highly unfavourable position.[287] Requirements for the opening of minority-language classes were also tightened, Albanian teachers who protested were dismissed and the Albanian teacher training college was closed. As a result, the number of Albanian-language secondary schools declined from ten in 1989 to only one in 1993.[288]

Thus, ethnolinguistic minorities in independent Macedonia claimed they increasingly felt like 'guests with certain rights'.[289] Some, such as the Turkish community, had participated in the 1991 independence referendum and had supported the new constitution in the hope that 'their support to the new regime in these dire times would be rewarded after the dust settled'.[290] Others, like the Albanians, challenged the legitimacy of the new state. By the early 1990s the Albanian community accounted for over 20 % of the population of Macedonia.[291] The main ethnic Albanian parties boycotted the independence referendum and the 1992 census, in protest at the new constitution.[292] Instead, in January 1992, the ethnic Albanian parties organised a referendum on the autonomy of North-Western Macedonia, in which the majority of the local ethnic Albanian population voted in favour.[293] The ethnic Albanian parties insisted that the 1992 referendum was purely demonstrative, and only called for recognition of the Albanians as an equal founding national group in Macedonia.[294] However, the results of the referendum rekindled fears of secession and partition among the Macedonian public.

The debate over the establishment of an Albanian-language university in Macedonia came to epitomise wider struggles for the inclusion and rights of the Albanian community. In contrast to the 1974 Yugoslav constitution, the first Macedonian constitution did not guarantee university education in Albanian. Mindful of how the Albanian-language University of Pristina had evolved into a nest of nationalist insurrection, the Macedonian authorities were determined to prevent the establishment of an Albanian-language university. Therefore, successive governments encouraged the Saints Cyril and Methodius University of Skopje to establish admission quotas for members of ethnolinguistic communities with considerable success: by 2005, about 150 Roma students attended university compared with only three students in 1993, and the proportion of Albanian students also increased.[295] In 1997, despite violent protests by Macedonian lecturers and students, the government also established an Albanian-language institute within the Pedagogical Faculty of the University of Skopje.

These concessions did not suffice, and in the mid-1990s, the Albanian Intellectuals Assembly in Macedonia called for the establishment of an independent Albanian-language university. The establishment of the University of Tetovo encountered considerable resistance: in 1994, the police bulldozed its buildings and arrested most of its leaders. In early 1995, the leaders of all the Albanian parties gathered for its opening ceremony but the following day the police stopped lessons and arrested the rector and several lecturers, jailing them on charges of sedition.[296] Most Albanian parties temporarily boycotted Parliament in protest: they argued that beyond entrenching the socio-economic inequality of ethnic Albanians, denial of the right to university education in the mother tongue 'reinforced the perception of ethnic Macedonian primacy of the state'.[297] Silently, the University of Tetovo continued its unrecognised activities and by 1999 it had enrolled over 4500 students.[298]

Macedonian authorities argued that the Tetovo University was illegal in two respects: it was private and it taught only in the Albanian language. Moreover, the government never received a proposal for its establishment and most of its academic staff did not meet the legal qualifications required for university lecturers.[299] The fact that most of the university staff graduated from the University of Pristina only compounded ethnic Macedonian suspicion that the University of Tetovo was the foundation stone for a parallel Albanian education system promoting nationalism and secession.[300] This may have been the case in Kosovo, where the Kosovo Liberation Army benefited from underground para-state Albanian-language institutions (such as schools) in its resistance against Serbian authorities. The situation in Macedonia was different: Albanian political parties demanded constitutional changes and insisted on the establishment of an Albanian-language university, but they had also participated in coalition governments from 1992. When tension between the ethnic Macedonian and ethnic Albanian communities escalated in the late 1990s, ethnic Albanian parties started complaining that the distribution of ministerial positions did not reflect their community's demographic and political weight.[301]

As in Lebanon and Macedonia, the intensification of inter-group tensions sharpened group boundaries and helped cement each community's identity markers. Thus, in the 1990s, religion emerged as a politically salient cleavage between ethnic Albanians and ethnic Macedonians and 'Albanianness and Macedonianness became rapidly and strongly associated with Islam and Christianity respectively'.[302] This is because in the ethnic Macedonian imagery, conflicts in Bosnia and Herzegovina (1992–1995) and Kosovo (1998–1999) became intertwined with Islam 'as a dangerous religion that favours irredentism and territorial expansionism'.[303] Whereas the conflicts in Bosnia and Herzegovina and Kosovo strengthened religious solidarity among local Muslim populations, the singling out of ethnic Albanians 'as embodying threat'[304] can only be understood in the context of inter-communal relations within the Macedonian state. Indeed, as early as 1995, ethnic Macedonian parties 'fear[ed] that the Kosovo intifada [was] moving South'.[305]

Reverberations of the Kosovo conflict, the increasing influx of Albanian refugees and the closure of borders certainly contributed to increasing tensions within Macedonia. Yet, despite the presence of Kosovar fighters and political leaders, the National Liberation Army's (NLA) insurgency in 2001 was primarily 'a struggle for greater inclusiveness and political authority' within Macedonia.[306] During the 2001 conflict, the speaker of the Macedonian Parliament disingenuously argued that 'Macedonians thought they were doing everything right in terms of inter-ethnic relations'.[307] In fact, the National Liberation Army (NLA) articulated its demands only in terms of the rights of ethnic Albanians within Macedonia: the insurgents demanded equal constituent status for their community, official status for their language, more representation in the state administration and police, and a state-funded Albanian-language university.[308]

3.3.3 *The Ohrid Agreement and Beyond (2001–Present)*

Macedonia's 'mini-war' of 2001 was settled before it could escalate into a civil war engulfing the whole territory.[309] More than in Lebanon and Northern Ireland, external powers were decisive in framing and enforcing the 2001 *Framework Agreement* (known as the Ohrid Agreement). In August 2001, the President of Macedonia, Boris Trajkovski, and the representatives of the four major ethnic Macedonian and ethnic Albanian political parties signed the agreement under the supervision of the European Union (EU) and US representatives.

The Ohrid Agreement sanctioned the equality of all ethnic groups in the state by redefining Macedonia as a 'multi-ethnic society' and removing notions of Macedonians as 'constituent people'.[310] It also established a complex liberal consociation in Macedonia. Macedonia's consociation is liberal because its provisions are designed to accommodate demographic changes. Members of Parliament are free to designate themselves as members of 'communities not in the majority in the population of Macedonia', and laws affecting the territorial and non-territorial autonomy of local communities can only be passed with the approval of those members of parliament who belong to minorities. Moreover, in contrast to the Taif and Belfast Agreements, the Ohrid Agreement does not grant cultural and political rights to specific communities named in the agreement, such as the Christian right to the presidency in Lebanon or the Unionist and Nationalist veto rights in Northern Ireland. Instead, the Ohrid Agreement provides certain enhanced collective cultural and political safeguards for any community accounting for over 20 % of the population. Currently, this means only the ethnic Macedonian and ethnic Albanian communities.

The agreement states that there are 'no territorial solutions to ethnic issues' but responds to long-standing Albanian demands for decentralisation of the public administration. Macedonia's consociation is complex precisely because it provides for the devolution of decision-making to the municipal level. The definition of municipal boundaries in 2001–2004 appeared to 'create communities in which either Macedonians or Albanians dominate'.[311] Thus, many ethnic Macedonians opposed the proposed municipal boundaries as 'ethnic gerrymandering': they argued that by granting territorial autonomy to ethnically homogeneous communities the proposed municipalities might inhibit inter-group conflict in the short term, but could exacerbate long-term demands for federalisation and partition.[312]

Education was one of the first responsibilities devolved to the municipalities from 2005, but it also figures prominently in the Ohrid Agreement. During the ethnic conflict, the NLA demanded expansion of mother tongue education and state funding for Albanian-language universities. This reflects that language remains the most politically salient marker of ethnic identity in Macedonia. Both demands were met: the Ohrid Agreement reaffirmed rights to primary and secondary education 'in the students' native languages' and to learning the Macedonian language, and granted state funding for universities teaching in the language of at least 20 % of the population.[313] By 2004, two state universities taught in the Albanian language: the trilingual South East European University and the now legal University of Tetovo. Alongside the Ohrid Agreement's provisions for positive discrimination in university enrolments,[314] higher education in the mother tongue facilitated ethnic Albanian access to university: Ragaru finds that between 2001 and 2004 the proportion of Albanian students in university increased from 4.9 to 14.9 %.³¹⁵ Similarly, Chap. 6 traces the success of provisions to expand mother tongue instruction in primary and secondary schools, but it shows that policymakers consistently overlooked the broader implications of this expansion until at least 2008. Indeed, as Chap. 7 highlights, post-Ohrid education policy furthered the separation of students of different ethnolinguistic backgrounds into different shifts (in which different groups of students attend school at different times of the day), buildings or schools. Thus, as in Lebanon and Northern Ireland, in consociational Macedonia, schools are becoming 'parallel, non-intersecting communities'.³¹⁶

In fact, successive power-sharing executives presented schools as an instrument for social cohesion in Macedonia, and the 2005–2015 education strategy nostalgically longed to 'restore the school's lost status as the dominant institutional agent for creating and conveying values'.³¹⁷ Chapters 4, 5 and 6 show that debates over history education, citizenship education and language ultimately concerned precisely discussions over which values should be created and conveyed by schools. As in Lebanon and Northern Ireland, education reform in consociational Macedonia has to juggle the promotion of 'belonging to the Republic of Macedonia' with the 'nurturing [*of communal*] national and cultural identity'.³¹⁸

The tendency to prioritise the latter prompted Koppa to suggest that perhaps the 2001 ethnic conflict was 'not a struggle for inclusion, but a struggle for boundaries'.³¹⁹ Continuing ethnic Albanian dissatisfaction with post-Ohrid political and cultural reforms substantiates this view and fuels ethnic Macedonian fears that ethnic Albanians see the agreement 'only as the first gain enabling them to formulate further demands at the expenses of Macedonians'.³²⁰

For their part, the majority of ethnic Macedonians perceived the agreement as being imposed upon the state by a pro-Albanian international community.³²¹ Ethnic Macedonian parties had emphasised the nature of the state as an expression of the ethnic Macedonian nation in the 1990s; the Ohrid Agreement did not tackle long-standing anxieties over the identity and integrity of the state, instead reviving fears of partition.³²² Thus, from 2001, the majority ethnic Macedonian party VMRO-DPMNE started reformulating Macedonian identity in two respects. First, it started relying on religious institutions as potential allies in fostering the internal cohesion of the ethnic, linguistic and political Macedonian community. This seeped into curricular policy, igniting violent debates over the introduction of religious education in state schools.³²³ Second, VMRO-

DPMNE politicians started portraying the ethnic Macedonian people as descending from a mythical Hellenistic past, and initiated an 'antiquisation campaign' which culminated in the megalomaniac urban revival project Skopje 2014.[324]

The Turkish community and other minorities were excluded from the negotiation of the Ohrid Agreement and argue that the agreement has promoted an Albanian-Macedonian binational society and marginalised smaller ethnolinguistic communities.[325] In education, as in many other political and non-political institutions, smaller communities 'fear being "squeezed" between what they see as an insecure Macedonian majority and an aggressive Albanian minority'.[326]

Since Yugoslav times, the ethnic Macedonian community has viewed the state both as its ultimate expression and as its protector in an insecure, predatory regional environment. In Socialist Yugoslavia, the hegemonic public education system was employed to convey overarching identities of belonging and allegiances to the state. These narratives were partially tempered by the recognition of the linguistic rights of ethnic communities.

Independence, forced upon Macedonia by the collapse of Yugoslavia, changed the parameters of inter-group relations. Schooling remained an instrument for nation-state building, but it was at the service of a new project: the Macedonian nation-state. In an effort to prevent the creation of parallel *para*-state institutions among ethnic Albanians, successive governments refused to establish an Albanian-language university and limited mother tongue schooling. Thus, in the 1990s, debates over education 'came to symbolise the struggle for all minority rights in the state'.[327] These culminated in the 2001 conflict.

The following chapters trace reforms of history education, citizenship education, languages and of the overall structure of the education system to determine whether the politics of consociation impacted on the manifest and hidden curricula of compulsory schools in the three jurisdictions in question.

3.4 Conclusion

This chapter has surveyed the history of education systems in Lebanon, Northern Ireland and Macedonia and traced the political function of schooling in these three societies. It highlights that the contested states in Lebanon, Northern Ireland and Macedonia faced similar challenges in three respects. First, France, Great Britain and Serbia established their borders on the fault lines of receding empires. Initially, borders appeared porous and negotiable, morphing into effective frontiers only decades later. Second, their borders cut through the homeland and 'imagined community' of certain ethnic, religious or national groups such as the Sunni Muslims in Lebanon, Irish Nationalists in Northern Ireland and ethnic Albanians in Macedonia. Third, the diverging identities and national aspirations of different ethnic, linguistic, confessional and national communities crystallised in the context of hardening frontiers and escalating inter-group conflict. Group identities came to cluster around certain, politically salient attributes: in Lebanon and Northern Ireland the primary inter-group boundary was religious denomination, in socialist Macedonia it was language.

Moreover, this chapter showed that education policy is deeply entangled with different nation-state building projects. Until the early twentieth century, in the territories of present-day Lebanon, Northern Ireland and Macedonia, education was a clerical and foreign prerogative, an instrument of socialisation into communal narratives and allegiances. In the 1920s, it became an instrument for nation-state building and in subsequent decades Beirut, Belfast and Skopje attempted to impose (or enforce) central control over the education system. Just as the state attempted to ensure its legitimacy by conveying overarching founding myths and encouraging the mixing of schoolchildren of different ethnic, religious and national backgrounds, local communities too set out to reproduce their existence by transmitting their (mutually exclusive and maximally different) histories and markers of identity in separate institutions.

Their success depended on the strength of the central state, on its ability to articulate overarching 'integrative doctrines' and, most importantly, on its permeability to communal interests and demands. For example, both Lebanon and Yugoslavia promoted overarching value systems to justify the existence of the state: pluralism and Marxism, respectively. Both doctrines provided for a legitimate role of confessional and ethnic communities in defining some of the contents of curricula (through Yugoslav devolution) or in running schools (through state subsidies to confessional schools in Lebanon). In contrast, in Northern Ireland (in the 1930s) and Macedonia (in the 1990s), the state constructed institutions and narratives impermeable to the demands of the Irish Nationalists and ethnic Albanians. Communities, in turn, jealously guarded (or even established) their parallel institutions, such as schools and universities.

In this regard, an important difference emerged. In Lebanon and Northern Ireland the solidification of territorial boundaries, the construction of state institutions, the exacerbation of ethnopolitical conflict and the expansion of compulsory education went hand in hand. In contrast, inter-communal conflict in independent Macedonia emerged only after a fully functioning state educational system was in place. Thus, in the 1990s ethnic Macedonian elites could appropriate the monopolistic state educational system to convey congruence between state and nation, projecting a Macedonian ethnonational identity on other communities.

This chapter demonstrated that the instruments employed by states and communities to convey narratives, identities and allegiances to children were remarkably similar in Lebanon, Northern Ireland and Macedonia. First, before the conflicts, states attempted to impose a uniform curriculum on all schools. Clashes with communal actors focused on the contents of the national subjects: history, citizenship education, religion and languages. Second, the history of the education system in Lebanon, Northern Ireland and Macedonia is also the history of communal attempts to maximise independence in educational affairs through separate schools reflecting and entrenching societal cleavages.

Similarly, the Taif, Belfast and Ohrid peace agreements aimed to employ schools for peace-building and reconciliation by mapping reforms of the curricula of three national subjects (history, citizenship and languages) and calling for new structures in the education system. On the one hand, the education reforms promoted in the three peace agreements reflect the relative strength of religious, national and ethnic communities at the end of conflicts: in Lebanon, curricular reforms mirror closely the demands of Muslims; in Northern Ireland, support for Irish-language education accommodates the calls of the Irish Nationalist community; in Macedonia, state funding for Albanian-language universities responds to core ethnic Albanian requests. On the other hand, the agreements aim, through schools, to construct and convey overarching narratives of belonging and allegiance to a new, inclusive state where different groups share political power.

Chapters 4, 5, 6 and 7 compare the experiences of consociational Lebanon, Northern Ireland and Macedonia in implementing the reforms mapped in their peace agreements. They consider debates over history education, citizenship education, the languages of instruction and over initiatives to promote common schools for children belonging to different backgrounds, respectively. Each of these chapters aims to determine whether schools can help the stability of consociations, and to highlight constraining factors to education reform in deeply divided societies.

Notes

1. Fay Chung, 'Education: A Key to Power and a Tool for Change – a Practitioner's Perspective', *Current Issues in Comparative Education* 2, no.1 (1999): 1.
2. Florian Bieber, 'Bosnia-Herzegovina and Lebanon: Historical Lessons of Two Multireligious States,' *Third World Quarterly* 21, no. 2 (2000): 271; Hanf, *Coexistence*, 61.
3. Mounir Bashshour, 'The Role of Education: A Mirror of Fractured National Image,' in Halim Barakat (ed.), *Toward a Viable Lebanon* (London: Croom Helm, 1988), 42–43; Hanf, *Coexistence*, 57.
4. Bieber, 'Bosnia-Herzegovina', 271.
5. Kamal Salibi, *A House of Many Mansions: The History of Lebanon Reconsidered* (London: Published by I.B. Tauris & Co 1988): 165.
6. Ussama Makdisi, 'Reconstructing the Nation-State: The Modernity of Sectarianism in Lebanon,' *Middle East Report*, no. 200 (1996): 24.
7. Mounir Bashshour, 'Chances for Conflict Regulation at the Grassroot Level in Lebanon,' in Hanf (ed.), *The Political Function of Education*, 185.
8. Mattar, 'Is Lebanese Confessionalism,' in Choueiri (ed.), *Breaking the Cycle*, 50; Salibi, *A House of Many Mansions*, 25.
9. Ibid., 169.
10. Hanf, *Coexistence*, 65–66.
11. Ibid., 67.
12. Michael C. Hudson, 'Democracy and Social Mobilisation in Lebanese Politics,' *Comparative Politics* 1, no. 2 (1969): 251; Makdisi, 'Reconstructing', 24.
13. The 1926 constitution also specified the 'temporary' nature of confessionalism. Anna Ziadeh, *Sectarianism and Intercommunal Nation-Building in Lebanon* (London: Hurst, 2006): 147.
14. R. Hrair Dekmejian, *Patterns of Political Leadership: Lebanon, Israel, Egypt* (Albany: State University of New York Press, 1975): 35.
15. Marie-Joëlle Zahar, 'Power Sharing in Lebanon: Foreign Protectors, Domestic Peace, and Democratic Failure,' in Donald Rothschild and Philip Roeder (eds.), *Sustainable Peace: Power and Democracy after Civil Wars* (Ithaca: Cornell University Press, 2005): 224–226.
16. Art. 8, 'French Mandate for Syria and the Lebanon', *The American Journal of International Law* 17, no.3 (1923): 177–182.
17. Nemer Frayha, 'Education and Social Cohesion in Lebanon,' *Prospects* XXXIII, no. 1 (2003): 80.
18. Ibid., 81.
19. Mounir Bashshour, 'Higher Education and Political Development in Syria and Lebanon,' *Comparative Education Review* 10, no. 3 (1966): 455.

20. David Gilmour, *Lebanon, the Fractured Country* (Oxford: Martin Robertson, 1983): 66.
21. Frayha, 'Education and Social Cohesion', 81.
22. Eric M. Dorrington, *Lebanese Historical Memory and the Perception of National Identity through School Textbooks*, 2010, http://www.Scribd.Com/Doc/27022561/Lebanese-Historical-Memory-and-the-Perception-of-National-Identity-through-School-Textbooks: 5
23. Salibi, *A House of Many Mansions*, 203.
24. Dorrington, *Lebanese Historical Memory*, 7.
25. Salibi, *A House of Many Mansions*, 203.
26. Frayha, 'Education and Social Cohesion', 78.
27. Gilmour, *Lebanon*, 18, 59–60.
28. Boutros Labaki, *Education Et Mobilite Sociale Dans La Societe Multicommunautaire Du Liban* (Larnara: Materialen zu Gesellschaft und Bildung in multikulturellen Gesellschaften, 1988): 58, 76.
29. Ibid., 85, 80; Frayha, 'Education and Social Cohesion', 80.
30. Ibid., 176.
31. Nemer Frayha, 'Developing Curriculum as a Means to Bridging National Divisions in Lebanon,' in Sobhi Tawil and Alexandra Harley (eds.), *Education, Conflict and Social Cohesion* (Geneva: UNESCO International Bureau of Education, 2004), 172.
32. Labaki, *Education*, 176.
33. Hanf, *Coexistence*, 445, 69; Bashshour, 'The Role of Education', in Barakat (ed.), *Toward a Viable Lebanon*, 44. Over 70 percent of students were Muslim. Labaki, *Education*, 86–87.
34. Frayha, 'Developing Curriculum', in Tawil and Harley (eds.), *Education, Conflict and Social Cohesion*, 172.
35. Hanf, *Coexistence*, 552.
36. Dekmejian, *Patterns of Political Leadership*, 35–36; Hudson, 'Democracy', 249.
37. Mattar, 'Is Lebanese Confessionalism', in Choueiri (ed.), *Breaking the Cycle*, 51; Ghassane Salamé, *Lebanon's Injured Identities. Who Represents Whom During a Civil War?* (Oxford: Centre for Lebanese Studies, 1986): 5; Salibi, *A House of Many Mansions*, 139.
38. Ibid., 27.
39. Ibid., 28.
40. Mattar, 'Is Lebanese Confessionalism', in Choueiri (ed.), *Breaking the Cycle*, 51.
41. Youssef Choueiri, 'Explaining Civil Wars in Lebanon,' in Choueiri (ed.), *Breaking the Cycle*, 27–28.
42. Georges Naccache, 'Deux Negations Ne Font Pas Une Nation' (1949), qtd. in Gilmour, *Lebanon*, 53.

43. Kerr, *Imposing Power-Sharing*, 124.
44. Mattar, 'Is Lebanese Confessionalism', in Choueiri (ed.), *Breaking the Cycle*, 52.
45. Salibi, *A House of Many Mansions*, 37.
46. Farid elKhazen, *The Breakdown of the State in Lebanon, 1967–1976* (London: IB Tauris Publishers, 2000): 383.
47. Fawwaz Traboulsi, *A History of Modern Lebanon*, 102.
48. elKhazen, *The Breakdown*, 379.
49. Beydoun, 'A Note,' in Hanf and Salam (eds.), *Lebanon in Limbo*, 76.
50. Hanf, *Coexistence*, 79.
51. Beydoun, 'A Note', Hanf and Salam (eds.), *Lebanon in Limbo*, 75.
52. Salibi, *A House of Many Mansions*, 195; Economic and Social Commission for Western Asia, *Unpacking the Dynamics of Communal Tensions*, 14.
53. Hanf, *Coexistence*, 71.
54. Frayha, 'Developing Curriculum', in Tawil and Harley (eds.), *Education, Conflict and Social Cohesion*, 172.
55. Lebanese Government Platform (1943) and Lebanese Government Platform (1944), qtd. in Frayha, 'Education and Social Cohesion', 82.
56. International Bureau of Education, *Annuaire International de L'Education et de L'Einsegnement* (Geneva: UNESCO, 1946): 94.
57. International Bureau of Education, *International Yearbook of Education* (Geneva: UNESCO, 1949): 211.
58. Chartouni, *Conflict Resolution*, 75; Hanf, *Coexistence*, 365.
59. Frayha, 'Education and Social Cohesion', 83.
60. Ziadeh, *Sectarianism*, 113; Bashshour, 'The Role of Education', in Barakat (ed.), *Toward a Viable Lebanon*, 47.
61. International Bureau of Education, *Annuaire International*, 94.
62. Frayha, 'Developing Curriculum', in Tawil and Harley (eds.), *Education, Conflict and Social Cohesion*, 173; Frayha, 'Education and Social Cohesion', 83.
63. International Bureau of Education, *International Yearbook of Education* (Geneva: UNESCO, 1951): 182; International Bureau of Education, *International Yearbook of Education* (Geneva: UNESCO, 1957): 251.
64. International Bureau of Education, *International Yearbook of Education* (Geneva: UNESCO, 1957): 251–252.
65. Decree 1436, qtd. in Bashshour, 'The Role of Education,' in Barakat (ed.), *Toward a Viable Lebanon*, 47–48.
66. Frayha, 'Developing Curriculum,' in Tawil and Harley (eds.), *Education, Conflict and Social Cohesion*, 173.
67. International Bureau of Education, *International Yearbook of Education* (Geneva: UNESCO, 1952): 200; Frayha, 'Developing Curriculum,' in Tawil and Harley (eds.), *Education, Conflict and Social Cohesion*, 173;

United Nations Development Programme, *Lebanon Human Development Report: Toward a Citizen's State, 2008–2009* (Beirut: UNDP, 2009): 162.
68. K. Abouchedid, R. Nasser, and J. Van Blommestein, 'The Limitations of Inter-Group Learning in Confessional School Systems: The Case of Lebanon,' *Arab Studies Quarterly* 24, no. 4 (2002).
69. Ibid.
70. Choueiri, 'Explaining Civil Wars', in Choueiri (ed.), *Breaking the Cycle*, 29.
71. Ibid.
72. Kerr, *Imposing Power-Sharing*, 127.
73. Traboulsi, *A History of Modern Lebanon*, 138.
74. Inam Raad, Qtd. in Hanf, *Coexistence*, 369; Traboulsi, *A History of Modern Lebanon*, 140.
75. Frayha, 'Education and Social Cohesion,' 82.
76. Labaki, *Education*, 131–136.
77. Traboulsi, *A History of Modern Lebanon*, 163.
78. Labaki, *Education*, 129; Gilmour, *Lebanon*, 29.
79. Kamal Abouchedid and Ramzi Nasser, 'The State of History Teaching in Private-Run Confessional Schools in Lebanon: Implications for National Integration,' *Mediterranean Journal of Educational Studies* 5, no. 2 (2000): 61.
80. Frayha, 'Developing Curriculum,' in Tawil and Harley (eds.), *Education, Conflict and Social Cohesion*, 173.
81. Dorrington, *Lebanese Historical Memory*, 9.
82. Frayha, 'Developing Curriculum,' in Tawil and Harley (eds.), *Education, Conflict and Social Cohesion*, 173.
83. Memorandum no. 262/7173 of 1973, Qtd in. Ibid., 196; Mounir Bashshour, 'The Deepening Cleavage in the Educational System,' in Hanf and Salam (eds.), *Lebanon in Limbo*, 160.
84. Hanf, *Coexistence*, 162, 168.
85. Kathleen Fincham, 'Nationalist Narratives, Boundaries and Social Inclusion/Exclusion in Palestinian Camps in South Lebanon,' *Compare* 42, no. 2 (2012): 9.
86. Hanf, *Coexistence*, 175; Gilmour, *Lebanon*, 89–90.
87. Hanf, *Coexistence*, 166.
88. Salamé, *Lebanon's Injured Identities*, 7–9.
89. Hanf, *Coexistence*, 109.
90. Mark Farha, 'From Beirut Spring to Regional Winter? ,' in Choueiri (ed.), *Breaking the Cycle*, 203; Hanf, *Coexistence*, 458.
91. Judith Harik, *The Public and Social Services of the Lebanese Militias* (Oxford: Centre for Lebanese Studies, 1994): 12.
92. Hanf, *Coexistence*, 167.

93. Rudy Jaafar, 'Democratic Reform in Lebanon: An Electoral Approach,' in Choueiri (ed.), *Breaking the Cycle*, 289.
94. Hanf, *Coexistence*, 130.
95. elKhazen, *The Breakdown*, 382.
96. Salibi, *A House of Many Mansions*, 165.
97. Hanf, *Coexistence*, 247; Interview with Charles Chartouni (Lebanese Academic and Political Analyst), Beirut, 6/07/2012.
98. Harik, *The Public and Social Services*, 51.
99. Judith Harik, 'Hizballah's Public and Social Services and Iran,' in E.H. Chehabi (ed.), *Distant Relations: Iran and Lebanon in the Last 500 Years* (London: IB Tauris, 2006), 282–283.
100. Ibid., 269, 276–277.
101. Harik, *The Public and Social Services*, 48.
102. Iliya Harik, 'Towards a New Perspective on Secularism in Multicultural Societies,' in Hanf and Salam (eds.), *Lebanon in Limbo*, 23.
103. Salibi, *A House of Many Mansions*, 201.
104. Ibid., 10, 202. See also: United Nations Development Programme, *Lebanon Human Development*, 168, 184.
105. Qtd. in Pamela Chrabieh, 'Breaking the Vicious Cycle! Contributions of the 25–35 Lebanese Age Group,' in Choueiri (ed.), *Breaking the Cycle*, 76.
106. Ministry of National Education and Arts, *Report of the Lebanese Delegation to the 38th Session of the International Conference on Education* (Beirut: Ministry of National Education and Arts, 1981): 5.
107. Ibid., 7; Frayha, 'Developing Curriculum,' in Tawil and Harley (eds.), *Education, Conflict and Social Cohesion*, 174.
108. Ex-President Camille Chamoun, 1984, qtd. in Bashshour, 'The Role of Education,' in Barakat (ed.), *Toward a Viable Lebanon*, 61.
109. Joint Islamic Position, 1984, qtd. in ibid., 62.
110. Part I, Section B, *Taif Agreement*.
111. *Lebanon-Syria Treaty of Cooperation*, 20/05/1991, http://www.jewishvirtuallibrary.org/jsource/arabs/LebSyrCoop.html
112. Traboulsi, *A History of Modern Lebanon*, 245.
113. Part III, Section C, *Taif Agreement*.
114. Hanf, *Coexistence*, 540.
115. Michael C. Hudson, 'Lebanon after Taif. Another Reform Opportunity Lost?,' *Arab Studies Quarterly* 21, no. 1 (1999): 27.
116. Ibid.
117. Part II, Section G, *Taif Agreement*, incorporated into Article 95 of the Lebanese Constitution of 1991.
118. Paul Salem, 'Framing Post-War Lebanon: Perspectives on the Constitution and the Structure of Power,' *Mediterranean Politics* 3, no. 1 (1998): 16.

119. Hannes Baumann, 'The 'New Contractor Burgeoisie' in Lebanese Politics. Hariri, Mikati and Fares,' in Knudsen and Kerr (eds.), *Lebanon after the Cedar Revolution*, 131.
120. Part III, Section F, *Taif Agreement*.
121. Abouchedid et al., 'The Limitations of Inter-Group Learning.'
122. International Bureau of Education, *World Data on Education, Sixth Edition*, 34, 32.
123. Hanf, Coexistence, 646.
124. Michael Kerr, 'Before the Revolution,' in Knudsen and Kerr (eds.), *Lebanon after the Cedar Revolution*, 31; Salibi, *A House of Many Mansions*, 221.
125. Knudsen and Kerr (eds.), *Lebanon after the Cedar Revolution*; also Halim Shebaya, 'Intifada 2005: A Look Backwards and a Look Forward,' in Choueiri (ed.), *Breaking the Cycle*, 261–263.
126. Knudsen and Kerr, 'Introduction' in Knudsen and Kerr (eds.), *Lebanon after the Cedar Revolution*, 7.
127. International Crisis Group, *Lebanon: Hizbollah's Weapons Turn Inward* (Brussels: ICG, 2008).
128. Frayha, 'Developing Curriculum,' in Tawil and Harley (eds.), *Education, Conflict and Social Cohesion*, 178.
129. John Darby, 'Conflict in Northern Ireland: A Background Essay,' in Seamus Dunn (ed.), *Facets of the Conflict*, 17.
130. Donald Harman Akenson, *Education and Enmity, the Control of Schooling in Northern Ireland 1920–1950* (Newton Abbot: David and Charles, 1973): 37.
131. Lord Edward Stanley, Chief Secretary of State for Ireland, qtd. in Priscilla Chadwick, *Schools of Reconciliation. Issues in Joint Roman Catholic-Anglican Education* (London: Cassell, 1994): 125.
132. Tony Gallagher, 'Balancing Difference,' 433; Michael Arlow, 'Citizenship Education in a Divided Society: The Case of Northern Ireland,' in Tawil and Harley (eds.), *Education, Conflict and Social Cohesion*, 271; Valerie Morgan et al., *Breaking the Mould: The Roles of Parents and Teachers in the Integrated Schools in Northern Ireland* (Coleraine: University of Ulster, 1992): 5.
133. John Darby, *Conflict in Northern Ireland: The Development of a Polarised Community* (Dublin: Gill and Macmillan, 1976): 125.
134. Interview with Andrew Bell (Community Relations Coordinator, Department of Education Northern Ireland), Bangor, 26/02/2013.
135. Darby, *Conflict in Northern Ireland*, 126; Seamus Dunn, 'The Role of Education in the Northern Ireland Conflict,' *Oxford Review of Education* 12, no. 3 (1986): 253.
136. Michael Kerr, 'Nations Apart,' in Hanf (ed.), *The Political Function of Education*, 22.

137. Alan Smith, 'Religious Segregation and the Emergence of Integrated Schools in Northern Ireland,' *Oxford Review of Education* 27, no. 4 (2001): 561.
138. Ibid., 562. Akenson, *Education and Enmity*, 60–61.
139. Lynn, qtd. in Ibid., 51.
140. Lord Londonderry, Minister of Education, qtd. in Darby, *Conflict in Northern Ireland*, 126.
141. Kerr, 'Nations Apart,' in Hanf (ed.), *The Political Function of Education*, 22.
142. John Darby, 1976, Qtd. in Chadwick, *Schools of Reconciliation*, 126.
143. Smith, 'Religious Segregation,' 561. Akenson, *Education and Enmity*, 44–45.
144. Ibid., 194.
145. Darby, *Conflict in Northern Ireland*, 126; Akenson, *Education and Enmity*, 78.
146. Ibid., 76.
147. Ibid., 64–84, 87, 99–100.
148. Darby, *Conflict in Northern Ireland*, 128.
149. Smith, 'Religious Segregation,' 562.
150. Akenson, *Education and Enmity*, 195–196.
151. Ibid., 108, 195–196.
152. Akenson, *Education and Enmity*, 194.
153. Smith, 'Religious Segregation,' 562.
154. Simpson and Daly, 'Politics and Education,' 169.
155. Akenson, *Education and Enmity*, 193–194.
156. Ibid., 198–199; Ian Colwill and Carmel Gallagher, 'Developing a Curriculum for the Twenty-First Century: The Experiences of England and Northern Ireland,' *Prospects* 37, (2007): 412.
157. Akenson, *Education and Enmity*, 168, 198.
158. Ibid., 198–199; Darby, *Conflict in Northern Ireland*, 132–133.
159. Kerr, 'Nations Apart,' in Hanf (ed.), *The Political Function of Education*, 26.
160. Smith, 'Religious Segregation,' 563.
161. O'Leary, Brendan and McGarry, John, *The Politics of Antagonism. Understanding Northern Ireland* (London: Athlone Press, 1993): 130.
162. Gallagher, qtd. in Alan Smith, 'Education and Conflict in Northern Ireland,' in Dunn (ed.), *Facets of the Conflict*, 177.
163. Maurice Hayes, 'Neither Orange March nor Irish Jig: Finding Compromise in Northern Ireland,' in Elliott (ed.), *The Long Road to Peace in Northern Ireland*, 99.
164. Marc Mulholland, 'Assimilation Versus Segregation: Unionist Strategy in the 1960s,' *Twentieth Century British History*, no. 11 (2000).

165. Anthony Oberschall, *Conflict and Peace Building in Divided Societies* (London: Routledge, 2007): 159.
166. John Darby, 'Northern Ireland: Bonds and Breaks in Education,' *British Journal of Educational Studies* 26, no. 3 (1978): 215.
167. John P. Darby, 'Divisiveness of Education,' 8.
168. Darby, 'Northern Ireland,' 223.
169. Lord Melchett, '*Secretary of State: Integrated Education*' (*3 June 1977*) *Memorandum by Lord Melchett, Minister of State at the Northern Ireland Office to the Secretary of State for Northern Ireland*, 1977, PRONI CENT/1/10/3.
170. Qtd. in Chadwick, *Schools of Reconciliation*, 129.
171. Ibid., 130.
172. Ibid., 169.
173. Lord Melchett, '*Secretary of State: Integrated Education*.' See also: J. Pitt-Brooke, '*Note for the Record: Shared Schools*' (*30 July 1976*). *Meeting between R. Moyle, Minister of State at the Northern Ireland Office, with Cardinal Conway, Catholic Primate of Ireland* 1976, PRONI ED/32/B/1/11/1.
174. J. McAllister, *Integration in the Education Service*, 1979, CENT/1/9/1.
175. Darby, 'Northern Ireland,' 216; Seamus Dunn and Valerie Morgan, 'A Fraught Path': Education as a Basis for Developing Improved Community Relations in Northern Ireland,' *Oxford Review of Education* 25, no. 1/2 (1999): 142.
176. Valerie Morgan and Grace Fraser, 'When Does 'Good News' Become 'Bad News'? Relationships between Government and the Integrated Schools in Northern Ireland,' *British Journal of Educational Studies* 47, no. 4 (1999): 367.
177. Dunn and Morgan, 'A Fraught Path,' 143. Chapter 7 explains the ethos and structure of integrated schools.
178. Morgan and Fraser, 'When Does 'Good News' Become 'Bad News'?,' 368.
179. Dunn and Morgan, 'A Fraught Path,' 150.
180. Ibid., 142–143.
181. Qtd. in Arlow, 'Citizenship Education', in Tawil and Harley (eds.), *Education, Conflict and Social Cohesion*, 279.
182. Darby, 'Northern Ireland,' 222.
183. Dunn and Morgan, 'A Fraught Path,' 142. See also Chap. 4 and 5.
184. Smith, 'Religious Segregation,' 570.
185. G. Fontana, 'Religious Education after Conflicts: Promoting Social Cohesion or Entrenching Plurality?', *Compare*, October 2015, http://www.tandfonline.com/doi/full/10.1080/03057925.2015.1099422
186. Morgan and Fraser, 'When Does 'Good News' Become 'Bad News'?,' 370.
187. Dunn and Morgan, 'A Fraught Path,' 146.

188. *Belfast Telegraph*, 15/03/1989, qtd. in B.K. Lambkin, *Opposite Religions Still?*, 80.
189. Smith, 'Religious Segregation,' 565.
190. Dunn and Morgan, 'A Fraught Path,' 146.
191. Arlow, 'Citizenship Education', in Tawil and Harley (eds.), *Education, Conflict and Social Cohesion*, 271.
192. Smith, 'Education and Conflict,' in Dunn (ed.), *Facets of the Conflict*, 180.
193. Ibid., 171.
194. McGarry and O'Leary, 'Iraq's Constitution of 2005,' 675.
195. *Northern Ireland (St Andrews Agreement) Act 2006*.
196. McGarry and O'Leary, 'Consociational Theory, Northern Ireland's Conflict, and Its Agreement. Part 1,' 57.
197. Andrew Finlay, 'Anthropology Misapplied? The Culture Concept and the Peace Process in Ireland,' *Anthropology in Action* 13, no. 1–2 (2006): 2; Andrew Finlay, 'The Persistence of the 'Old' Idea of Culture and the Peace Process in Ireland,' *Critique of Anthropology*, no. 28 (2008): 281.
198. Stephen Farry, qtd. in Oberschall, *Conflict and Peace Building*, 179.
199. McGarry and O'Leary, 'Consociational Theory, Northern Ireland's Conflict, and Its Agreement Part 2,' 275.
200. Rights, Safeguards and Equality of Opportunity, Economic, Social and Cultural Issues, Art.4, *Belfast Agreement*.
201. Rights, Safeguards and Equality of Opportunity, Reconciliation and Victims of Violence, Art.13, *Belfast Agreement*.
202. United Nations Economic and Social Council, *The Right to Education. Report Submitted by Katarina Tomasevski, Special Rapporteur, in Accordance with Commission Resolution 2002/23. Mission to the United Kingdom (Northern Ireland) 24 November–1 December 2002* (Geneva: United Nations, 2003): 6.
203. Personal Communication with Ex-Principal in a Catholic Maintained School, 21/02/2013; Interview with Chris Hazzard (Sinn Féin MLA and Member of the Education Committee), Belfast, 18/09/2013. Darby, 'Divisiveness of Education,' 5; Interview with Tony Gallagher (Pro-Vice Chancellor, Queen's University Belfast), Belfast, 26/02/2013.
204. Simpson and Daly, 'Politics and Education,' 173; Interview with Danny Kinahan (Ulster Unionist Party MLA and Member of the Education Committee), Belfast, 19/09/2013; Interview with Mervyn Storey (Democratic Unionist Party MLA, Chair of Education Committee), Belfast, 27/02/2013.
205. Simpson and Daly, 'Politics and Education,' 172; Department of Education Northern Ireland, *Timeline on the Development of Transfer Policy*, http://www.deni.gov.uk/index/schools-and-infrastructure-2/admission-and-transport/6-post-primary-transfer-and-wider-reform.htm; Tony Gallagher,

'Results of the Consultation on the Burns Report', paper presented to the Graduate School of Education, Queen's University Belfast, 6/12/2002.
206. Ibid., 173.
207. Alan Smith, 'Education and the Peace Process in Northern Ireland,' paper presented at the *Annual Conference of the American Education Research Association* (Montreal: Conflict Archive on the Internet Web Service, 1999): 9.
208. Akenson, *Education and Enmity*, 19.
209. Ibid, 193.
210. Jan Briza, *Minority Rights in Yugoslavia* (London: Minority Rights Group, 2000): 7.
211. Bieber, 'Bosnia-Herzegovina,' 271; Franke Wilmer, *The Social Construction of Man, the State and War: Identity, Conflict and Violence in Former Yugoslavia* (New York: Routledge, 2002): 47.
212. John R. Lampe, *Yugoslavia as History: Twice There Was a Country* (Cambridge: Cambridge University Press, 1996).
213. Peter John Georgeoff, *The Educational System of Yugoslavia* (Washington: National Institute of Education, US Department of Education, 1982), 9; Victor Roudometof, *Collective Memory, National Identity and Ethnic Conflict* (Westport: Praeger, 2002), 197.
214. Lampe, *Yugoslavia*, 94.
215. Ibid., 114.
216. Ibid.; Lampe, *Yugoslavia*, 187.
217. Ibid., 145–146.
218. Wolfgang Höpken, 'History Education and Yugoslav (Dis-) Integration,' in Melissa K. Bokovoy, Jill A. Irvine, and Carol S. Lilly (eds.), *State-Society Relations in Yugoslavia, 1945–1992* (New York: St Martin's Press, 1997): 81.
219. Lampe, *Yugoslavia*, 146, 188.
220. Andrew Rossos, *Macedonia and the Macedonians, a History* (Stanford: Hoover Institution Press, 2008): 249; Ben Fowkes, *Ethnicity and Ethnic Conflict in the Post-Communist World* (London: Palgrave, 2002): 57.
221. Lampe, *Yugoslavia*, 140–141, 114.
222. This was the case particularly the Internal Macedonian Revolutionary Organisation (VMRO), Lampe, *Yugoslavia*, 140–141.
223. Aydin Babuna, 'The Albanians of Kosovo and Macedonia: Ethnic Identity Superseding Religion,' *Nationalities Papers* 28, no. 1 (2000): 68.
224. The 1923 Treaty of Lausanne regulated population transfers with Turkey after World War I. Gëzim Krasniqi, 'The 'Forbidden Fruit': Islam and the Politics of Identity in Kosovo and Macedonia,' *Southeast European and Black Sea Studies* 11, no. 2 (2011): 193–194; Fowkes, *Ethnicity*, 57.
225. Babuna, 'The Albanians,' 68–69.

226. Ibid., 69.
227. John Phillips, *Macedonia. Warlords and Rebels in the Balkans* (London: Yale University Press, 2004): 35; Fowkes, *Ethnicity*, 58.
228. Fowkes, *Ethnicity*, 58.
229. 'Bratstvo i jedinstvo' was a Yugoslavia's foremost motto. See: Ronny Myhrvold, *Former Yugoslav Republic of Macedonia: Education as a Political Phenomenon*, Nordem Report (Oslo: Norwegian Centre for Human Rights, 2005), 3.
230. The most notable example of unrecognized ethnic group are the Roma.
231. Sasho Ripiloski, *Conflict in Macedonia*, 52; Wilmer, *The Social Construction*, 42.
232. Höpken, 'History Education', in Bokovoy et al. (eds.), *State-Society Relations in Yugoslavia*, 82.
233. International Bureau of Education, *International Yearbook of Education* (Geneva: UNESCO,1952): 318.
234. International Bureau of Education, *International Yearbook of Education* (Geneva: UNESCO,1952): 320; International Bureau of Education, *International Yearbook of Education* (Geneva: UNESCO, 1959): 496–497.
235. John Georgeoff, 'Social Studies in Yugoslav Elementary Schools,' *The Elementary School Journal* 66, no. 8 (1966): 436; John Georgeoff, 'Nationalism in the History Textbooks of Yugoslavia and Bulgaria,' *Comparative Education Review* 10, no. 3 (1966): 442.
236. Höpken, 'History Education', in Bokovoy et al. (eds.), *State-Society Relations in Yugoslavia*, 81–82; Klaus Buchenau, 'What Went Wrong? Church–State Relations in Socialist Yugoslavia,' *Nationalities Papers: The Journal of Nationalism and Ethnicity* 33, no. 4 (2005): 551.
237. Georgeoff, 'Social Studies,' 434, 436; Georgeoff, 'Nationalism,' 446.
238. International Bureau of Education, *Annuaire international*, 167.
239. Ibid., 166.
240. International Bureau of Education, *International Yearbook of Education* (Geneva: UNESCO, 1953): 382.
241. Paul Shoup, *Communism and the Yugoslav National Question* (London: Columbia University Press, 1968): 189.
242. Phillips, *Macedonia*, 41.
243. Rossos, *Macedonia*, 250; Stefan Troebst, 'Yugoslav Macedonia: 1943–1953. Building the Party, the State and the Nation,' in Bokovoy et al. (eds.), *State-Society Relations in Yugoslavia*, 245–246.
244. Shoup, *Communism*, 159.
245. Phillips, *Macedonia*, 41.
246. Paolo Quercia, 'Bordeline Religion: The Role of Churches in Balkan Nation Building,' *CeMiSS Quarterly* II, no. 1 (2004), 24–25.

247. Christian Voss, 'The Macedonian Standard Language: Tito-Yugoslav Experiment or Symbol for 'Great Macedonian' Ethnic Inclusion?,' paper presented at the conference on *Language and the Future of Europe: Ideologies, Policies and Practices*, University of Southampton, 2004.
248. Shoup, *Communism*, 178–179; Troebst, 'Yugoslav Macedonia', in Bokovoy et al. (eds.), *State-Society Relations in Yugoslavia*, 255.
249. Rossos, *Macedonia*, 252.
250. According to the 1948 census, Albanians accounted for 17.1 % of the total population of the republic of Macedonia. Ibid., 256–257.
251. Nazif Mandaci, 'Turks of Macedonia: The Travails of the 'Smaller' Minority,' *Journal of Muslim Minority Affairs* 27, no. 1 (2007): 6–7.
252. Shoup, *Communism*, 194.
253. Babuna, 'The Albanians,' 69–70.
254. Rossos, *Macedonia*, 288–289.
255. Babuna, 'The Albanians,' 69.
256. Vasiliki P. Neofotistos, 'Beyond Stereotypes: Violence and the Porousness of Ethnic Boundaries in the Republic of Macedonia,' *History and Anthropology* 15, no. 1 (2004): 60.
257. Ibid.
258. Fabian Schmidt, 'Ethnic Albanians: Balancing the Power Triangle,' *Transitions Online*, 26/05/1995.
259. Ellen Comisso, 'Now That the Fighting in the Balkans Is over, Did We Learn Anything? A Retrospective Analysis of Yugoslavia's Dissolution,' paper presented at the conference on *East European Studies*, Woodrow Wilson International Centre for Scholars, 20/04/2005.
260. Wilmer, *The Social Construction*, 45. Babuna, 'The Albanians,' 71.
261. Georgeoff, *The Educational System of Yugoslavia*, 24, 10, 19.
262. Ibid.; Höpken, 'History Education', in Bokovoy et al. (eds.), *State-Society Relations in Yugoslavia*, 88; Lampe, *Yugoslavia*, 334.
263. Ibid., 333.
264. Höpken, 'History Education', in Bokovoy et al. (eds.), *State-Society Relations in Yugoslavia*, 82–84.
265. Ibid., 89.
266. Ibid., 89–91.
267. Myhrvold, *Former Yugoslav Republic of Macedonia*, 25.
268. Rossos, *Macedonia*, 289. Phillips, *Macedonia*, 45.
269. Myhrvold, *Former Yugoslav Republic of Macedonia*, 4; Elizabeth Sidiropoulos, 'Minority Protection in the Former Yugoslav Republic of Macedonia: Will It Preserve the State?,' *Cambridge Review of International Affairs* 12, no. 2 (1999): 142; Barany, 'Ethnic Mobilisation in the Postcommunist Context,' in Barany and Moser (eds.), *Ethnic Politics after Communism*, 89; Neofotistos, 'Beyond Stereotypes,' 61.

270. Phillips, *Macedonia*, 45; Myhrvold, *Former Yugoslav Republic of Macedonia*, 25–26.
271. Phillips, *Macedonia*, 45.
272. Ingrid Vik, *Divided Communities: A Study of Inter-Ethnic Relations and Minority Rights in Macedonia* (Oslo: The Norwegian Helsinki Committee, 2001): 46.
273. Bieber, 'Bosnia-Herzegovina,' 271.
274. Wilmer, *The Social Construction*, 46.
275. Ibid., 26.
276. Ripiloski, *Conflict in Macedonia*, 24.
277. Ripiloski, *Conflict in Macedonia*, 27; Ramet, *Balkan Babel*, 184; Sabrina P. Ramet, *Balkan Babel. The Disintegration of Yugoslavia from the Death of Tito to the Fall of Milošević* (Boulder: Westview Press, 2002): 184.
278. Ulf Brunnbauer, 'The Implementation of the Ohrid Agreement,' 10.
279. Phillips, *Macedonia*, 15.
280. Ripiloski, *Conflict in Macedonia*, 31.
281. Hugh Poulton, *Who Are the Macedonians?* (London: Hurst, 1995): 172; International Crisis Group, *Macedonia's Ethnic Albanians: Bridging the Gulf* (Brussels: International Crisis Group, 2000): 9.
282. Rossos, *Macedonia*, 278.
283. Brunnbauer, 'The Implementation of the Ohrid Agreement,' 9.
284. International Crisis Group, *Macedonia's Ethnic Albanians*, 7. Poulton, *Who are the Macedonians?*, 184. Quercia, 'Bordeline Religion,' 25.
285. Ann Low-Beer, *Report. Seminar on 'the Reform of History Teaching: Curriculum, Textbook and Teacher Training'*. Mavrovo, the Former Yugoslav Republic of Macedonia, 19–21 October 1999 (Strasbourg: Council of Europe, 1999): 6.
286. Phillips, *Macedonia*, 58. This refers to the Pirin and Aegean portions of historic Macedonia, occupied in 1913.
287. Merle Vetterlein, 'The Influence of the Ohrid Framework Agreement on the Educational Policy of the Republic of Macedonia,' paper presented at the *8th Annual Kokkalis Graduate Student Workshop*, Cambridge, 2-3/02/2006, 9.
288. Poulton, *Who Are the Macedonians?*, 187, 183.
289. Brunnbauer, 'The Implementation of the Ohrid Agreement,' 10.
290. Mandaci, 'Turks of Macedonia,' 8.
291. International Crisis Group, *The Macedonian Question: Reform or Rebellion* (Brussels: International Crisis Group, 2001): 19.
292. Poulton, *Who Are the Macedonians?*, 138. For a fuller discussion of motivations for the boycott, including Albanian resistance to a potential Macedonian realignment with Serbia, see: Jenny Engström, 'Multi-

Ethnicity or Bi-Nationalism? The Framework Agreement and the Future of the Macedonian State,' *Journal of Ethnopolitics and Minority Issues in Europe*, no. 1 (2002).
293. Figures vary between 72 percent and 99 percent in favour out of over 276,000 voters. Ramet, *Balkan Babel*, 189; Maria-Eleni Koppa, 'Ethnic Albanians in the Former Yugoslav Republic of Macedonia: Between Nationality and Citizenship,' *Nationalism and Ethnic Politics* 7, no. 4 (2001): 44; Fowkes, *Ethnicity*, 118.
294. Babuna, 'The Albanians,' 80–81.
295. Risto Karajkov, 'Roma in Macedonia: A Decade of Inconclusion?,' *Osservatorio Balcani e Caucaso*, 16/05/2005; From 4 percent in 1993 to over 7 percent in 1997, Sidiropoulos, 'Minority Protection,' 146.
296. Vetterlein, 'The Influence of the Ohrid Framework Agreement', 11; Fabian Schmidt, 'Macedonia: From National Consensus to Pluralism,' *Transitions Online*, 29/03/1995; Duncan M. Perry, 'Republic of Macedonia: On the Road to Stability – or Destruction?,' *Transitions Online*, 25/08/1995; Schmidt, 'Macedonia': 79.
297. Ripiloski, *Conflict in Macedonia*, 58; Perry, 'Republic of Macedonia'.
298. Koppa, 'Ethnic Albanians,' p. 51.
299. Perry, 'Republic of Macedonia'; Premysl Rosūlek, 'Macedonia in 2011 – on the Way Towards Stabilisation or before the New 'Grand Agreement'?,' in Marja Risteska and Zhidas Daskalovski (eds.), *One Decade after the Ohrid Agreement: Lessons (to Be) Learned from the Macedonian Experience* (Skopje: Centre for Research and Policymaking 2011): 72.
300. Perry, 'Republic of Macedonia'; Koppa, 'Ethnic Albanians,' 50–51.
301. Ripiloski, *Conflict in Macedonia*, 171.
302. Mandaci, 'Turks of Macedonia,' 12.
303. Neofotistos, 'Beyond Stereotypes,' 52.
304. Ibid.
305. Perry, 'Republic of Macedonia'.
306. Ripiloski, *Conflict in Macedonia*, 142.
307. Stojan Andov, qtd. in International Crisis Group, *Macedonia: The Last Chance for Peace* (Brussels: International Crisis Group, 2001), 19.
308. Phillips, *Macedonia*, 87, 90.
309. Engström, 'Multi-Ethnicity or Bi-Nationalism?,' 11.
310. Florian Bieber, 'Introduction,' in Risteska and Daskalovski (eds.), *One Decade after the Ohrid Agreement*, 20; Nadège Ragaru, 'The Former Yugoslav Republic of Macedonia: Between Ohrid and Brussels,' in Judy Batt (ed.), *Is There an Albanian Question?* (Paris: European Union Institute for Security Studies, 2008): 44.
311. Engström, 'Multi-Ethnicity or Bi-Nationalism?,' 17.

312. Myhrvold, *Former Yugoslav Republic of Macedonia*, 11–12.
313. Article 6.1 of the *Ohrid Agreement*, Article 48 of the Constitution.
314. Article 6.3, *Ohrid Agreement*.
315. Ragaru, 'The Former Yugoslav Republic of Macedonia', in Batt (ed.), *Is There an Albanian Question?*, 45.
316. Myhrvold, *Former Yugoslav Republic of Macedonia*, 18.
317. Ministry of Education and Science, *National Programme for the Development of Education in the Republic of Macedonia 2005–2015* (Skopje: Ministry of Education and Science, 2004): 44.
318. *Law on Primary Education*, qtd. in Ministry of Education and Science of the Republic of Macedonia, *Manual for the Prevention and Protection against Discrimination in the Educational System in the Republic of Macedonia* (Skopje: Ministry of Education and Science, 2010): 23; Ministry of Education and Science of the Republic of Macedonia, *Steps Towards Integrated Education*, 2010, 3 and in Ministry of Education and Science, *National Programme for the Development of Education in the Republic of Macedonia 2005–2015*, 45.
319. Koppa, 'Ethnic Albanians,' 58.
320. Rosūlek, 'Macedonia in 2011' in Risteska and Daskalovski (eds.), *One Decade after the Ohrid Agreement*, 68.
321. Engström, 'Multi-Ethnicity or Bi-Nationalism?,' 2; Myhrvold, *Former Yugoslav Republic of Macedonia*, 9; Ripiloski, *Conflict in Macedonia*, 118.
322. Ibid., 118.
323. Giuditta Fontana, 'State Building and Religious Education in the Former Yugoslav Republic of Macedonia', in Hanf, Theodor and Karim El Mufti (eds.), *Policies and Politics of Teaching Religion* (Baden-Baden: Nomos, 2013). See also Fontana, 'Religious Education after Conflicts.'
324. Bieber, 'Introduction,' 21.
325. Engström, 'Multi-Ethnicity or Bi-Nationalism?,' 9; The position of the Turkish community is well explained in Mandaci, 'Turks of Macedonia.'
326. Ragaru, 'The Former Yugoslav Republic of Macedonia', in Batt (ed.), *Is There an Albanian Question?*, 48.
327. Phillips, *Macedonia*, 70.

CHAPTER 4

Reforming History Education

In 1999, an article posited that 'the permanence of the peace process in Northern Ireland may depend on which model of history teaching emerges'.[1] Militia leaders made similar arguments about Lebanon in the 1980s.[2] Analysing debates over history education in Lebanon, Northern Ireland and Macedonia since the Taif, Belfast and Ohrid Agreements, this chapter confirms that history education was expected to contribute to the construction of overarching identities and to the promotion of reconciliation in the three societies.

This chapter also shows that the model of history education adopted by Lebanon, Northern Ireland and Macedonia was affected by the consociational political system in three ways. First, the lack of consensus over the end of conflict hindered the formulation of consensual overarching narratives of the past. Second, debates over the political function of history education mirrored wider tensions between the principles of pluralism and parity of esteem at the heart of consociations. Finally, the deregulation of curricula (in Lebanon), multiperspective curricula (in Northern Ireland) and proportional curricula (in Macedonia) contributed to the reproduction of the different (and potentially mutually exclusive) communal narratives of the past. Before analysing the three case studies, this chapter briefly surveys the literature on the political function of history education.

4.1 History Education in Deeply Divided Societies: Theoretical Debates

Most states devote very little time and financial resources to history education. Moreover, the effective impact of history education upon children's values and attitudes has never been quantified. Some argue that history education at school has a minimal impact compared with the politicised oral narratives of families and communities.[3] In fact, recent research shows that schools can contribute to the development of tolerant and inclusive views of the past in deeply divided societies. Seixas found that families and communities influence 'the process of establishing historical fact, assessing historical interpretation, and hypothesising about historical patterns', while schools provide historical information for children.[4] In Northern Ireland, Barton and McCully found that until the age of 11, children's identification with historical events and figures eludes political, national or communal alignments. It comes to reflect their background only between the ages of 11 and 13.[5] This would explain why history education is at the core of the most heated debates over education reform: it remains an effective instrument for shaping individual and group identity and influencing inter-group relations.

Theories of ethnicity and nationalism recognise that historical narratives help construct ethnic and national groups and contribute to their internal cohesion: a 'long common past' may make group identities 'more stable' and 'integrative'.[6] Cohesive ethnic and cultural communities reproduce their founding historical narratives, remember formative collective events and forget the inconvenient past, effectively becoming 'communities of memories'.[7] In a state, history education may help integrate and homogenise citizens, 'tell[ing] the nation what their memories are supposed to be', and reproduc[ing] collective identity across generations.[8] Cultural homogeneity, in turn, serves to enable, or at least legitimise, life within the common political community of the democratic nation-state.

Historical narratives also help delineate the group and construct its boundaries by excluding and delegitimising its rivals. Narratives contributing to nation-building are often ethnocentric, and may convey a sense of collective victimhood, portraying ethnic or cultural minorities as foreigners and free-riders.[9] During violent conflicts, historical narratives often erase past experiences of coexistence and cultural hybridity and project upon the past distinctive and mutually exclusive 'identity categories and classifications that are essentially modern socio-political formations'.[10] This is because, as Bell et al. put it, 'stories about the past are inevitably prescriptive and instruct people how to think and act'.[11] By enshrining a political consensus over legitimate identities and reflecting power imbalances in societies, history curricula can help sustain a political order, maintain elite cohesion, legitimise control over the population and prevent structural change. They can also sanction marginalisation, political domination or even violence against minority groups. Above all, historical narratives can inhibit peaceful change through the weight of the past and the 'fear of betraying the sacrifices of one's ancestors'.[12]

If history education offers an interpretation of 'the past to suit contemporary needs',[13] it also reflects changing inter-group relations. After conflicts, reform of history curricula may exemplify a wider intent to address 'the legacies of conflict', shape a new 'common sense of national identity', and signal a 'changed identity on the part of the state'.[14] Thus, history education can promote reconciliation, mutual understanding and trust by addressing the roots of the past conflict, and prevent them from poisoning the future. It can promote tolerance and equality by teaching the core historical narratives of rival communities and can encourage children to 'see themselves as active forces for historical change'.[15]

Generally, in post-conflict societies history education is entrusted with two responsibilities. First, it is expected to provide a positive collective narrative of the past and help social cohesion through the socialisation of children in a new patriotic collective memory.[16] Second, it is expected to contribute to long-term reconciliation. The dilemma is that in a deeply divided society, history education can promote long-term peace only by acknowledging the different history of groups 'to designate their place not only in the past but also in present and future society'.[17]

The model of history teaching employed in a society, therefore, can shed light on the main political function of history education. Peter Seixas identifies three approaches to history education: 'the collective memory/best story approach', the 'postmodern approach' and the 'disciplinary approach'.[18] The 'best story' approach focuses on the contents of the curriculum rather than on its pedagogical approach, and provides a single narrative of the past.[19] After conflicts, unified historical narratives can reformulate group identity inclusively, offer a balanced account of the past, discredit divisive narratives and remind citizens of peaceful past coexistence. Yet, it may be challenging to formulate a curriculum before historians have established an acceptable record of the past conflict. Moreover, elites may have a 'vested interest in retaining simple narratives that flatter their own group and promote group unity by emphasising sharp divergences between themselves and other groups'.[20] Finally, a curriculum with explicit social and political objectives often fuels tensions and accusations of social engineering. For these reasons, McCully argues that 'a traditional narrative approach to teaching history [is] especially unsuited to a divided society'.[21]

The 'postmodern' approach to history education consists of multi-perspectivity: the presentation of the narratives of the past formulated by different groups in society, and evaluation of 'how these stories serve present aims'.[22] It addresses family and community narratives of the past directly and attempts to tackle 'emotional dimensions' and maximise history's impact on attitudes and values.[23] It aims to help students criticise and build on their background knowledge, and highlights the dialectical relationship between different communal histories. It promotes history education as a 'means of collective self-discovery', concerned with 'the examination of values, not their transmission', eroding present 'emotional barriers' and promoting empathy.[24] Critiques of postmodern approaches argue that multiperspectivity can further relativism and the denial of established but politically inconvenient truths.[25]

Finally, the 'disciplinary' approach to history education aims to convey familiarity with the sources and methods through which historical accounts are constructed.[26] McCully argues that trust-building and reconciliation are best promoted through a curriculum building skills and values, rather than a content-oriented one.[27] This is because a skills-based curriculum would teach that the value and meaning of documents and accounts changes over time, that interpretations of the past can be challenged through primary and secondary sources, that diversity can be understood and empathy can be developed, and that individual choices can affect history. Students would acquire the ability to express moral judgement, to respectfully engage in debates over the past and future, and learn self-control.[28] Disciplinary and multiperspective approaches to history education could, in Maha Yahya's words, contribute to social cohesion if social cohesion is 'not about imposing a heterogeneous [sic] identity on all these different groups but about ... promoting a sense of shared understanding, respect of difference and mutual dialogue'.[29]

The political function of history education largely determines the curricular approach to the study of history, but is in turn affected by wider sociopolitical conditions. In particular, Höpken shows that there are five sociopolitical preconditions to the production of a history textbook (or curriculum) furthering reconciliation.[30] First, 'conflict has to be at an end'. This in itself is problematic as forms of structural violence and separation persist in society after peace agreements are signed (see Chap. 7). Cole and Barsalou argue that reform can be hampered if school structures reproduce inequalities.[31]

Second, political elites must endorse a multiperspective approach to the past and avoid interference with curricula and textbooks. Yet, Cole and Barsalou point out that political elites in post-conflict societies rarely wish to promote critical thinking or undermine established hierarchies and traditions.[32] Religious institutions and the media can have an equally detrimental impact on the drafting process.

Third, society needs to be open to constructive reflection over the past to address 'certain elements that served state-building needs but now stand in the way of reconciliation'.[33] Thus, reform of history education requires a minimum level of trust within society, permitting open challenges to established narratives, revisions and discussion, without sparking violence within and outside the classroom.

Fourth, emotions must be manageable, otherwise a moratorium on history teaching might be necessary. In the immediate aftermath of conflicts, states often promote 'amnesia' to uphold stability and 'move on'.[34] Yet, the silence of official institutions can create a vacuum filled with competing and mutually exclusive communal narratives of history.

Fifth, the international community should refrain from 'top-down' interventions, but also monitor the short- and long-term impact of reforms of history education.[35] Cole and Barsalou add that successful reforms of history education need to be a political and educational priority and to be backed by widespread agreement over the aim of history education.[36] Each of these provisos affected the process and outcomes of the initiatives to reform history education in Lebanon, Northern Ireland and Macedonia: they did so to different extents, and nowhere more destructively than in Lebanon.

4.2   Lebanon

In the 1980s, PSP leader Walid Jumblatt argued that the civil war, as a struggle over identity, could only end after agreement on a consensual history for Lebanon.[37] Chapter 3 has shown that before and during the war history books emphasised Arab identity in Muslim schools, Phoenician roots in Christian schools and 'unclear' allegiances in state schools, where neither narrative prevailed.[38] The conflicting narratives conveyed by schools had partly contributed to citizens' 'confusion about their identity' and to the violent conflict over the state's identity and destiny.[39]

Fortunately, the Taif Agreement preceded consensus over Lebanese history. It attempted to reconcile two visions of Lebanon: that of Lebanon as an Arab state and that of Lebanon as a historical refuge for persecuted religious communities which coexisted and shared power.[40] In Taif, Lebanese deputies advocated the unification of history curricula and textbooks to 'develop the national spirit'.[41] Rather than embracing the suggestion of some scholars to present multiple narratives of the past in schools, Lebanese deputies favoured a 'best story' approach. They maintained that a common history book would strengthen allegiance to the state at the expense of religious and political alignments, mend the fractures caused by the war, and reflect the new inter-communal power equilibrium.[42]

Frayha sees the decision to employ history, alongside civic education, to promote reconciliation and social cohesion after the war, as a shift in 'the role of schooling from one of institutionalised divisions to one endeavouring to construct national identity'.[43] The 1995 *New Framework for Education in Lebanon* appears to confirm this view: it reiterated that the education system was to contribute to building trust and a cohesive society and that history education was to instil understanding of a common Lebanese history, highlighting the negative impact of conflict among Lebanese citizens and 'establishing an awareness that the needs of the present and ambitions [for] the future rely on the promotion of national unity'.[44] Yet the Ministry of Education allocated only one hour per week to history education at the post-primary level and only two weekly hours of *social studies* at the primary level.[45] This suggests that in fact 'the socialisation of students along national unitary lines' was not a political priority in post-Taif Lebanon.[46]

4.2.1   Mission Impossible

As director of the Centre for Educational Research and Development (CERD), Munir Abu Assali was tasked with initiating a full curricular reform, including what many saw as the 'impossible mission' of tackling the history curriculum, which had remained untouched since 1968–1970.[47] Abu Assali argues that he insisted on some ground rules for reform. He maintained that all political and religious groups should be involved in debates aimed at reaching 'a new consensus' based on an allegiance to

Lebanon superseding previous confessional compromises. He insisted reforms should fulfil the promises of the Taif Agreement. He promoted transparent decision-making, with solutions reached by consensus rather than by majority voting to 'preserve unity among different communities', arguing that 'we have different belongings so we cannot impose our point of view' and that majority voting could 'break' the committee. Finally, he insisted on swift implementation of decisions, to avoid any political volte-face, and on involving the public in policy evaluation and debate.[48]

A committee including political and religious representatives was convened to finalise and publish the main aims and principles of a new history curriculum. According to a CERD officer, the committee also started drafting textbooks, completing six books.[49] Abu Assali argues that the books drafted under his supervision reminded children that conflict among Lebanese citizens, and calls for external help could lead to 'catastrophe' and to the collapse of the state. He maintains that the books presented Lebanon's history as 'the mixture of the different histories' of the many religious communities, and encouraged respect for different perspectives. He also claims that they were designed to stimulate critical thinking through informed research, debate and group presentations.[50] Still, between 1997 and 1999, curricula for every subject were published and distributed, except for history.

4.2.2 A State Secret

When government changed in 1999, the directorship of CERD changed hands and Nemer Frayha replaced Abu Assali. Sidelining the existing curricula, a new education minister asked Frayha to create a new committee to review and 'renew' the history curricula and textbooks.[51] The new committee was composed of different members, regulated by different procedures and, according to Abu Assali, employing a different method of decision-making. Abu Assali argues that Frayha abandoned decision-making by consensus and that this explains his failure to finalise new history curricula.[52] The new committee, which convened in 1999 to draft a new history curriculum, did include representatives of the many religious groups, but its operations were 'handled almost like a state secret'.[53]

It is known that the works of the committee were punctuated by deep disagreements and frequent resignations. Bashshour suggests that debates centred on whether to emphasise Lebanese unity or the contribution of each specific community to Lebanese history.[54] The then secretary of the drafting committee admitted that initial conflicts were primarily due to members' attempts to impose their 'own ideology' over others and that the bone of contention was Lebanese identity: 'some wanted to consider the Lebanese Arab since 4000 BC', while others insisted on the importance of the Arab conquest of 636 AD and of later social and linguistic transformations.[55] Frayha, who chaired the committee, confirms that the struggles involved balancing two narratives of the past, and determining the extent of Arab-ness and of Lebanese cultural and ethnonational specificity. Still, he maintains that the committee managed to establish a common understanding of controversial events and figures, from the characters of Emir Fakhreddine and Emir Bashir Shihab II, to the Palestinian involvement in Lebanon since 1948; from the causes of the 1975–1989 Civil War to the roots of Lebanese national identity.[56]

Once the committee completed it, the curriculum was approved by an advisory council, examined by the Education minister, inspected by the Judicial Consulting Council, checked by the Cabinet and finally published in June 2000.[57] Frayha recalls that the 2000 curriculum was founded on three guiding principles: Lebanese independence, Arab identity and opposition to the forces upsetting inter-communal coexistence.[58] Similar to its predecessor, it promoted pride in Lebanese identity, encouraged belonging to Lebanon rather than to confessional communities, stimulated affiliation to the Arab world, and warned students as to the detrimental impact of conflict among Lebanese and foreign intervention, with emphasis on the 'Zionist danger'.[59] According to Frayha, the history curriculum published in 2000 could help build a 'common national memory'.[60]

After finalising the history curriculum, CERD formed 11 textbook drafting committees, each comprising one historian, a textbook writer, a specialist in teaching methods and a class teacher, representing different religious groups. A further committee, including three Christian and three Muslim scholars and headed by the CERD director, was formed to review the books. While Frayha admits, 'I'm not proud of it, it's not pure academia', he maintains that consensus among the six members was essential to ensure schools would adopt the books.[61]

According to Frayha, the history books drafted during his mandate at CERD focused primarily on social rather than political and military history. The curriculum looked at contemporary local history and family history, before considering the history of Lebanon from Phoenician times to the Taif Agreement. Frayha insisted on including the civil war in the history books, as the war had become the 'cornerstone' of family histories, with personal time often measured in terms of 'before/after the war'. He also maintains that the textbooks attempted to be politically 'neutral', to encourage students to draw lessons from history without apportioning blame for past events.[62]

In fact, while they were being distributed in 2001, the textbooks *A Window unto History*, for grades 2 and 3, were besieged by controversy, illustrating that their contents were far from uncontroversial. In particular, Education Minister Abd-al-Rahim Murad claims he asked Frayha to delay distribution of the textbooks because he found some major mistakes, which could lead to 'political problems'.[63] Murad insists that there were several major factual inaccuracies, but controversy focused on Chap. 11 of the grade 3 textbook, titled: 'They All Went and Lebanon Stayed: Independence of the Nation'. The chapter showed a timeline of invasions of Lebanon's territory, from 2000 BC to 1943 AD, including the 636 AD 'Arab conquest'.[64] The timeline and chapter title, according to Murad, portrayed Arabs as conquerors on a par with the French, denied the Arab identity of Lebanon and suggested that 'the Arabs were expelled from Lebanon' like other conquerors.[65] This, he declared at the time, ensured that 'Lebanon has no identity, it was lost or blurred'.[66]

Frayha recognises that emphasis on Lebanese identity in the textbooks may have been 'interpreted by some people as underplaying the Arab identity', but he objected that most countries use the idiom *Al-Fatih Al-Arabi* ('the Arab conquest') to describe the events of 636 AD.[67] Prominent Muslim figures also publicly supported the textbooks and pointed out that they clearly did not claim that the Arabs had left Lebanon.[68] Moreover, Frayha offered to cut the relevant page out of the textbook and CERD issued a statement that page 88 of the grade 3 textbook contained mistakes and would be removed.[69]

Still, the education minister insisted that the history textbooks should be seized and Frayha should be fired because he printed and distributed textbooks without direct ministerial approval.[70] Frayha maintains that direct ministerial approval was not needed before publishing the textbooks and that Murad fuelled the controversy because he wanted to 'get back at' Frayha for obstructing the minister's plans to open some private schools. He also recalls that a group of Lebanese historians lobbied the minister directly, arguing that the textbooks were not appropriate for students, but he claims their protests were 'ideological' and motivated by financial interests (defending the continued existence of a number of different textbook series).[71] Yet others who participated in the drafting process recognise that disagreements over the interpretation of certain events ran deep between members of the drafting committee and among different religious communities.[72] Local observers confirm that the education minister exaggerated a marginal problem 'for political reasons' and that the withdrawal of history books owed more to Sunni political opposition and Syrian pressure than to any procedural concerns.[73] Ultimately, copies of every grade 2 and 3 books were withdrawn, the printing of other textbooks was stopped and Frayha was 'relieved' of his duties.[74]

Education minister Murad formed a new drafting committee to revise the curriculum and produce new textbooks. Before the new books were finalised, Murad was approached with complaints that their contents did not do equal justice to all the confessional communities of Lebanon.[75] Work on the history curriculum and textbooks was simply suspended: Frayha comments ironically that the minister was clearly not 'ready to fight' for his new textbooks in such a politicised context.[76]

4.2.3 *Political Disagreement Versus Historical Events*

In 2009, the new Education Minister Hassan Mneimneh formed a new committee for the drafting of history curricula and books. He convened representatives of the main religious groups and political parties and asked them to 'extract' a new curriculum from that of 2000.[77] A new history curriculum for grades 2–9 was completed in 2010 and presented to the Council of ministers for approval in early 2011.[78] Already a low priority, approval of the history curriculum was sidelined during negotiations over the composition of a new executive in January–June 2011.

In mid-2011, a new education minister presented the history curriculum to the cabinet and ministers started examining it with a view to 'having their share in history and being presented positively'.[79] The political representatives of each confessional community came face to face with the many divergent perspectives on Lebanon's past and, as Daw put it, 'every minister wanted to add points to the book to support his sect'.[80] Thus, the process of 'cleaning up the dirty details, and putting the dirty laundry away'[81] dragged on and even spilled over into Lebanon's streets.

In January 2012, it emerged that the new curriculum described the events of 2005, leading to Syrian withdrawal from Lebanon, as 'a wave of protests', rather than the 'Cedar revolution'.[82] It was argued that the phrase 'Cedar revolution' had been coined by an American diplomat and was 'sensitive to many in the country'.[83] Supporters of the March 14 coalition (particularly the Christian Kataeb and Lebanese Forces) staged a demonstration, protesting that their parties' contribution to independence was being expunged from official accounts of Lebanon's history, while Hizbollah's resistance to Israel was given a place of honour.[84] Echoing the street, Kataeb deputy Samy Gemayel equated the Cedar Revolution to Lebanon's second independence and asked whether 'we have the right to remove Hizbollah's liberation of South Lebanon from the history curriculum'.[85] In the midst of the controversy, Walid Jumblatt wondered, 'does disagreement in politics erase historical events?'[86] The answer is probably affirmative: unable to mediate an agreement, Prime Minister Najib Mikati declared a moratorium on history curricula and textbooks, and to this day, a unified history curriculum is one of Taif's unfulfilled promises.

Beyond highlighting deep disagreements over the state's identity and foreign orientation among Lebanese elites, the failure to formulate a sanctioned history curriculum and unified textbook means that schools are free to choose not to teach history. Indeed, most students are taught history only in grades 9 and 12, when they sit an official exam including a test based on the 1968–1970 curriculum.[87] When history is taught in other grades, controversial topics are often avoided to prevent fights.[88] Moreover, publishing houses are free to produce history textbooks on the basis of the 1968–1970 curriculum.[89] Books are approved by CERD on the basis of three criteria: they have to follow the 1968–1970 curriculum, comply with the Lebanese constitution and avoid offence or discrimination on religious and communal grounds.[90] CERD also checks imported textbooks to ensure that they do not include illegal pictures and do not have Israeli authors.[91] However, CERD is often unaware of the contents of textbooks used in private schools, especially when they are imported: in 2012, for example, it was found that a history book in use in an international school in Beirut listed Hizbollah as a terrorist organisation.[92]

Most textbooks, as well as the questions posed in official exams, consider history only up until 1943, as 'Lebanese parties have different points of view' on later events.[93] By reaching 'the end of history in 1943',[94] textbooks overlook contemporary developments, including the 1958 and 1975–1989 civil wars and the roots and formation of the present political parties and consociational political system. Thus, the civil war remains the 'gaping hole' in Lebanese history education.[95] Different communal narratives of the war are conveyed in an institutional void where they interact and compete, perpetuating each community's sense of victimhood and myth of resistance.[96] At the same time, these narratives fall short of encouraging patriotism, democratic participation and even an understanding of the origins and workings of Lebanon's political system.

Indeed, a 1994 study of history textbooks in Catholic schools highlighted that most books avoided controversial issues and emphasised multireligious coexistence even at the expense of factual accuracy.[97] Messara confirms that history textbooks portray Lebanon as a 'tolerant society whose members love one another and associate as brothers'.[98] However, different textbooks devote varying proportions of time to local, Arab, European and World history and emphasise different events.[99] Even when they consider the same event, books employed in different schools often provide different interpretations: for example, the Lebanese nationalists executed by the Ottomans in 1916 are heroes in some books and traitors in others.[100] History teachers also admit that their communal background influences their teaching: Christian teachers tend to present the French Mandate positively and to draw the origins of Greater Lebanon to Fakhreddine's emirate in the early seventeenth century, while teachers in Muslim schools generally present Greater Lebanon as an artificial French creation. Thus, history education circumvents controversial issues and rhetorically emphasises inter-communal coexistence and cooperation, but it also reproduces and legitimises communally specific, and mutually exclusive, narratives of events.[101]

Abouchedid and Nasser confirm that students' identities and their perceptions of the past are affected by school history in Lebanon.[102] This substantiates the observation that, by promoting divisive rather than overarching narratives of the past, Lebanon may be 'raising another generation of children who identify themselves only with their communities and not their nation'.[103] Moreover, present arrangements for history education do not build skills conducive to reconciliation and peacebuilding: they do not promote empathy and affection, convey multiple perspectives, or encourage acceptance that 'you will never be able to convert everyone to your beliefs'.[104] Instead, Bashshour warns that history education furthers 'a culture of memory [which] is very likely [a] breeding ground for submission and dependence'.[105]

4.2.4 Fragmented Pasts

In 1996 Abu Assali explained to a journalist that Lebanon had survived the war but 'we are now in the [intensive] care unit'. He argued that, rather than curing Lebanon, an injection of historical reality 'may kill the patient'.¹⁰⁶ In 2014, the Lebanese patient is still waiting for an injection of historical reality. This is partly because, according to a CERD senior officer, policymakers missed the political honeymoon of the early 1990s, which provided a window of opportunity for the formulation of unified history textbooks.¹⁰⁷ Hereafter, the politicisation of debates over the history curriculum has exacerbated a wider tendency to disregard previous achievements in educational reform.

But the stalemate over formulation of a unified history curriculum signals wider conflicts over Lebanon's history and over the origins of its consociation. Debates over the history curriculum mirror shifting political cleavages: in 2001, controversies focused on the familiar disagreement over the Arab or Lebanese roots of identity, reflecting the Muslim-Christian divide during the civil war. Mirroring the political polarisation between the March 14 and March 8 coalitions after 2008, recent debates about the history curricula have focused on the relative importance of the March 14 resistance to Syrian occupation as compared with the Hizbollah resistance to Israeli occupation. Thus, Yahya argues that by delaying the formulation of a unified history curriculum 'it's almost as if we wanted to apply to history the amnesty laws that we applied after the civil war'.¹⁰⁸ As an amnesty, silence over Lebanon's recent history may help protect the integrity and stability of the political system, whose elites represent the groups involved in past violence.¹⁰⁹ Current arrangements for history education certainly help the internal cohesion of Lebanon's confessional and political communities: in 2009 most parties employed 'selective memory of the war' for political campaigns.¹¹⁰

Moreover, Beydoun argues that attempts to create a unified history textbook exemplify the Lebanese state's weakness, and the desire to 'solve the problem once and for all because at the end of the day the state is in control of nothing'.¹¹¹ Akar admits that 'we're never going to agree on a history' and suggests that a single narrative history textbook may undermine the very historical skills which contribute to reconciliation and peacebuilding.¹¹² It would present a questionable account of the past, without promoting individual or group self-esteem.¹¹³ Indeed, it may be time to recognise that Taif, rather than a detailed plan for education reform, 'was [simply] a political text'.¹¹⁴ It reflected the balance of power among Lebanon's communities at the end of the civil war and long-standing Muslim insistence on employing schools as instruments of nation-state building. A move away from the 'best story' approach to history education would open new avenues for the Lebanese history curriculum: for example, teaching could be based on historical sources, on the presentation of the pasts of Lebanon's many communities, and on the offer of 'even opposing narratives of the same past event', encouraging 'students to gravitate toward their own version'.[115] Curiously, this is precisely the approach adopted in Northern Ireland.

4.3 Northern Ireland

As in Lebanon, there is no consensus in Northern Ireland over the past: the Unionist/Protestant and Nationalist/Catholic communities disagree on the roots of the Troubles, the most formative events of the past and the portrayal of historical figures.[116] Until the 1990s, history education reflected this divergence. As Chap. 3 explained, controlled schools (catering predominantly for Unionist/Protestant children) endorsed a British perspective on history and taught little or no Irish history: as a CCMS officer put it, 'denying access to Irish history [was] a means of consolidating [children's] Britishness'.[117] Conversely, Catholic maintained schools emphasised the historical connections to the Republic of Ireland, thus strengthening the identity of 'Catholic people [who] strongly identified themselves as Irish people'.[118]

This is why the publication of a statutory core history curriculum in 1990 appeared as a 'little miracle'.[119] First, the new curriculum bridged the gap between the histories taught in controlled and Catholic maintained schools, by imposing more focus on Irish history. Moreover, in an attempt to further overarching European identifications, most topics were presented through three geographical prisms: that of the island of Ireland, that of the British Isles, and that of Europe.[120] Second, the 1990 curriculum abandoned previous narrative, 'best story' approaches to history education and adopted multiperspectivity and a skills-based disciplinary approach. Hereafter, history education aimed to present and legitimise different perspectives, promote individual and collective self-esteem and confidence, further empathy and understanding of different views and tackle controversial issues and events related to the conflict.[121]

Indeed, Kitson observed that both the curriculum and the textbooks available for history were so balanced as to be 'almost apolitical'.[122] By focusing on social and material life, history education circumvented political divisions and avoided debates over controversial historical personalities.[123]

However, the long-term social impact of the new curriculum was criticised on three grounds. First, a history education that overlooks individual agency may convey a nihilistic view of the past to children.[124] Second, the curriculum's lack of narrative accounts of the past and of explicit links between the past and the present and its 'aversion to national history fails to provide students with the one thing they may need most – a sense of shared identity'.[125] This might make teenagers vulnerable to the politicised narratives they encounter in their family or community. Indeed, confirming Seixas' hypothesis, research in Northern Ireland found that students often employ the factual information provided by history education to support their communal and partisan narratives, especially in Key Stage (KS) 3 and 4.[126] Because they see school history as unbiased, students draw from the curriculum to 'support their developing identities' and to inform views acquired outside class.[127]

Third, Barton and McCully found that the curriculum provided more sources of identification and empathy for children of Unionist/Protestant background than for those of Nationalist/Catholic background. They even proposed that 'a balanced and neutral course of study standardised for the whole region may not be up to the task of dealing with the emotionally charged uses of history in Northern Ireland'.[128] These three criticisms informed the curricular revision announced in 1999.

4.3.1 *The 2005 Curriculum and Its Weaknesses*

The curricular reform initiated in 1999 aimed to 'cherish diversity, understand diversity and regard it as being a good thing rather than try and make everybody the same'.[129] At the primary level, history is studied through the subject *The World Around Us* (including also science and geography). It aims to develop familiarity with historical sources, ability to identify different time periods and an understanding of historical change and knowledge of some historical figures.[130] The 2005 curriculum does not prescribe how much time and emphasis should be devoted to history and does not prescribe topics or study units, but schools are expected to offer a 'broad and balanced curriculum'.[131] At the post-primary level, history is generally studied as a freestanding subject. KS3 requires students to 'investigate the long and short term causes and consequences of the partition of Ireland and how it has influenced Northern Ireland today',[132] while KS4 offers the choice between studying 'Britain, Northern Ireland and Ireland' in 1932–1949 or in 1965–1985.[133] Like its predecessor, the 2005 curriculum aims to foster multiperspectivity, enquiry, problem-solving and the 'ability to challenge stereotypical, biased or distorted viewpoints with appropriately sensitive, informed and balanced responses'.[134]

The 2005 curriculum is often presented as a model for other societies emerging from conflict, for two key reasons. First, while the curriculum 'is not a free for all', it is flexible enough to allow schools to focus on a local history which 'connects them to their community'. At the primary level, the Council for the Curriculum, Examinations and Assessment (CCEA) provides support materials, but principals are allowed to frame a curriculum relevant to pupils' lives, including for example the history of local sites.[135] Second, the Northern Ireland history curriculum adopts a disciplinary and multiperspective approach. It expects children to 'be critical' and 'come to their conclusions' based on evidence, and encourages teachers to deal with diversity and address the recent past.[136] To this end, CCEA produces a variety of support materials to help teachers tackle challenging issues.[137] The curriculum offers many opportunities to challenge misconceptions and misperceptions of history, for example by pointing out that about a quarter of the men who enlisted in World War I from Ulster were Catholics, or that William of Orange's army was multireligious and multicultural.[138]

However, the implementation of the 2005 statutory curriculum for history education in Northern Ireland is still criticised. Like its predecessor, the 2005 curriculum can appear aspirational in its ambition to employ history education to tackle societal attitudes and inter-communal prejudice. In fact, in 2012 only about 4.5 % of pupils in Northern Ireland chose history as a subject at KS4, so a minuscule minority of students learned about post-1922 history and the Troubles in school.[139] Yet children are surrounded by the physical and ritual remains of the conflict, and often know their meaning only 'if they have some personal connection with it, and they are much more likely to remember the atrocities committed by the other side'.[140] Additionally, despite findings to the contrary, many teachers argue that student attitudes reflect the political background of their family and cannot be altered in school.[141] Thus, teachers often sidestep controversial issues to avoid offending students and some schools even avoid teaching modules on Northern Ireland at KS3 and KS4 as 'it entails a study of the "isms" of Northern Ireland's political parties'.[142] As a consequence, many observers assume that history education does not tackle Northern Ireland's controversial past and that this partly explains why teenagers have a distorted understanding of the conflict.[143] Indeed, as recently as 2009, Magill et al. found that many teenagers thought that the Troubles were about religion.[144]

The 2005 curriculum has also been criticised on pedagogical grounds. In particular, its focus on static units of study at the primary level and its lack of explicit connections to the present may hamper children's understanding of change, and of the relationship between the past and the present.[145] It may also encourage students to draw selectively from the curriculum to support their developing political perspectives.[146] Finally, the lack of an overarching historical narrative in the curriculum allows the persistence of different interpretations of the past between students belonging to different communities. Thus, Bell et al. found that, depending on their background, some students described partition as 'England separating from Ireland', others as 'Northern Ireland getting independence' and still others as 'Ireland breaking with Britain'.[147]

Some students even argue that controlled schools still avoid nationalist perspectives of the past and vice versa, and that history classes can be arenas for the expression of prejudices and verbal attacks against 'the other side'.[148] Certainly, the separation of pupils of different denominational, political and national backgrounds into different schools makes it hard to employ history to challenge prejudices and communal narratives of the past. In contrast, teachers in integrated schools maintain that the mixed background of their students facilitates discussion, furthers debate over controversial issues and leads to drawing connections between the past and present.[149] Thus, initiatives for *shared education*, discussed in Chap. 7, may impact positively on history teaching.

4.3.2   An Escapable Connection?

Surveys in Northern Ireland found that students regard school as an important, if not the most important, source of information about history.[150] However, this section has shown that the impact of Northern Ireland's history curriculum upon children's political, communal and national identities remains unclear and that debates continue over whether history education is 'stemming the tide' of extremism or providing ammunition for it.[151]

This is because, in contrast to the 'best story' approach adopted in Lebanon, Northern Ireland's history curriculum does not aim to endorse or supplant Unionist/Protestant and Nationalist/Catholic interpretations of the past. Rather, it suggests that 'the connection between history and national identity is not an inescapable one'.¹⁵² The 1990 and 2005 history curricula attempt to circumvent the thorny issue of national identity by focusing on the development of historical skills, critical thinking and multiperspectivity. These skills are instrumental to mutual understanding, tolerance and even reconciliation in post-conflict societies.

A comparison with Lebanon confirms that a skills-based history curriculum is more likely to contribute to mutual understanding and reconciliation than a 'best story' approach, embodied in Lebanon's controversial curricula of 2001 and 2011. This may be due to the lack of consensus over the end of conflict in both societies: Magill et al. found that in Northern Ireland many respondents born in the 1990s thought that the Troubles had not ended in 1998.¹⁵³ Indeed, Barton predicts the failure of a 'best story' approach to history education in a deeply divided society where communities have 'diametrically opposed interpretations' of the past, which 'continue to be the source of political controversy and even violence'.¹⁵⁴

4.4 Macedonia

Rather than attempting to deconstruct the relationship between history and national identity, the Yugoslav state employed history education for nation-state building in the Republic of Macedonia. Similarly, the newly independent Macedonian state, under the strategic and diplomatic pressures of the 1990s, attempted to employ history to legitimise its sovereignty and independence, and even prove the existence of a distinct ethnic Macedonian people. This task proved arduous in a multi-ethnic, multilinguistic and mutlireligious country, whose past events are interpreted differently by the different ethnic communities, and whose historical heroes are 'claimed' by Greece and Bulgaria as their national heroes.¹⁵⁵

The first post-independence curriculum aimed at building a national identity founded on Slavism: it presented the past as the linear 'story' of the emergence of 'state institutions and symbols' associated with the ethnic Macedonian community.¹⁵⁶ Textbooks were drafted and published by a government commission, but a local historian argues they mainly contained 'recycled history lessons', drawn from previous curricula.¹⁵⁷ Moreover, Jordanovski found that the textbooks implanted 'retrospective national feelings and strivings' on the inhabitants of the territory of present-day Macedonia¹⁵⁸ and Koren found that 'contemporary borders [were] projected on earlier periods'.¹⁵⁹ Thus, Macedonia was presented as unified and ethnically homogeneous throughout history: textbooks ignored that the Turks were a majority of its inhabitants during the Ottoman empire, and that Muslim Albanians have long inhabited the territory of present-day Macedonia. They focused on the history of Greater Macedonia, emphasised the territorial losses from every military conflict and traced the fate of ethnic Macedonians in neighbouring states. They portrayed positively institutions and events conducive to the foundation of an independent Macedonian state, such as the creation of the Macedonian Republic as part of Yugoslavia and the creation of an independent Macedonian Orthodox Church.[160] Finally, the curriculum sidelined those facts that deviated from a linear narrative of the past culminating in Macedonian statehood, such as the violent implosion of Yugoslavia and the history of ethnic Albanians in Yugoslavia.[161] Most of these criticisms of the 1992 curriculum and textbooks are actually wider critiques of a 'best story' approach to history education and to the use of the past to foster the construction of a nation-state.

4.4.1   *A Proportional Curriculum*

In contrast to the Taif Agreement, Macedonia's Ohrid Agreement impacted history education only indirectly. An Albanian historian explained that with the expansion of education in the language of ethnic communities 'it was logical to have something about their culture and history' in the curricula.[162] Thus, rather than simply recycling old content, the education minister convened a group of experts to fully revise the history curriculum.[163]

The ten-member curriculum drafting committee included educational specialists, university experts (including four Albanian-speaking academics) and representatives of the main political parties.[164] Rapidly, controversy ensued on the number of lessons to be devoted to the history of ethnic Macedonians and of ethnic Albanians in the history curricula. Thus, Mladenovski summarises the process of curriculum drafting as a protracted negotiation over the percentage of the contents devoted to each community, a game of 'give us 20 percent [of the curriculum], we'll give you 30 percent [of the curriculum]'.[165] Ultimately, ethnic Albanian members of the curriculum drafting committee approved a new curriculum only because, for the first time, it provided for lessons on the history of ethnic Albanians for students in Macedonian-, Turkish- and Serbian-language classes.[166]

The new history curriculum was introduced in primary schools and in academic secondary schools in 2005. History is part of *Nature and*

Society up to the fifth grade of primary school, and is taught as an independent subject from sixth grade upwards for 80 minutes a week in academic secondary schools.[167] The 2005 curriculum is highly prescriptive: it includes the title, aims and contents of every lesson but the topics are often disjointed.[168] Compared with its predecessor, it includes more lessons about non-majority ethnolinguistic communities. However, most of the curriculum focuses on 'national history', meaning the history of the territory of historic Macedonia until its partition during the Balkan wars, and the history of the Socialist Republic of Macedonia and its irredent lands in Greece and Bulgaria since 1913.[169] Similar to the Lebanese 1968–1970 history curriculum, the Macedonian 2005 curriculum ends with Macedonia's independence in 1991.

The new curriculum and the new history textbooks were criticised on pedagogical grounds in four respects. First, the History Teachers' Association of Macedonia complained that the curriculum was drafted behind closed doors, without involving primary and secondary school teachers. As a consequence, the language and activities prescribed are often too complex for students and generally require some prior knowledge of historical events.[170] Second, the curricula paid little attention to historical skills such as analysis of primary sources, critical thinking, identification of the causes and consequences of events, interpretation of change and continuity and development of empathy.[171] Third, history teachers were not offered training, despite the introduction of new contents on ethnic Albanian history in 2005. Thus, teachers, in classes of up to 40 pupils, still adopt a knowledge-based, mnemonic and chronological approach to history teaching, relying fully on the textbook.

Finally, the new history textbooks contained major factual mistakes.[172] The inadequacy of teaching resources was exacerbated by teachers' limited freedom of choice: since 2008 the state has published one history textbook for each language of instruction and distributed it for free in compulsory schools.[173] The formal procedure for the adoption of the history textbook is unclear, and most institutions, including the Bureau of Educational Development (BoE), deny any role in their drafting and revision.[174] It appears that the education minister issues calls for textbook proposals by independent groups of authors, evaluates them, and selects a proposal for each language of instruction. Author groups then write textbooks in a very short time with very little monitoring. Ethnic Albanian and ethnic Macedonian authors rarely cooperate in drafting books: different authors are tasked with the writing of the Albanian-language and of the Macedonian-language textbook, as books written by Macedonians would be 'set aside' in Albanian-language classes and vice versa.[175]

Local and international observers criticised the potential social impact of the 2005 history curriculum. The proportional approach to curriculum writing, partially rooted in Yugoslav traditions, also reflects the political and administrative proportionality enshrined in the Ohrid Agreement. Thus, in Macedonia's history curricula the amount of lessons devoted to each ethnic community is generally 'based on [its] demographic scope', with ethnic Albanians granted about 20 % of lessons in the Macedonian-language history curriculum.[176] Curriculum-sharing according to proportional considerations generally satisfied the ethnic Macedonians and ethnic Albanians.[177] Still, the Macedonian-language curriculum devotes only one lesson to the Vlachs and one to the Jews, but no lessons to the Roma, Turk and Serb communities.[178] By minimising the diversity of Macedonia's population, some argue that history education undermines the self-esteem of children belonging to smaller minorities.[179] Indeed, historian Boban Petrovski explains that Romas, because of their disadvantaged socio-economic status, 'are not in such a position that they can make demands' on the history curriculum.[180] This suggests that, rather than simply reflecting the demographic weight of a community, the history curriculum also mirrors and reproduces the power hierarchies among Macedonia's ethnolinguistic communities.

Furthermore, observing the lack of lessons about ethnic Turks in the history curriculum, Petrovski explains that Turks are expected to 'identify' with the history of the Ottoman Empire.[181] The assumption that certain ethnic groups have a historical homeland outside the Macedonian territory also informs the Turkish- and Albanian-language curricula, which include more information about each community's 'country of origin'.[182] Rather than looking at ethnic Albanians in Macedonia, the Albanian-language curricula focus on the history of 'Albanian lands' (primarily Albania and Kosovo).[183] This backs Mladenovski's view that the history curricula portray ethnic Albanians and ethnic Macedonians as if 'we were talking about two separate states' and substantiates an international observer's warning that history books seem to teach that 'this country is monoethnic'.[184] Indeed, the curricula and textbooks do not present past events as common to all the communities in Macedonia and often ignore local history. For example, the curriculum contains a lesson about the Macedonians during World War I and a separate one about the Albanians.[185]

Thus, history education does not address the entangled history of Macedonia's mixed populations, and presents the pasts of local ethnic communities as fully separate. In fact, the 2005 curriculum explicitly allows teachers to sidestep Macedonia's diversity: out of 48 lessons, teachers only have to teach 36 of their choice, making 25 % of the curriculum optional. Because of the limited number of lessons on non-ethnic Macedonian communities, the choice to teach about them is up to individual teachers.[186] Macedonian teachers can avoid teaching Albanian history, while Albanian teachers can focus primarily on 'ethnic Albanian history'.[187] No state exam or central monitoring system exists to prevent children being taught the unchallenged historical narratives of Macedonia's two largest ethnolinguistic communities.

Indeed, local observers warn that schools may be creating and reproducing two parallel and mutually exclusive histories for these two communities.[188] In Macedonian-language textbooks, national history is generally the history of the ethnic Macedonian community, mobilised to convey a glorified and mythical (if often factually debatable) past. It helps define the roots of the Macedonian people, project them onto the past, and establish ownership of Macedonia's territory.[189] Despite recent improvements, some Albanian activists also argue that Macedonian-language textbooks still contain false information and biased and discriminatory attitudes towards local minorities and bordering countries. For example, Xabir Deralla mentioned that all Albanians are presented as fascists in the lessons on World War II.[190] For their part, Albanian-language curricula contain very little Macedonian history, and even less about the Albanian community in Macedonia. If Albanian-language textbooks are less derogatory than the Macedonian-language ones, it is probably because they need to be approved by the ethnic Macedonian education minister before being distributed.[191] Similar to the Macedonian-language curriculum, the Albanian-language curriculum conveys a sense of victimhood and immemorial ownership of the Macedonian territory, delegitimising visions for a common, interdependent future.[192] In sum, through two parallel 'best stories', history education in Macedonia's state schools helps consolidate the internal cohesion of the ethnic Albanian and ethnic Macedonian communities.

4.4.2 *We Are Not Touching History*

In 2008, the Ministry of Education initiated a revision of all curricula in an attempt to update them and to introduce more 'multicultural' contents. However, as one of the participants of the revision put it, 'when it came to the history curriculum, [the government] said we are not touching this because it is a political decision'.¹⁹³

In fact, a special committee was formed to produce a revised history curriculum.¹⁹⁴ It finalised the new curriculum for sixth grade which, mirroring evolving ethnic Macedonian narratives of identity, focused more than its predecessor on ancient myths and heroes (particularly the figure of Alexander the Great).¹⁹⁵ Albanian historians complained that emphasis on antiquity has come at the expense of Albanian history and that history education was being used to sanction ethnic Macedonian ownership of the state. Additionally, Greek and Bulgarian historians questioned the veracity of facts and interpretations in the new curriculum.¹⁹⁶ Debates reached the European Parliament, where Bulgarian ambassador Dimitar Tsanchev threatened to block Macedonia's European Union (EU) accession over the contents of the history curriculum.¹⁹⁷

Moreover, the curriculum drafting committee failed to produce new history curricula for grades 7–9 because of 'some misunderstanding between communities'.¹⁹⁸ In particular, some argue that new drafts of the curriculum described Albanians as 'mountain people', thus inflaming ethnic Albanian media, public opinion and politicians.¹⁹⁹ Others maintain that the committee split over the number of lessons on Albanian history in the new curriculum.²⁰⁰ The BoE declines knowledge of and responsibility for the process. However, it is credible that the process broke down over the attempt to once again apply (political and demographic) proportionality to curriculum writing. As of 2013, teachers were still employing the 2005 curricula and making use of curricular provisions to avoid teaching 25 % of the lessons.

Lazarevska argues that, because of Macedonia's political and strategic instability, 'it will never be a good enough time' for a full revision of the history curricula.²⁰¹ In Macedonia's consociation, the present history curricula serve an important political function: they contribute to cement and delimit the ethnic Albanian and ethnic Macedonian communities by reproducing their parallel 'best stories'. History education provides a glorious past for ethnic Macedonians, it proves their ownership of the Macedonian territory and legitimises Macedonia's statehood and independence. It also entrenches the image of ethnic Albanians and ethnic Macedonians as each other's victims and rivals: as an international officer notes, children 'do not have a curriculum that tells them you live in a culturally and ethnically diverse country, embrace it, in fact, they're telling them the opposite'.²⁰² Ultimately, calls for 'more emphasis on a history that unites', rather than parallel communal narratives, have long fallen on deaf ears. As in Lebanon, in Macedonia the reform of history education is politicised, but also marginal in political priorities.[203]

4.5 Conclusion

Marthoz argues that 'if geography provides an excuse to make war, history's role is to prepare and justify it'.[204] This also applies to peace. Yet, this chapter demonstrates that the reform of history education is rarely a political and financial priority for post-war governments.

This chapter has compared initiatives with reform history education in consociational Lebanon, Northern Ireland and Macedonia. It shows first that it is difficult to determine whether curricular reforms promote or just reflect conflict transformation and reconciliation. Höpken's suggestion that textbooks promoting reconciliation can only be produced once conflict has ended exemplifies this chicken-and-egg problem. This vicious circle affects deeply divided societies such as Lebanon, Northern Ireland and Macedonia, where there is no consensus over whether conflicts have ended. In fact, their consociational political systems are premised on the management rather than the resolution of violent inter-group conflicts.

This chapter confirms that 'if the political conflict is not resolved, it is impossible to elaborate' an 'institutionally legitimised version of what took place'.[205] This explains why schools in Macedonia and Lebanon reach 'the end of history' before their respective conflicts. It also suggests that Macedonia's emphasis on nation-building through the history curricula is detrimental to mutual trust and reconciliation among the local ethno-linguistic communities. Similarly, the obstinate attempt to formulate a unified history curriculum in Lebanon has, if anything, further polarised opinions over the past. In both societies, historical narratives are easily mobilised by political and communal elites in the context of pervasive insecurity, fear of state collapse and relapse into violence. In contrast, Northern Ireland's experiment in decoupling history and national identity through a skills-based approach to history education has allowed the formulation of modules on the Troubles. However, Northern Ireland's approach also highlights the challenges in promoting political stability in the absence of overarching narratives of the past, and confirms that a multiperspective history can be taught in schools only if political elites (and the communities they represent) endow alternative narratives of the past with a modicum of legitimacy.

Moreover, debates over history education in these three deeply divided societies reveal a lack of consensus over the political function of history education. On the one hand, history is expected to promote unity and social cohesion among citizens belonging to different ethnic, confessional, linguistic and political communities. On the other hand, it is expected to further reconciliation by reflecting, acknowledging and valuing the specific narratives of each community. Thus, this chapter demonstrates that initiatives for the reform of history education fail when they contradict the principles of pluralism and parity of esteem. The failure to produce a unified textbook presenting a narrative, homogeneous history of Lebanon is an obvious example. This chapter also shows that reforms take hold when they reflect and reproduce the sociopolitical building blocks of the three consociations by accommodating different narratives of the past (in Northern Ireland) or applying consociational expedients to curriculum drafting (as with Macedonia's proportional curriculum).

Finally, this chapter confirms that history education in consociational Lebanon, Northern Ireland and Macedonia does not challenge the socialisation of children into separate and potentially antagonistic narratives of the past. Divergent histories are associated with the ethnic, confessional and national communities that participated in violent conflict and now share political power. This consolidates the communities on which consociational politics is founded and legitimises, or at least does not challenge, the authority of those political leaders who participated in war. Thus, history education may help stabilise the consociational political system in the short term.

Notes

1. Robert Phillips et al., 'Four Histories, One Nation? History Teaching, Nationhood and a British Identity,' *Compare* 29, no. 2 (1999): 162.
2. Kamal Salibi, *A House of Many Mansions*, 201.
3. Peter Seixas, 'Historical Understanding among Adolescents in a Multicultural Setting,' *Curriculum Enquiry* 23, no. 3 (1993): 301; Jean-Damascène Gasanabo, *Fostering Peaceful Co-Existence through Analysis and Revision of History Curricula and Textbooks in Southeast Europe, Preliminary Stocktaking Report* (Geneva: UNESCO, 2006): 7; Alan McCully, 'The Contribution of History Teaching to Peace Building,' in Salomon and Cairns (eds.), *Handbook on Peace Education*, 214.
4. Seixas, 'Historical Understanding', 320.

5. Keith Barton and Alan McCully, 'History, Identity and the School Curriculum in Northern Ireland: And Empirical Study of Secondary Students' Ideas and Perspectives,' *Journal of Curriculum Studies* 37, no. 1 (2005).
6. Max Weber, *The Essential Weber: A Reader*, ed. Sam Whimster (New York: Routledge, 2007), 150; Smith, *The Ethnic Origins of Nations*; Höpken, 'History Education,' in Bokovoy et al. (eds.), *State-Society Relations in Yugoslavia*, 80.
7. Qtd. in Ibid.
8. Dennis Hart, qtd. in Roland Bleiker and Hoang Young-Ju, 'On the Use and Abuse of Korea's Past: An Inquiry into History Teaching and Reconciliation,' in Cole (ed.), *Teaching the Violent Past*, 254.
9. Gasanabo, *Fostering Peaceful Co-Existence*, 7, 32, 63, 65; Elizabeth A. Cole and Judy Barsalou, *Unite or Divide? The Challenges of Teaching History in Societies Emerging from Violent Conflict* (Washington: United States Institute of Peace, 2006): 1; Maria Donkova, 'Teaching History Differently: A Lesson from the Balkans,' *History: Beyond the Battlefield. UNESCO Sources* 120, (2000): 9.
10. Davies, *Education and Conflict*, 89.
11. John Bell, Ulf Hansson, and Nick McCaffery, *The Troubles Aren't History Yet. Young People's Understanding of the Past* (Belfast: Community Relations Council, 2010), 16.
12. Lambkin, *Opposite Religions Still?*, 62.
13. Qtd. in Penney Clark, 'Representations of Aboriginal People in English Canadian History Textbooks: Toward Reconciliation,' in Cole (ed.), *Teaching the Violent Past*, 93.
14. Smith and Vaux, qtd. in McCully, 'The Contribution of History,' in Salomon and Cairns (eds.), *Handbook on Peace Education*, 213; Elizabeth A. Cole, 'Introduction: Reconciliation and History Education,' in Cole (ed.), *Teaching the Violent Past*, 14.
15. Peter Seixas and C. Peck, 'Teaching Historical Thinking,' in A. Sears and I. Wright (eds.), *Challenges and Prospects for Canadian Social Studies*, (Vancouver: Pacific Educational Press, 2004): 114; Bell et al., *The Troubles*, 15. Cole and Barsalou, *Unite or Divide*, 1,4.
16. Cole, 'Introduction', Cole (ed.), *Teaching the Violent Past*, 18, 20; Alan McCully, Brendan Hartop, and Keith Barton, *Teaching History in Societies Emerging from Conflict* (Coleraine: University of Ulster, 2003): 10.
17. Jean-Paul Marthoz, 'The Hidden History of Latin America,' *History: Beyond the Battlefield. UNESCO Sources* 120, (2000).
18. Arthur Chapman et al., 'Developing Historical Thinking: Theory and Research,' in Arthur Chapman et al. (eds.), *Thinking Historically About Missing Persons: A Guide for Teachers*, (Cyprus: International Centre for Transitional Justice, 2011): 5.

19. Ibid., 6.
20. Cole and Barsalou, *Unite or Divide*, 9.
21. McCully, 'The Contribution of History Teaching', in Salomon and Cairns (eds.), *Handbook on Peace Education*, 216.
22. Chapman et al., 'Developing Historical Thinking', in Chapman et al. (eds.), *Thinking Historically About Missing Persons*, 6.
23. McCully, 'The Contribution of History Teaching', in Salomon and Cairns (eds.), *Handbook on Peace Education*, 218; Seixas, 'Historical Understanding', 302.
24. Cole, 'Introduction', Cole (ed.), *Teaching the Violent Past*, 21; John Slater, qtd. in Jacqueline Dean, 'History and Citizenship: Concepts and Practice,' *Educational Evaluation and Policy Analysis* 3, no. 13 (2002): 11; McCully, 'The Contribution of History Teaching', in Salomon and Cairns (eds.), *Handbook on Peace Education*, 218.
25. Bleiker and Young-Ju, 'On the Use', in Cole (ed.), *Teaching the Violent Past*, 269.
26. Chapman et al., 'Developing Historical Thinking', Chapman et al. (eds.), *Thinking Historically About Missing Persons*, 6.
27. McCully et al., 'History Education', 5, 8.
28. Peter Seixas, 'Conceptualising the Growth of Historical Understanding,' in David Olson and Nancy Torrance (eds.), *The Handbook of Education and Human Development*, (Oxford: Blackwell Publishers, 1996): 773; Cole and Barsalou, *Unite or Divide*, 1.
29. Interview with Maha Yahya (ESCWA Regional Advisor and Editor of the 2008 UNDP Human Development Report), Beirut, 3/07/2012.
30. McCully et al., *Teaching History*, 12.
31. Cole and Barsalou, *Unite or Divide*, 14.
32. Ibid., 10.
33. Cole, 'Introduction,' in Cole (ed.), *Teaching the Violent Past*, 19.
34. Cole and Barsalou, *Unite or Divide*, 2.
35. Ibid.,14.
36. Ibid., 6, 14.
37. Salibi, *A House of Many Mansions*, 201.
38. Interview with Nemer Frayha (Lebanese Academic and Former CERD Director), Beirut, 19/06/2012.
39. Nemer Frayha, 'Education as a Means of Building Societal Cohesion in Lebanon: An Unfinished Task,' in Maha Shuayb (ed.), *Rethinking Education for Social Cohesion. International Case Studies.*, (New York: Macmillan, 2013): 176; Interview with Senior Officer, CERD, Beirut, 27/06/2012.
40. Sune Haugbolle, 'Memory as Representation and Memory as Idiom,' in Choueiri (ed.), *Breaking the Cycle*, 127–8.

41. Interview with Anwar Daw (PSP Member, Member of the Advisory Committee on History Books), Beirut, 10/07/2012.
42. Interview with Khaled Qabbani (Lebanese Jurist and Former Education Minister), Beirut, 17/07/2012; Anwar Daw, in an interview, argued that the 1968 curriculum was pro-Maronite and dismissed the contributions of other communities to the history of Lebanon.
43. Nemer Frayha, 'Developing Curriculum', in Tawil and Harley (eds.), *Education, Conflict and Social Cohesion*, 198.
44. Abu Assali, 'Education for Social Cohesion', in Shuayb (ed.), *Rethinking Education for Social Cohesion*, 160; Telephone Interview with Mounir Abu Assali (Lebanese Academic and Former CERD Director), 6/09/2012.
45. Mounir Abu Assali, 'Education for Social Cohesion in Lebanon: The Educational Reform Experiment in the Wake of the Lebanese War,' in Shuayb (ed.), *Rethinking Education for Social Cohesion*, 155.
46. Kamal Abouchedid and Ramzi Nasser, 'The State of History Teaching'.
47. Abu Assali Interview.
48. Abu Assali Interview; Mounir Abou Assali, 'Education for Social Cohesion', in Shuayb (ed.), *Rethinking Education for Social Cohesion*, 147–148.
49. Senior Officer, CERD, Interview.
50. Abu Assali Interview.
51. Senior Officer, CERD, Interview.
52. Abu Assali Interview.
53. Munir Bashshour, 'History Teaching and History Textbooks in Lebanon,' paper presented at the conference on *Learning about the Other and Teaching for Tolerance in Muslim Majority Societies*, Istanbul: Centre for Values Education, 10/11/2005, 6.
54. Ibid., 7–8.
55. Joseph Abi Rached, qtd. in Frayha, 'Developing Curriculum', in Tawil and Harley (eds.), *Education, Conflict and Social Cohesion*, 186.
56. Frayha, 'Developing Curriculum', in Tawil and Harley (eds.), *Education, Conflict and Social Cohesion*, 186–7.
57. The committee was composed of three Christians and three Muslims, representing several different political parties. Frayha, 'Developing Curriculum', in Tawil and Harley (eds.), *Education, Conflict and Social Cohesion*, 186; Frayha, 'Education as a Means', in Shuayb (ed.), *Rethinking Education for Social Cohesion*, 177; Frayha Interview.
58. Frayha, 'Developing Curriculum', in Tawil and Harley (eds.), *Education, Conflict and Social Cohesion*, 194.
59. Bashshour, 'The Deepening Cleavage,' in Hanf and Salam (eds.), *Lebanon in Limbo*, 165–6.
60. Frayha, 'Developing Curriculum', in Tawil and Harley (eds.), *Education, Conflict and Social Cohesion*, 195.

61. Frayha Interview; Frayha, 'Education as a Means', in Shuayb (ed.), *Rethinking Education for Social Cohesion*, 177.
62. Frayha Interview.
63. Interview with Abd-Al-Rahim Murad (Lebanese Politician and Former Education Minister), Beirut, 27/06/2012.
64. Ibid.; Frayha Interview; Bashshour, 'The Deepening Cleavage', in Hanf and Salam (eds.), *Lebanon in Limbo*, 167; Frayha, 'Developing Curriculum', in Tawil and Harley (eds.), *Education, Conflict and Social Cohesion*, 187.
65. Murad Interview; Daw Interview; Bashshour, 'History Teaching', 9.
66. Hassan M. Fattah, 'Lebanon's History Textbooks Sidestep Its Civil War,' *New York Times*, 10/01/2007.
67. Frayha, 'Education as a Means', in Shuayb (ed.), *Rethinking Education for Social Cohesion*, 178; Frayha Interview.
68. Senior Officer, CERD, Interview.
69. Bashshour, 'The Deepening Cleavage', in Hanf and Salam (eds.), *Lebanon in Limbo*, 167.
70. Murad Interview.
71. Frayha Interview; Frayha, 'Developing Curriculum', in Tawil and Harley (eds.), *Education, Conflict and Social Cohesion*, 188; Frayha Interview.
72. Senior Officer, CERD, Interview.
73. Frayha, 'Education as a Means', in Shuayb (ed.), *Rethinking Education for Social Cohesion*, 177; Daw Interview. Fattah, 'Lebanon's History'.
74. Frayha Interview.
75. Murad Interview.
76. Frayha Interview.
77. Ibid.
78. Daw Interview.
79. Frayha Interview.
80. Daw Interview; Senior Officer, CERD, Interview.
81. Yahya Interview.
82. 'Mikati: History Curriculum No Place for Narrow Interests,' *The Daily Star*, 28/02/2012.
83. Culture Minister Gaby Layyoun qtd. in Van Meguerditchian, 'History Curriculum Revision Sparks Controversy,' *The Daily Star*, 31/01/2012. The phrase was coined by US Under Secretary of State for Global Affairs Paula J. Dobriansky.
84. Daw Interview.
85. Meguerditchian, 'History Curriculum'.
86. Ibid.
87. Interview with Adnan El-Amine (Lebanese Association for Educational Studies Director and Curriculum Specialist), Beirut, 22/06/2012; Interview with Walid Al-Khatib (Director, UNRWA Field Education Office), Beirut, 3/07/2012.

88. Paige Kollock, 'Lebanese Children Learn Abbreviated National History,' *Voice of America*, 11/11/2012.
89. Senior Officer, CERD, Interview.
90. Ibid; Frayha, 'Developing Curriculum', in Tawil and Harley (eds.), *Education, Conflict and Social Cohesion*, 185.
91. Senior Officer, CERD, Interview.
92. Abouchedid et al., 'The Limitations of Inter-Group Learning'; Franklin Lamb, 'Why Did Palestinian Refugees Come to Lebanon?,' *Eurasia Review* (2012).
93. Senior Officer, CERD, Interview.
94. Antoine Messara, qtd. in Craig Larkin, 'Beyond the War? The Lebanese Postmemory Experience,' *International Journal of Middle Eastern Studies* 42, (2010): 620.
95. Yahya Interview.
96. Ibid.; Larkin, 'Beyond the War?', 618, 620, 628.
97. Bashshour, 'History Teaching', 4.
98. Qtd. in Larkin, 'Beyond the War?', 620.
99. Abouchedid and Nasser, 'The State of History', 69–70.
100. Abouchedid et al., 'The Limitations of Inter-Group Learning'.
101. Abouchedid and Nasser, 'The State of History', 72, 75.
102. Abouchedid et al., 'The Limitations of Inter-Group Learning'.
103. Ohaness Goktchian, qtd. in Lamb, 'Why Did Palestinian Refugees Come to Lebanon?'; Yahya Interview; United Nations Development Programme, *Education and Citizenship*.
104. Interview with Elie Awad (Project Manager, Youth for Tolerance), Beirut, 20/06/2012; interview with Christalla Yakinthou (Consultant at International Centre for Transitional Justice), Beirut, 21/06/2012.
105. Bashshour, 'History Teaching', 11.
106. Abu Assali Interview.
107. Senior Officer, CERD, Interview.
108. Maha Yahya, qtd in Rima Maktabi, 'Lebanon's Missing History: Why School Books Ignore the Past,' *CNN*, 8/06/2012.
109. Yakinthou Interview.
110. Economic and Social Commission for Western Asia, *Unpacking the Dynamics of Communal Tensions*, 15.
111. Jim Quilty, 'Separate Learning.'
112. Interview with Bassel Akar (Lebanese Academic and Civic Education Specialist), Beirut, 28/06/2012; Senior Officer, CERD, Interview.
113. Quilty, 'Separate Learning'; Bashshour, 'History Teaching', 1.
114. Adnan El-Amine, qtd. in Frayha, 'Developing Curriculum', in Tawil and Harley (eds.), *Education, Conflict and Social Cohesion*, 188.

115. Quilty, 'Separate Learning'; Simona Sikimic, 'Debate over History Curriculum Reignites,' *The Daily Star*, 30/04/2011.
116. Barton and McCully, 'History', 86; Interview with Richard Hanna (Chief Executive Council for Curriculum, Examination and Assessment and Expert on History Curriculum), Belfast, 19/02/2013.
117. Interview with Terry Murphy (Head of Education Standards, Council for Catholic Maintained Schools), Holywood, 19/02/2013.
118. Ibid; Hanna Interview.
119. Michael Arlow, 'Citizenship Education,' in Tawil and Harley (eds.), *Education, Conflict and Social Cohesion*, 293.
120. Karin Fischer, 'University Historians and Their Role in the Development of a 'Shared' History in Northern Ireland Schools 1960s–1980s: An Illustration of the Ambiguous Social Function of Historians,' *History of Education* 40, no. 2 (2011): 241; Phillips et al., 'Four Histories', 60.
121. Alan McCully, 'The Northern Irish Curriculum and National Identity,' in David Kerr and Cliff O'Neill (eds.), *Professional Preparation and Professional Development in a Climate of Change*, (Lancaster: 1995), 14; Arlow, 'Citizenship Education', 295–6; Hanna Interview; Keith C. Barton, 'History Education and National Identity in Northern Ireland and the United States: Differing Priorities,' *Theory into Practice* 40, no. 1 (2001): 50.
122. Qtd. in Bell et al., *The Troubles*, 24; Alison Kitson, 'History Teaching and Reconciliation in Northern Ireland,' in Elizabeth A. Cole, *Teaching the Violent Past. History Education and Reconciliation*, (Plymouth: Rowman and Littlefield Publishers, 2007): 135, 149.
123. Keith C. Barton, 'A Sociocultural Perspective on Children's Understanding of Historical Change: Comparative Findings from Northern Ireland and the United States,' *American Educational Research Journal* 38, no. 4 (2001): 896, 902; Kent Den Heyer, 'Between Every 'Now' and 'Then': A Role for the Study of Historical Agency in History and Citizenship Education,' *Theory and Research in Social Education* 31, no. 4 (2003): 421.
124. Barton, 'A Sociocultural Perspective', 907.
125. Ibid., 906; Barton, 'History Education', 42. Barton and McCully, 'History', 108; Kitson, 'History Teaching', in Cole (ed.), *Teaching the Violent Past*, 131.
126. McCully et al., *Teaching History*, 6; Barton and McCully, 'History', 108.
127. Alan McCully, Keith C. Barton, and Margaret Conway, 'History Education and National Identity in Northern Ireland,' *International Journal of Historical Learning, Teaching and Research* 3, no. 1 (2003): 9–10; Barton and McCully, 'History', 101–2, 111. Bell et al., *The Troubles*, 33.

128. Barton and McCully, 'History', 110–111.
129. Telephone Interview with Senior Officer (Education and Skills Authority), 13/03/2013.
130. Council for Curriculum Examination and Assessment, 'Progression Framework: The World around Us – History. Key Stages 1–2', *Northern Ireland Curriculum*, http://www.nicurriculum.org.uk/docs/key_stages_1_and_2/areas_of_learning/the_world_around_us/WAUGridHistory.pdf
131. Hanna Interview.
132. Council for Curriculum Examination and Assessment, 'Environment and Society: History. Minimum Statutory Content Key Stage 3.', *Northern Ireland Curriculum*, http://www.nicurriculum.org.uk/docs/key_stage_3/areas_of_learning/statutory_requirements/ks3_history.pdf
133. Council for Curriculum Examination and Assessment, *CCEA GCSE Specification in History*, Belfast: Council for Curriculum Examination and Assessment, 2012.
134. Council for Curriculum Examination and Assessment, 'Environment and Society,' *Northern Ireland Curriculum*, http://www.nicurriculum.org.uk/docs/key_stages_1_and_2/areas_of_learning/the_world_around_us/WAUGridHistory.pdf
135. Murphy Interview; Hanna Interview.
136. Interview with Michael Arlow (Director, the Spirit of Enniskillen Trust and Former Curriculum Developer for Local and Global Citizenship), Belfast, 22/02/2013; Murphy Interview.
137. Hanna Interview.
138. Kitson, 'History Teaching', in Cole (ed.), *Teaching the Violent Past*, 144.
139. Joint Council for Qualifications, *Provisional GCSE (Full Course) Results – June 2012 (Northern Ireland Only)*, Belfast: Council for the Curriculum, Examinations and Assessment, 2012.
140. Arlow Interview.
141. McCully et al., 'History Education', 9–10; Bell et al., *The Troubles*, 33–34; Cole and Barsalou, *Unite or Divide*, 13.
142. Bell et al., *The Troubles*, 26.
143. Telephone Interview with Project Manager (Teaching Divided Histories, Nerve Centre, Derry/Londonderry), 10/04/2013.
144. Most of the students of age 11, and just under a third of respondents in their late teens and twenties. Magill et al., *The Role of Education*, 46–8.
145. Barton, 'A Sociocultural Perspective,' 907; Arlow Interview.
146. Kitson, 'History Teaching', in Cole (ed.), *Teaching the Violent Past*, 149.
147. Bell et al., *The Troubles*, 53, 88, 85.
148. Ibid., 61; Interview with Conall McDevitt (SDLP MLA and Member of the Education Committee), Belfast, 1/03/2013; Project Manager (Nerve Centre) Interview.

149. Kitson, 'History Teaching', in Cole (ed.), *Teaching the Violent Past*, 150.
150. McCully et al., 'History Education', 9; Bell et al., *The Troubles*, 7, 29; Magill et al., *The Role of Education*, 2.
151. McCully et al., 'History Education', 10.
152. Ibid., 54.
153. Magill et. Al., *The Role of Education*, 12, 31.
154. Barton, 'History Education', 50.
155. The foremost examples are the ancient king Alexander the Great (claimed by Greece) and the nineteenth-century anti-Ottoman revolutionary Goce Delchev (claimed by Bulgaria).
156. Interview with Albert Hani (Executive Director Training Centre for Management of Conflicts, Deputy Country Director Forum ZFD Skopje), Skopje, 13/09/2012; Nikola Jordanovski, 'The Common Yugoslav History and the Republic of Macedonia,' in Christina Koulouri (ed.), *Clio in the Balkans. The Politics of History Education*, (Thessaloniki: Centre for Democracy and Reconciliation in SouthEast Europe, 2002): 259.
157. Interview with Albanian Historian, Skopje, 14/09/2012.
158. Nikola Jordanovski, 'Medieval and Modern Macedonia as Part of a 'Grand Narrative',' in Koulouri (ed.), *Clio in the Balkans*, 109–115.
159. Snežana Koren, 'Yugoslavia: A Look in the Broken Mirror. Who Is the 'Other'?,' in Koulouri (ed.), *Clio in the Balkans*, 199.
160. Nikola Jordanovski, 'Between the Necessity and the Impossibility of a 'National History',' in Koulouri (ed.), *Clio in the Balkans*, 274; Jordanovski, 'The Common Yugoslav History', in Koulouri (ed.), *Clio in the Balkans*, 257, 259; Koren, 'Yugoslavia', in Koulouri (ed.), *Clio in the Balkans*, 199.
161. Jordanovski, 'The Common Yugoslav History', in Koulouri (ed.), *Clio in the Balkans*, 260; Koren, 'Yugoslavia', in Koulouri (ed.), *Clio in the Balkans*, 200; Hani Interview; Jordanovski, 'Between the Necessity', in Koulouri (ed.), *Clio in the Balkans*, 274.
162. Ibid.; Joke van der Leeuw-Roord, *A Key to Unlock the Past. History Education in Macedonia: An Analysis of Today, Suggestions for the Future* (Skopje: EuroClio, 2012), 12.
163. Albanian Historian Interview.
164. Ibid., Gasanabo, *Fostering Peaceful Co-Existence*, 38; van der Leeuw-Roord, *A Key*, 17.
165. Interview with Mire Mladenovski (President of the History Teachers' Association of Macedonia), Skopje, 13/09/2012.
166. van der Leeuw-Roord, *A Key*, 17.
167. Ibid., 12.
168. Albanian Historian Interview; van der Leeuw-Roord, *A Key*, 14.
169. Albanian Historian Interview; Gasanabo, *Fostering Peaceful Co-Existence*, 38; Interview with Boban Petrovski (Macedonian Historian and Professor,

Saints Cyril and Methodius University), Skopje, 19/09/2012; Gasanabo, *Fostering Peaceful Co-Existence*, 38; Albanian Historian Interview.
170. Ibid; Mladenovski Interview.
171. van der Leeuw-Roord, *A Key*, 18; Albanian Historian Interview; Ky Krauthamer, 'Reconciling Differences in Macedonian Classrooms,' *Transitions Online*, 3/09/2012.
172. Mladenovski Interview; Petrovski Interview.
173. Albanian Historian Interview; Mladenovski Interview.
174. van der Leeuw-Roord, *A Key*, 9, 20.
175. van der Leeuw-Roord, *A Key*, 20; Albanian Historian Interview; Interview with Xabir Deralla (President of Civil - Centre for Freedom), Skopje, 18/09/2012.
176. van der Leeuw-Roord, *A Key*, 15; Mladenovski Interview.
177. Petrovski Interview.
178. van der Leeuw-Roord, *A Key*, 20; Petrovski Interview; Interview with Recep Ali Cupi (Director of the Directorate for the Development and Promotion of the Languages of the Nationalities), Skopje, 19/09/2012.
179. Interview with Spomenka Lazarevska (Education Program Director, Foundation Open Society Macedonia), Skopje, 17/09/2012.
180. Petrivski Interview.
181. Ibid.
182. Emilija Simoska, 'FYR Macedonia,' in Koulouri (ed.), *Clio in the Balkans*, 496.
183. Petrovski Interview; Albanian Historian Interview.
184. Interview with an Officer in an International Mission, Skopje, 10/09/2012; Mladenovski Interview.
185. van der Leeuw-Roord, *A Key*, 13, 16; Mladenovski Interview.
186. Albanian Historian Interview; Mladenovski Interview; Officer in an International Mission Interview; van der Leeuw-Roord, *A Key*, 21.
187. Mladenovski Interview; Interview with Nora Sabani (Education for Development Specialist, UNICEF), Skopje, 18/09/2012.
188. Hani Interview; Mladenovski Interview.
189. Gasanabo, *Fostering Peaceful Coexistence*, 65; Mladenovski Interview.
190. Deralla Interview; van der Leeuw-Roord, *A Key*, 18.
191. Deralla Interview; Mladenovski Interview.
192. Cole and Barsalou, *Unite or Divide*, 6; Mladenovski Interview; Hani Interview.
193. Sabani Interview; Mladenovski Interview.
194. Ibid.; van der Leeuw-Roord, *A Key*, 17.
195. Hani Interview; van der Leeuw-Roord, *A Key*, 12, 18; Jean Arnault Dérenset and Laurent Geslin, 'The Nationalist Movement Rewriting Macedonia's History,' *Le Temps*, 13/08/2012; Mladenovski Interview.

196. van der Leeuw-Roord, *A Key*, 15, 20, 24.
197. Veselin Zhelev, 'Skopje's Attitude to Neighbours Causes Worry: Bulgaria's EU Ambassador,' *Focus Information Agency*, 30/04/2013.
198. Albanian Historian Interview.
199. Ibid.
200. Mladenovski Interview.
201. Lazarevska Interview.
202. Officer in an International Mission Interview.
203. van der Leeuw-Roord, *A Key*, 10.
204. Marthoz, 'The Hidden History', 7.
205. Cole, 'Introduction', in Cole (ed.), *Teaching the Violent Past*, 18.

CHAPTER 5

Formulating Citizenship Education

Shared values and beliefs transcending identification with ethnic, confessional or national groups help states further social cohesion and political stability.[1] Political stability, particularly in democratic societies, also depends on the active engagement and support of individuals, attainable only when individuals feel represented in (and by) state institutions.[2] Thus, the teaching of citizenship education may contribute to political stability by conveying overarching values and beliefs, preparing children for 'their roles and responsibilities as citizens', and establishing a direct relationship between the state and its citizens.[3]

However, in deeply divided societies, the roles and responsibilities of good citizens and the legitimacy of the state are contested. Even the definition of citizenship is problematic when religious, ethnic or national groups mediate the relationship between the state and its citizens and, as in Lebanon, citizenship becomes 'hyphenated'.[4] This complicates the formulation of curricula for citizenship education in consociations. After surveying the available theories on citizenship education in deeply divided societies, this chapter will trace the initiatives to reform citizenship education after the three peace agreements in Lebanon, Northern Ireland and Macedonia.

© The Editor(s) (if applicable) and The Author(s) 2017
G. Fontana, *Education Policy and Power-Sharing in Post-Conflict Societies*, DOI 10.1007/978-3-319-31426-6_5

5.1 Citizenship Education in Deeply Divided Societies: Theoretical Debates

Osler and Starkey argue that in democracies citizenship is composed of three essential and complementary elements: status, feelings and practice.[5] Citizen status encompasses legal nationality: this may reflect biological heritage and the subordination of certain racial, gender and class groups.[6] Citizenship practices are the skills and behaviours deriving from democratic and human rights values.[7] Feelings of citizenship are part and parcel of identity, but also depend on the inclusiveness of society and on its specific expressions of nationalism.[8]

Leenders and Veugelers observe that 'different citizenship concepts appear to be related to different pedagogical aims' of citizenship education, as identified on a spectrum between minimal and maximal citizenship education.[9] David Kerr shows that minimal citizenship education (or civic education) promotes a narrow definition of citizenship, often supports the exclusive interests of some groups, employs didactic teaching and focuses on knowledge acquisition. It focuses primarily on citizenship status, conveying the rights and duties of citizens within the predefined legal framework of the state, and concentrates on political and governmental institutions, mechanisms for decision-making and governance, and only occasionally on information about human and individual rights.[10]

Leenders and Veugelers argue that minimal civic education assumes the homogeneity of the population and aims to transmit fixed values to children in an attempt to promote loyalty and obedience and 'to help integrate a diverse population into a single national culture'.[11] The promotion of minimal and contested notions of citizenship, the emphasis on assimilation rather than diversity, and the attempt to erode group attachments through loyalty to the state and the promotion of individual rights can exacerbate inter-group tensions, especially if dominant groups 'subordinate the very aim of educating children as civic equals, to perpetuate their own power'.[12] Indeed, defining citizenship in terms of loyalty to the state can exclude certain communities in deeply divided societies.

In contrast, maximal citizenship education (or citizenship education) defines citizenship broadly and inclusively, conveying the contents and knowledge components of civic education, but also questioning the processes leading to the emergence of current definitions of citizenship.[13] To cultivate citizenship status, maximal citizenship education provides knowledge about the political system and society. To promote citizenship practices, it encourages involvement in civil society, and actions improving the local and wider community. Finally, to stimulate feelings of citizenship, it fosters debate, investigation, critical thinking about inclusive notions of citizenship, 'socially useful qualities' and value dispositions.[14] Tawil argues that 'method and content in the area of values education are inseparable', so maximal citizenship education requires participatory methods, critical thinking, open communication and debate, independent learning and group work.[15] Above all, it requires the practising of citizenship skills.[16]

Maximal citizenship education aims to show that identities are 'multiple, nested and overlapping'.[17] Rather than breaking the link between individuals and ethnic, religious or national groups, it strives to construct superordinate identities and transversal loyalties, reconciling citizenship, individual rights and group membership.[18] In this approach, pride in citizenship and commitment to the state can only be developed if students are proud of their ethnic, national or religious identity and if the state recognises and values each of its cultural communities.[19] This is why, after a violent conflict, maximal citizenship education can act 'as a positive transformative force, rather than a means for indoctrination'.[20]

It is widely accepted that children can be introduced to the values and principles underpinning citizenship in primary school, but the best time for political socialisation and the tackling of issues related to conflicts is after 10–11 years of age.[21] In schools, civic and citizenship education can be taught as a separate subject: this ensures teacher training, provides a protected environment to practise values and behaviours, and endows civic and citizenship education with a higher status (as do official exams).[22] Citizenship can also be 'integrated' into a social studies course, allowing students to extrapolate findings from other subjects.[23] Finally, citizenship can be a cross-curricular theme: this encourages coordination across several subject areas and a 'whole school' approach to certain founding values and principles. Yet, a cross-curricular approach tends to be fragmented and weak, and risks marginalising citizenship in favour of higher status subjects.[24]

Moreover, citizen status, practice and feelings are not only conveyed through the manifest curriculum: beyond content (the curriculum), Kerr points at the influence of culture (from societal norms and traditions to the professional culture of teachers) and climate (school ethos, opportunities to practise values and explore controversial issues).[25] Building on these three categories, Shuayb argues that Lebanese schools adopt one of five approaches to citizenship education. The *passive approach* promotes a subject approach to citizenship education, with few school activities and focusing on exam preparation. The *avoidance or apolitical approach* attempts to depoliticise the school by banning debates over politics and current affairs, teaching citizenship education didactically, offering limited extracurricular activities, and physically separating students belonging to different communities. The *extracurricular approach* relies on extracurricular activities to practise some citizenship skills, but rarely allows students to plan activities or reflect upon them. The *multidimensional/structured approach* integrates citizenship education in every aspect of school life and organisation, encompassing the relationship with the wider community, a democratic management system, an inclusive admission and hiring policy, extensive social and civic activities, active student councils and critical classroom pedagogies. Finally, the *paradoxical approach* emphasises active pedagogies, provides a voice for students and extracurricular activities, but it does so within the confines of one community.[26]

Shuayb proposes a correlation between schools' approaches to citizenship education and students' political attitudes: she maintains that students in schools applying the *passive* and *apolitical* approaches are more likely to express sectarian opinions and prefer the exclusive company of students and teachers from their own community, and less likely to trust people belonging to other communities. Students in schools applying the *multidimensional* and *extracurricular* approaches are less likely to trust sectarian parties and are more reticent to join them, preferring voting as a form of social participation. In contrast, students in schools adopting the *paradoxical* and *apolitical* approaches tend to trust sectarian parties and aim to join them. Thus, Shuayb suggests that, to promote social cohesion in Lebanon, schools should move from a subject-based approach to citizenship education to a more holistic and multidimensional approach.[27] Analysis of initiatives to reform citizenship education in Lebanon, Northern Ireland and Macedonia shows that the three societies are moving towards more maximal approaches to citizenship education.

5.2 Lebanon

The Taif Agreement demanded the unification of the curricula and textbooks for both history education and citizenship education to 'help bring [students] together around the same sense of national and civic identity'.[28]

Civic education had been an instrument for nation-state building since Lebanese independence. The 1946 and 1968 curricula unsuccessfully attempted to establish the primacy of national identity over confessional belonging, overlooking inter-communal cooperation and ignoring the tension between confessional allegiance, communal belonging and national identity.[29] Curricular contents also mirrored evolving inter-communal relations: the 1946 curriculum emphasised a collective 'Lebanese identity', but its successor, reflecting the gradual redistribution of power from the Christian to the Muslim community after the 1958 civil war, favoured an overarching 'Arab identity'.[30] Moreover, in 1973 the Ministry of Education suspended the civic education exams due to the increasing ideological polarisation of students over pan-Arab allegiances.[31] After the exam was cancelled most schools stopped teaching civic education.

After the civil war, the Center for Educational Research and Development (CERD) allocated 30 yearly hours to the teaching of *civic education*, and tasked the subject with 'shap[ing] a new generation of informed and responsible citizens who can contribute to post-war social reconstruction'.[32] If history education was expected to ground Lebanese national identity in a consensual narrative of the past, citizenship education was to convey 'common principles based on national feelings of freedom, respect for others' opinions, forgiveness, openness, equality, understanding of democracy and the meaning of citizenship'.[33]

5.2.1 Citizenship and Civic Education

Similar to the history education working group, the curriculum drafting committee for citizenship education included seven representatives of different confessional and political groups, with the notable exception of Hizbollah, which refused to participate, in opposition to the very 'notion of 'secular civic values'.[34] During its works, CERD director Abu Assali insisted on decision-making by consensus and an emphasis on the core values and principles of the Taif Agreement.[35]

In contrast to the stalemate over history education, CERD succeeded in producing a unified curriculum for *citizenship and civic education*, approved and published in 1997. *Citizenship and civic education* would be taught only in Arabic and would develop skills of criticism and debate, peaceful conflict resolution and tolerance, empathy for diversity, and participation in collective life. It would nurture loyalty to 'Lebanese identity, land and country' and further 'awareness' of Arab identity and openness 'to the whole world'.[36]

The unified *Morals and Civic Education* textbook was developed by an equally diverse working group and approved by the government before being published and distributed in 2000.[37] According to Frayha the textbook had 'more of an impact than curriculum objectives at school, since students and teachers deal with textbooks on a daily basis'.[38]

Most experts, including those who participated in the drafting process, assert that formulating a curriculum for civic education was easier than for history because it had 'less stakeholder interest', was completed during a 'golden period' of political consensus, and enshrined collective aspirations over how citizens should behave in the future.[39] Akar adds that the curriculum embodies and furthers the nationalist objective of shaping a 'Lebanese and Arab citizen' and of employing nationalism and national identity to promote social cohesion, transcending communal divisions. It grounds the concept of citizenship in the relationship between the state and individuals and furthers 'unity' on the basis of collective belonging to a 'dual Lebanese-Arab identity'.[40] Expectations to 'enhance' an ambiguously defined national identity and further exclusive allegiance to the state overshadow the values of freedom, justice, tolerance, human rights, intercivilisational dialogue and peaceful conflict resolution.[41]

Akar notes that, with some minor exceptions, the curriculum and textbooks approximate closely the ideal type of civic education in their focus on developing knowledge of local political institutions and of laws and rights essential to political participation.[42] Frayha agrees that the *citizenship and civic education* 'curriculum [aims] for social and institutional education' but argues that it can also be employed to stimulate debates on the operation of state institutions or on controversial themes such as the issue of Palestine and the resistance to Israeli occupation of Southern Lebanon.[43] In contrast, Abu Assali insists that *citizenship and civic education* aims to convey important skills such as debate, dialogue and critical thinking through active learning methods.[44]

5.2.2   *The Weaknesses of a Nationalist Civic Education*

Lebanon's political instability since 2005 confirms that *citizenship and civic education* has not succeeded in wrestling citizen allegiance away from communities and towards the Lebanese state. Surveys confirmed that most students trust religious institutions and sectarian political leaders above government and state institutions.[45] A senior officer at CERD argued that *citizenship and civic education* is ineffective because the curriculum is not fully applied in schools.[46] In fact, Akar and Shuayb question whether, even when fully applied, the 1997 curriculum can promote education for democratic and inclusive citizenship in Lebanon. They point at curricular contents and pedagogical approaches to show that the unified curriculum and textbook contribute very little to social cohesion, and may even erode the maximal notions of citizenship held by some students, discouraging their participation in public life and further fragmenting the Lebanese population.[47]

This is because the contents of the textbook and curriculum are 'too idealistic and unrealistic' in contrast to daily reality in Lebanon.[48] A 2003 evaluation confirmed that the 'aims for citizenship and social cohesion were part of a political agenda aimed at satisfying the conscience of the different sectarian and political parties'.[49] Thus, ironically, the curriculum does not promote awareness of the concept and contents of citizenship as a fundamental value and does not discuss citizenship until grade 6.[50] Even then, citizenship is narrowly defined as a legal relationship between the state and the individual, and textbooks further a rigid nationalistic notion of citizenship founded on a dual Lebanese-Arab identity at the expense of individual allegiance to confession and community. This minimises opportunities to reflect on multiple and interacting identities and allegiances.[51]

Indeed, the curriculum overlooks concepts relevant to Lebanon, such as 'plural society', meritocracy, sovereignty and 'institutional independence'.[52] For example, it discusses and advocates majoritarian democracy rather than examining Lebanon's consociation, its proportional distribution of institutional positions and communal control of personal status laws: this prevents debate over the benefits and shortcomings of consociation.[53] Thus, the curriculum does not offer practical guidelines for constructive participation in Lebanese society and politics.[54] Adonis Accra suggests that this stems from a focus on the principles embodied in the Taif Agreement, including transition towards majoritarian democracy, rather than on those institutionalised in the Lebanese constitution.[55]

El-Amine reflects that in a deeply divided society, unified 'textbooks cannot create unity': rather, they create cognitive dissonance.[56] Students passively memorise and repeat the *Morals and Civic Education* textbook but deem its contents hypocritical and irrelevant to their daily lives. By embodying institutional hypocrisy the curriculum can even demotivate students from participating in Lebanese political life.[57]

Moreover, curricula and textbooks focus on individual duties and obligations to the state rather than on individual rights, and place the expectations of society above individual needs and desires.[58] Thus, surveys found that students see knowledge of laws as the primary aim of *citizenship and civic education*: this reflects emphasis on knowledge and obedience rather than analysis and participation in textbooks.[59]

Finally, Accra criticises curricular contents for focusing excessively on security rather than peace.[60] As a consequence, students come to understand the characteristics of model citizens as abiding by laws and working towards national unity, but also fighting for the country and armed resistance.[61] The textbooks avoid the civil war but contain a chapter on Lebanon's enemies (focusing on Israel) and on its friends (focusing on the Arab League).

The *citizenship and civic education* curricula are also criticised for being technically weak because of a 'disarticulation in the process of writing' them, which resulted in a disharmonious curriculum and 'schizophrenic' books.[62] Thus, curriculum goals are inconsistent and do not match the contents of textbooks, and even the contents of textbooks lack coherence. El-Amine reflects that he does not see how the textbooks can promote citizenship, but observes that they clearly promote a 'general understanding that we have to avoid such terms, such ideas, [such] pictures'.[63]

Indeed, despite the consensus on a nationalist notion of citizenship, technical weaknesses in the curriculum and textbooks blur teachers' understanding of the skills associated with citizenship education.[64] In some extreme cases, this leads to schools only teaching *citizenship and civic education* in grades 9 and 12, before state exams.[65] More frequently, teachers rely on frontal teaching of the overloaded curriculum in a hierarchical environment, and on memorisation and rote learning of the textbook. They rarely promote active methods or extracurricular activities, and they avoid existing opportunities for debate, discussion, interaction and participation.[66] This does not stimulate the internalisation of values and principles, and limits the exploration, practising and learning of active citizenship.[67]

Akar argues that the current pedagogical approach erodes rather than cultivates students' engagement with society and their motivation to act in the public arena.[68] It may undermine the aims of the 1997 curriculum by depriving students of opportunities for critical thinking and breeding obedient rather than active individuals.[69] Avoidance of current affairs, entrenchment of undemocratic practices and denial of opportunities for practising citizenship may also hamper the development of a sense of belonging.[70] This is particularly the case in the state sector because of the lower quality of teaching, because activities organised in public schools require direct CERD approval, and because of a diffused policy of 'no politics on campus'.[71]

Indeed, some argue that *citizenship and civic education* is taught differently in schools because of the 'sectarian split'.[72] However, Shuayb maintains that the divide runs between public and private schools rather than along communal lines.[73] She finds that public schools provide a less favourable environment to foster citizenship among students: they tend to be undemocratic and hierarchical, lacking opportunities to express opinions and practise democratic decision-making for both students and teachers. In addition, principals are often affiliated to political parties and generally afraid of the political opinions of students. Public schools with a uniform student population adopt a *passive approach* to citizenship education, underpinned by the assumption that 'sects are naturally cohesive'. Public schools that have experienced sectarian or political conflict tend to adopt an *avoidance and apolitical approach*, banning debate over political and current affairs, teaching citizenship education didactically, offering limited extracurricular activities and attempting to physically separate students according to their religious or political affiliation. In contrast, private schools are more likely to adopt a *multidimensional/structured approach* to education for citizenship, including participatory management structures, democratic school environments, structured school/community relationships, inclusive student admissions, analytical and critical pedagogy and extensive extracurricular activities. As mentioned, Shuayb found that school approaches to citizenship education are correlated with students' political attitudes, and called for a 'move from subject-based approach to a multi-dimensional one'.[74]

Increasing social tensions led the Lebanese government to formulate a comprehensive *Education Sector Development Plan* in 2010, which included a 'new approach' to citizenship education.[75] In the same year, the Ministry of Education proposed a draft law requiring 'all students in public schools to sing the national anthem every Monday morning and to perform the national oath in the first hour of each school day'.[76] A comprehensive project for *citizenship and civic education* reform, funded by the EU, was launched in September 2012 and includes the evaluation of curricula and teaching resources, the training of teachers and administrators to implement active citizenship, and the development of democratic school communities.[77]

5.2.3 Moral Preaching

To El-Amine, the limits of *citizenship and civic education* in Lebanon exemplify the fact that education cannot be expected to 'direct[ly] impact on the society... in terms of value and political content'.[78] Indeed, most of the weaknesses of citizenship education in Lebanon can be traced back to the nationalistic and minimalist approach to the subject adopted in the curriculum and textbook. The Taif Agreement entrusted civic education with social cohesion and nurturing a sense of national belonging after the war. It was to do so through a notion of national identity, displacing religious and political allegiances. This approach left no space for reflection on the multiplicity and layering of identities that characterises any plural society: *citizenship and civic education* ignored communal values and allegiances and did not question the power relations within and between different confessional and political communities.

Thus, according to Frayha, CERD succeeded in formulating a unified *citizenship and civic education* curriculum because its contents were 'mainly statements about laws, rhetoric and moral preaching'.[79] The divergence between curricular contents and the reality of Lebanese civic and political life undermines the internalisation of feelings of citizenship. Moreover, *citizenship and civic education* does not cultivate skills conducive to the building of a cohesive democratic state. In particular, it does not provide space for debate or the formulation and conveying of shared, agreed values central to citizenship, despite the clear 'potential danger in not having, at least, a common aim or universal principles for living together'.[80]

Ultimately, this analysis of *citizenship and civic education* confirms that in Lebanon, as in other Arab states, 'the political commitment to produce independent, creative students has been weak for reasons of self-preservation – doing so would produce citizens capable of challenging authority – be it political, religious or traditional'.[81]

5.3 Northern Ireland

As in Lebanon, Wylie argues that in Northern Ireland, 'political conflict over the very existence of the state makes citizenship education necessary but extremely difficult to implement'.[82] Indeed, Arlow recalls that after the Belfast Agreement, 'society was challenged to define' democracy and to formulate 'shared values capable of underpinning a sustainable peace.[83] In 2005, the secretary of state for Northern Ireland pointed out that 'retaining the "status quo" was not an option' and a new *Government Policy and Strategic Framework for Good Relations in Northern Ireland (A Shared Future*) mapped the way to an ambiguously defined 'normal, civic society'.[84] The document reaffirmed the right to oppose societal integration and to assert communal identities, but also envisaged 'a shared society in which people are encouraged to make choices in their lives that are not bound by historical divisions'.[85]

From this context emerged the first curricula for *personal development and mutual understanding* and for *local and global citizenship*. Participants in its formulation recognised that 'it would be naïve to think that changing curriculum is going to change an entire culture and generation', but felt that they were contributing to the promotion of peace and social cohesion.[86] After all, in an education system fragmented along communal lines, curricular reforms were one of the few instruments for 'mak[ing] some difference'.[87]

5.3.1   Elusive Bird: EMU

Local and global citizenship and *personal development and mutual understanding* were not the first initiatives aiming to foster peaceful coexistence and reconciliation through school curricula. As mentioned in Chap. 3, in the 1980s the Department of Education Northern Ireland (DENI) introduced and expanded *Inter-School Contact Schemes*.[88] The 1989 Education Reform Order (ERO) also established *Education for Mutual Understanding* (EMU) as a statutory cross-curricular theme in all grant-aided schools.[89] EMU attempted to 'steer clear of political indoctrination or social engineering',[90] but promoted 'self-respect and respect for others, and the improvement of relationships between people of differing cultural traditions'.[91] Its objectives included understanding conflict and appreciating interdependence: it focused on intercultural learning and on understanding the complex relationship between the two main confessional and national communities in Northern Ireland.[92]

According to Smith and Robinson, EMU succeeded in changing the dominant discourse in Northern Ireland and in introducing a language that 'allows people to express their support for cultural pluralism and political dialogue rather than sectarianism and political violence'.[93] However, Wylie found that EMU was 'treating the conflict as the by-product of individual prejudice and intolerance, rather than recognising it as a deep-seated communal conflict, essentially political in nature'.[94] As a consequence, EMU almost ignored human rights and political literacy and, in focusing on the two main communities, neglected other forms of prejudice, such as racism and homophobia.[95]

Moreover, initially EMU was accused of having a political agenda and of attempting to dilute cultural identities.[96] Arlow argues that 'many found EMU to be an elusive bird' underpinned by vague, general and aspirational values and objectives.[97] Indeed, the implementation of EMU as a cross-curricular theme curbed its impact: schools often lacked a comprehensive approach to EMU, associating it with discrete inter-school visits and pushing it to the margins of the curriculum, leading to fragmented experiences.[98] In an attempt to create 'oases of peace', some schools avoided controversial issues and a 2000 study found that only a third of students had discussed sectarianism in class.[99]

In the late 1990s, a DENI working group confirmed that the impact of EMU was undermined by its cross-curricular approach, the schools' culture of avoidance and lack of teacher training.[100] The 1999 report *Towards a Culture of Tolerance: Education for Diversity* called for schools to promote the values of pluralism, social justice, human rights, and responsibility and democracy.[101] In the same year, the Council for the Curriculum, Examinations and Assessment (CCEA) called for the introduction of modules in citizenship education to contribute to the peace process.[102]

5.3.2 Formulating and Implementing Personal Development and Mutual Understanding and Local and Global Citizenship

A 2001 consultation report found only limited support for the introduction of citizenship education in Northern Ireland.[103] Educational practitioners also worried about the commitment of the controversial Sinn Féin Education Minister McGuinness 'to support lessons in citizenship when they [Sinn Féin] were quite clear that ... at that time they didn't support the state'.[104] An officer involved in the debate over the introduction of citizenship education recalls that it was 'an interesting discussion, but it wasn't a difficult discussion': there was a broad consensus on the need for students to understand their rights and responsibilities, to appreciate the issues dividing them and to respect different cultures and identifications.[105] In contrast to his outspoken position over the 11-plus test, Arlow recalls that McGuinness avoided expressing explicit support for citizenship education: 'he was perceptive enough to realise if Sinn Féin was seen to be pushing this, then it would just immediately get opposition from the Unionist parties'.[106]

Thus, compared with the introduction of EMU in the 1990s, the introduction of *local and global citizenship* at the secondary level and of *personal development and mutual understanding* at the primary level were 'astonishingly uncontroversial'.[107] Arlow argues that the Belfast Agreement established a new political context and stimulated a political will to enact change. The introduction of citizenship education thus reflects both the genuine desire to contribute to the newly established peace and the political need, with exclusive local control of education policy for the first time since 1974, 'to show that they really did address peace and social cohesion'.[108]

The *local and global citizenship* curriculum was based on models developed by the University of Ulster's *Social, Civic and Political Education Project* and adapted according to the results of extensive consultations and piloting.[109] To address the substantial criticism that there had not been enough training for EMU, approximately five teachers from each post-primary school were trained on *local and global citizenship*.[110] Trainings for *personal development and mutual understanding* were also offered to primary school teachers.[111] During the piloting phase, the contents of the curriculum were criticised only once in a political forum and, despite the worries of teachers and educational authorities, there were no complaints from parents. In fact, Arlow admits that 'sometimes I wonder if actually we were pushing things far enough'.[112]

Local and global citizenship recognises that the population of Northern Ireland may not have a 'shared history, but we've got to have a shared future' and that citizenship education may encourage students to contribute to the society they are part of.[113] *Personal development and mutual understanding* and *local and global citizenship* were introduced in schools between 2003 and 2009. Citizenship is also implemented through cross-curricular themes, including EMU and the cross-subject aim of 'developing pupils as contributors to society'.[114]

In the early curriculum drafting stages, the University of Ulster and CCEA had called for the allocation of dedicated time for *local and global citizenship* to ensure that it didn't 'fall between the stones' as EMU had. Ultimately, *personal development and mutual understanding* and *local and global citizenship* were introduced as statutory requirements, but their mode of delivery is not specified. Thus, schools can allocate a specific period, embed them as modules within another subject (generally *Learning for Life and Work* at the secondary level and *The World around Us* at the primary level) or teach them as cross-curricular themes.[115]

At the primary level, *personal development and mutual understanding* deals mainly with community relations and with the handling of conflicts.[116] Reflecting the developmental stage of children and their understanding of groups and individuals, it avoids abstract notions, focusing on identities, attachments and personal relationships.[117] At KS1, it introduces children to the local and wider community, discusses group similarities and differences and relationships with family and friends, and debates appropriate behaviour in conflict situations. At KS2 it discusses how to develop and nurture relationships and debates human rights, social responsibilities and the many causes of conflict. Some have suggested that this may put 'sectarianism into children's heads', but teachers argue that controversial issues can be discussed with primary school children sensitively and by focusing on children's immediate experience.[118]

In contrast, *local and global citizenship* at the post-primary level considers four themes: inclusion and diversity, human rights and responsibilities, equality and social cohesion and democracy and active participation.[119] It aims to investigate each issue in the local, European and global context, in an effort to 'avoid parochialism but maintain a local focus'.[120] It is flexible enough to allow students and teachers to explore their areas of interest, and to discuss the more legal and political aspects of citizenship only when they impact on individual rights and citizens' interaction with institutions. *Local and global citizenship* is to be process-oriented: the values underpinning it 'cannot be taught, they must arise from experience'.[121]

At KS3, the minimum requirements of *local and global citizenship* are usually taught as part of the compulsory module *Learning for Life and Work*. They include analysis of expressions of group identities, the impact of conflict on prejudice and racism and ways to manage conflicts. By encouraging students' understanding of human rights values, equality and power relations, and teaching them how to influence their immediate environment, *local and global citizenship* aims to encourage the construction of superordinate overarching identities.[122] At KS4, in preparation for the General Certificate of Secondary Education (GCSE), *Learning for Life and Work* is neither a compulsory subject nor a popular one and encompasses areas such as *local and global citizenship*, but also employability and personal development.[123]

When compared to EMU, *local and global citizenship* is more structured, less focused on conflict and reconciliation, less concerned with national and cultural identities and more focused on 'moving beyond the conflict... to active citizenship'.[124] In contrast to the Lebanese *citizenship and civic education*, it reminds students of the multiplicity and layering of identities, including global and European identifications.[125] Indeed, Northern Ireland's curriculum drafters recognised that excessive emphasis on a common identity can be perceived as a threat to communal belonging. In contrast to their Lebanese counterparts, they maintained that it was neither possible nor desirable to 'draw up a specification for an ideal citizen and frame that as a curriculum objective'.[126] Thus, similar to history education, *local and global citizenship* attempts to sidestep patriotism, national belonging and loyalty to the state, referring primarily to international human rights instruments. Citizenship is defined in terms of equal rights and responsibilities rather than religious, national or cultural identity.[127]

Curriculum drafters admitted that 'it has yet to be tested whether a concept of citizenship based on equal rights and responsibilities can help transcend these deeper, emotionally based loyalties', but they hoped to construct democracy as a viable alternative to violence.[128] Indeed, Arlow reflects that *local and global citizenship* was 'a product of its time': during the piloting phase, in the early years of the peace agreement, 'it felt like nothing was fixed'. Through *local and global citizenship*, students are encouraged to imagine 'a perfect world' and provided with instruments to 'narrow the gap' between their ideals and reality. *Local and global citizenship* aimed to move beyond politically correct answers and debate students' sincere opinions, to employ critical thinking, access emotional dimensions, and deconstruct the culture of avoidance and silence.[129] Despite the limits of hierarchical school settings, students are to be trained for life in a non-violent democracy, for active participation and for activism on local issues.[130] In sum, *local and global citizenship* aimed 'to be transformative without being prescriptive about the outcome'.[131]

5.3.3 Still 'Patchy': The Limits of Personal Development and Mutual Understanding and Local and Global Citizenship

Despite their ambitious aims, *personal development and mutual understanding* and *local and global citizenship* did not have a decisive impact on the community relations approach of most schools. This is mainly because of the failure to allocate specific curricular time for them.[132] Some argue that the primary and secondary curricula have been developed separately so there is no progression or consistency of approach.[133] Arlow notes that *personal development and mutual understanding* allows teachers to avoid key controversial issues, but *local and global citizenship* at KS4 is an assessment-based and traditional subject, 'almost like a watered-down politics' course.[134] Others call for more discussion of conflict resolution, reconciliation and peace in the context of Northern Ireland, for more analysis of the 'positive use of traditional politics' to enact changes locally and focus on the development of alternative and cross-cutting identities.[135]

In fact, the concepts and values underpinning *local and global citizenship* and *personal development and mutual understanding* remain contentious: for example, each community tries to appropriate the language of human rights to its own ends.[136] Moreover, Niens and Reilly found that school ethos impacts on the delivery of the curriculum: investigating empirically the 'global dimension' of *local and global citizenship*, they suggest that maintained schools emphasise the global Catholic community and its missionary activities, integrated schools focus on diversity and mutual understanding within Northern Ireland, and controlled schools concentrate on international links and exchanges.[137] This reflects the reality of the separation of children from different backgrounds in schools, and may hamper the effectiveness of *local and global citizenship*.[138] As Chaps. 3 and 7 explain, most schools in Northern Ireland are by default noninclusive: they are generally imbued with the values, traditions and symbols associated to one community. In this context, the concepts of democracy, social justice and universal human rights may appear remote and hypocritical.[139]

Finally, an expert observed that recent emphasis on literacy and on subjects about Science, Technology, Engineering and Mathematics has eroded the time devoted to subjects with a community relations component.[140] Training for *local and global citizenship* and *personal development and mutual understanding* teachers has also diminished, but many teachers still struggle to understand key values and principles, from 'social cohesion' to 'human rights'.[141] As a consequence, teaching is 'patchy, in some schools it is excellent, and in others it is barely done at all'.[142]

More broadly, experts have noted that the 'feeling that we have peace, [and] sectarianism is a thing of the past' has weakened emphasis on citizenship education, mutual understanding and community relations work.[143] A 2008–2009 DENI review found that community relations initiatives remain marginal to curricular and non-curricular activities, and that teachers struggle to embed them, tend to avoid them and to treat them superficially.[144] Thus, in 2011 DENI initiated a *Community Relations, Equality and Diversity Policy* to coordinate initiatives associated to EMU, to the *Cross-Community Contact Scheme*, to youth organisations and to the formal school curriculum. The *Community Relations, Equality and Diversity Policy* aims to introduce students to 'others they perceive to be different' and to support them in dealing with difference and appreciating diversity. It is flexible enough to focus on a variety of issues, from bullying to flags and emblems, and aims to act as 'a tray that holds everything together'.¹⁴⁵

5.3.4   Transformative, Not Prescriptive

It remains difficult to estimate the long-term impact of citizenship education in Northern Ireland. However, the existence of multilayered and multidimensional policies, from *Cross-Community Contact Schemes*, to EMU, to the *Community Relations, Equality & Diversity Policy* is an impressive achievement.

A CCEA officer reflected that the introduction of *local and global citizenship* 'slip[ped] by almost unnoticed'.¹⁴⁶ Indeed, *local and global citizenship* and *personal development and mutual understanding* could be introduced because they aim 'to be transformative without being prescriptive about the outcome'.¹⁴⁷ In contrast to their Lebanese counterparts, curriculum drafters in Northern Ireland did not aim to shape an ideal citizen, develop allegiance and loyalty to the state, or encourage patriotism and nationalism. Rather than proposing overarching identifications to suppress communal allegiances, *local and global citizenship* and *personal development and mutual understanding* are, like the Belfast Agreement, underpinned by the principle of individual free choice between two equally legitimate and equally valued political, cultural and national traditions.

Citizenship education in Northern Ireland does not offer a solution to the fundamental question of 'whether 'our common future' will be about 'integration' and 'shared development' or whether it will be about 'peaceful coexistence' and 'separate development'.¹⁴⁸ Rather, it aims to encourage students to imagine a future society, to stimulate their independent reflection, analysis and questioning of dogmas. Experts hope that, indirectly, this approach will contribute to fostering common belonging and a desire for shared future development.¹⁴⁹

5.4   Macedonia

In Macedonia the outlines of a debate over the status, practices and feelings associated with citizenship crystallised at independence, when ethnic Albanians boycotted the independence referendum and organised an alternative referendum on territorial autonomy. For their part, ethnic Macedonians often assumed they could rejoin Yugoslavia at a later stage.¹⁵⁰

In 1998 the Ministry of Education created a commission to oversee and implement all activities related to civic education. If 'centralisation was a strong sign of distrust' towards those domestic and international experts who had piloted previous civic education initiatives, it nonetheless ensured top-down introduction of civic education in schools. Civic education was officially introduced in 1998, and mainstreamed in 2001–2002 as a separate subject in grades 7 and 8 of primary school and in all grades of secondary vocational schools and as 'curriculum inserts' in all grades of academic secondary schools.[151]

Trajkovski argues that 'the [2001] war spoiled the very ideas of citizenship, diversity and human rights'.[152] The National Liberation Army's (NLA) appeal to human rights as the justification for its insurrection undermined inter-communal trust and stimulated a widespread 'feeling that others [were] out to get them'.[153] The Ohrid Agreement's provisions for proportional allocation of positions in the public administration left ethnic Macedonians marginalised and embittered, and ethnic Albanians increasingly determined to redress past discrimination.[154] This further problematised the definition of citizenship and the articulation of the relationship between the state and individuals.

5.4.1   Lost in the Curriculum: Civic Education

When asked about civic education, local analysts and practitioners disagree not only on its quality and impact, but also on its very existence. Some think that the government eliminated *civic education* classes when it introduced *religious education* in 2008, others think that *civic education* is a cross-curricular theme, and still others argue that it exists but admit that it is 'very experimental' and its contents and aims are unclear.[155] In fact, arrangements for *civic education* in Macedonia are quite complex. According to curricular documents, it is taught as an independent subject for 36 periods per year in grades 8 and 9. In the early years of primary school and in secondary school, according to a senior officer of the Bureau of Educational Development (BoE), it is implemented as a cross-curricular theme.[156]

The *civic education* curriculum for grades 8 and 9 is very detailed, and lists activities and objectives for each lesson. Petrova-Gjorjeva argues that *civic education* focuses on problem-solving and on instructing children on societal norms and values; it refers more to action than to abstract knowledge and 'reflects social expectations'. She argues that through *civic education* 'rules of living in a community are determined for young people'.[157]

Petrova-Gjorjeva's observations contrast with the official contents of the curriculum, which emphasise active learning methods, debate and discussion of controversial issues, and current affairs. Formally, the curriculum invites analysis and discussion of a variety of topics, from human rights and responsibilities to democracy, from the European Union to the responsibilities of institutions and authorities, from public participation to obedience to laws, from the constitution to the role of the media in society, from international humanitarian law to the resolution of conflicts 'caused by cultural, ethical and religious differences'. The curriculum aims to convey knowledge, respect and tolerance for the different communities in Macedonia, to further respect for human rights and democracy, and to strengthen collective social and cultural identities.[158]

The objectives of citizenship and multiculturalism also infuse the curricula of other subjects at every level, particularly the national subjects. Educational strategies and legal documents similarly reflect a desire to develop mutual understanding, tolerance and allegiance to the Macedonian state. For example, the 2008 *Law on Elementary Education* calls for the development of cooperation, respect for diversity, understanding of human rights and freedoms, awareness of belonging to the state and development of pupils' identities and personalities. The *Concept of Nine-Year Elementary Education* also calls for focus on democracy and multiculturalism.[159] Thus, Lazarevska summarises that 'on paper it looks like everything is fine'.[160]

However, Sabani reflects that *civic education* 'got a bit lost in the curriculum'.[161] This is certainly the most substantial critique of citizenship education in Macedonian schools: because of the poor implementation of curricula and educational strategies, as mentioned, many analysts and practitioners are not even aware of its existence as a subject.

Sabani argues that 'small changes' are needed to ensure implementation of the *civic education* curriculum: long-term funding, the production of specific and comprehensive teaching materials (Macedonia still lacks a comprehensive resource pack for *civic education*), and the revision of existing textbooks. In fact, current textbooks may further prejudice by ignoring some ethnicities (generally the Roma) and portraying others negatively (particularly Albanians and Turks).[162] Textbooks often include mistakes such as the statement that every ethnic group in Macedonia has a state, or wrong depictions of flags, including the Macedonian flag.[163]

Moreover, Carta et al. call for teacher training as teachers frequently lack the skills and capacity to promote multiculturalism and equality in the classroom.¹⁶⁴ A wider culture of avoidance and hypocrisy may discourage teacher engagement in discussions about peace and tolerance, but didactic, memory-based teaching also hampers the development of democratic and active citizenship.¹⁶⁵ In fact, the Organisation for Security and Cooperation in Europe (OSCE) found that some teachers encourage prejudices with their derogatory comments about other ethnic groups.¹⁶⁶ Thus, the introduction of inspections of *civic education* may improve the quality and effectiveness of the subject.¹⁶⁷

Finally, as in the case of Lebanon, in Macedonia the contents of the *civic education* curriculum may not be relevant to everyday life. For example, in the context of increasing residential and educational separation, curricular emphasis on the multi-ethnic character of Macedonia is not accompanied by contact between children belonging to different communities or visits to 'places from other communities'.¹⁶⁸ Moreover, as in Lebanon, the grade 8 curriculum presents majoritarian democracy but it does not discuss or even mention consociation.¹⁶⁹ This may be because citizenship education projects have been often 'imported' from abroad rather than being developed in Macedonia, and because books are frequently translations of 'American' textbooks.¹⁷⁰

Some argue that it is a deliberate political decision not to employ teachers, books and financial resources to encourage peaceful multiculturalism and inclusive citizenship through *civic education* in Macedonia.¹⁷¹ More probably, the weakness of *civic education* reflects a lack of local capacity as well as wider disagreement over visions for Macedonia's future: as Schenker puts it, when they look at the future, 'Albanians see one thing, Macedonians see 13 other things'.¹⁷²

5.4.2 The Strategy for Integrated Education

In 2010, the Ministry of Education approved the *Strategy for Integrated Education*, which aimed at the 'education of youth of all ethnic groups in a multi-ethnic environment for the preparation [for] life in a multi-ethnic society'.¹⁷³ The strategy (considered in more depth in Chaps. 6 and 7) addressed most of the criticisms levelled at *civic education*. To provide opportunities for children belonging to different ethnolinguistic backgrounds to mix in schools, it called for the mainstreaming of joint extracurricular activities and suggested running mixed classes for some subjects, such as sports, foreign languages, music and art education. To strengthen the teaching of *civic education*, the strategy mapped extensive teacher training in active learning skills and methods and in 'interethnic' communication. It also demanded the 'cleaning' of existing textbooks and curricula and the establishment of standards to avoid stereotyping and discrimination of ethnic and linguistic communities in future educational materials. Finally, the strategy called for the introduction of *civic education* as a discrete subject in every year of primary and secondary school.[174]

The strategy was sidelined because of controversies over language rights and policies.[175] However, the United Nations Children's Emergency Fund (UNICEF) and the BoE examined existing textbooks and curricula and established guidelines and methods for the drafting of future books, with the hope that by 2015 all textbooks in Macedonia will be evidence-based and include multicultural contents.[176] Moreover, while *civic education* was not introduced in all grades of primary and secondary schools, the BoE and UNICEF formulated the compulsory cross-curricular theme of *Life-Skills Based Education* for primary school. The theme includes interactive methods and activities and is very similar to *personal development and mutual understanding* in Northern Ireland in its focus on five themes: personal development, interpersonal relationships, social relations, health and the environment. Themes deal with a variety of issues, from confidence building to expressing opinions, from dealing with emotions to conflict resolution, from hygiene to attitudes to the media. *Life-Skills Based Education* also envisages the 'building [of] a positive attitude to the nation'.[177]

It is too soon to estimate the long-term impact of these initiatives. Some critics, observing the flurry of activity, argue that international donors are simply employing Macedonia as a laboratory for experimental education policies.[178]

5.4.3 Towards a Civic Culture

In Macedonia, there is considerable debate over whether it is time to move 'beyond the Ohrid Framework Agreement', but citizenship education is not employed to stimulate discussion about the future.[179] The attempts to reform aspects of schooling related to citizenship education highlight two tendencies in the Macedonian education system. First, international actors such as the OSCE, European Union (EU) and the United States Agency for International Development (USAID) often urge local policymakers to frame and implement initiatives for stereotype reduction, inter-group contact and reconciliation. This is often interpreted locally as a capricious foreign interference.[180] Donor strategies are often met with local bureaucratic and political resistance and projects are rarely implemented or mainstreamed comprehensively. Failures in reforming education are blamed on the fact that 'education is politicised' and that local politicians are unaccountable.[181]

Second, most observers would agree that 'the situation is better than ten years ago'.[182] Yet, schools do not challenge the socialisation of children into the values and practices sustaining and reproducing inter-communal conflict. Above all, Georgieva notes that schools do not teach students that politicians who belong to different ethnolinguistic communities can represent them and protect their interests.[183] As such, rather than conveying an overarching civic culture, they contribute to cementing ethnic and political cleavages.

5.5 Conclusion

Analysis of citizenship education in Lebanon, Northern Ireland and Macedonia substantiates Lynn Davies' bitter observation that 'the most important threats to our survival are war, disease and environmental degradation. Yet, peace education, health education and ecology are not the top curriculum areas'.[184] No society puts citizenship education at the top of the educational agenda. In fact, despite rhetorical emphasis on a values dimension in education, and on the need for development of citizenship skills, schools are not assessed on the quality of their citizenship education programmes or on 'the quality of the citizens they graduate'.[185] The recent introduction of the *Community Relations, Equality & Diversity Policy* in Northern Ireland may be an exception.

Moreover, this chapter confirms Smith's observation that 'citizenship education is inextricably linked to the political milieu in which it is introduced'.[186] More than with history education, the effectiveness of citizenship education depends on the structure of schools and on their hidden curriculum. Schools have the potential to impact students' attitudes, allowing them to 'model some of the democratic ideals' and pluralist practices of consociations.[187] However, participatory methods, critical thinking and a culture of debate challenge the ingrained structures of schools, society and politics. It also remains unclear how far schools can promote democracy through their hierarchical and undemocratic structures. In Lebanon, Northern Ireland and Macedonia, schools also struggle to promote inclusive citizenship within exclusive establishments separated along linguistic, confessional or national lines. Thus, school exchanges across communal lines may help the internalisation and development of practices and feelings of citizenship.

Finally, effective citizenship education also requires a minimal definition of the concept of citizenship. This chapter has shown that the lack of consensus over national identity and the future of the state in deeply divided societies problematises this definition. As with history education, reaching a consensus over citizenship in consociations is challenging because of the tension between the 'diversity agenda' and the 'social inclusion' agenda.[188] Thus, in Lebanon, *citizenship and civic education* emerged as a vehicle to promote patriotism and a unified but 'hyphenated' Arab-Lebanese identity after the civil war. Emphasis on individual human rights and unmitigated loyalty to the state contrasts with the social and political reality of 'a country where people are captives of the religious sects to which they belong: they are born in their sect's hospital, taught at their sect's schools, given employment through the assistance of the sect's leadership, and end up being buried in the sect's cemetery'.[189] Akar suggests that the 'hypocritical' curriculum discourages students from participating in transformative politics.[190]

In contrast, citizenship education in Northern Ireland and Macedonia strives towards a more multidimensional approach to the construction of an inclusive, equal and diverse community. This approach requires local involvement in formulating curricula, extensive teacher training, allocated curricular time and appropriate teaching materials. Without these things, citizenship education gets pushed to the margins of the curriculum, as in Macedonia. Moreover, attention to subnational identities is often perceived to undermine allegiance to the state, so the 'balance between the preservation of cultural identity and allegiance to a shared vision' remains problematic.[191] English introduces a further dilemma when he points out that in Northern Ireland, equal legitimacy and recognition is granted to 'a tradition whose instinct is to support and maintain the state and ... to a tradition aiming at some form of dismemberment of the state'.[192]

However, Smith suggests that opportunities to question the values and principles at the heart of citizenship, publicly and legitimately, facilitate the formulation of inclusive notions of citizenship in deeply divided societies.[193] In this sense, *local and global citizenship* in Northern Ireland may offer a substantial contribution to the formulation of a consensual notion of citizenship, by providing space for the renegotiation and expression of the meanings and contents of identities and citizenship. No comparable space exists in Lebanon or Macedonia.

Notes

1. Ken Wylie, 'Citizenship, Identity and Social Inclusion', 238.
2. Audrey Osler and Hugh Starkey, 'Education for Democratic Citizenship: A Review of Research, Policy and Practice 1995–2005,' *Research Papers in Education* 21, no. 4 (2006): 434.
3. David Kerr, 'Citizenship Education in the Curriculum. An International Review,' *The School Field* X, no. 3/4 (1999): 6–7; Sobhi Tawil, 'Exploring Humanitarian Law: Armed Conflict and Education for Social Cohesion,' *Prospects* XXXI, no. 3 (2001): 295.
4. Augustus Richard Norton, 'Foreword,' in Knudsen and Kerr (eds.), *Lebanon after the Cedar Revolution*, xvi.
5. Bassel Akar, 'The Space between Civic Education and Active Citizenship in Lebanon,' in Shuayb (ed.), *Rethinking Education for Social Cohesion*, 156. The International Civic and Citizenship Education Study, the main instrument for international assessment of citizenship education, aso measures knowledge, skills and values.
6. Bassel Akar, 'The Space between Civic Education', in Shuayb (ed.), *Rethinking Education for Social Cohesion*, 156; Banks, 'Preface,' in Banks (ed.), *Diversity and Citizenship Education*, xx; Osler and Starkey, 'Education for Democratic Citizenship,' 441.
7. Akar, 'The Space between Civic Education', in Shuayb (ed.), *Rethinking Education for Social Cohesion*, 156.
8. Ibid., 156; Bassel Akar, 'Citizenship Education in Lebanon: An Introduction into Students' Concepts and Learning Experiences,' *Educate* 7, no. 2 (2007): 3.
9. Kerr, 'Citizenship Education,' 12–13.
10. Ibid.; Muhammad Faour and Marwan Muasher, *Education for Citizenship in the Arab World. Key to the Future* (Washington D.C.: Carnegie Endowment, 2011): 8; Margaret Sinclair, *Learning to Live Together: Building Skills, Values and Attitudes for the Twenty-First Century* (Paris: UNESCO IBE, 2004): 45; Ulrike Niens and Marie-Hélène Chastenay, 'Educating for Peace? Citizenship Education in Quebec and Northern Ireland,' *Comparative education Review* 52, no. 4 (2008): 520.
11. Wylie, 'Citizenship, Identity and Social Inclusion,' 237; Hélène Leenders and Wiel Veugelers, 'Different Perspectives on Values and Citizenship Education,' in J. Zajda and H. Daun (eds.), *Global Values Education*, (Springer, 2009): 23–24.
12. Amy Gutmann, 'Unity and Diversity', in Banks (ed.), *Diversity and Citizenship Education*, 74; Walter C. Parker, 'Diversity, Globalisation and Democratic Education,' in Banks (ed.), *Diversity and Citizenship Education*, 441; Banks, 'Preface', in Banks (ed.), *Diversity and Citizenship*

Education, xx; Akar, 'The Space between Civic Education,' in Shuayb (ed.), *Rethinking Education for Social Cohesion*, 160.
13. Kerr, 'Citizenship Education,' 13.
14. Faour and Muasher, *Education for Citizenship*, 8–9; Leenders and Veugelers, 'Different Perspectives', in Zajda and Daun (eds.), *Global Values Education*, 22.
15. Tawil, 'Exploring Humanitarian Law,' 303; Kerr, 'Citizenship Education,' 13.
16. Sinclair, *Learning to Live Together*, 46–48; Leenders and Veugelers, 'Different Perspectives', in Zajda and Daun (eds.), *Global Values Education*, 26–29.
17. Will Kymlicka, 'Foreword,' in Banks (ed.), *Diversity and Citizenship Education*, xiv.
18. Ulrike Niens and Lorraine McIlrath, 'Understandings of Citizenship Education in Northern Ireland and the Republic of Ireland: Public Discourses among Stakeholders in the Public and Private Sectors,' *Education, Citizenship and Social Justice* 73, no. 5 (2010): 74; Niens and Chastenay, 'Educating for Peace?,' 521.
19. Kymlicka, 'Foreword', in Banks (ed.), *Diversity and Citizenship Education*, xiv; Banks, 'Democratic Citizenship Education,' in Banks (ed.), *Diversity and Citizenship Education*, 9.
20. Niens and McIlrath, 'Understandings of Citizenship Education,' p.84.
21. For example: Niens and Chastenay, 'Educating for Peace?,' 521–522.
22. Sinclair, *Learning to Live Together*, 135; Kerr, 'Citizenship Education,' 26.
23. Leenders and Veugelers, 'Different Perspectives', in Zajda and Daun (eds.), *Global Values Education*, 22.
24. Sinclair, *Learning to Live Together*, 135.
25. Kerr, 'Citizenship Education,' 19.
26. Maha Shuayb, 'Current Models and Approaches to Social Cohesion in Secondary Schools in Lebanon,' in Shuayb (ed.), *Rethinking Education for Social Cohesion*, 141–147.
27. Ibid., 149–152.
28. Nemer Frayha, 'Developing Curriculum,' in Tawil and Harley (eds.), *Education, Conflict and Social Cohesion*, 198.
29. Qabbani Interview; Abu Assali Interview.
30. Frayha, 'Developing Curriculum', in Tawil and Harley (eds.), *Education, Conflict and Social Cohesion*, 173; Akar Interview.
31. Frayha, 'Developing Curriculum', in Tawil and Harley (eds.), *Education, Conflict and Social Cohesion*, 196.
32. Centre for Educational Research and Development, *Approach to Citizenship and Civic Education*, http://www.crdp.org/CRDP/all%20curriculum/Civic%20Education/Civic%20Education%20Curriculum%20_ar.htm; Tawil, 'Exploring Humanitarian Law,' 300.

33. Qabbani Interview.
34. Mark Farha, 'The Historical Legacy and Political Implications of State and Sectarian Schools in Lebanon,' in Shuayb (ed.), *Rethinking Education for Social Cohesion*, 78.
35. Mounir Abou Assali, 'Education for Social Cohesion in Lebanon: The Educational Reform Experiment in the Wake of the Lebanese War,' in Shuayb (ed.), *Rethinking Education for Social Cohesion*, 87.
36. For a full list of aims, see: Akar, 'The Space between Civic Education,' in Shuayb (ed.), *Rethinking Education for Social Cohesion*, 161; Interview with Adnan El-Amine (Laes Director and Curriculum Specialist), Beirut, 22/07/2012; Centre for Educational Research and Development, *Civic Education Curriculum*, (Beirut: CERD, 1997).
37. El-Amine Interview; Abu Assali Interview.
38. Frayha, 'Developing Curriculum', in Tawil and Harley (eds.), *Education, Conflict and Social Cohesion*, 193.
39. Akar Interview; Senior Officer, CERD, Interview; Abu Assali Interview.
40. Akar Interview; Akar, 'The Space between Civic Education,' in Shuayb (ed.), *Rethinking Education for Social Cohesion*, 160, 164; Frayha, 'Developing Curriculum', in Tawil and Harley (eds.), *Education, Conflict and Social Cohesion*, 194.
41. Ibid., 191, 194; Mounir Abu Assali, 'Education for Social Cohesion in Lebanon: The Educational Reform Experiment in the Wake of the Lebanese War,' in Shuayb (ed.), *Rethinking Education for Social Cohesion*, 93.
42. Akar Interview; Akar, 'The Space between Civic Education,' in Shuayb (ed.), *Rethinking Education for Social Cohesion*, 160.
43. Ibid., 159–160; Akar Interview; Frayha, 'Developing Curriculum', in Tawil and Harley (eds.), *Education, Conflict and Social Cohesion*, 196.
44. Abu Assali Interview.
45. Shuayb, 'Current Models,' in Shuayb (ed.), *Rethinking Education for Social Cohesion*, 138.
46. Senior Officer, CERD, Interview.
47. El-Amine Interview; Akar Interview.
48. Maha Shuayb, 'Education: A Means for the Cohesion of the Lebanese Confessional Society,' in Choueiri (ed.), *Breaking the Cycle*, 169; El-Amine Interview.
49. Shuayb, 'Current Models,' in Shuayb (ed.), *Rethinking Education for Social Cohesion*, 139.
50. Centre for Educational Research and Development, *Civic Education Curriculum*.
51. Akar, 'The Space between Civic Education,' in Shuayb (ed.), *Rethinking Education for Social Cohesion*, 161, 164; Frayha, 'Developing Curriculum,' in Tawil and Harley (eds.), *Education, Conflict and Social Cohesion*, 164.

52. Ibid.,192.
53. Shuayb, 'Education,' in Choueiri (ed.), *Breaking the Cycle*, 169.
54. Akar, 'Citizenship Education in Lebanon,' 13.
55. Frayha, 'Developing Curriculum,' in Tawil and Harley (eds.), *Education, Conflict and Social Cohesion*, 192.
56. El-Amine Interview.
57. Akar, 'Citizenship Education in Lebanon,' 13; Akar Interview; Akar, 'Teacher Reflections on the Challenges of Teaching Citizenship Education in Lebanon: A Qualitative Pilot Study', *Reflecting Education* 2, No.2 (2006): 55; Bassel Akar, 'Exploring the Challenges and Practices of Citizenship Education in National and Civic Education Grades Ten and Eleven in Lebanon,' *Compare* 39, no. 5 (2009): 685.
58. Akar, 'Teacher Reflections,' 49; Shuayb, 'Education,' in Choueiri (ed.), *Breaking the Cycle*, 176, 191.
59. Akar, 'Citizenship Education in Lebanon,' 8; Akar, 'Teacher Reflections,' 61.
60. Frayha, 'Developing Curriculum,' in Tawil and Harley (eds.), *Education, Conflict and Social Cohesion*, 192.
61. Akar, 'Citizenship Education in Lebanon,' 12.
62. El-Amine Interview.
63. Ibid.; Shuayb, 'Current Models,' in Shuayb (ed.), *Rethinking Education for Social Cohesion*, 139.
64. Akar, 'The Space between Civic Education,' in Shuayb (ed.), *Rethinking Education for Social Cohesion*, 164; El-Amine Interview.
65. Abu Assali Interview; Abou Assali, 'Education for Social Cohesion in Lebanon', in Shuayb (ed.), *Rethinking Education for Social Cohesion*, 94.
66. El-Amine Interview; Akar Interview; Frayha, 'Developing Curriculum,' in Tawil and Harley (eds.), *Education, Conflict and Social Cohesion*, 192; Awad Interview; Akar, 'Teacher Reflections,' 59; Abu Assali Interview; Shuayb, 'Education', in Choueiri (ed.), *Breaking the Cycle*, 186; Abou Assali, 'Education for Social Cohesion', in Shuayb (ed.), *Rethinking Education for Social Cohesion*, 94.
67. Akar Interview; Akar, 'Teacher Reflections,' 61; Akar, 'The Space between Civic Education,' in Shuayb (ed.), *Rethinking Education for Social Cohesion*, 155.
68. Akar Interview.
69. Akar, 'The Space between Civic Education,' in Shuayb (ed.), *Rethinking Education for Social Cohesion*, 155,166.
70. Shuayb, 'Education,' in Choueiri (ed.), *Breaking the Cycle*, 168.
71. Awad Interview; Akar, 'Citizenship Education in Lebanon,' 13; Senior Officer, CERD, Interview.
72. Daw Interview.

73. Shuayb, 'Education,' in Choueiri (ed.), *Breaking the Cycle*.
74. Shuayb, 'Education,' in Choueiri (ed.), *Breaking the Cycle*, 235, 178–182, 222–230.
75. Akar Interview.
76. Ministry of Education and Higher Education, *Achievements: 2010*, https://www.google.co.uk/search?q=Ministry+of+Education+and+Higher+Education%2C+Achievements%3A+2010&oq=Ministry+of+Education+and+Higher+Education%2C+Achievements%3A+2010&aqs=chrome..69i57.164j0j4&sourceid=chrome&es_sm=91&ie=UTF-8: 27.
77. Ibid., 15; Akar Interview; El-Amine Interview.
78. Ibid.
79. Nemer Frayha, 'Education as a Means' in Shuayb (ed.), *Rethinking Education for Social Cohesion*, 105.
80. Akar, 'Teacher Reflections,' 61.
81. Faour and Muasher, *Education for Citizenship*, 13.
82. Wylie, 'Citizenship, Identity and Social Inclusion,' 238.
83. Michael Arlow, 'Citizenship Education,' in Tawil and Harley (eds.), *Education, Conflict and Social Cohesion*, 266.
84. Paul Murphy, qtd. in Office of the First Minister and Deputy First Minister, *A Shared Future. Policy and Strategic Framework for Good Relations in Northern Ireland*, (Belfast: OFMDFM, 2005) 3.
85. Arlow, 'Ctizenship Education', in Tawil and Harley (eds.), *Education, Conflict and Social Cohesion*, 260.
86. Hanna Interview.
87. Interview with Expert of Religious Education and Citizenship Education, Belfast, 19/02/2013.
88. Sinclair, *Learning to Live Together*, 94; Arlow, 'Citizenship Education', in Tawil and Harley (eds.), *Education, Conflict and Social Cohesion*, 280.
89. *The Education Reform (Northern Ireland) Order 1989*, 19/12/1989; Alan Smith and Alan Robinson, *Education for Mutual Understanding: The Initial Statutory Years* (Belfast: University of Ulster, 1997), 1.
90. Wylie, 'Citizenship, Identity and Social Inclusion,' 239.
91. Smith and Robinson, *Education for Mutual Understanding*, 1.
92. Ibid., 13; Wylie, 'Citizenship, Identity and Social Inclusion,' 239.
93. Smith and Robinson, qtd. in Arlow, 'Citizenship Education', in Tawil and Harley (eds.), *Education, Conflict and Social Cohesion*, 282.
94. Wylie, 'Citizenship, Identity and Social Inclusion,' 239.
95. Ibid; Michael Arlow, *The Challenges of Social Inclusion in Northern Ireland: Citizenship and Life Skills* (Geneva: IBE, 2000), 2; Niens and Chastenay, 'Educating for Peace?,' 525.
96. Sinclair, *Learning to Live Together*, 239; Arlow, 'Citizenship Education', in Tawil and Harley (eds.), *Education, Conflict and Social Cohesion*, 280; Arlow, *The Challenges of Social Inclusion*, 2.

97. Arlow, 'Citizenship Education,' in Tawil and Harley (eds.), *Education, Conflict and Social Cohesion*, 282.
98. Sinclair, *Learning to Live Together*, 96; Interview with Expert of Religious Education and Citizenship Education; Niens and Chastenay, 'Educating for Peace?,' 525.
99. Terence Duffy, 'Peace Education in a Divided Society: Creating a Culture of Peace in Northern Ireland,' *Prospects* XXX, no. 1 (2000): 25; Arlow, *The Challenges of Social Inclusion*, 3.
100. Alan Smith, 'Citizenship Education in Northern Ireland: Beyond National Identity?,' *Cambridge Journal of Education* 33, no. 1 (2003): 22.
101. Sinclair, *Learning to Live Together*, 93.
102. Arlow, *The Challenges of Social Inclusion*, 3.
103. Ibid., 5.
104. Senior Officer (Education and Skills Authority) Interview.
105. Ibid.
106. Arlow Interview.
107. Ibid.
108. Arlow Interview; Arlow, 'Citizenship Education,' in Tawil and Harley (eds.), *Education, Conflict and Social Cohesion*, 283.
109. Expert of Religious Education and Citizenship Education Interview; Arlow Interview; Expert of Religious Education and Citizenship Education Interview.
110. Ibid.; Arlow Interview.
111. Expert of Religious Education and Citizenship Education Interview.
112. Arlow Interview.
113. Hanna Interview; Senior Officer (Education and Skills Authority) Interview; Arlow, 'Citizenship Education,' in Tawil and Harley (eds.), *Education, Conflict and Social Cohesion*, 285.
114. Bell Interview.
115. Niens and Chastenay, 'Educating for Peace?,' 526.
116. Bell Interview; Expert of Religious Education and Citizenship Education Interview.
117. Ibid.
118. Bell Interview; Expert of Religious Education and Citizenship Education Interview; Christopher Oulton et al., 'Controversial Issues: Teachers' Attitudes and Practices in the Context of Citizenship Education,' *Oxford Review of Education* 30, no. 4 (2004): 498.
119. Expert of Religious Education and Citizenship Education Interview; Arlow, *The Challenges of Social Inclusion*, 8.
120. Arlow, 'Citizenship Education,' in Tawil and Harley (eds.), *Education, Conflict and Social Cohesion*, 284.

121. Arlow, *The Challenges of Social*, 9; Niens and McIlrath, 'Understandings of Citizenship Education,' 77; Arlow Interview.
122. Bell Interview; Niens and Chastenay, 'Educating for Peace?,' 526.
123. Bell Interview; Arlow Interview.
124. Sinclair, *Learning to Live Together*, 94; Niens and Chastenay, 'Educating for Peace?,' 526.
125. Hanna Interview; Wylie, 'Citizenship, Identity and Social Inclusion,' 240.
126. Arlow, *The Challenges of Social Inclusion*, 8; Niens and Chastenay, 'Educating for Peace?,' 532.
127. Arlow, *The Challenges of Social Inclusion*, 8; Smith, 'Citizenship Education,' 24–25.
128. Ibid., 25.
129. Arlow Interview; Arlow, *The Challenges of Social Inclusion*, 9–13; Expert of Religious Education and Citizenship Education Interview.
130. Ibid.; Niens and Chastenay, 'Educating for Peace?,' 525–526.
131. Arlow, *The Challenges of Social*, 10.
132. Niens and McIlrath, 'Understandings of Citizenship Education,' 80.
133. Arlow Interview; Expert of Religious Education and Citizenship Education Interview.
134. Arlow Interview; Expert of Religious Education and Citizenship Education Interview.
135. Niens and Chastenay, 'Educating for Peace?,' 531, 533.
136. Wylie, 'Citizenship, Identity and Social Inclusion,' 242.
137. Ulrike Niens and Jacqueline Reilly, *The Global Dimension: School Approaches, Teaching and Learning in Northern Ireland* (Belfast: DfID, 2010): 28–29, 72.
138. Arlow Interview.
139. Niens and Chastenay, 'Educating for Peace?,' 531; Niens and McIlrath, 'Understandings of Citizenship Education,' 82.
140. Arlow Interview; Expert of Religious Education and Citizenship Education Interview; Oulton et al., 'Controversial Issues,' 498.
141. Expert of Religious Education and Citizenship Education Interview; Arlow Interview.
142. Arlow Interview.
143. Expert of Religious Education and Citizenship Education Interview.
144. Bell Interview.
145. Ibid.
146. Qtd. by Michael Arlow.
147. Bell Interview.
148. Wylie, 'Citizenship, Identity and Social Inclusion,' 241.
149. Ibid., 242; Smith, 'Citizenship Education,' 27–28.
150. Officer in an International Mission Interview.

151. Ilo Trajkovski, 'The Place and the Role of Civic Education in the Republic of Macedonia,' *Journal of Social Science Education* 2, (2003), 1–4.
152. Ibid., 4.
153. Officer in an International Mission Interview.
154. Hani Interview.
155. Interview with Harald Schenker (Independent Consultant and Drafter of the Strategy for Integrated Education), Skopje, 12/09/2012; Hani Interview; Interview with Ljubica Grodzanovska (Journalist, Transitions Online, Edno Magazine), Skopje, 9/09/2012.
156. Interview with Silvana Veteroska (Head of Sector for Professional Development, Bureau for Development of Education), Skopje, 14/09/2012; Bureau for the Development of Education of the Republic of Macedonia, *Curriculum: Civic Education.* (Skopje: Ministry of Education and Science, 2008).
157. Emilija Petrova-Gjorgjeva, 'Democratic Society and Moral Education' paper presented at the *World Conference On Educational Sciences* (Istanbul, Turkey, 6/05/2010): 52.
158. Bureau for the Development of Education of the Republic of Macedonia, *Curriculum: Civic Education.*
159. Vera Stojanovska and Biljana Krsteska-Papic, 'Multicultural Component in Elementary Education in the Republic of Macedonia,' *Practice and Theory in Systems of Education* 5, no. 1 (2010): 29, 31.
160. Lazarevska Interview.
161. Sabani Interview.
162. Interview with Loreta Georgieva (Executive Director, Macedonian Civic Education Centre),' Skopje, 11/09/2012; Stojanovska and Krsteska-Papic, 'Multicultural Component,' 36; Sabani Interview; Ali Cupi Interview; Lazarevska Interview; Organisation for Security and Co-operation in Europe Spillover Mission to Skopje, *Age, Contact, Perceptions: How Schools Shape Relations between Ethnicities* (Skopje: OSCE, 2010): 17.
163. Respectively in a social studies and in a sociology textbook. 'Macedonia Awaits Results of Schoolbook Revision,' *Balkan Insight*, 23/02/2011; Zaklina Ahadzi-Zafirova, 'Macedonia's Textbook Trauma,' *Transitions Online*, 30/11/2011.
164. Alessia Carta, Carla Podda, and Claudia Secci, 'Cittadinanza Democratica in Construzione. Lettura Dei Rapporti Di 'Esclusione/Inclusione' in Macedonia,' *Ricerche di Pedagogia e Didattica* 7, no. 1 (2012): 4.
165. Hani Interview; Lazarevska Interview.
166. Sabani Interview; Stojanovska and Krsteska-Papic, 'Multicultural Component,' 33; Carta et al., 'Cittadinanza Democratica,' 4; Officer in an International Mission Interview; Organisation for Security and

Co-operation in Europe Spillover Mission to Skopje, *Age, Contact, Perceptions*, 33.
167. Officer in an International Mission Interview; Trajkovski, 'The Place and the Role of Civic Education,' 4.
168. Georgieva Interview.
169. Stojanovska and Krsteska-Papic, 'Multicultural Component,' 36.
170. Trajkovski, 'The Place and the Role of Civic Education,' 5; Carta et al., 'Cittadinanza Democratica,' 4.
171. Albanian Historian Interview.
172. Schenker Interview.
173. Ministry of Education and Science, *Interethnic Integration in Education*, http://www.mon.gov.mk/index.php/component/content/article/1112; Ministry of Education and Science of the Republic of Macedonia, *Steps Towards Integrated Education*.
174. Schenker Interview; Officer in an International Mission Interview; Ministry of Education and Science, *Plan of Activities of the Donor Organisations in the Area of Inter-Ethnic Education for 2012*, (Skopje: Ministry of Education and Science, 2013).
175. See Chaps. 6 and 7.
176. Interview with an Officer, Ministry of Education and Science, Skopje, 18/09/2012; Sabani Interview.
177. Bureau for the Development of Education of the Republic of Macedonia, *Curriculum: Life-Skills Based Education* (Skopje: Ministry of Education and Science, 2008); Sabani Interview.
178. Interview with Nenad Novkovski (Academic and Former Minister of Education), Skopje, 11/09/2012.
179. Schenker Interview.
180. Novkovski Interview.
181. Officer in an International Mission Interview.
182. Lazarevska Interview.
183. Georgieva Interview.
184. Lynn Davies, 'Teaching About Conflict through Citizenship Education,' *International Journal of Citizenship and Teacher Education* 1, no. 2 (2005): 29.
185. Awad Interview.
186. Smith, 'Citizenship Education,' 29.
187. Wylie, 'Citizenship, Identity and Social Inclusion,' 246.
188. Wylie, 'Citizenship, Identity and Social Inclusion,' 237.

189. Rehab Moukahal, 'Values and Experience', *Lebanese Association for Educational Studies*, http://www.laes.org/_publications.php?lang=en&id=13
190. Akar, 'Citizenship Education in Lebanon,' 13.
191. Niens and Chastenay, 'Educating for Peace?,' 535.
192. Qtd. in Wylie, 'Citizenship, Identity and Social Inclusion,' 242.
193. Smith, 'Citizenship Education,' 30.

CHAPTER 6

Languages of Instruction

De Varennes reflects that state-building makes it extremely hard 'for a state to remain language neutral'.[1] Indeed, the construction of state institutions, especially if they are democratic, drives states to choose one or more official languages to communicate with their citizens. Official languages are not necessarily the languages spoken by members of local confessional, ethnic and national communities. However, the choice of languages is rarely politically neutral in deeply divided societies. Here, schools can help construct and spread the official languages of the state, but can also contribute to preserving and reproducing the traditional vernaculars of local communities.

This chapter considers debates over the choice of languages of instruction in compulsory schools in Lebanon, Northern Ireland and Macedonia since their peace agreements. It shows that these debates reflected the new inter-communal power hierarchies emerging out of the three conflicts and enshrined in the new consociational arrangements. These debates also mirror two important differences. First, the three societies have different degrees of linguistic diversity: in Northern Ireland, the overwhelming majority of the population speaks English as a mother tongue; in Lebanon, Arabic is the only official language but French and English are widely spoken; Macedonia is more diverse linguistically: Macedonian is the official language, Albanian is spoken by over 20 % of the population, and smaller communities speak Turkish, Romani, Serbian, Bosniak and Vlach. Second, as Chaps. 1 and 3 explained, Lebanon, Northern Ireland and Macedonia differ in the political saliency of their linguistic cleavages.

The concept of mother tongue informs educational and political debates in the three consociations, despite continuing theoretical debates over its precise definition.[2] This chapter employs the concept of mother tongue to denote an individual's native language, the language learnt first by a child, or even a community's heritage language. However, it refutes the differentiation between the 'national language' (as an instrument of socialisation into national identity) and 'foreign languages' (as tools for socio-economic mobility), common in the literature.[3] Indeed, this distinction is blurred in Lebanon, Northern Ireland and Macedonia. Therefore, this chapter considers all local, national and foreign languages.

6.1 Teaching Languages in Deeply Divided Societies: Theoretical Debates

The time allocated to languages in school curricula is far superior to the time devoted to other 'national subjects'. Moreover, debates over languages in education impact three core functions of schooling: the promotion of a shared identity, the achievement of 'equality or at least a sense of social inclusion' and the creation of human capital.[4]

Theories of nationalism highlight the intimate and exclusive relationship between the state and its official language(s). Gellner argues that standardised languages facilitated industrialisation, and later, through mass schooling, became identified with states and their cultures.[5] Conversely, Anderson sees the existence of a common vernacular and of print media as key to the birth of the first nations as 'imagined communities'.[6] J.S. Mill presented official languages as instruments for democracy, essential to the emergence of 'the united public opinion necessary to the working of representative government'.[7] Hobsbawm adds that by teaching a language, schools provide children with tools to communicate with the state.[8]

However, the state's selection of official languages favours some linguistic groups while disadvantaging others: certain local languages may become 'dialectalised' and associated with 'tradition and obsolescence' and, over time, become extinct.[9] In multilingual societies this choice reflects inter-group hierarchies: the more prestigious languages (spoken by the dominant communities) are used for official functions such as government and education, while less prestigious vernaculars (spoken by marginalised or excluded groups) are relegated to the private domain.[10] Thus, the status of language in the education system often mirrors the status of linguistic communities in plural societies.

Linguistic policy also reproduces the socio-economic and political status of communities and is 'implicated in ... competition between groups for material and symbolic resources'.[11] Schools that teach only in the official state language entrench the social hierarchies between individuals belonging to different linguistic communities. This is because non-native speakers are 'understood not as having a different competence, but as being incompetent'.[12] Children may face comprehension difficulties, frustration, cultural and cognitive dissonance, and be deprived of their identity, creativity and expressive potential.[13] In the long term, Skuttnabb-Kangas argues that education in languages other than the mother tongue leads to worse educational performances, higher dropout rates and higher unemployment.[14]

Beyond its detrimental impact on individuals, 'the one-language-one-nation ideology of language policy and national identity'[15] also contributes to violent conflict in plural societies, where linguistic cleavages coincide with ethnic, religious or national fractures. On the one hand, the teaching of certain traditional languages may be perceived as threatening the integrity and very existence of a state. On the other hand, schooling in the official state language limits access to education and employment opportunities for some linguistic communities: Brown shows that this fuels violent inter-communal conflict.[16]

Conversely, mother tongue education provides a link between school, home and the local community, involves families in school life, allows the transmission of values and boosts self-esteem. It also aids the acquisition of a second language and educational achievement.[17] Indeed, Thomas and Collier have found that the single most influential factor predicting the educational success of bilingual students is the number of years of schooling in the mother tongue they experienced.[18]

This substantiates the claim that for liberal societies to be just, members of different communities should be endowed with different rights. For example, a just society would provide 'promotion-oriented rights' for linguistic minorities (such as instruction in the mother tongue in state schools), thereby adapting 'the nation-building process to the liberal postulate of equality of all citizens'.[19] Mother tongue education should be provided at least up to the secondary school level, to guarantee some social mobility.

However, instruction in minority or indigenous languages may be 'regressive' if it promotes self-ghettoisation and the long-term socio-economic exclusion of a linguistic community.[20] Advanced learning of the official state language should complement the right to mother tongue education to ensure that members of all linguistic communities can participate in economic, social and political life.[21]

The long-term sociopolitical impact of language learning depends on which model of language teaching is adopted in schools. Models of language teaching vary along a continuum, from assimilation or monolingualism to full pluralism or multilingualism. Freeman Field confirms that language policies 'reflect ideological assumptions about language, speakers of language, and the role of schools in society'.[22] Thus, monolingual programmes generally reproduce existing power structures and are often implemented in polities that deny the legitimacy or very existence of linguistic minorities. As mentioned, monolingual education often hampers educational achievement, especially when children are forced to learn in the official language, regardless of their mother tongue ('submersion education'). It may also further socio-economic exclusion through 'segregation programmes', which force children from minority backgrounds to be instructed through their low-status mother tongue without learning the official language.[23]

In contrast, pluralistic approaches to languages generally rely on bilingual education, meant as 'the use of two (or more) languages of instruction at some point in a students' school career'.[24] However, they vary widely in the 'methods for coordinating the relationships' between the different languages.[25] These variations, according to Ruiz, reflect three broad societal 'ideological orientations' towards languages.[26] When the existence of non-official languages is perceived as a problem, schools adopt transitional programmes for 'subtractive bilingualism'. In subtractive bilingualism, children initially learn in the mother tongue but shift to the official language in the course of primary education to gain proficiency in the official language.[27]

When non-official languages are enshrined as a human right, schools adopt 'additive bilingualism' and provide instruction in the mother tongue and in the state official language at all levels. For example, the 'language shelter' model allows children belonging to a linguistic minority to learn in their mother tongue while learning the official language as a subject.

Conversely, 'immersion programmes for indigenous people and minorities' instruct children through the medium of a lost ancestral language to revive a native language community.[28] These approaches legitimise communal rights and strengthen group identity, so they gain broad political support only 'when the risk of provoking divided loyalties, stoking secessionist fires, or sustaining cultural autonomy is low'.[29]

Finally, when societies perceive language as a resource, schools offer enrichment bilingual programmes. For example, language immersion programmes for speakers of the official language allow children to be instructed through a minority or foreign language.[30] This is rarely controversial because it 'serves the interests of dominant groups in the society' by allowing middle-class children to learn prestigious languages.[31]

In plural societies, bilingual education furthers communal equality and mutual understanding by, at the very least, legitimising the culture and language of different ethnic, national or religious communities.[32] Byram also claims that language learning can promote 'intercultural competence' by relativising dichotomies of 'us against them', encouraging perspective-taking, challenging stereotypes, and bringing two or more cultures into a dialectical relationship.[33] Ultimately, the impact of bilingual education on inter-group conflict largely depends on the model of bilingualism adopted and its effect upon the educational and socio-economic opportunities of members of different communities. Maintenance and additive bilingual programmes have shown the best educational results, with better linguistic competences in the official language than immersion programmes.[34]

Despite this evidence, debates over languages of instruction in most divided societies remain linked primarily to the struggle for power and recognition of communities. Interestingly, this is not the case in Lebanon.

6.2 Lebanon

About 95 % of Lebanon's population speaks Arabic as their mother tongue, but linguistic plurality is 'entrenched in the Lebanese psyche and the Lebanese education system'.[35] Indeed, Chap. 3 explained that modern schooling was born multilingual: since the nineteenth century, foreign missions adopted French or English as languages of instruction and confessional communities 'learnt the language of their tutelary nations'.[36] Thus, most Christian schools adopted French, Muslim schools emphasised Arabic, and American schools, generally attracting children of wealthy Sunni and Greek Orthodox backgrounds, employed English and Arabic.

The French Mandate further entrenched bilingualism by introducing French and Arabic as official languages and requiring schools to teach sciences and social studies in French.[37] However, after Lebanese independence, Arabic was established as the sole official national language, and all schools were encouraged to teach the Arabic language and to employ Arabic as a language of instruction for all subjects at all levels, including sciences.

Emphasis on Arabic-medium education expressed a 'zeal for independent national identity' after decolonisation.[38] Yet, Diab suggests that this 'hasty expression of national pride ... did not result from careful planning': it overlooked the deep rooting of foreign languages in Lebanon's education system and the long tradition of teaching sciences in French and English.[39] Thus, many private schools ignored government directives and retained French- or English-medium education. Rather than enforcing its decisions, in 1950 the government exempted foreign private schools from teaching Arabic, which remained compulsory only for Lebanese citizens.[40] Moreover, the 1968 curricula affirmed that schools should '*in principle* use Arabic as [the] medium of instruction for all subjects' but *in practice* allowed state schools to teach science in English and French.[41]

The educational debate over languages of instruction reflected a wider conflict over the identity and the regional orientation of the Lebanese state. Instruction in Arabic aimed 'to [stimulate] Arab unity and identity'.[42] Conversely, by challenging the use of Arabic, 'the defenders of a non-Arab Lebanon ... [were] challenging Arabness on linguistic grounds'.[43] Unsuccessfully, certain Christian Maronite intellectuals even attempted to construct a 'Lebanese' language as distinct from the Arabic language.[44] More successfully, in the 1960s Christians largely insisted on multilingual education while Muslims favoured Arabic monolingualism.[45] As Chap. 3 mentioned, this mirrored the clash between Muslim pan-Arab identifications and Christian 'double heritage, the Arab and the Western'.[46] It also reflected the political clash between 'Muslims calling for cultural homogeneity' and 'Christians championing cultural heterogeneity'.[47]

These tensions culminated in the 1975–1989 civil war, which accelerated the linguistic fragmentation of the Lebanese education system. Some schools taught every subject at every level in Arabic to convey the 'heritage and historical depth of the Arab language' to children.[48] Most of the newly founded private schools adopted English as their language of instruction.

6.2.1 Enrichment Bilingual Education

Chapters 4 and 5 have shown that the civil war did not solve fundamental debates over the identity of Lebanese citizens and the foreign orientations of the state. Yet it largely solved past clashes over language policy. Chartouni argues that after the Taif Agreement, arabisation did not appeal to a 'Muslim community [that] has become more pluralistic in its cultural orientation and ethos and engaged in a massive policy of educational modernisation'.[49] Similarly, Bizri demonstrates that Christian political parties abandoned the idea of a Lebanese language as distinct from Arabic as 'utopian and economically harmful for Lebanon'.[50] A consensus emerged over Arabic as the mother tongue and language of national affiliation, English as the language of business and science, and French as the language of high culture.[51]

The 1995 *New Framework for Education* established that schools should ensure proficiency in the Arabic language 'as the official national language', but also teach at least one foreign language to further children's 'openness to foreign cultures'.[52] The 1997 curriculum effectively ratified the unofficial practice of multilingualism: schools could choose their language of instruction and the new curriculum entrenched bilingual education according to an enrichment model.[53] Thus, Arabic and one foreign language (English or French) are studied from first grade: foreign languages join Arabic as languages of instruction from grade 7 (and a second foreign language is taught from grade 7). As clear in Fig. 6.1, 52 % of schools teach in Arabic and French, about 24 % teach in Arabic and English and about 24 % offer instruction in the three languages.

In this Arabic-French-English trilingual education system, Arabic remains the only language of instruction that all students share. This is partly because successive governments have insisted that the Arabic language is the only effective instrument by which to teach an overarching identity and affiliation to Lebanon. Thus, the national curriculum requires schools to teach the national subjects (*Citizenship and Civic Education*, *Geography*, *History* and *Arabic*) in the Arabic language and students sit these four official exams in Arabic.[54]

Still, Shaaban found that the quality of Arabic teaching in state schools declined steadily since the 1970s and that despite political rhetoric, Arabic 'occupies a second place' in most Lebanese schools.[55] This may be due to mnemonic and passive methodologies and to the lack of interesting contents in curricula and textbooks, which, according to some teachers, hinder

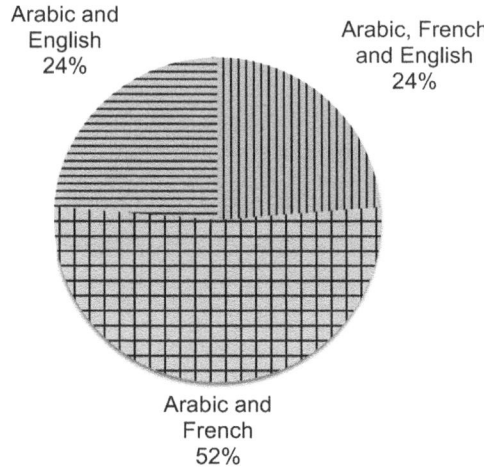

Fig. 6.1 Lebanese schools by language of instruction in 2010 (Central Administration of Statistics, *State Statistical Yearbook* (Beirut: Central Administration of Statistics, 2010))

the learning of Arabic *fusha*.[56] Moreover, deprived households and communities rarely speak standard Arabic and this hampers children's learning. The conflict between different forms of spoken Arabic (*ammiyya*), together with the lack of teacher training programmes and reference materials, also sustains the preconception that Arabic is barely 'good enough' for national subjects and not suitable to teach sciences.[57] Ultimately, many Lebanese students struggle with reading and writing Arabic *fusha*.

Even many Islamic schools, which previously taught only in Arabic, started employing English and French as languages of instruction since 1999. For example, the Makassed schools, pressed by the 'reality' of student desire to master a foreign language, abandoned the 'dream' of Arabic instruction.[58] Terc argues that this decision exemplifies an ideological shift from viewing students as bearers of Arab unity and cultural heritage, towards a desire to form modern, adaptable, technologically savvy students who can combine 'religion with national affiliation'.[59]

Indeed, in contrast to history, language policy has been largely depoliticised in Lebanon and parents often send their children to schools affiliated with different communities to learn English or French.[60] The Arabic language has also emerged as an overarching marker of Lebanese identity, and is employed as a medium of instruction for the national subjects, in domestic life and in religious activity.[61]

6.2.2 Old and New Cleavages in Language Policy

Bizri argues that 'the choice of French and/or English as second and third languages in Lebanon is no longer associated with confession or class, but with aspirations to social success'.[62] Surveys confirm that students view the study of English as an essential instrument of socio-economic mobility and policymakers often agree: they perceive English as the language of business and science. While being associated with high culture, to an extent, the French language remains also an expression of affiliation to French culture, particularly among Christians.[63] Thus, being French-educated or English-educated remains a secondary marker of communal identity for certain Christians who value Arabic-French bilingualism.

However, more than reflecting communal fractures, language policy in consociational Lebanon cements socio-economic cleavages. Bizri confirms that 'the famous Lebanese trilingualism with French, Arabic and English in reality [is] not accessible to all members of the nation'.[64] Indeed, access to multilingual education is a function of socio-economic status and the quality of language teaching in Lebanon's 'elitist educational system' depends on individual ability to 'afford ... expensive private schools with strong English programmes'.[65]

In most schools, the quality of English and French teaching is poor: in 1993 only 25 % of students passed their English Baccalaureate exam.[66] Foreign language teaching is largely based on text, memory and repetition, employs academic and artificial language and favours writing over speaking, particularly when classes are crowded and children have different proficiency levels.[67] Moreover, students in public schools have access to fewer foreign language learning opportunities than students in private schools. Children are rarely exposed to French or English after school, and lack opportunities to practise these foreign languages, particularly in 'low socio-economic status schools'.[68] In fact, pupils of middle-class backgrounds often speak French or English at home.[69] Thus, despite the curriculum being nominally the same, students in 'low socio-economic status schools' achieve lower levels of French and English and are unable to employ the foreign languages in science class.[70] In the long term, this entrenches socio-economic cleavages and hampers social mobility.

6.2.3 *'Practicality Won over Principle'*

Shabaan reflects that in the debates over languages of instruction, 'practicality won over principle'.[71] After the Taif Agreement, a consensus emerged over reconstructing Lebanon as a multilingual society and language policy was depoliticised. Thus, Lebanon's multilingual schools reflect the functional trilingualism of Lebanese society: Arabic is the mother tongue and language of national affiliation, and English and French remain the languages of business and science.

When it is successfully implemented, as in several private schools, Lebanon's additive bilingualism creates citizens 'whose mother-tongue is neither Arabic, nor French, nor English but the movement between all of them'.[72] Multilingualism cuts across confessional lines and may even strengthen an overarching Lebanese identity among a select group of wealthy trilingual citizens. However, due to the weakness of language teaching in state schools, Lebanon's multilingual education also entrenches socio-economic inequality and strengthens class cleavages. This may fuel communal grievances and further long-term political instability when, as in the case of the Shia community, socio-economic and confessional cleavages coincide.

6.3 Northern Ireland

Like Lebanon, contemporary Northern Ireland is a largely monolingual region: just 3.7 % of residents can speak, understand, read and write Irish and less than 1 % have a similar knowledge of Ulster-Scots. However, Northern Ireland's linguistic homogeneity is relatively recent: 'the Irish-speaking community collapsed to the point of extinction' only in the late nineteenth century.[73] Declining numbers of native speakers paralleled the increasing 'symbolic and to a degree … cultural status' of Irish and its political relevance.[74]

Indeed, after partition, the consolidation of Northern Ireland as distinct from the Irish Free State became the main thrust of local language policies.[75] In 1915 the Gaelic League had called for a Free Gaelic-speaking Ireland, thereby associating the Irish language with an Irish Nationalist project.[76] In contrast, the new Northern Ireland state education system, as Chap. 3 explained, aimed to form loyal British citizens. Thus, new curricula immediately marginalised the Irish language and by 1936 Prime Minister James Craig openly opposed funding Irish teaching in schools on the grounds that 'we do not see that these boys being taught Irish would be any better citizens'.[77] His successor added that the state should not pay for the teaching of Irish, 'chief object of which is to foment antagonism to Great Britain'.[78]

The Irish language in Northern Ireland remained taught in Catholic maintained schools. However, by the 1960s, it became relegated to a symbol of resistance to the state, and only the Troubles provided impetus for its 'revival'.[79] In 1971, 'without any involvement by church and state', a group of parents established the first Irish-medium school in West Belfast.[80] They presented Irish-medium schooling as part of a right to freedom of expression for the Catholic/Nationalist minority and called for access to the Irish language as part and parcel of 'parity of esteem'.[81] Unionists remained suspicious of Irish, associating it with resistance to the Union.[82] However, the 'minority rights discourse' adopted by Irish-language activists resonated with the British state. In the late 1980s the British government started presenting Irish as part of one of the two native cultural traditions of Northern Ireland rather than as a 'foreign and subversive' element.[83]

Education policy expressed the 'reinvented' role of the state 'as a "promoter" of the Irish language'.[84] Irish was introduced in the 1989 curriculum and in 1994–5 the Department of Education Northern Ireland (DENI) provided funding for Irish-medium schools and curriculum material in Irish. The British government argued that the Irish language was 'an important strand in the complex cultural inheritance of Northern Ireland … [and should] be valued as such by all sections of the community'.[85]

6.3.1 Irish-Language Education: Not in the Cold Anymore

The Belfast Agreement recognised 'the importance of respect, understanding and tolerance in relation to linguistic diversity, including in Northern Ireland, the Irish language, Ulster-Scots and the languages of the various ethnic communities'. The British government also pledged to 'take resolute action to promote' the Irish language, to 'facilitate and encourage the use of the language in speech and writing in public and private life' and to 'place a statutory duty on the Department of Education to encourage and facilitate Irish-medium education'.[86]

Figure 6.2 shows that the number of pupils in Irish-medium education has more than tripled in a decade. In 2000, the sector accounted for less

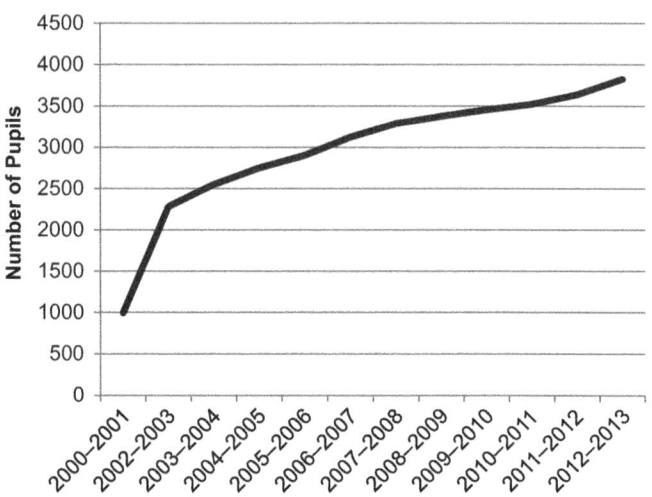

Fig. 6.2 Number of primary and secondary school students in Irish-medium education between 2001 and 2013 (Department of Education Northern Ireland, 'Children in Irish-Medium Education 2001/02-2012/13,' *Northern Ireland summary data*, http://www.deni.gov.uk/index/facts-and-figures-new/education-statistics/32_statistics_and_research-numbersofschoolsandpupils_pg/32_statistics_and_research-northernirelandsummarydata_pg.htm)

than 1 % of pupils in primary and secondary schools; in 2012–2013 it accommodated about 3 % and was available in every county.

Micheal O'Duibh of the Council for Irish-Medium Education (Comhairle na Gaelscolaíochta, CnaG) argues that Irish-medium schools expanded because of increasing parental demand. He adds that before 1998, Irish-medium education was underfunded, but the establishment of a statutory duty on DENI to 'encourage and facilitate' Irish-medium education, increased funding, and the creation of the CnaG in 2000 contributed to raising the profile of Irish-medium education.[87] The political influence of the Irish-medium sector on the Nationalist leadership also helped secure favourable concessions: for example, shortly after the Belfast Agreement, under the initiative of Education Minister McGuinness, the viability criteria for new schools were lowered to an intake of as little as 12 pupils.[88] Ultimately, as O'Duibh summarises, Irish-medium schools 'are not in the cold anymore'.[89]

CnaG portrays the Irish language as a powerful instrument for fostering cultural understanding and mutual respect among children belonging to different traditions in Northern Ireland.[90] Yet, CnaG still perceives 'a certain element of negativity from Stormont' towards Irish-medium education.[91] Indeed, Unionist parties remain suspicious of Irish-medium education, and often portray investment in the Irish language as a 'waste of money when there is English-medium education'.[92] While they do not dispute the right to learn Irish, they believe it should be 'treated like all other proper languages rather than being given a special preference, it should be like whether you're learning French or Italian'.[93]

In fact, Irish is different from 'French or Italian' in two respects. First, to a substantial portion of Northern Ireland's population, Irish is not a foreign language, but their lost native vernacular. This is why Irish-medium education adopts the immersion method.[94] Total immersion education in the Irish language for children whose mother tongue is English is offered in free-standing Irish-medium schools and in Irish-medium units in some English-medium schools. Irish-medium streams in some post-primary schools allow pupils to learn some subjects in Irish.[95]

CnaG promotes the benefits of immersion education and bilingualism for pupils. As mentioned, immersion education produces worse academic performances than both mother tongue education (English-medium in this case) and a dual-language bilingual approach.[96] However, the immersion model is the most effective method to ensure the revival of an almost extinct linguistic community. This explains why an immersion model was adopted in Irish-medium schools. These schools closely resemble language immersion programmes for indigenous minorities in their attempt to produce new speakers of a community's heritage language. Thus, the teaching of Irish remains largely confined to Catholic maintained schools and Irish-medium schools: only 6 % of Irish-medium schools are controlled and most of their pupils have a Catholic/Nationalist background.[97]

The second difference between 'French or Italian' and Irish in Northern Ireland is that, while pools of Italian and French speakers transmit their languages to their children, in Northern Ireland the 'acquisition of the Irish language will continue to depend upon the educational system rather than intergenerational transmission within family units'.[98] Irish-medium education is therefore helping cement the Catholic/Nationalist community by reviving a linguistic community that largely coincides with a denominational and national tradition. Thus, O'Duibh aptly qualifies Irish-medium as a 'cultural immersion method'.[99]

A recent ministerial *Review of Irish-Medium Education* recommended future expansion of Irish-medium education through Irish-medium streams within English-language schools.[100] Thus, O'Duibh reflects that the sector's future expansion will depend on its ability to 'normalise Irish-medium education … [so that] it's for all communities': in a predominantly 'loyalist' school, 'you may have to redefine the ethos of an Irish-medium school'.[101]

Future expansion of Irish-medium education also partly depends on DENI's fulfilment of its statutory duties: in 2011, a high court decision criticised its performance, reiterating that the duty to facilitate Irish-medium education is not 'merely aspirational' but actually 'intended to have practical consequences and legislative significance'.[102] For example, the immersion method requires different curricular approaches from those appropriate to other educational sectors, but according to CnaG, the Irish-medium sector is rarely consulted before DENI's decisions.[103]

6.3.2 Ulster-Scots: Cashing in the Cheque

An officer at the Ulster-Scots Agency suggests that the increasing profile of Ulster-Scots culture, heritage and vernacular since the Belfast Agreement is due to the fact that 'the peace process is freeing people'. He argues that decreasing fear and insecurity eased pressures for Unionists to conform to a monolithic British identity and that the recognition of Ulster-Scots culture and vernacular promoted public interest.[104]

In fact, attention to Ulster-Scots is better interpreted as 'a cultural "response" by Unionists to Nationalists'.[105] At the insistence of Unionist parties, the 2006 St Andrews Agreement redressed previous emphasis on the Irish language, establishing that 'the Government firmly believes in the need to enhance and develop the Ulster Scots language, heritage and culture'.[106]

Thus, since 2007, language policy in Northern Ireland has reflected the maxim that 'if you do it for Irish you have to do it for Ulster-Scot'.[107] However, advocates of the Ulster-Scots language recurrently call for more use of the vernacular in public life: recalling promises of parity of esteem, they complain that 'over the years we have not been able to cash in that cheque'.[108] The Ulster Scots Agency offers extracurricular modules on Ulster-Scots language, heritage and culture for schools. Newspapers periodically announce the imminent introduction of Ulster-Scots language modules in schools.[109] Indeed, reflecting the political function of the

Ulster-Scots vernacular, a prominent Unionist politician suggests that the teaching of Ulster-Scots in schools could consolidate Unionist identities: by transmitting key values and identities to children, it could 'engineer you to be... a Unionist'.[110]

In fact, there are very practical reasons why the 'cheque' of full parity of esteem for Ulster-Scots has not been cashed in. In particular, despite the wording of the St Andrews Agreement, a single, codified, 'Ulster-Scots' language does not exist. The Ulster Scots Agency sponsors an Ulster-Scots Language Forum to standardise the many dialects and vernaculars, but the forum has not produced tangible results yet.[111] Ultimately, the lack of a standard Ulster-Scots language means that Ulster-Scots cannot be employed as a language of instruction.

6.3.3 Parity of Languages

As Chaps. 1 and 3 explained, religious denomination and national allegiance emerged as the primary markers of communal identity before and during the Troubles. Vernacular languages (Irish and Ulster-Scots) remain only one of the attributes of communal belonging, and not necessarily the most significant or politically salient one in Northern Ireland.

However, the expansion of Irish-medium education and the emergence of calls for Ulster-Scots-medium education suggest that these heritage languages are being constructed as a further marker of mutually exclusive communal (and political) identities. Rather than emerging as sources of overarching identification, as Arabic in Lebanon, the Irish and Ulster-Scots vernaculars add a linguistic dimension to the confessional and national cleavages of Northern Ireland's communities. These vernaculars are rarely taught at home: by teaching them, schools help socialise children into mutually exclusive Catholic/Nationalist and Protestant/Unionist 'cultures'.

6.4 Macedonia

In Macedonia, language is the most politically salient identity marker and linguistic cleavages largely coincide with ethnic differences. As Chap. 3 explained, the codification of a Macedonian language was essential to the construction of an ethnic Macedonian collective identity. Albanian nationalism also employed language as an overarching marker of belonging.[112] Thus, after Macedonia's independence, 'the struggle over language rights constitute[d] efforts to legitimise the [Albanian] minority group itself and to alter its relationship to the [Macedonian] state'.[113] This struggle also affected education policy through long-standing debates over instruction in the mother tongue.

In Yugoslavia, children were taught in different classes depending on the language of instruction.[114] The 1991 constitution of independent Macedonia granted the right to mother tongue education, and the state provided primary and secondary education in Macedonian, Albanian, Turkish and Serbian. However, this right was severely restricted in practice.[115]

If most of the reforms included in the Ohrid Agreement were in the making before 2001, this was certainly not the case for linguistic reforms, which were implemented only because of the National Liberation Army (NLA) demands during the 2001 conflict.[116] As Chap. 3 explained, linguistic reforms reflected the new power relations between the ethnic Macedonian and ethnic Albanian communities in the context of the newly established consociation.

6.4.1 The Unintended Consequences of Increasing Access

The Ohrid Agreement established 'state funding ... for university level education in languages spoken by at least 20 percent of the population of Macedonia', and reiterated the right to compulsory education 'in the students' native languages' and to learning the Macedonian language.[117] Hereafter, the entire thrust of education policy would shift towards expanding access to mother tongue education for children of Turkish, Serbian and Albanian backgrounds.

These provisions had a limited direct impact on primary schools, which had enrolled over 90 % of children by 1999.[118] Moreover, the right to mother tongue instruction at primary school level had long been remarkably uncontroversial and students were not prevented from freely choosing their language of instruction. Figure 6.3 confirms that the Ohrid Agreement did not impact on the proportion of children attending primary school in Macedonian, Albanian, Turkish or Serbian. For example, just over 31 % of pupils studied in Albanian in 2000–2001: the proportion increased to about 32 % in 2006–2007 and about 33 % in 2011–2012.[119]

The picture is different at the secondary level, as Fig. 6.4 shows. Post-agreement governments concentrated on expanding access to secondary education for students of ethnic minority backgrounds by, for example,

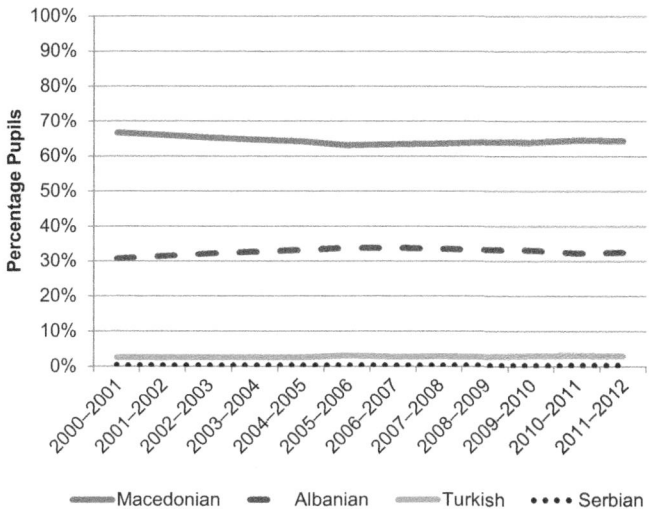

Fig. 6.3 Percentage students by language of instruction in primary and lower secondary schools in Macedonia between 2000 and 2012 (State Statistical Office, *Statistical Yearbook* (Skopje: State Statistical Office, 2006); State Statistical Office, *Statistical Yearbook* (Skopje: State Statistical Office, 2008); State Statistical Office, *Primary, lower secondary and upper secondary schools at the end of the school year, 2011/2012* (Skopje: State Statistical Office, 2013); State Statistical Office, *Statistical Yearbook* (Skopje: State Statistical Office, 2013))

building more secondary schools in deprived areas.[120] They also lowered the minimum number of children required to open an Albanian-, Turkish- or Serbian-language class, and made secondary education free and compulsory in 2008. Thus, the proportion of students attending school in Albanian grew steadily from 16 % in 2000–2001, to 18 % in 2006–2007 and 29 % in 2011–2012.[121]

Expansion of mother tongue education at the secondary level may have 'increased respect for the state' among members of some ethnic communities.[122] Certainly, it signals that consociational Macedonia recognises, values and protects the different languages of its ethnic communities and by extension their cultural specificity.

However, the successful expansion of secondary education in Albanian and Turkish had some unintended consequences for the wider education

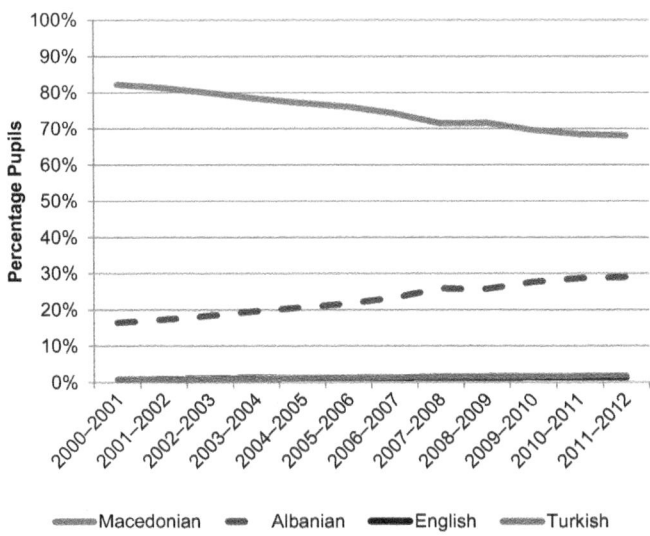

Fig. 6.4 Percentage students by language of instruction in upper secondary education in Macedonia between 2000 and 2012 (State Statistical Office, *Statistical Yearbook* (Skopje: State Statistical Office, 2006); State Statistical Office, *Statistical Yearbook* (Skopje: State Statistical Office, 2008); State Statistical Office, *Primary, lower secondary and upper secondary schools at the end of the school year, 2011/2012* (Skopje: State Statistical Office, 2013); State Statistical Office, *Statistical Yearbook* (Skopje: State Statistical Office, 2013))

system. The growing number of students forced schools to operate several shifts (with different groups of students attending school at different times of the day) or to create satellite schools. To this day, students are often divided into different shifts or buildings on the basis of their language of instruction, so the provision of 'quality mother-tongue education … usually involves having no contact with the other community'.[123] Private 'pilot' English-medium schools are ethnically mixed but only cater for upper-middle-class children.[124] Exceptions to the separation of children of different ethnic backgrounds in state schools are rare: a high-profile example is the trilingual elementary school Bashimi/Brastvo/Birlik in Gostivar.[125] Lack of contact between children of different backgrounds, as Chap. 7 discusses in more depth, may foster stereotypes and inter-group rivalry.

Moreover, in ethnically and linguistically separate school environments, children of ethnic minority background struggle to learn the Macedonian language. Since 2008, children attending school in Albanian, Turkish and Serbian have learnt English before the official state language. The constitution guarantees the right to learn Macedonian at all levels of education, but in 2007 the ethnic Albanian Education Minister Suleiman Rushiti introduced the English language from first grade and delayed Macedonian-language classes to fourth grade.[126] This reform indicated a shift from a language shelter model of bilingualism (with pupils studying in the mother tongue but learning the Macedonian language as a subject) to a voluntary segregation model (with children instructed in their mother tongue without gaining proficiency in the official language).

The delay of Macedonian-language classes to fourth grade may also have been 'a message' from the ethnic Albanian Education Minister to the ethnic Macedonian elites and the wider public: 'I want to learn a foreign language before I learn the official language'.[127] Thus, linguistic reforms in Macedonia's education system remain an expression of, or even a tool for, wider power struggles in the consociation.[128] Current arrangements are not only detrimental to language learning, but also hold potentially destabilising consequences for the peace process. First, they are depriving children of the basic means of communication across communal lines: a shared language. The poor quality of English-language education in all schools hampers the emergence of English as a shared language in Macedonia. Second, young Albanians struggle to express themselves in Macedonian, and this may hamper their employment prospects in a Macedonian-dominated labour market.[129] For their part, most ethnic Macedonians 'want other communities to want to learn the state language', but refuse to learn Albanian or other local languages.[130]

There are only two, very original, models for bilingual education in Macedonia: Mozaik kindergartens and Nansen schools. In both cases, parents often enrol children in bilingual schools because of their better infrastructure, superior quality of education 'and educated personnel'. They only come to appreciate the benefits of bilingualism at a later stage.[131] In the Mozaik kindergartens, two teachers work in parallel, speaking two languages to children.[132] In schools adopting the *Nansen model of integrated bilingual primary education*, students belonging to two communities are taught in their mother tongue in separate classes but every day they attend extracurricular activities in mixed groups. Two teachers supervise the extracurricular activities, speaking the two working languages and paraphrasing each other. Nansen Dialogue Centre Project Manager, Veton Zenkolli maintains that although students are never forced to speak languages other than their mother tongue, they generally learn the school's second language.[133] He argues that the Nansen model performs a balancing act on the 'thin line between integration and assimilation'.[134] This is because Mozaik kindergartens and Nansen schools accommodate both the principle of parity of esteem (by granting equal value, legitimacy and authority to both working languages and upholding the right to mother tongue education), and the principle of pluralism (by promoting contact and cooperation). As Chap. 7 shows, in deeply divided societies, initiatives for integration are particularly successful when, beyond fostering equality and relationship-building, they provide added value in terms of the quality of education.

The expansion of access to education has also benefited the smaller communities (the Roma, Vlachs, Serbs, Bosniaks and Turks), allowing more children to access secondary education.[135] Yet children belonging to smaller communities often struggle in primary school: Turkish- and Serbian-language education may be available, but most children attend classes in Albanian or Macedonian.[136] These students often underperform and are excluded and sometimes even discriminated against, as they do not have sufficient proficiency in the language of instruction.[137] As a consequence, dropout rates among children belonging to smaller communities are higher than the national average: in 2008 only 44.6 % of Roma children completed primary school, compared with a national rate of 82.6 %.[138]

Thus, smaller communities have criticised post-Ohrid education policy for appeasing the demands of the ethnic Macedonian and ethnic Albanian communities, while appearing to 'forget the others'.[139] They point out that the Ohrid Agreement's provisions for administrative decentralisation favour Albanian-language schools in municipalities controlled by Albanian parties and Macedonian-language schools in municipalities controlled by Macedonian parties.[140] Moreover, schools are instrumentalised in wider power struggles: for example, in September 2012, the Macedonian daily *Dnevik* reported that the Democratic Union for Integration (DUI)-controlled municipalities intended to close several Macedonian-language classes as a payback for the closure of an Albanian-language class in a Macedonian-controlled municipality.[141] Preoccupied with the ethnic Albanians and Macedonians, the government underinvested in areas populated by smaller communities, where schools accommodate even thousands of students in three or four daily shifts.[142]

6.4.2   Corrective Measures

An international observer explained that the Ohrid Agreement did not build 'bridges' between the communities only 'because it is a peace accord, it wasn't an intensive, detailed reform package'.[143] Yet by 2008, the Macedonian government was under strong international pressure to introduce 'corrective measures' in its education policy. It attempted to do so through the *Strategy for Integrated Education* (intended to reverse the ethnolinguistic separation in schools) and through the creation of a new Directorate for Development and Promotion of Education in the Languages of the Communities.

The *Strategy for Integrated Education* was formulated by the Organisation for Security and Cooperation in Europe (OSCE) and the Ministry of Education to address the increasing separation of children of different ethnic backgrounds into parallel schools, and avoid 'comparative disadvantages among the ethnic groups' in future employment prospects.[144]

While the strategy was being drafted, ethnic Albanian parties 'spoke quite clearly against it politically' and expressed their worries that integration would amount to assimilation into a Macedonian culture and language. They temporised and 'came up with all kinds of excuses', including complaints about the lack of preliminary consultation and local involvement, protesting that learning further languages would burden children.[145] In particular, ethnic Albanian parties resisted the strategy's proposal to teach Macedonian as a subject 'as soon as possible' in Albanian-, Serbian- and Turkish-medium classes. As a political counterweight, the strategy proposed offering the languages of 'communities over 20 percent and the other communities' as elective courses.[146] Ethnic Albanian parties argued that the strategy was asymmetrical: it forced children attending Albanian-, Serbian- and Turkish-medium classes to study Macedonian from first grade, but it did not require children studying in Macedonian to learn another local language.[147] Such asymmetry was inevitable: the constitution demands the teaching of Macedonian to all citizens, but does not 'give [anyone] means to force' Macedonian native speakers to learn other local languages.[148] Thus, as one of the drafters of the strategy put it, forcing every pupil to learn Albanian would be 'political suicide'.[149]

Even before the strategy was completed, Minister of Education Nikola Todorov announced that from September 2009, every child would learn Macedonian from first grade. The OSCE High Commissioner on

National Minorities Knud Vollebaek admitted that 'this initiative has caused some disquiet among non-majority communities'.[150] In fact, 'non-majority communities' interpreted the announcement as a 'pure provocation based on ethnic dominance'.[151] Ethnic Albanian political parties cried assimilation and the Democratic Party of Albanians (DPA) appealed to the Constitutional Court. Ethnic Albanian parents and teachers protested against the decision, and from January 2010, students enrolled in Albanian-language classes boycotted Macedonian lessons.[152] In July 2010, Macedonia's Constitutional Court declared that teaching the Macedonian language from first grade contradicted existing laws and annulled the provision.[153] Todorov, who had emerged as 'the saviour of Macedonian identity against the Albanians', promised to 'seek other ways to enforce the program'.[154]

Meanwhile, the *Strategy for Integrated Education* had 'basically died with language'.[155] After Todorov's announcement, the strategy remained identified with one politically controversial provision: the introduction of Macedonian-language lessons from first grade. As explained in Chaps. 5 and 7, some aspects of the strategy were later implemented, but 'language is a political issue, so it's left aside'.[156]

Recep Ali Cupi explains that when the gulf between the ethnic Albanian and ethnic Macedonian communities deepened and violent incidents started occurring in schools, governments began focusing on educational initiatives for children of Roma, Turkish, Serb, Vlach and Bosniak backgrounds. Attention to the smaller communities increased after the sidelining of the *Strategy for Integrated Education*: they emerged as a potential political buffer between the ethnic Albanians and ethnic Macedonians. Reform initiatives could be 'tested' on smaller communities and evaluated in a less politicised environment before being mainstreamed.[157] Similarly, smaller communities could provide badly needed legitimacy and support for educational change.

To tackle the sense of political and educational exclusion of the Roma, Turks, Serbs, Vlachs and Bosniaks, the Directorate for Development and Promotion of Education in the Languages of the Communities (DDPELC) was created in 2002. The DDPELC was tasked with furthering education in the Roma, Vlach and Bosniak languages, but initially maintained a low profile.[158]

The curriculum was also amended to introduce the elective subject in *Language and Culture* of the Roma, Vlach and Bosniak communities. From 2008, the subject was offered one hour per week in third grade and two hours per week between fourth and ninth grade.[159] The Ministry of Education maintains that the elective subject is only open to children belonging to the Roma, Vlach and Bosniak communities.[160] Indeed, Cupi argues that the elective subject aims to benefit children who do not speak the language of the community they belong to at home or, as he puts it, 'don't know their own language'. The elective course aims to 'strengthen [children's] belonging, their identity, which is very important. Not to give a space for cultural assimilation'.[161] This suggests that schools are employed to foster the internal cohesion and collective esteem of smaller communities in Macedonia's consociation, in the hope that this will temper their sense of political exclusion.

This approach produced negligible results. For one, very few students selected the elective course in 2008–2009, leaving the Ministry of Education and international observers puzzled.[162] In fact, a study on *Roma Language and Culture* found that the elective subject was 'more a declarative commitment of the government and relevant state institutions than [a] reality'.[163] Between 2008 and 2010, information about the subject often did not reach illiterate families, those taking seasonal work abroad or those without a permanent address.[164] The BoE, the ministry and individual schools provided contradictory information over who could select the subject, and the minimum number of students required to establish a class was sometimes set at 15, sometimes at 20.[165] Even when classes were established, teachers lacked pedagogical training and teaching qualifications.[166] Curricula existed but no one had responded to the call for textbooks, so no teaching materials were available.[167] Finally, schools often discouraged parents from signing up and parents feared overburdening their children and singling them out as different from other pupils. The study concluded that 'the State has not secured [the] necessary preconditions for the implementation of the said elective subject'.[168]

Since 2010, the DDPELC has worked to address the shortcomings in the implementation of the elective subject in *Language and Culture* of the Roma, Vlach and Bosniak communities. It organises meetings with parents in schools and has appointed textbook authors and published textbooks. The DDPELC has also attempted to provide better training for teachers of *Language and Culture* of the communities, and to create University chairs in the languages of the smaller communities. In 2012, it succeeded in introducing an elective course in *Roma Culture and Language* in the Pedagogical Faculty of the Saints Cyril and Methodius University.[169]

Enrolments in the elective classes have increased since 2010 but a fundamental dilemma remains. The state provides education in the Macedonian, Albanian, Turkish and Serbian languages according to a language shelter (or even voluntary segregation) model. Yet children from smaller ethnic communities are forced to study in a language that is not their mother tongue. They can only study their mother tongue or heritage language as an additional subject. This reflects the inter-communal power hierarchy in Macedonia's consociation and contributes to reproducing it. Children from smaller minorities face greater difficulties at school because of their limited proficiency in the language of instruction, but they also have an additional workload compared with children of Macedonian, Albanian, Turkish and Serbian backgrounds. Thus, the Foundation Open Society Macedonia observes that 'the right of these communities to study their language and culture is being provided to the detriment of the principle of equality among pupils'.[170]

Ironically, these considerations are of limited interest to many parents, who often would prefer additional classes in English or Macedonian to the elective *language and culture* of the Roma, Vlach and Bosniak communities.[171] While appreciating opportunities to cultivate their mother tongues and community traditions, members of smaller communities are deeply aware that 'the market forces say you have to know Macedonian and if you want more you have to know Albanian'.[172]

6.4.3 Walking the Line

Debates over language policy in Macedonia exemplify the need, in deeply divided societies, to walk the 'very thin line between enjoying language rights and complete separation'.[173] The language of instruction in Macedonia's state schools remains a bone of contention in highly symbolic debates over ownership of the state and its institutions, and the relationships between different communities, as demonstrated by the *Strategy for Integrated Education*.

Debates over languages in Macedonia's schools reflect the evolving status and hierarchy of different ethnolinguistic communities in the state, to an even greater extent than language debates in Lebanon and Northern Ireland. Thus, post-Ohrid language policies have hampered the learning of the Macedonian language among children of Albanian background and fostered the separation of Albanian and Macedonian children into different schools or shifts. These are the unintended consequences of the newly established parity of esteem between the ethnic Albanian and ethnic Macedonian communities. Yet debates over the language of instruction in schools also highlight the marginalisation of the Turkish, Serbian, Roma, Bosniak and Vlach communities in consociational Macedonia.

6.5 Conclusion

This analysis of language policies in compulsory schools in Macedonia, Northern Ireland and Lebanon confirms that language is the nexus between the economic, cultural and political function of education in consociations. Debates over languages of instruction reflect both the political saliency of languages and the tension between two functions of education. On the one hand, education is expected to provide the skills for future employment and full participation in society. This requires the mastering of the state language, as well as international languages. Thus, in Lebanon schools have adopted a model of dual-language enrichment bilingualism (Arabic-French or Arabic-English) and in Macedonia English-medium education is demanded and valued. Even in deeply divided societies, when bilingualism is seen as key to social mobility and when it serves the 'interests of dominant groups in the society', it is less politically contentious and more 'socially rewarded and recognised' than the teaching of indigenous languages.[174] In contrast, the latter often musters 'little support or opprobrium'.[175]

On the other hand, education reflects and reproduces inter-group relations and hierarchies. Küper reflects that 'political power and domination are not exercised in the language of those who are dominated'. He adds that it is 'quite normal that a change of political power be accompanied by a change of language'.[176] This chapter confirms that the Belfast and Ohrid Agreements inaugurated new language policies, mirroring altered political relationships and new inter-group hierarchies. In consociational Macedonia, language policy reflects the demographic weight, political assertiveness and different political status of ethnolinguistic communities. Communities 'over 20 percent' (the ethnic Macedonians and Albanians) are provided with state-funded university education in the mother tongue. Moreover, the state has long protected the right to mother tongue education of the Macedonian, Albanian, Turkish and Serb communities through a 'language shelter' model of primary and secondary education. Since 2007, this has evolved into a voluntary monolingual 'segregation programme'. In contrast, children belonging to the smaller and less assertive Roma, Vlach and Bosniak communities attend monolingual submersion education in the Macedonian or Albanian language. Thus, schools reflect and reproduce inter-group hierarchies.

Finally, this chapter shows that choices of languages of instruction can help create overarching markers of identity (as with Arabic in Lebanon), but also cement mutually exclusive ethnic, national and confessional communities. The latter is the case when language is a politically salient marker of identity, as in Macedonia, and when it overlaps with other salient cleavages, as in Northern Ireland. Indeed, in Northern Ireland, schools are helping to construct heritage languages (Irish and Ulster-Scots) as further markers of communal identity. As evident in Macedonia, decisions about the language of instruction and model of language teaching in deeply divided societies can further the physical and psychological separation between children belonging to different communities.

Notes

1. Fernand De Varennes, Qtd. in Zhidas Daskalovski, 'Language and Identity: The Ohrid Framework Agreement and Liberal Notions of Citizenship and Nationality in Macedonia,' *Journal on Ethnopolitics and Minority Issues in Europe* 1, (2002): 9.
2. Fasold, in Adama Ouane, 'The Discourse on Mother Tongues Education and National Languages,' in Adama Ouane (ed.), *Towards a Multilingual Culture of Education*, (Hamburg: UNESCO Institute for Education, 2003): 37; D.P. Pattayak, 'Mother Tongues: The Problem of Definition and the Educational Challenge,' in Ouane (ed.), *Towards a Multilingual Culture of Education*, 27; Tove Skutnabb-Kangas and Teresa L. McCarty, 'Key Concepts in Bilingual Education: Ideological, Historical, Epistemological and Empirical Foundations,' in Jim Cummins (ed.), *Encyclopedia of Language and Education Volume 5. Bilingual Education* (Philadelphia: Springer, 2008): 11.
3. Ibid., 104–105.
4. Byram, *From Foreign Language Education to Education for Intercultural Citizenship. Essays and Reflections* (Toronto: Multilingual Matters, 2008): 5.
5. Stephen May, 'Language Education, Pluralism and Citizenship,' in Stephen May and Nancy H. Hornberger (eds.), *Encyclopedia of Language and Education Volume 1. Language Policy and Political Issues in Education*, (Philadelphia: Springer, 2008): 18; Byram, *From Foreign Language Education*, 107.

6. Ibid.
7. Caoimhghin Ó Croidheáin, *Language from Below. The Irish Language, Ideology and Power in the 20th Century* (Oxford: Peter Lang, 2006): 106.
8. Byram, *From Foreign Language Education*, 28.
9. May, 'Language Education', in May and Hornberger (eds.), *Encyclopedia of Language and Education Volume 1*, 18, 24.
10. Rebecca Freeman Field, 'Identity, Community and Power in Bilingual Education,' in Cummins (ed.), *Encyclopedia of Language and Education Volume 5*, 78.
11. Byram, *From Foreign Language Education*, 82; Jim Cummins, 'Introduction,' in Cummins (ed.), *Encyclopedia of Language and Education Volume 5*, xiv.
12. Hillary Janks, 'Teaching Language and Power,' in Marilyn Martin-Jones and Anne-Marie de Mejia, *Encyclopedia of Language and Education Volume 3. Discourse and Education*, (Philadelphia: Springer, 2008): 201, 203; Patricia Baquedano-Lopez and Shlomy Kattan, 'Language Socialisation in Schools,' in Nancy H. Hornberger (ed.), *Encyclopedia of Language and Education Volume 8. Language Socialisation*, (Philadelphia: Springer, 2008): 165.
13. Herbert Weiland, 'Education and Political Change in Namibia. Equality and Inequality,' in Hanf (ed.), *The Political Function of Education*, 115; Tove Skutnabb-Kangas, 'Language Rights and Bilingual Education,' in Cummins (ed.), *Encyclopedia of Language and Education Volume 5*, 125; Brown, 'The Influence of Education on Violent Conflict and Peace', 197; Wolfgang Küper, 'The Necessity of Introducing Mother Tongues in Education Systems of Developing Countries,' in Ouane (ed.), *Towards a Multilingual Culture of Education*, 96.
14. Skutnabb-Kangas, 'Language Rights', in Cummins (ed.), *Encyclopedia of Language and Education Volume 5*, 118.
15. Qtd. in Freeman Field, 'Identity', in Cummins (ed.), *Encyclopedia of Language and Education Volume 5*, 82.
16. Brown, 'The Influence of Education on Violent Conflict and Peace,' 195–196.
17. Cummins' Theory of Developmental Interdependence, explained in Ouane, 'The Impossible Debate,' in Ouane (ed.), *Towards a Multilingual Culture of Education*, 68; Küper, 'The Necessity', in Ouane (ed.), *Towards a Multilingual Culture of Education*, 92.
18. Stephen May, 'Bilingual/Immersion Education: What the Research Tells Us,' in Cummins (ed.), *Encyclopedia of Language and Education Volume 5*, 27.
19. Will Kymlika, in May, 'Language Education,' in May and Hornberger (eds.), *Encyclopedia of Language and Education Volume 1*, 25; Daskalovski, 'Language and Identity,' 13.

20. May, 'Language Education,' in May and Hornberger (eds.), *Encyclopedia of Language and Education Volume 1*, 20–21.
21. Ouane, 'By Way of Conclusion,' in Ouane (ed.), *Towards a Multilingual Culture of Education*, 250.
22. Freeman Field, 'Identity', in Cummins (ed.), *Encyclopedia of Language and Education Volume 5*, 77.
23. Skutnabb-Kangas and McCarty, 'Key Concepts', in Cummins (ed.), *Encyclopedia of Language and Education Volume 5*, 12–13.
24. Cummins, 'Introduction', in Cummins (ed.), *Encyclopedia of Language and Education Volume 5*, xiii.
25. Ouane, 'By Way of Conclusion,' in Ouane (ed.), *Towards a Multilingual Culture of Education*, 252.
26. Qtd in Freeman Field, 'Identity', in Cummins (ed.), *Encyclopedia of Language and Education Volume 5*, 78.
27. May, 'Bilingual/Immersion Education,' in Cummins (ed.), *Encyclopedia of Language and Education Volume 5*, 20.
28. Skutnabb-Kangas and McCarty, 'Key Concepts', in Cummins (ed.), *Encyclopedia of Language and Education Volume 5*, 7–8, 13; May, 'Bilingual/Immersion Education,' in Cummins (ed.), *Encyclopedia of Language and Education Volume 5*, 22.
29. Joseph Lo Bianco, 'Bilingual Education and Socio-Political Issues,' in Cummins (ed.), *Encyclopedia of Language and Education Volume 5*, 44; May, 'Bilingual/Immersion Education,' in Cummins (ed.), *Encyclopedia of Language and Education Volume 5*, 22.
30. Skutnabb-Kangas and McCarty, 'Key Concepts', in Cummins (ed.), *Encyclopedia of Language and Education Volume 5*, 6.
31. Cummins, 'Introduction', in Cummins (ed.), *Encyclopedia of Language and Education Volume 5*, xiv; Lo Bianco, 'Bilingual Education', in Cummins (ed.), *Encyclopedia of Language and Education Volume 5*, 41.
32. Alan Smith, 'Education in the Twenty-First Century', 380.
33. Byram, *From Foreign Language Education*, 68–70.
34. May, 'Bilingual/Immersion Education,' in Cummins (ed.), *Encyclopedia of Language and Education Volume 5*, 20, 27; Cummins, 'Introduction', in Cummins (ed.), *Encyclopedia of Language and Education Volume 5*, xv.
35. Kassim Ali Shaaban, 'Bilingual Education in Lebanon,' in Jim Cummins and David Corson (eds.), *Encyclopedia of Language and Education Volume 5. Bilingual Education*, (London: Kulwer Academic Publishers, 1998): 252. Other languages are Armenian, Syriac, Kurdish and Assyrian.
36. Fida Bizri, 'Linguistic Green Lines in Lebanon,' *Mediterranean Politics* 18, no. 3 (2013): 451.

37. Ghazi M. Ghait and Kassim A. Shaaban, 'Language-in-Education Policy and Planning: The Case of Lebanon,' *Mediterranean Journal of Educational Studies* 1, no. 2 (1996): 99–100.
38. Shaaban, 'Bilingual Education in Lebanon', in Cummins and Corson (eds.), *Encyclopedia of Language and Education Volume 5*, 253; Ghait and Shaaban, 'Language-in-Education,' 101.
39. Rula L. Diab, 'University Students' Beliefs About Learning English and French in Lebanon,' *System* 34, (2006): 82; Shaaban, 'Bilingual Education in Lebanon', in Cummins and Corson (eds.), *Encyclopedia of Language and Education Volume 5*, 253; Ghait and Shaaban, 'Language-in-Education,' 101.
40. Ibid., 100; Shaaban, 'Bilingual Education in Lebanon', in Cummins and Corson (eds.), *Encyclopedia of Language and Education Volume 5*, 253.
41. Ghait and Shaaban, 'Language-in-Education,' 100–101.
42. Zeena Zakharia, '(Re)Constructing Language Policy in a Shi'i School in Lebanon,' in Kate Menken and Ofelia Garcia (eds.), *Negotiating Language Policies in Schools*, (London: Routledge, 2010): 164.
43. Bizri, 'Linguistic Green Lines,' 446.
44. Ibid.
45. Chartouni Interview.
46. Chartouni, *Conflict Resolution*, 75; Theodor Hanf, *Coexistence*, 365.
47. Ibid., 365.
48. This was the case in the (Sunni) Makassed Schools according to Mandy Terc, 'Iconisation and Linguistic Ideologies in Lebanon's Makassed Schools,' Unpublished Research Paper (American University of Beirut, 2006).
49. Chartouni, *Conflict Resolution*, 82.
50. Bizri, 'Linguistic Green Lines,' 448.
51. Shaaban, 'Bilingual Education,' in Cummins and Corson (eds.), *Encyclopedia of Language and Education Volume 5*, 259.
52. Ibid., 255.
53. Ghait and Shaaban, 'Language-in-Education,' 104.
54. Shaaban, 'Bilingual Education,' in Cummins and Corson (eds.), *Encyclopedia of Language and Education Volume 5*, 255.
55. Ibid., 257–258.
56. *Fusha* is the standard Arabic employed in writing, schools and official communication. *Ammiyya* is the spoken vernacular. Zakharia, '(Re)Constructing Language,' in Menken and Garcia (eds.), *Negotiating Language Policies*, 175; Rima Bahous, 'Multilingual Educational Trends and Practices in Lebanon: A Case Study,' *International Review of Education* 57, (2011): 747.

57. Ghait and Shaaban, 'Language-in-Education,' 102; Bahous, 'Multilingual Educational Trends and Practices in Lebanon: A Case Study,' 741.
58. Terc, 'Iconisation', 3 (focusing on the Sunni Makassed schools), 16; Bahous, 'Multilingual Educational Trends,' 741.
59. Terc, 'Iconisation,' 21, 5.
60. Interview with Munir Bashshour (American University of Beirut), Beirut, 18/06/2012.
61. Bahous, 'Multilingual Educational Trends,' 740.
62. Ibid., 452.
63. Diab, 'University Students' Beliefs,' 82–83; Bahous, 'Multilingual Educational Trends,' 740; Murad Interview.
64. Bizri, 'Linguistic Green Lines,' 451.
65. Ghait and Shaaban, 'Language-in-Education,' 103.
66. Shaaban, 'Bilingual Education,' in Cummins and Corson (eds.), *Encyclopedia of Language and Education Volume 5*, 251.
67. Ibid., 256; Bahous, 'Multilingual Educational Trends,' 744.
68. Shaaban, 'Bilingual Education,' in Cummins and Corson (eds.), *Encyclopedia of Language and Education Volume 5*, 256, 258; Jocelyne Bahous, 'What Language Should a Lebanese Child Learn First?,' paper presented at the conference on *Multilingualism and Multiculturalism in Lebanon* (Beirut, 3/12/1999), 5.
69. Bahous, 'Multilingual Educational Trends,' 746.
70. Bahous, 'What Language', 5.
71. Shaaban, 'Bilingual Education', in Cummins and Corson (eds.), *Encyclopedia of Language and Education Volume 5*, 253.
72. Bizri, 'Linguistic Green Lines,' 452.
73. Diarmait Mac Giolla Chríost, *The Irish Language in Ireland. From Goídel to Globalisation* (London: Routledge, 2005): 136, 253; Philip McDermott, 'Irish Isn't Spoken Here?' Language Policy and Planning in Ireland '*English Today* 27, no. 2 (2011): 26. Cathair Ó Dochartaigh, 'Irish in Ireland', in Glanville Price (ed.), *Languages in Britain & Ireland* (Malden: Blackwell: 2000): 7–8.
74. Ibid.
75. Ó Croidheáin, *Language from Below*, 192.
76. Sarah McMonagle, 'Deliberating the Irish Language in Northern Ireland: From Conflict to Multiculturalism?,' *Journal of Multilingual and Multicultural Development* 31, no. 3 (2010): 254.
77. Qtd. in ibid., 193.
78. John Miller Andrews, qtd in ibid., 194.
79. Mac Giolla Chríost, *The Irish Language*, 235, 16; McDermott, 'Irish Isn't Spoken Here?', 28; Ó Croidheáin, *Language from Below*, 123.

80. Bunscoil Phobal Feirste, McMonagle, 'Deliberating the Irish Language,' 255; Irish Reporter, qtd. in Ó Croidheáin, *Language from Below*, 256.
81. Ibid., 256, 123.
82. McDermott, 'Irish Isn't Spoken Here?,' 28.
83. Ó Croidheáin, *Language from Below*, 259.
84. Ibid., 260.
85. Central Community Relations Unit, 2 June 1997, qtd. in ibid., 136.
86. Rights, Safeguards and Equality of Opportunity, Reconciliation and Victims of Violence, Art.3, Art.13, *Belfast Agreement*.
87. Telephone Interview with Micheal O'Duibh (Chief Executive, Council for Irish-medium Schools), 5/03/2013.
88. Mcilwaine Interview. 15 pupils in Belfast and Derry/Londonderry. Eurydice, *Foreign Language Teaching in Schools in Europe* (Brussels: Euridyce, 2000): 29.
89. O'Duibh Interview.
90. Ibid.
91. Ibid.
92. McDermott, 'Irish Isn't Spoken Here?,' 29; O'Duibh Interview.
93. Interview with Danny Kinahan (UUP MLA and Member of the Education Committee), Stormont, 19/09/2013.
94. O'Duibh Interview.
95. Personal Correspondence with Micheal O'Duibh (Chief Executive, Council for Irish-Medium Education), 2/10/2013.
96. Cummins, 'Introduction', in Cummins (ed.), *Encyclopedia of Language and Education Volume 5*, xv.
97. According to information provided by Micheal O'Duibh, 22 % are Catholic maintained and 72 % are Irish-medium maintained; Noel Purdy, Laurence Siberry, and George Beale, 'Primary Languages in Northern Ireland: Too Little, Too Late?,' *The Language Learning Journal* 38, no. 2 (2010): 152; Mac Giolla Chríost, *The Irish Language*, 162.
98. Ibid., 170.
99. O'Duibh Interview.
100. Ibid.
101. Ibid.
102. 'Court Orders Department of Education to Reconsider Its Transport Policy for Irish-medium Secondary School. Summary of Judgment' (25/10/2011), http://www.courtsni.gov.uk/en-GB/Judicial%20 Decisions/SummaryJudgments/Documents/Summary%20of%20judgment%20-%20In%20re%20Colma%20McKee/j_sj_RE_Colm_ McKee_251011.html
103. O'Duibh Interview.
104. Interview with Officer (Ulster-Scots Agency), Belfast, 20/02/2013.
105. McMonagle, 'Deliberating the Irish Language,' 257.

106. *Northern Ireland (St Andrews Agreement) Act 2006*, 16.
107. O'Duibh Interview.
108. Robbie Meredith, 'School Children 'Could Study Ulster-Scots for GCSE',' *BBC News*, 25/07/2012.
109. For example, Robbie Meredith, 'School Children 'Could Study Ulster-Scots for GCSE',' *BBC News*, 25/07/2012.
110. Interview with Mervyn Storey (Democratic Unionist Party MLA, Chair of Education Committee), Stormont, 27/02/2013.
111. Officer (Ulster-Scots Agency) Interview.
112. David Levinson, *Ethnic Groups Worldwide. A Ready Reference Handbook* (Phoenix: Oryx Press, 1998), 8; Babuna, 'The Albanians'.
113. May, 'Language Education,' in May and Hornberger (eds.), *Encyclopedia of Language and Education Volume 1*, 26.
114. Sabani Interview; Interview with an Officer in an International Delegation, Skopje, 11/09/2012.
115. Merle Vetterlein, 'The Influence of the Ohrid Framework Agreement', 8.
116. Schenker Interview.
117. Article 6, *Ohrid Agreement*.
118. The World Bank, *School Enrolment, Primary (percentage net)*, http://data.worldbank.org/indicator/SE.PRM.NENR?page=2
119. State Statistical Office, *Statistical Yearbook* (Skopje: State Statistical Office, 2006); State Statistical Office, *Statistical Yearbook* (Skopje: State Statistical Office, 2008); State Statistical Office, *Statistical Yearbook* (Skopje: State Statistical Office, 2013).
120. Novkovski Interview; Sabani Interview.
121. State Statistical Office, *Statistical Yearbook* (Skopje: State Statistical Office, 2006); State Statistical Office, *Statistical Yearbook* (Skopje: State Statistical Office, 2008); State Statistical Office, *Statistical Yearbook* (Skopje: State Statistical Office, 2013).
122. Officer in an International Delegation Interview.
123. Officer in an International Mission Interview. See also Chap. 7.
124. Officer in an International Delegation Interview; Sabani Interview.
125. Georgieva Interview.
126. Veteroska Interview.
127. Officer in an International Mission Interview.
128. Interview with an Officer, Ministry of Education and Science, Skopje, 18/09/2012.
129. Officer in an International Mission Interview; Grodzanovska Interview.
130. Officer in an International Mission Interview; Georgieva Interview.
131. Teacher qtd. in Dawn Tankersley, 'Bombs or Bilingual Programmes? Dual-Language Immersion, Transformative Education and Community Building in Macedonia,' *International Journal of Bilingual Education and*

Bilingualism 4, no. 2 (2011): 113. Interview with Veton Zenkolli (Project Manager, Nansen Dialogue Centre), Skopje, 12/09/2012.
132. Children are aged 3 to 7. Officer, Ministry of Education and Science, Interview.
133. Ibid. Nansen Dialogue Centre, 'Nansen Model for Integrated Education' http://www.nansen-dialogue.net/index.php?option=com_content&view =article&id=475&Itemid=549
134. Zenkolli Interview.
135. Ali Cupi Interview.
136. Ibid; Sam Vaknin, 'The Education of Macedonia. Interview with Ljubica Grozdanovska of BID Consulting,' 2007 http://www.globalpolitician. com/default.asp?23540-macedonia/
137. Most discrimination is reported against Roma children according to Spomenka Lazarevska; Grodzanovska Interview.
138. United Nations International Children's Emergency Fund, *Child-Focused Public Expenditure Review* (Skopje: UNICEF Country Office, 2009): 43.
139. Grodzanovska Interview; Interview with Ana Mickovska (Policy Analyst, Centre for Research and Policymaking), Skopje, 10/09/2012; Ali Cupi Interview.
140. Sabani Interview.
141. Gotse Dechev School in Aerodrom. 'Dnevik: Action for Eliminating Macedoanian Classes in Albanian Municipalities Continues,' *Focus Information Agency*, 21/09/2012.
142. Grodzanovska Interview.
143. Officer in an International Mission Interview.
144. Tamara Grncarovska, 'Ambassador Herrero Interview in *Utrinski Vasnik*: Learning of the Language Should Not Bring These Divisions,' http:// www.osce.org/skopje/67529?download=true
145. Ibid; Schenker Interview; Interview with a Coordinator in the Ministry of Education, Skopje, 19/09/2012; Zenkolli Interview; Sinisa-Jakov Marusic, 'Macedonia 'Very Surprised' by OSCE Letter,' *Balkan Insight*, 28/01/2010.
146. Schenker Interview.
147. Ibid.; Zenkolli Interview.
148. Schenker Interview.
149. Schenker Interview.
150. Sinisa-Jakov Marusic, 'Macedonia Court Annuls Controversial Classes,' *Balkan Insight*, 15/07/2010.
151. Deralla Interview; Interview with an Officer, Ministry of Education and Science, Skopje, 18/09/2012, Interview; Schenker Interview; Lazarevska Interview.

152. Ibid.; Marusic, 'Macedonia 'Very Surprised"'; Deralla Interview.
153. Marusic, 'Macedonia Court'.
154. Ibid.; Schenker Interview.
155. Ibid.
156. Officer, Ministry of Education and Science, Interview.
157. Ali Cupi Interview.
158. Ibid.
159. Foundation Open Society Macedonia, *Analysis of the Implementation of Roma Language and Culture as an Elective Subject* (Skopje: FOSIM, 2010), 15.
160. Ali Cupi Interview; Lazarevska Interview.
161. Ali Cupi Interview.
162. Lazarevska Interview.
163. Foundation Open Society Macedonia, *Analysis*, 23.
164. Lazarevska Interview.
165. Foundation Open Society Macedonia, *Analysis*, 15–19.
166. Lazarevska Interview.
167. Ali Cupi Interview; Foundation Open Society Macedonia, *Analysis*, 17.
168. Foundation Open Society Macedonia, *Analysis*, 7.
169. Ali Cupi Interview.
170. Foundation Open Society Macedonia, *Analysis*, 16.
171. Ibid., 21.
172. Officer in an International Delegation, Interview.
173. Interview with Officer in an International Donor, Skopje, 14/09/2012.
174. Cummins, 'Introduction', in Cummins (ed.), *Encyclopedia of Language and Education Volume 5*, xiv.
175. Lo Bianco, 'Bilingual Education', in Cummins (ed.), *Encyclopedia of Language and Education Volume 5*, 41.
176. Küper, 'The Necessity', in Ouane (ed.), *Towards a Multilingual Culture of Education*, 95.

CHAPTER 7

Inter-group Contact and Separation in Schools

This chapter analyses the structure of the education system in consociational Lebanon, Northern Ireland and Macedonia to determine whether schools foster contact or separation between children from different backgrounds. It first introduces the theoretical debate over the political function of separate schools in deeply divided societies, whose essence 'concerns the right to a separate education ... against the role that separate schools are perceived to play in perpetuating divisions and sectarianism'.[1] Then, it considers initiatives to reform the structure of the education system in Lebanon, Northern Ireland and Macedonia after the Taif, Belfast and Ohrid Agreements.

This chapter shows that education policy in the three consociations navigated between the dual aims of protecting communal identities through a plurality of separate schools and promoting social cohesion through plural mixed institutions. It demonstrates that ultimately the three 'consociational' education systems privileged a plurality of separate schools over plural common schools. Thus, as in curricular policy, successful initiatives to promote reconciliation through mixed schools also accommodated demands for group equality and a better quality of education.

7.1 SEPARATE AND COMMON SCHOOLS IN DEEPLY DIVIDED SOCIETIES: THEORETICAL DEBATES

Tracing the history of education systems in Lebanon, Northern Ireland and Macedonia, Chap. 3 demonstrated that the difference between educational separation and segregation is ambiguous when the boundary between imposition of and demand for separated schools is blurred. Indeed, communities in deeply divided societies have historically viewed separate schools as tools to nurture and transmit specific aspects of group identity (such as history, language or religion). Thus, many plural societies, including Lebanon and Northern Ireland, recognise the right to schools that protect and reproduce the cultural specificities of local communities.

However, each society regulates the relationship between the state and communal schools in a different way. For example, Lebanon's education system approximates a model of *communally based schooling*, with subsidised schools fully managed by confessional communities, and state institutions 'for the unaffiliated'.[2] *Communally based schooling* is criticised for furthering the 'fragmentation of citizens into silos with unequal freedom, opportunity and civic status attached to each silo or citizen'.[3] In contrast, Northern Ireland approximates *civic minimalism*, which maximises school choice but enforces basic common educational standards through a common statutory curriculum.[4] Both in *communally based* and in *civic minimalist schooling*, 'too many of those with the power to choose opt for separate environments', and schools generally cater for uniform student bodies in terms of their income, ethnicity or religion.[5] Such informal separation 'based on customs and practice' is harder to erode than legally enforced segregation.[6]

Research suggests that separate schooling is an important expression of provisions for communal autonomy and group equality in consociations.[7] This chapter confirms that separate schools reflect the principles underpinning political consociations. It adds that consociational education systems are typically characterised by the existence of a plurality of state-funded schools catering for children from different backgrounds. This is, first, because separate schools can provide precious channels for upward social mobility in deeply divided societies. Second, equally funded and equally legitimate separate schools may contribute to peace by enhancing feelings of citizenship and stimulating loyalty to a state that 'reflects and values their cultural group'.[8] Thus, Skutnabb-Kangas claims that 'accepting temporary physical segregation as a means for achieving educational, psychological, societal and political integration of minorities and majorities later on is an absolute necessity for a human rights oriented education'.[9]

Actually, separate institutions need to be carefully managed to ensure that 'physical segregation' remains a temporary expedient and that they contribute to positive inter-group relations. If mismanaged, separate schools can perpetuate socio-economic inequality through, for example, lower quality education for certain communities. Thus, they can act as the 'seal' to iniquity rather than as an instrument for emancipation.[10] In turn, iniquity exacerbates inter-group conflicts when socio-economic cleavages overlap with communal cleavages.

Beyond contributing to material inequality, Gallagher maintains that separate schools can have a detrimental impact on social cohesion in two respects. First, separate schools can socialise children into different cultures through politicised or nationalised curricula ('cultural hypothesis').[11] Previous chapters have considered the 'cultural hypothesis' and demonstrated that even common history and citizenship education curricula can be employed to convey different and mutually hostile allegiances to children from different backgrounds, particularly when they attend separate schools.

This chapter considers the second perspective on how separate schools contribute to the perpetuation of inter-group conflicts. The 'social hypothesis' holds that the very fact of separation along ethnic, religious or linguistic lines may 'initiate pupils into conflict' by validating group differences and encouraging prejudice, hostility and fear.[12]

Indeed, evidence suggests that separate schools, regardless of their manifest curricula, 'may not rebuild social cohesion as readily as integrated schools where contact between children is sustained'.[13] First, in attempting to protect distinctive elements of group culture, schools may nurture 'essentialist identities', which are easily mobilised for conflict.[14] Thus, separate schools may convey mutually exclusive political identities, reproduce images of communities as 'homogeneous and fixed' and ignore those identities that are ambiguous, multilayered and overlapping, in order 'to maintain social harmony'.[15]

Second, Hughes shows that 'cultural and physical isolation' in school is correlated to feelings of 'suspicion and fear' towards members of other communities in Northern Ireland.[16] Indeed, separate schools can benignly accept 'long-standing prejudices' and discourage debate over the roots of conflict, thereby hampering mutual understanding and trust.[17] Combined with physical separation, this can perpetuate stereotypes, such as the belief that members of different communities have different physical characteristics.

Third, separate schools 'set up processes that maintain separation in the school and out into life beyond school'.[18] They prevent the development of inter-group friendships and further endogamy, thereby preserving the symbolic and practical security of communities.[19] Moreover, when separate schools reflect the residential separation of communities into different areas, schools can become institutional symbols of communal hold over territory.

Critics of separate schooling generally support the 'contact hypothesis', which also informs many educational initiatives in Lebanon, Northern Ireland and Macedonia. Allport's 'contact hypothesis' holds that 'prejudice (unless deeply rooted in the character structure of the individual) may be reduced by equal status contact between majority and minority groups in the pursuit of common goals'.[20] By extension, mixed schools would contribute to reconciliation in deeply divided societies.[21]

However, more tolerant individuals cannot be produced 'by osmosis': recent refinements to Allport's initial hypothesis provide important insights on what kinds of contact are beneficial.[22] They hold that optimal contact situations fulfil four basic conditions: equality between individuals or groups; cooperative contact activities presenting a common goal; avoidance of competitive situations; and legitimation of contact through institutional support.[23] Moreover, research suggests that when communal identities are salient during contact, prejudices are reduced 'via generalisation'.[24] It also proposes that when contact encourages meaningful engagement with divisive issues, it furthers mutual knowledge and understanding and helps define 'who we are in relation to them'.[25] Finally, it is argued that sustained and regular interaction among individuals from different backgrounds in a variety of social contexts can further 'recategorisation' or the adoption of overarching superordinate group identities.[26] In sum, recent empirical research found that when it meets certain conditions, as Hughes puts it, 'contact is good, and the more of it the better'.[27]

Indeed, according to recent empirical investigations, contact between individuals of different backgrounds helps reduce prejudices and anxiety in mixed environments; it encourages the exploration of personal and group identities and the understanding of multiple perspectives; and it provides opportunities to debate sensitive issues and further inter-group friendships.[28] In contrast to common misconceptions, contact does not dilute national or religious identifications.[29] Yet it results in more positive inter-group attitudes, increased empathy and respect for diversity, propensity for forgiveness, and more ability to appreciate, and even to take, alternative perspectives in a debate.[30] Contact may also affect long-term social attitudes: former integrated school students in Northern Ireland, regardless of their socio-economic background, are more supportive of mixed schools and mixed marriages, and more likely to adopt 'neutral political position[s]'.[31]

Moreover, the beneficial impact of contact may extend beyond the immediate participants. Recent research addressed the 'transfer problem', explaining how contact among a limited number of people can impact on wider society.[32] It found that the knowledge that a friend or a family member has friends from a different community moderates and improves the inter-group attitudes of individuals. By reducing fear and anxiety, 'vicarious friendship' in turn contributes to prejudice reduction.[33]

Despite its benefits, contact is not a panacea. First, contact may impact differently on different components of social cohesion and reconciliation. For example, Janmaat shows that classroom diversity is positively correlated with tolerance, but not with trust and civic participation.[34] Thus, initiatives to promote reconciliation through schools cannot be limited to inter-group contact. Second, contextual factors affect the impact of contact initiatives. For example, mixed education reduces anxiety and prejudices to a greater degree in mixed residential areas than in separated residential areas. This is because in the former, inter-group contact is consistent with the values and norms promoted by families and local communities.[35]

Third, Donnelly points out that in post-conflict plural societies, individuals belonging to minority and majority groups perceive contact differently, and contact impacts them differently.[36] Referring to Northern Ireland, she argues that members of minority groups tend to be less enthusiastic about mixed activities, and their attitudes are less affected by experiences of contact. This may reflect each group's interpretation of conflict: groups that view conflicts as the result of state-sanctioned inequality perceive personal relationships as irrelevant to peace-building.[37] Thus, they resist overemphasis on contact as a mechanism for conflict resolution, arguing that it absolves the state from its responsibility 'in the construction and maintenance of racial and ethnic divisions'.[38] Their political representatives are likely to 'believe that as long as you have equality, everything else will fall into place'.[39] Conversely, when groups view conflict as resulting from dysfunctional inter-communal relations (as majority communities often do), their members tend to favour contact as a peace-building mechanism and report more benefits from it.[40] Their political representatives generally maintain that 'we cannot hope to move beyond our present community divisions while our young people are educated separately'.[41]

This chapter shows that the tension between aspirations to encourage inter-group contact and the desire to further group equality underpinned debates over structural reforms in the education systems of Lebanon, Northern Ireland and Macedonia after the Taif, Belfast and Ohrid Agreements.

7.2 Lebanon

Bashshour argues that the 'issue of public versus private' is key to understanding the relationship between the state, confessional communities and the education system in Lebanon. He believes the following story exemplifies this relationship. In 1947, notables in a small town were offered the opportunity to establish a free state school. They refused, arguing it would threaten the viability of an existing private school, but accepted a cash gift from the state. Bashshour explains that they 'wanted money from the government but they [didn't] want the government to open a school for them'.[42] This chapter shows that nowadays, international donors face similar attitudes when they set out to finance state schools.

Indeed, private schools have a long tradition in Lebanon and are a source of national pride and prestige: since independence they have embodied the principle of freedom of education, enshrined in Article 10 of the Lebanese Constitution, but also promoted 'their own divergent views of national identity and sense of civic loyalty'.[43] Chapter 3 explained that successive Lebanese governments declared they would establish state control over private education, but in practice they diminished state supervision over private institutions and entrenched the position of private schools by subsiding them. When demands for equal opportunities for children from deprived backgrounds emerged in the 1960s, rather than investing in state education, governments expanded subsidies for private free schools. Until the 1970s, private schools competed against an expanding state education sector, but during the civil war state education dwindled and private institutions grew exponentially (Fig. 7.1).

The Taif Agreement called for the expansion of state education, but also declared that 'private education shall be protected and state control over private schools … shall be strengthened'.[44] As explained in Chapter 3, Muslim educational councils had long called for the expansion of public education and state control over private schools. Conversely, representatives of Christian schools and political parties insisted on maximally independent private institutions. The Taif Agreement attempted to square this circle.

7.2.1 Private versus Public?

The 1993 *Education Development Plan* reformulated the objectives of the Taif Agreement: it set out 'to reinforce the public sector of education', but also 'to protect private education'.[45] Bashshour commented: 'protect it against what?'[46] Indeed, Fig. 7.1 shows that the exponential growth in the number of private schools in Lebanon continued after the Taif Agreement. Most observers would agree that, since 1989, private education has continued to expand at the expense of a weakening state network. This is because private schools have a better reputation than their state counterparts.[47] Moreno found that private school students perform 10–15 % better than public school students in most exams.[48] Thus, by 2010, about

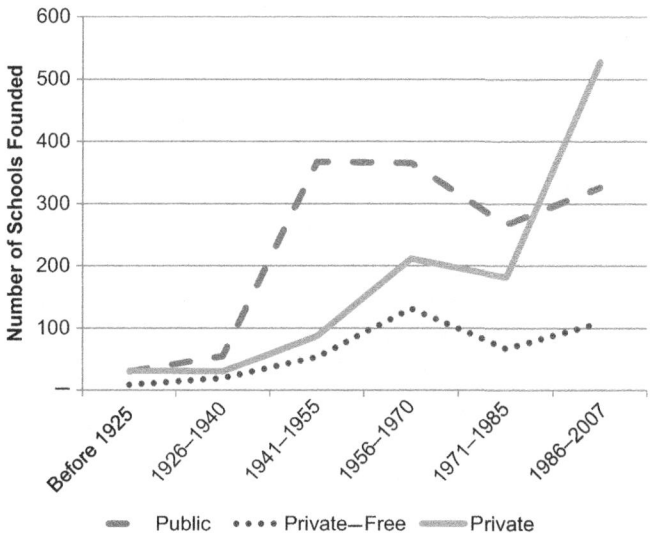

Fig. 7.1 Distribution of schools by foundation year in Lebanon (Central Administration of Statistics, *Education* (Beirut: Central Administration of Statistics, 2008))

half of Lebanese schools were private or private free (Fig. 7.2), catering for the overwhelming majority of Lebanese children (Fig. 7.3).

Despite the Taif Agreement, government institutional and financial support for state schools has been weak at best: World Bank consultant Moreno estimates that out of the 11 % of Lebanese GDP spent on education, just over 2 % of GDP 'is public money into public schools'.[49] In a 'surreal' policy, the Lebanese government provides extensive subsidies to private and private free schools, including educational grants to civil servants allowing state employees to send their children to private schools.[50]

Poor investment in state schools reveals the post-1989 diminished view of state responsibilities: rather than a provider of welfare, the state emerged simply as the facilitator of 'a good business environment'.[51] It also reflects the inability of successive governments to implement their plans in a politically unstable context. Finally, successive governments may have failed to redirect investment from the private into the public sector because of the political influence of confessional communities, whose interests lay in the survival of private confessional schools.[52]

However, donors agree that the quality gap between public and private schools, and the weakness of public education, hampers social cohesion and trust in the Lebanese state. In this view, private schools cannot promote 'national unity' if they only cater to one confessional commu-

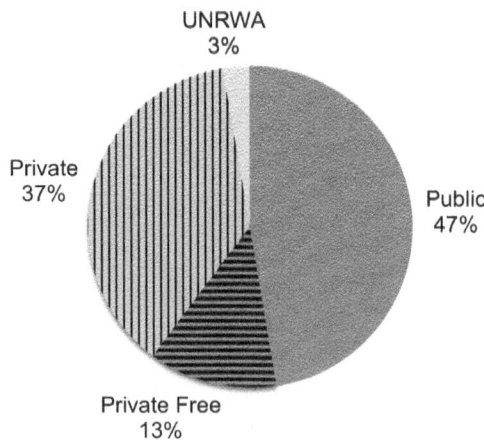

Fig. 7.2 Lebanese schools by type in 2010 (Central Administration of Statistics, *State Statistical Yearbook*)

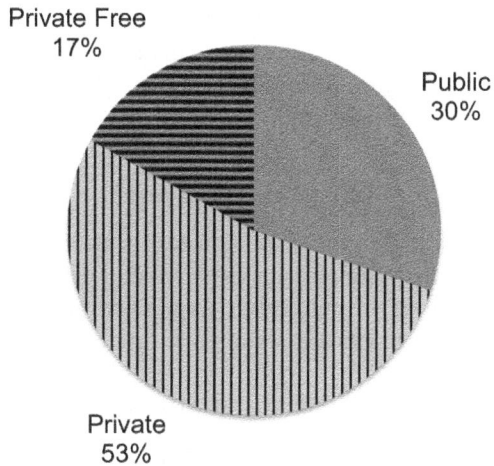

Fig. 7.3 Percentage students by type of school in Lebanon in 2010 (Central Administration of Statistics, *State Statistical Yearbook*)

nity.[53] Thus, the World Bank attempted to 'generate some [social] glue' by investing in a ten-years Education Development Project. The project aimed to improve the quality of state education and change the perception that public schools are only for the 'leftovers of society'.[54] Its impact was limited because most of its components were not institutionalised, embedded or implemented in the wider education system.[55] The United States Agency for International Aid (USAID) similarly attempted to overcome the 'atrophy' of the public educational sector through infrastructural investment, teacher trainings, community involvement in school activities, and extracurricular activities in 151 state schools throughout Lebanon.[56]

Officers in international organisations admit that in the initial stages of projects, local community leaders often campaign to divert part of the funding to private schools.[57] Reflecting on the competition between state institutions and private communal schools for international funding, Kotob suggested that perhaps education is 'a micro-dimension of what the country is'.[58] Indeed, donors appear to assume that confessional communities and the state are rivals. For example, a USAID official explained that better state services, including schools, could help construct the Lebanese state as a reference point for citizens. In turn, this would erode allegiance to confessional communities and encourage individuals to 'think about themselves as Lebanese'.[59] This perspective overlooks the fact that in

Lebanon, national and communal identities are 'hyphenated' and that the consociational state exists in a complex, dialectical and interdependent relationship with its communities. Education policy is an expression of this interdependent relationship.

7.2.2 Sterilised Jars?

Despite rhetorical support for state schools as tools to promote social cohesion, the Lebanese state remains protective of private schools: the latter are part and parcel of the cultural heritage of confessional communities and 'it would be anathema to allow the government to mingle and tamper with their things'.[60]

In contrast to Northern Ireland and Macedonia, in Lebanon, private schools largely drive initiatives for contact among children from different communal and socio-economic background. For example, in Sidon the private Hariri schools are encouraging 'economic and social' mixing by cooperating with state schools.[61] The United Nations Relief and Works Agency (UNRWA) is also promoting extracurricular activities to promote contact between Palestinian and Lebanese children. Al-Khatib argues that contact activities contribute to 'promoting the mutual understanding [between Lebanese and Palestinian children as] a prerequisite to avoid the other face of the coin, the confrontation'.[62]

El-Amine adds that even separate private schools can contribute to social cohesion if they disseminate 'a minimal level of common ideology about the state' and 'a minimum culture about citizenship'.[63] Previous chapters have shown that views of the state and of understandings of citizenship remain contested in Lebanon and that schools do not even convey a minimal sense of multiple and nested identity. However, a 2008 survey of ninth-grade students suggests that both state and private schools convey some components of citizenship: public school students expressed more 'trust in government institutions' and 'love of country', but private school students displayed more knowledge and understanding of citizenship.[64]

However, despite the Taif Agreement, the Ministry of Education has little or no control over private institutions, with three important consequences.[65] First, Daw blames private, and especially religious, schools for the diverging outlooks of Lebanon's citizens on 'moral and ethical issues'.[66] A senior officer at CERD confirms that private schools use the national curricula to convey 'their point of view, their view of Lebanon, the coexistence between Lebanese parties'.[67] Moreover, the affiliation of private religious schools impacts on their hidden curriculum: prayers, readings from the scriptures, religious symbols and exclusive extracurricular activities and summer colonies help socialise children into self-contained confessional communities.[68] Thus, Khalife argues that private religious schools are 'like sterilised jars' that insulate children from the reality of Lebanese pluralism.[69]

Second, schools affiliated to confessions and political parties can be employed to socialise children in particular political or religious orientations. For example, Erlich and Kahati reported that in a Shia religious school affiliated to Hizbollah in a Lebanese village, 'judging from appearances, one might think that [it] was in Iran'.[70] Fincham adds that UNRWA schools contribute to 'construct "difference" between "Palestinians" and "others"' because the atmosphere of UNRWA schools is affected by the history, politics and current events in the Palestinian Occupied Territories.[71] This does not hamper consociational stability unless the manifest and hidden curriculum of schools questions the legitimacy and very existence of the Lebanese state.

Third, Shuayb argues that confessional schools convey a sense of belonging and 'care by the sect' while 'the passive education in public schools will lead to negative feelings towards the secular state'. As a consequence, she shows that most children wish they attended private religious schools rather than public institutions.[72] This suggests that, beyond socialising children into communal and political identities, private religious schools also help entrench communities as the main provider of services to individuals. In contrast, the weakness of state education fosters resentment towards the state.

Moreover, Qabbani proposes that the private-public divide may reflect and entrench socio-economic divisions rather than communal fractures.[73] El-Amine adds that 'I don't think those who fought in 1975 were from private schools, they were I assume from public schools from each side, poor people'.[74] In fact, Mneimneh observes that 'public schools are not civic schools'.[75] They recruit from the most deprived socio-economic groups but they are also generally separated along communal lines.[76] Despite being secular and open to all applicants, they largely reflect the demography of their area and, due to the residential separation, children belonging to different communities attend different schools.[77] When a school caters predominantly for the members of a confessional community, teachers belonging to other confessions tend not to seek employment there.[78] Ultimately, public sector appointments often reflect the clientele of politicians: a wider patronage system instrumentalises 'state institutions to promote one's individual, factional, and communal interests'.[79]

In this light, it is easier to explain continuing state subsidies to private free schools that compete with public institutions. Private free schools are major channels for corruption and patronage.[80] Access to private free schools depends on the goodwill of local politicians or charitable organisations. Moreover, the United Nations Development Programme (UNDP) found that citizens ignore that subsidised services are financed and effectively provided by the state. Therefore, as UNDP put it, 'rights are repackaged as "favours"'.[81] Indirect subsidies to private institutions strain government resources while entrenching the role of communities as intermediaries between the state and its citizens.

7.2.3 A Communal Backyard

Yahya argues that the Taif Agreement provided an opportunity to shape a stronger, civic state, but in the following decades 'the sectarian communities have entered into the state and they have sort of turned it into their own backyard'.[82] Lebanon's consociational state and its institutions became 'extensions of … [communal] politics and negotiations'.[83]

This analysis of Lebanese education reforms substantiates Yahya's view. First, despite the reforms mapped in the Taif Agreement, the state has little or no control over private institutions. Second, the Lebanese state finances both public and (indirectly) private schools. The public education sector remains 'the weak and sick guy' and the inferior quality of public services delegitimises the state.[84] In contrast, subsidies to private schools entrench the role of confessional communities and political parties as intermediaries between individuals and the state. Thus, the fragmented structure of Lebanon's education system has an important political function: it helps consolidate confessional communities and legitimises their political elites. This confirms Moreno's view that the obstacles to education reform lie 'outside the education sector': he suggests that reforms which 'erode the confessional system would threaten the political leadership'.[85]

7.3 NORTHERN IRELAND

In contrast to Lebanon, Northern Ireland has virtually no private schools.[86] Yet, Gallagher summarises that 'for such a small place if you can think of any way of dividing the kids, we do it. We divide them in terms of class, academic selection, we divide them in terms of religion, we divide them very often in terms of gender … [and] on the basis of language'.[87] Indeed, Figs. 7.4 and 7.5 show the proportion of pupils in each sector of Northern Ireland's fragmented education system.

Chapter 3 traced the emergence of Northern Ireland's many state-funded education sectors, which differ in terms of their ethos and the backgrounds of their pupils, teachers and administrators. State-controlled schools avoid formal 'ownership of Protestant identity' but they have a 'de facto Protestant status'.[88] Similarly, Irish-medium schools are ambiguous about their ethos but accommodate primarily pupils of Catholic and Nationalist background.[89] Regardless of their communal affiliation, grammar schools have a good reputation for quality education and selectively admit pupils on the basis of their 11-plus test results.[90] In contrast, Catholic maintained schools are explicitly faith-based and openly express and convey a 'shared sense of belonging to the Catholic faith community' as well as elements of Irish identity.[91] Finally, integrated education aims at the 'education together in equal numbers of children who are more usually educated separately' and has 'constitutional and structural safeguards to encourage ownership [of schools] by the two traditions'.[92]

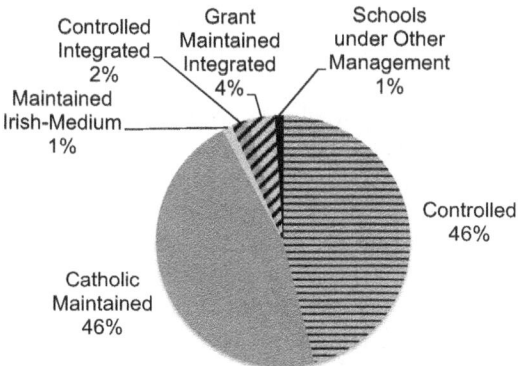

Fig. 7.4 Primary school pupils by school type in Northern Ireland in 2012–2013 (Department of Education Northern Ireland, 'Pupil Enrolment by School Type,' *Northern Ireland Summary Data*, http://www.deni.gov.uk/index/facts-and-figures-new/education-statistics/32_statistics_and_research-numbersofschoolsandpupils_pg/32_statistics_and_research-northernirelandsummarydata_pg.htm)

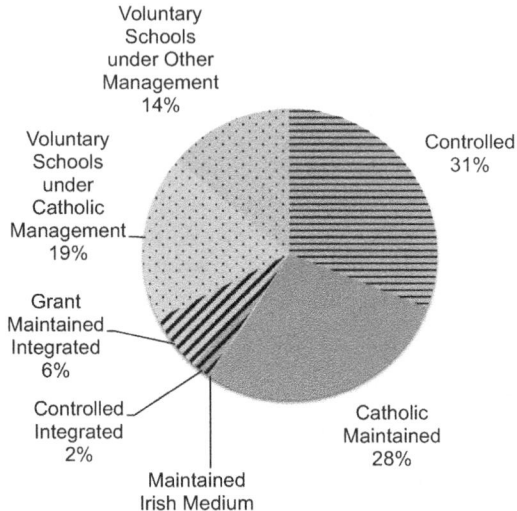

Fig. 7.5 Post-primary students by school type in Northern Ireland in 2012–2013 (Central Administration of Statistics, *State Statistical Yearbook*)

Recent data show that in 2011, half of the children in Northern Ireland studied at schools where over 95 % of students belonged to one community.[93] Figures 7.6 and 7.7 confirm that Catholic maintained schools cater primarily for children of Catholic (and by extension Nationalist) backgrounds, while controlled schools accommodate primarily children of Protestant (and Unionist) backgrounds.

This section considers successive attempts to reform the fragmented structure of Northern Ireland's education system since 1998. Reform initiatives responded to two fundamental concerns. First, as mentioned, some argue that separate schools perpetuate inter-communal conflict by limiting interaction between people of different backgrounds, allowing differential teaching of the common curriculum, and hampering dialogue over controversial topics.[94] Accordingly, separate schools 'initiate children into separate customs and attitudes' and 'crystallise the religious and political differences of the two communities'.[95] Conversely, mixed schools would contribute to social cohesion and reconciliation or, as the Belfast Agreement puts it, 'a culture of tolerance'.

Second, demographic changes have cast doubts over the long-term financial feasibility of Northern Ireland's education system. In 2011–2012, the

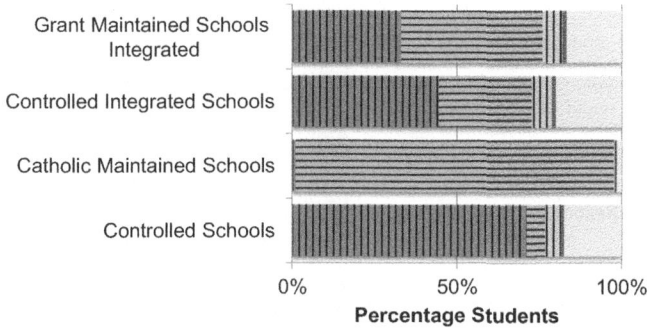

Fig. 7.6 Religion of primary school pupils by school type in Northern Ireland in 2012–2013 (Department of Education Northern Ireland, 'Pupil Religion by School Type and Management Type', *Northern Ireland Summary Data*, http://www.deni.gov.uk/index/facts-and-figures-new/education-statistics/32_statistics_and_research-numbersofschoolsandpupils_pg/32_statistics_and_research-northernirelandsummarydata_pg.htm)

Department of Education for Northern Ireland (DENI) found 82,472 empty spaces in schools, equating about 150 empty schools.[96] The 2006 Independent Strategic Review of Education suggested that school collaborations could lead to savings of up to 79.6 million British pounds in the education budget.[97] Successive rationalisation reports also underlined the financial benefits of 'a unified system of common schools'.[98] Ultimately, in the current economic climate, Storey claims, 'we can't have four of everything'.[99]

7.3.1 Facilitate and Encourage Integrated Education

In 1998, the Belfast Agreement called for 'the promotion of a culture of tolerance at every level of society, including initiatives to facilitate and encourage integrated education'. Following this, DENI established a *Towards a Culture of Tolerance: Integrating Education* working group, which included representatives of different educational sectors and educational experts. When the working group met, the representatives of the Council for Catholic Maintained Schools (CCMS) proposed looking into 'ways of promoting tolerance through all types of schools' rather than

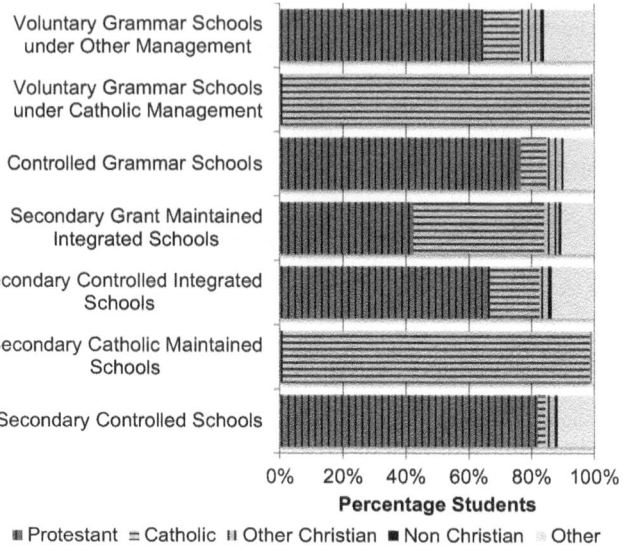

Fig. 7.7 Religion of secondary school students by school type in Northern Ireland in 2012–2013 (Central Administration of Statistics, *State Statistical Yearbook*)

only considering how to expand integrated schools.[100] The terms of reference of the working groups were amended accordingly.

This anecdote exemplifies the main challenge to the promotion of integrated schools in Northern Ireland: integration is understood in a myriad of ways. Indeed, public opinion polls highlight strong public support for integrated education, mixed schooling and more contact between children of different backgrounds.[101] However, polling questions present integrated education, mixed education and shared education as interchangeable, when in fact they are completely different methods of promoting intergroup contact through schools. Integrated schools are 'common schools attended by children of different traditions'.[102] As Chap. 3 explained, they were created by parents and are founded, according to the Northern Ireland Council for Integrated Education (NICIE), on principles of equality, faith and values, social responsibility, and parental involvement. They enrol equal numbers of children belonging to the Catholic and Protestant traditions: far from being an empty 'box-ticking' exercise, this ensures that no community feels assimilable.[103] In contrast, mixed schools are 'separate schools with a significant minority from other tradition'.[104] Finally, shared education is 'separate schools with some shared resources, pupil contact and collaboration between them'.[105]

This terminological ambiguity partly explains why, despite overwhelming support for more mixing in education, integrated education stagnates. Indeed, integrated schools have expanded from the 28 pupils in Lagan College in 1981 to the current 21,503 students in integrated education (or 7 % of total enrolments).[106] Yet Fig. 7.8 shows that expansion peaked before the Belfast Agreement and has slowed since 1999.

There are also practical challenges to the expansion of integrated education. In particular, demographic and financial constraints hamper the establishment of new integrated schools. Since the late 1990s, DENI has increased financial incentives for existing schools wishing to transform into integrated establishments.[107] Transformation 'is a longer journey': it requires progressive change in staff, integration of library contents, timetable changes and a new approach to curricula of, for example, religious education. The procedures for transformation also remain complex: they involve a decision by the boards of governors, a public meeting, a public vote, a vote among parents and the approval of schools within a ten-mile radius.[108] This discourages transformation. Indeed, DENI reports that 42 schools in Northern Ireland are mixed (with 10 % or more pupils of a different tradition) but have no intention of transforming.[109] Finally, DENI refuses a request for transformation if it threatens the viability of an existing controlled or Catholic maintained school. In this case, children demanding integrated education are diverted into a different school sector. As Fitsimmons notes, 'that would not happen in any other sector; you would not force a Catholic child who wanted to go to a Catholic maintained school into a Protestant controlled school'.[110]

Thus, DENI has been accused of interpreting its statutory duty to 'encourage and facilitate' integrated education as 'a requirement only to be responsive to parental demand rather than … actively seeking opportunities to increase the number of integrated or common schools'.[111] The Integrated Education Fund argues that parents would send their children to integrated schools if more places were available and reports that applications to integrated schools are frequently turned down because of the lack of places (1000 applications were refused in 2001, and 500 in 2005).[112] Still, not all integrated schools are oversubscribed, most parents 'will choose a good school over an integrated school' and there are relatively few demands for the transformation of existing schools into integrated status.[113] McDevitt points out that if there was a strong desire

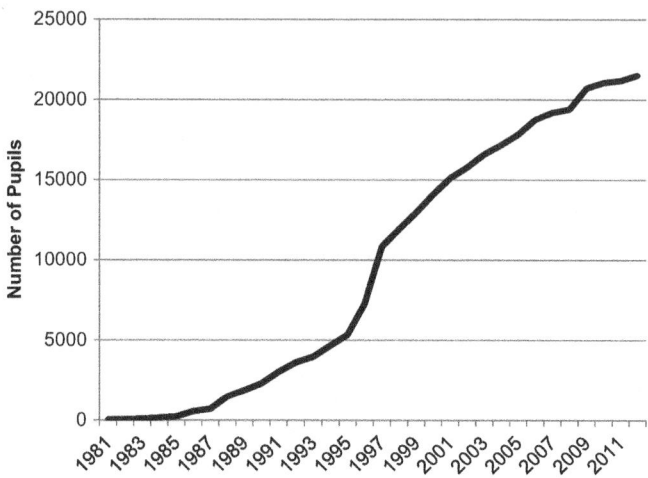

Fig. 7.8 Number of students in integrated schools in Northern Ireland between 1981 and 2012 (Department of Education Northern Ireland, *Northern Ireland Summary Data*, http://www.deni.gov.uk/index/facts-and-figures-new/education-statistics/32_statistics_and_research-numbersofschoolsandpupils_pg/32_statistics_and_research-northernirelandsummarydata_pg.htm)

for integrated education, 'all of our schools would be integrated by now, because we've had the option to … [integrate] for nearly forty years, and for 20-odd years we've had a duty'.[114]

7.3.2 A Sterile Debate?

The most fundamental achievement of the integrated education movement is undoubtedly that 'attacking the aim of educating children together has become increasingly difficult if not impossible in mainstream religion and politics'.[115] However, despite the Belfast Agreement, the expansion of integrated schools remains highly controversial.

First, it is criticised because of the purported impact of integrated schools on national and religious identities. McDevitt observes that integrated schools convey 'a common allegiance to a state', thereby effectively privileging Unionist over Nationalist narratives of the state.[116] This may explain why the Catholic Church and CCMS maintain that mixing does not require integrated education.[117] Moreover, integrated schools have been criticised for neutralising identities by, for example, not displaying symbols of national and confessional belonging.[118] Research confirms that integrated education affects social attitudes, generates more 'positive positions' on politics, religion, identity, mixed marriages and integrated schooling, and produces 'less extreme attitudes'.[119] It may even facilitate the emergence of a complementary and overarching 'integrated identity' among students.[120] Yet inter-group contact does not impact national, religious or sociopolitical self-identification among students.[121] Thus, political opposition to integrated schools may reflect more worry about electoral results than concern with religious and national integrity. Indeed, Farry reflects that 'political parties who are organised and who appeal to an electorate based on a sectional basis' have no interest in promoting initiatives that would 'undermine the cohesion of what are essentially separate constituencies'.[122]

Second, reflecting a long-standing tradition of Unionist insistence on integration through state-controlled schools, in 2010 First Minister Peter Robinson called Northern Ireland's education system 'a benign form of apartheid' and blamed the fragmented education system for the continuing divisions in society.[123] The DUP and other Unionist parties argue that integrated schools receive preferential treatment, endanger state schools and contribute to their demise. In particular, Storey views transformation into integrated status as a survival strategy, 'a vehicle to try and squeeze out of the system all the benefits'.[124] Echoing Bashshour's view of private education in Lebanon, he adds that 'the state system is good enough to give the money but it ain't good enough for them [integrated and Catholic maintained schools] to be part of it'.[125] The rigid quotas and complex process of transformation discourage many schools from becoming integrated, but all of the 17 schools that have transformed to date are state-controlled schools.[126] Thus, some argue that transformation is depriving the Protestant community of its schools while leaving the Catholic maintained sector intact.[127] As noted in Chap. 3, the asymmetric impact of integrated education on the state-controlled and Catholic maintained sectors has, since 1998, added to Protestant/Unionist feelings of relative deprivation.

However, integration through the state-controlled sector is not a realistic option. The state-controlled system is 'deemed as [religiously, culturally and politically] Protestant' by all communities in Northern Ireland and this hampers the potential both for genuine integration and for beneficial inter-group contact in state-controlled schools.[128] Indeed,

NICIE maintains that children belonging to minority traditions in both state-controlled schools and Catholic maintained schools experience assimilation and hide their identities.[129] Even Robinson's call for the end of educational 'apartheid' appeared to some as the expression of 'anti-Catholic' or anti-Irish attitudes.[130]

Moreover, Fig. 7.9 confirms that enrolment in primary state-controlled schools has declined steadily since the Belfast Agreement. The picture is similar for post-primary schools.[131] Yet this has little to do with the expansion of integrated education: it reflects the overall demographic decline and the shrinking of the Protestant/Unionist community. Additionally, pupils in Catholic maintained schools perform better than their peers in controlled schools: in non-selective Catholic maintained schools, 73.7 % of pupils gain five or more good GCSEs (General Certificate of Secondary Education), compared with only 59.2 % in non-selective controlled schools.[132] Due to the better quality of Catholic maintained schools, increasing numbers of children of Protestant/Unionist background attend Catholic maintained schools.

Third, integrated schools are criticised for having failed to produce 'wonderful citizens' and 'bring communities together'.[133] Research suggests that, in its emphasis on the benefits of contact per se rather than on schools' contributions to tackling differences, the integrated education movement may have 'lost a sense of purpose'.[134] In fact, until the recent introduction of the *Community Relations, Equality and Diversity Policy*, inspections did not assess the depth of integration and the contribution of schools to mutual understanding and reconciliation. Thus, different integrated schools adopted different approaches to diversity and integration: at one end of the spectrum, *proactive approaches* involved planned policies and activities to further integration. At the other end, *passive approaches* allowed integration to happen naturally.[135] *Passive approaches* were more frequent in transformed integrated schools than in schools founded as integrated, particularly at the primary level.[136] They can make inter-group contact ineffective by, for example, neutralising rather than making salient the identities of Protestant/Unionist and Catholic/Nationalist.[137]

To critics, the failure of integrated schools to produce 'wonderful citizens' confirms that social integration should be allowed to happen naturally rather than be encouraged.[138] In fact, recent research suggests that, despite its limits, integrated education has an overwhelmingly positive social impact in deeply divided societies. Unlike short-term cross-community projects, it provides sustained and positive contact.[139] The

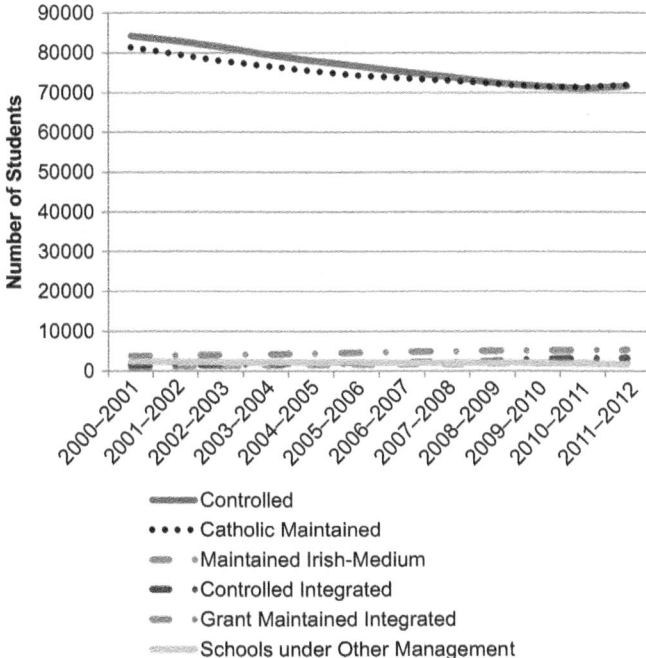

Fig. 7.9 Pupil enrolments by primary school type in Northern Ireland between 2000 and 2012 (Department of Education Northern Ireland, *Northern Ireland Summary Data*, http://www.deni.gov.uk/index/facts-and-figures-new/education-statistics/32_statistics_and_research-numbersofschoolsandpupils_pg/32_statistics_and_research-northernirelandsummarydata_pg.htm)

quantity and quality of inter-group contact predicts children's attitudes to different others and propensity to forgive. Thus, integrated school students display more respect for diversity, greater empathy and increased appreciation of different sides of an argument.[140] Mixed schooling also promotes security and confidence in mixed groups as well as mixed friendships.[141] Finally, recent research has demonstrated that friends and family members of individuals involved in sustained and positive contact through integrated education also experience reduced prejudice and anxiety.[142] Despite these findings, even wholehearted supporters of integrated education admit that the integrated education movement did not create momentum for the integration of the whole education system and remains 'a small sector that's very closed within itself'.[143]

Indeed, Gallagher argues that the politicisation of arguments over separate and integrated schools in Northern Ireland has led to an increasingly 'sterile debate'.[144] Despite public opinion polls, it is clear that parents and communities treasure particular school sectors. In Northern Ireland, schools remain an expression of identity and culture and there is very little appetite for a non-denominational integrated system. As McDevitt puts it, 'people relate to schools that they feel uphold their positive sense of identity, be that national, be that religious … be that cultural, be that social, be that political'.[145] For example, the Catholic/Nationalist community views Catholic maintained schools as a symbol of its successful struggle for social mobility and political equality. On the one hand, the CCMS defensively claims that separate sectors are 'not necessarily working against the objectives of what was the Good Friday Agreement'.[146] On the other hand, Sinn Féin, holder of the education portfolio since 1999, maintains that 'respecting diversity means respecting diversity of provision'.[147] Reflecting its view of the conflict as resulting from state-sponsored inequality, Sinn Féin emphasises communal equality and parity rather than inter-group contact as the key to conflict management.[148] This results in the promotion of a plurality of equally funded education sectors.

Moreover, if common schools existed, they would probably reflect the demographic realities of their separate catchment areas (as they do in Lebanon). Indeed, over 90 % of Northern Ireland's public housing is separated.[149] In separate residential areas, schools can serve as bulwarks in wider 'battles for territory'.[150] For example, during the 2001 Holy Cross School dispute, Protestant residents picketed the entrance to a Catholic primary school in north Belfast to prevent Catholic parents and children from walking through 'their' area.[151] This suggests that alternative models to accommodate group equality while building trust, confidence and tolerance may be necessary before promoting a mixed education system.

7.3.3 Sharing

According to the Ministerial Advisory Group on Shared Education, *shared education* is 'two or more schools … from different sectors working in collaboration, with the aim of delivering educational benefits to learners, promoting the efficient and effective use of resources, and promoting equality of opportunity, good relations, equality of identity, respect for diversity and community cohesion'.¹⁵² As mentioned, *shared education* is fundamentally different from integrated education: integrated education applies an immersion model, while shared education is limited cooperation between different institutions.¹⁵³

Gallagher traces the idea of *shared education* back to the reflection that separate schools institutionalise boundaries between children of different backgrounds, while integrated schools eliminate these boundaries. 'But would there be a way of leaving those boundaries in place but making them less important? Making them porous?'¹⁵⁴ The idea of *shared education* also emerged from the finding that 'it is the cross-community contact of integrated education, rather than the ethos of integrated education, which promotes positive out-group attitudes'.¹⁵⁵ Thus, *shared education* attempts to provide opportunities for sustained, meaningful and positive inter-group contact without challenging the ethos and affiliation of schools. In contrast to integrated education, which evolved into a third educational sector, it aims to permeate every existing sector of schooling by 'bring[ing] the separate schools together on a curricular basis and offer[ing] children an opportunity to study together for a sustained period of time'.¹⁵⁶ Participating schools share their facilities and expertise and students move between schools for their classes. For example, Shimna Integrated College, a school with 'specialist status in modern languages', employed *shared education* activities to share its language teachers with local primary schools.¹⁵⁷

Recent evaluations confirm that sharing provides some of the same benefits as integrated education. It allows children to meet different others, and provides sustained and regular contact even in very tense areas. This results in less prejudice, increased trust and forgiveness, an increase in mixed friendships and declining anxiety.¹⁵⁸ In the short term, superficial contact may increase inter-group tensions, but schools are supported in managing the diversity created through cooperation.¹⁵⁹

Moreover, sharing helps schools deliver the full range of the Entitlement Framework and complements Area Planning. The Entitlement Framework requires every school to provide a minimum of 24 courses at GCSE level and a minimum of 27 courses at A-level.¹⁶⁰ Its primary aim was to provide students with more educational opportunities, but very few schools are large enough to provide such a variety of academic and vocational subjects without collaborating with other institutions.¹⁶¹ Thus, inter-school and inter-sector cooperation 'was a good thing that we didn't anticipate when the policy was being developed'.¹⁶² Similarly, *shared education* encourages collaborative school networks and furthers teachers' sharing of good practices across sectors.[163] This aids Area Planning, which aims to create positive interdependence between self-constituted networks of schools. In turn, school networks are expected to plan to reduce the number of empty desks while delivering a 'range of options' to pupils so they can help institutionalise the inter-sectoral networks established through *shared education*.[164]

Most education sectors support *shared education*: its academic and financial benefits make it appealing for school managers, parents and school principals.[165] Moreover, sharing is appreciated, but not 'to such an extent that it would call into question whether or not their separate schools should exist'.[166] Indeed, some schools worry that *shared education* will erode their institutional identity or dilute their quality.[167] Yet Murphy reflects that 'no one has really asked the question how is this affecting our value-based education': most assume that the impact will be minimal.[168] Actually, *shared education* presents an important challenge to Catholic maintained schools: the need to 'protect the distinctiveness of Catholic education as [it enters] a shared future with other sectors'. This effectively 'mirrors the challenge for society generally'.[169] *Shared education* also challenges the state-controlled sector. As mentioned, inter-group contact is most beneficial when identities are salient and 'we define who we are in relation to them'.[170] By avoiding ownership of a Protestant/Unionist identity, state-controlled schools may be 'denying Protestant children a basis on which to engage with their Catholic peers'.[171]

In contrast, supporters of integrated education view *shared education* as a 'watered down version' of integration and worry that it may further legitimise the fragmented education system.[172] Integrated education and *shared education* appear to be competing for pupils, political support and financial resources.[173] Moreover, in 2013 the Ministerial Advisory Group on Shared Education argued against promoting an integrated education system because 'promoting one sector over others would be divisive'.[174] Thus, NICIE is justified in its 'concerns that shared education is very much on the agenda and integrated education appears to be almost a dirty word'.[175]

Undoubtedly, public and political discourse has shifted from expanding integrated schools to furthering *shared education*. The 2011–2015 Programme for Government includes no commitments to integrated education. Rather, it promises more sharing of facilities and more opportunities to participate in *shared education* activities by 2015.[176] Recent polls also show higher public support for sharing in education than for integrated education.[177] This is perhaps because shared education respects the institutional integrity of schools, allows parents to enrol children in the school of their choice, does not threaten the school as an expression of community identity and does not express explicit community relations aims. In short, 'it doesn't have the same connotations as integrated education'.[178]

Public support may also reflect the fact that 'the language of *shared education* is a catch-all term which all the key stakeholders can buy into'.[179] All main political parties declared support for *shared education* in their recent manifestos.[180] Yet, there are a variety of interpretations of the ultimate aim of sharing: some envisage a single education system while others welcome only more connections between distinctive institutions. Indeed, the most fundamental criticism of *shared education* is that there is no 'end-game' to sharing and this perpetuates acceptable levels of segregation.[181] Thus, some warn that sharing facilities may simply lead to 'two schools under one roof', an arrangement rarely conducive to better understanding and inter-communal relations.[182] In contrast, advocates of *shared education* argue that no ultimate aim can be stated, as local models are allowed to develop organically within each network of schools.[183]

Therefore, Gallagher sees several 'possible futures here': if *shared education* is mainstreamed, it could lead to a system of common schools or allow the survival of separate sectors which routinely cooperate.[184] In either case, *shared education* would help build relationships and cooperative networks across communal lines: these have been proven to contribute to peace in plural societies. Through inter-group cooperative networks, *shared education* may help move society 'out of conflict and into a space where relations are different'.[185] The risk is that *shared education* initiatives may also get diluted to the point that 'anything becomes shared education'.[186] Ultimately, echoing the peace process, Gallagher argues that 'what we are doing is creating a process with enough guarantees in it that people won't be forced to go somewhere they don't want to go and leave it up to people to make their own decisions later down the line'.[187]

7.3.4 Change in the Air?

Shared education is not the only innovation in Northern Ireland's education system and most policymakers, experts and politicians recognise that currently, reforms 'are all in the air'.[188] However, McCallister warns that current reforms may only be 'reinforcing what you're trying to move from': the fragmentation of Northern Ireland's education system.[189]

For example, during direct rule, the Education and Skills Authority (ESA) was planned as a technocratic body. It was expected to rationalise and streamline the structures of educational management in Northern Ireland, provide consistency of access to services and tackle educational underachievement.[190] Yet its establishment fell hostage to clerical and political interests. In 2007, the ESA governing board and wider structure were reframed to reflect the interests of owners of school buildings (the Methodist, Church of Ireland, Presbyterian and Catholic Churches) and political parties.[191]

Further reforms to the ESA structure were presented to the Education Committee in 2012. However, the 2012 Education Bill encountered the staunch opposition of Unionist parties. Controversies mounted over the exclusion of integrated and Irish-medium schools from the ESA governing body and over the extent of autonomy of voluntary grammar schools.[192] Political representatives also debated the creation of a unified body to represent state-controlled schools within ESA. On the one hand, a unified controlled governing body could redress the fragmentation of the state sector and improve its performance. On the other hand, it appeared to further 'this other thing, that never existed before' in state schools: a Protestant ethos.[193] Through its governing board and supporting structures, the proposed ESA appeared to consolidate rather than erode the barriers between different education sectors.

By September 2013, Kinahan summarised that 'the Sinn Féin Minister knows that when the bill comes through we [UUP] will put in massive amendments, the DUP will put in massive amendments, and so the negotiations are going on'.[194] In April 2014, after a seven-year stalemate, Education Minister O'Dowd sounded the 'death-knell' for ESA and ordered DENI to stop working on its establishment 'at this stage'.[195]

The continuing stalemate over ESA exemplifies the difficulties in eroding the structural barriers between institutions affiliated to different communities in a consociation. It also highlights the failure of Sinn Féin's approach to education policy. As with the abolition of the 11-plus test, Unionist parties resented that Sinn Féin had 'decided education is going to be one way and one way only, and they're going to get there, whatever means they need to choose'.[196] While Sinn Féin eroded the resistance of all professional and educational bodies, Unionist parties still maintained that they would veto the Bill.[197] No educational considerations explain the

ESA stalemate: the *Belfast Telegraph* summarised that 'what this shambles demonstrates is the dysfunction of politics at Stormont when it comes to compromise over party dogma or vested interests'.[198]

7.3.5 *Less Divided but Not Less Diverse*

In 1998, the Belfast Agreement called for 'initiatives to facilitate and encourage integrated education'. Yet most politicians argue that Northern Ireland's fragmented education system has changed very little since 1998.[199] Ultimately, many accept that 'the system will continue to be segregated along religious lines certainly for the foreseeable future'.[200] Certainly the duplication of services is straining Northern Ireland's finances, but a system of common schools is not a 'realistic option'.[201]

Education reforms explicitly aimed at 'community[-relations] outcomes' generally fail when they challenge existing identities, communal institutions or religious establishments in consociations.[202] Northern Ireland's *shared education*, with its emphasis on academic and financial benefits, may have succeeded in squaring the circle and placing sustained and meaningful inter-group contact at the heart of education reform strategies. Yet it has also signalled a shift in political rhetoric 'to education policies that plan for separate development rather than structural change'.[203] Indeed, in 2013 the Ministerial Advisory Group on Shared Education concluded that 'while the vision of a plurality of schools is respected and encouraged this must be within the context where strong efforts are made to ensure that different types of school collaborate together in a sustained and meaningful manner'.[204]

There is still considerable disagreement on whether education reform should tackle the separation of schools along religious and national lines. In particular, Hazzard summarises that 'to separate our kids either on cultural background, religious background, even social background, is wrong', but it is equally 'wrong to say that a faith based school can't promote the ideals we want society to have'.[205] Thus, Sinn Féin has promoted education reforms aimed at encouraging socio-economic equality and socio-economic mixing in schools rather than attempting to employ schools for relationship-building between Protestants/Unionists and Catholics/Nationalists.[206] This approach has led to the 'charade, that exists only in Northern Ireland, of academic selection' and the 'costly white elephant' of ESA.[207] In turn, the stalemate over ESA validates the fear of many politicians that it is important that 'sharing does not become owned by any party, because once a party tries to own an issue, by definition, it excludes other parties from being able to support it'.[208]

Ultimately, this analysis of initiatives to encourage mixing in schools in Northern Ireland shows that education reform cannot change society, but it can make schools flexible enough to accommodate rather than hinder social change and reconciliation. After all, as McDevitt puts it, 'you want [Northern Ireland] less divided but you don't want it less diverse'.[209]

7.4 MACEDONIA

Compulsory education emerged as a tool for building a nation-state in independent Macedonia. Here, as Chaps. 3 and 7 show, the right to education in the mother tongue became a symbol of wider struggles for the inclusion of ethnic minorities in the institutions and narratives of the new state. These struggles culminated in the 2001 conflict, which hampered the operation of some schools, created tensions within mixed schools and accelerated the residential separation of ethnic communities.

The Ohrid Agreement aimed to tackle the sociopolitical inequality between ethnic Albanians and ethnic Macedonians and to expand access to state services, including schools, for all citizens. Chapter 6 demonstrated that after 2001, shared government succeeded in expanding access to mother tongue education for children of Albanian, Turkish and Serbian backgrounds. However, the agreement 'does not provide any linkages' between Macedonian-, Albanian-, Turkish-, and Serbian-language schools.[210] This section focuses on the impact of the Ohrid Agreement on the overall structure of Macedonia's education system, examining provisions for decentralisation first, and initiatives to expand mother tongue education second.

7.4.1 Devolving Education

Sabani argues that the Ohrid Agreement impacted on primary education mainly through its provisions for decentralisation.[211] Indeed, the agreement called for enhanced 'powers of elected local officials' and enlarged 'competencies in … public services' including education. This decentralisation was expected to allow educational change, to depoliticise decisions over schooling reforms, and to produce policies reflecting more closely the needs of all citizens, including the members of smaller ethnic communities.[212] In fact, decentralisation did not alter the basic centralised structure of Macedonia's education system. Rather, it facilitated the evolution of its schools from instruments for nation-state building to tools for cementing the mutually exclusive ethnic, linguistic and political communities in the state.

Education was one of the first responsibilities devolved to municipalities in 2005. Hereafter, municipalities became school founders and owners with the power to appoint school directors and pay for the salaries of teachers and supporting staff.[213] Despite the official political discourse, Macedonia's educational decentralisation was quite limited: the government could revoke unilaterally the powers of municipalities over education, and Skopje determined funding allocations, curricular contents and pedagogical approaches.[214]

Moreover, the impact of decentralisation was curtailed by the lack of local capacity among school directors, school boards and parent councils. Indeed, despite the creation of the ambiguous professional figures of municipal education instructor and municipal education officer, some mayors recognised their lack of local capacity and attempted to return their responsibilities to Skopje.[215] Additionally, school appointments came to reflect the clientelistic networks of politicians: new mayors repeatedly dismissed school directors and staff to replace them with individuals affiliated to their political party.[216]

Furthermore, decentralisation has not depoliticised the financing of education: critics report that unclear procedures for the allocation of block grants translate into higher financing for municipalities ruled by majority parties.[217] Similarly, procedures for the allocation of funding do not make the school network more adaptable to changing demography. Decentralisation may have made it easier to open Turkish-, Albanian- or Serbian-language classes. Yet decisions on whether to open new classes and build new schools are still in the hands of the Education minister. These decisions are dictated by political as much as financial concerns. Thus, Sabani and Lyon observe that the school network still reflects the demography of the 1960s and has not adapted to urbanisation or to the demographic growth of ethnic Albanians.[218] As a consequence, almost a third of Macedonia's primary schools have less than 20 pupils, while many urban schools are overcrowded and operate in shifts (with different groups of students attending school at different times of the day).[219] Lyon proposes that this is because successive governments have deliberately avoided redistributing resources from underpopulated areas to overpopulated ones. Such a decision would be 'understandably sensitive': ethnic Albanians inhabit overpopulated regions, while ethnic Macedonians are the majority in underpopulated zones.[220] Small schools in mountainous areas exemplify this problem, because the closure of a 'monolingual' school 'means losing out to the other community'.[221] Thus, rather than depoliticising education policy, decentralisation is contributing to the perception of schools as symbols of a community's hold over a territory.

Finally, decentralisation has furthered an ethnic division of labour in education. Frequently, the ethnic Albanian deputy minister of education deals with Albanian-majority municipalities and Albanian-language schools, while the ethnic Macedonian education minister tackles issues in Macedonian-majority municipalities and Macedonian-language schools.[222] To the public, the Ministry of Education appears 'ethnically split'.[223] Far from enhancing its legitimacy, this hampers public trust in the Ministry of Education: it creates perceptions of a marginalised Albanian deputy minister and discredits ministerial initiatives in the eyes of the Albanian community.[224] However, the ethnic division of labour also serves to construct an ethnic Albanian elite as the only political referent for the ethnic Albanian community, and ethnic Macedonian politicians as the only referent for the ethnic Macedonian public. As such, it supports the short-term legitimacy and stability of consociational politics.

7.4.2 Separating Education

As explained in Chap. 6, post-Ohrid governments have attempted to narrow the educational gap between children belonging to different ethnic communities. They have done so by expanding mother tongue education and making primary and secondary school compulsory and free. These reforms succeeded in expanding access to education for pupils of non-Macedonian ethnic backgrounds, particularly at the secondary level.[225] This may have legitimised the state in the eyes of ethnic communities, but it has not appeased criticisms for the differential distribution of educational resources.[226] Indeed, most initiatives did not tackle the quality of education, and 'both sides complain of unequal treatment'.[227] Albanian-language classes are overcrowded, and education in Albanian, Turkish and Serbian is deemed worse than Macedonian-language schooling.[228] Conversely, teachers and pupils in Macedonian-medium classes complain that Albanian-language pupils pass exams with lower academic standards.[229] Perceptions of inequality add to wider inter-communal tensions.

Moreover, the expansion of mother tongue education has resulted, as the 2010 *Strategy for Integrated Education* puts it, in 'a set of almost four parallel education systems, depending on the language of tuition'.[230] A tendency to separate pupils of different backgrounds into different shifts and buildings started in 2001, when an ethnic Albanian teacher was attacked and beaten by students in a multi-ethnic school in Kumanovo. As a response, ethnic Albanian students boycotted the school and, with their teachers and parents, initiated a hunger strike to lobby for a new, separate building.[231] Zenkolli asserts that 'the Minister of Education at the time did not have the capacity to deal with the problem'.[232] The Minister sanctioned the construction of new primary and secondary Albanian-language schools located in an area inhabited predominantly by ethnic Albanians. By 2006, Vetterlein observed that in Kumanovo 'the segregation ... [was] complete and both sides seem[ed] to be satisfied with the solution'.[233] This decision created a precedent: hereafter policy would reflect the maxim, if 'they don't mix ... there's no problem'.[234]

Thus, in post-Ohrid Macedonia, 'ethnic separation is seen as a measure of conflict prevention'.[235] In 2009, the United Nations Children's Emergency Fund (UNICEF) reported that the number of multi-ethnic schools teaching in Albanian and Macedonian declined by over 10 % between 2001 and 2009.[236] By 2010 only half of Macedonia's secondary schools offered instruction in multiple languages. To this day, however ethnically mixed their student body, most schools are far from being 'integrated'.[237] Even in multilingual and multi-ethnic schools, students are often separated into different shifts depending on their language of instruction. A 2010 Organisation for Security and Cooperation in Europe (OSCE) study confirms that ethnic Albanian and ethnic Macedonian students rarely interact in school.[238] Similarly, Tomovska reports that in a multilingual primary school (Albanian and Macedonian), children are separated into different parts of the building and the timetable ensures that they do not use the yard at the same time.[239] Indeed, in most schools the hidden curriculum prevents students from forming friendships with peers of a different background: administration and planning are often separate, resulting in separate celebrations, extracurricular activities and school trips.[240] This, in addition to worsening Macedonian-language skills among ethnic Albanian pupils, hampers knowledge of others' customs, mutual understanding and tolerance.[241]

Thus, Tomovska argues that violent incidents are often 'the only experience children have of the shared yard and their peers' from the other side of the school.²⁴² Arshinkovska adds that since 2008, the Ministry of Education has paid for private security to monitor school shifts and breaks.²⁴³ For example, the Nikola Karev High School in the Karpos III municipality operates a first shift for Macedonian-language students, followed by a one-hour break with police guards and a second shift for Albanian-language students.²⁴⁴ This has not necessarily allayed violent conflict: Deralla warns that the presence of security guards may exacerbate tensions in mixed schools.²⁴⁵

Violent clashes between students are a persistent feature of pre-election Macedonia, but wider political inability to tackle these fights has accelerated the fragmentation of schools into different buildings or 'ethnic shifts'.²⁴⁶ For fear of violent conflict, parents often demand separate shifts and buildings even in the absence of manifest conflict. Others withdraw their children from mixed schools, transferring them to more uniform institutions 'and then immediately the municipality will react and will close the whole Macedonian-language class or vice versa'.²⁴⁷ Beyond security concerns, these demands reflect a 'widespread fear' of assimilation.²⁴⁸ Thus, new schools tend to open as monolingual.²⁴⁹ This furthers the fragmentation of Macedonia's education system into parallel, linguistically homogeneous institutions. It also hampers the expansion of successful initiatives for mixed and multilingual education such as the *Nansen model of integrated education*. 'To be on the safe side', even after successful cooperation in curricular and extracurricular activities, school principals generally prefer to avoid joint planning and refrain from encouraging mixing between students of different backgrounds and from amending staggered timetables that prevent inter-group contact.²⁵⁰

Opportunities to meet peers of different backgrounds are equally limited outside school. This is partly because separate schooling reflects increasing residential separation.²⁵¹ For example, children of Roma backgrounds generally attend schools in 'the ghetto', where they are not exposed to 'different cultures'.²⁵² Separate schools are not equal: as an example, the Brakja Ramiz i Hamid school has a 90 % Roma population and is the only school in Macedonia operating on four shifts, with a clear impact on the quality of instruction.²⁵³ In an attempt to improve the quality of education and promote co-education between children of different ethnic backgrounds, Roma intellectuals called for the building of schools with mixed catchment areas.²⁵⁴ These calls fell largely on deaf ears.

Thus, according to Tomovska, schooling helps to cement the 'parallel worlds' of primary school children.²⁵⁵ Parallel schools deprive students of the opportunity to interact across community lines and may further inter-communal fear and mistrust, encouraging different opinions about the political and security situation, and compounding negative mutual perceptions.[256]

In particular, observers agree that Macedonia's fragmented education system isolates children of ethnic Albanian backgrounds.[257] Figure 7.10 confirms that children belonging to the Roma, Vlach, Serb and Bosniak communities frequently attend Macedonian-language classes, where they mix with peers of multiple backgrounds. Multilingual schools also generally combine Turkish- and Serbian-language classes with Macedonian-language classes in mixed shifts. In contrast, the overwhelming majority of ethnic Albanian students attend Albanian-medium classes and are often separated into different shifts or buildings.[258] The building of new Albanian-language schools in Albanian-majority residential areas furthers the isolation of ethnic Albanian students and has even prompted accusations that the state is ghettoising the Albanian community.[259]

For their part, ethnic Macedonian political parties claim that ethnic Albanians employ schools 'to conquer new territories'.[260] The 'Autumn of Albanians' in September 2012 appeared to validate this claim: Albanian-language schools opened the academic year by flying the flag and singing the national anthem of the Albanian state.[261] Schools are emerging as institutional markers of communal territory, and violent debates over school names exemplify this function. Fierce controversies erupted over school name changes, particularly over attempts to rename Albanian-language schools after members of the National Liberation Army (NLA), and Macedonian-language schools after members of the Macedonian security forces who fought in the 2001 ethnic conflict.[262]

7.4.3 *The Strategy for Integrated Education*

By 2009, international donors had reached a broad consensus on the need for more mixing between children belonging to different ethnolinguistic groups in schools. The resulting *Strategy for Integrated Education*, drafted by a working group of the Ministry of Education and a OSCE consultant, was conceived of as 'part of a much wider strategy for promoting integration in the process of building a multi-ethnic society'.[263] As Chaps. 5 and 6 mentioned, the strategy suggested extensive curricular reforms and amendments to language teaching. It also aimed to 'provide corrective measures' to redress the increasing fragmentation of the education sys-

260 G. FONTANA

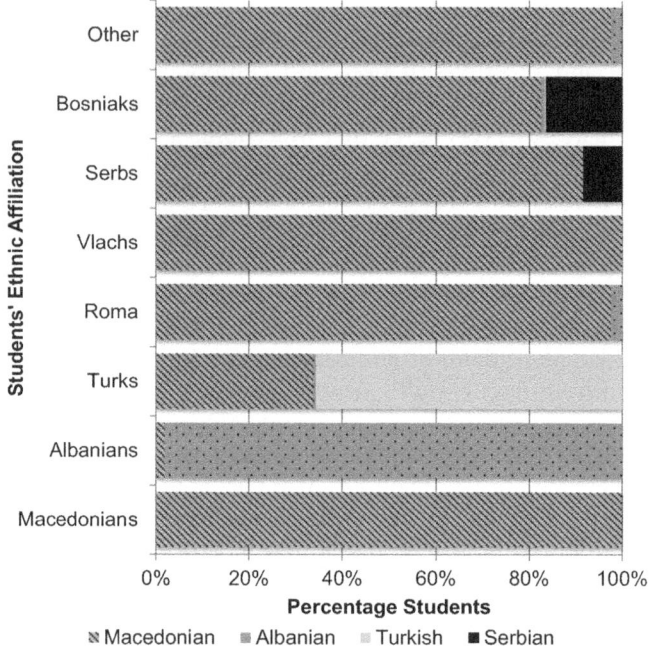

Fig. 7.10 Students by ethnic belonging and language of instruction in primary and lower secondary schools in Macedonia in 2011–2012 (State Statistical Office, *Primary, Lower Secondary and Upper Secondary Schools at the End of the School Year, 2011/2012*, Skopje: State Statistical Office, 2013. No comparable data are available for upper secondary schools)

tem, to 'safeguard community rights … [while] provid[ing] linkages' and opportunities for interaction.[264] It was to provide impetus for new policies, standards and practices, based on the importance of contact between students belonging to different ethnolinguistic groups. It claimed that 'primary schools are the proper terrain to start with integration processes, and secondary schools are the space where they should be deepened'.[265]

In contrast to Northern Ireland's *shared education* initiative, Macedonia's *Strategy for Integrated Education* employed 'the ethnic side [as] the glue' and then 'implicitly… touche[d] on a lot of other qualitative things' such as educational quality and modernisation.[266] It attempted to reverse the ethnolinguistic separation of children in schools by, in the first instance, calling for municipalities to avoid opening 'monoethnic schools', building new schools in 'monoethnic areas', or establishing shifts 'along linguistic or ethnic lines'.[267] Second, it proposed incentives to 'promote and reward' the institutionalisation of joint extracurricular activities in schools.[268] Finally, it planned for the introduction of joint classes in the least 'language-sensitive' subjects, such as IT, English, art, technical laboratories and physical education.[269] The strategy also addressed the changing of school names, the training of municipal education inspectors and officers, and the creation of new inspection criteria to reward schools' contributions to interethnic relations. The breadth of proposals substantiates Sabani's view that the main weakness of the strategy was that 'it was too ambitious, it had too many goals'.[270] Indeed, OSCE consultant Schenker recalls that 'at some stage we were thinking if ten percent of this gets implemented it's a revolution', but says that 'now zero percent is implemented'.[271]

Chapter 6 explained that the *Strategy for Integrated Education* 'basically died with [controversies over] language'.[272] The strategy spelt its own demise by treating the Albanian and Macedonian languages asymmetrically, despite them being the most politically salient identity markers of the ethnic Albanian and ethnic Macedonian communities. The introduction of Macedonian-language classes from first grade was perceived as crossing the 'thin line between integration and assimilation'.[273] Thus, in 2012 Lazarevska honestly reflected that 'we do think about [the *Strategy for Integrated Education*], when ... the High Commissioner comes here to check what is happening, then for two days the journalists talk about that, everybody talks about integrated education'.[274]

Actually, the Ministry of Education is also implementing those few aspects of the strategy that the government 'has found appropriate and more easy to implement'.[275] The most high-profile initiative is the *Interethnic Integration in Education Project*, financed by USAID and managed by the Macedonian Centre for Civic Education.[276] The project provides for community outreach, including work with the local media to encourage positive reporting on education. It also builds capacity at a local level by training municipal staff involved in education planning, helping them develop local strategies and creating monitoring mechanisms and indicators for local inspectors. Local officers are encouraged to develop context-specific activities to promote inter-group contact: for example, ethnically homogeneous municipalities may decide to invest in student exchanges rather than in extracurricular activities. To help allay parental resistance to mixed activities, the project provides earmarked funding for the refurbishment of schools engaging in interethnic activities.[277] Finally, the project focuses on six 'demonstration schools' (including four schools catering for mixed student populations and two paired-up monolingual schools) to provide models 'of best practices and lessons learned'.[278]

According to Schenker, the *Interethnic Integration in Education Project* was originally part of the *Strategy for Integrated Education* but 'because the political side [of the strategy] is dead … [many] regard the USAID project as the strategy'. He laments that as a consequence 'they're not pushing for the implementation of the strategy'.[279] In fact, the most apparent difference between the strategy and the *Interethnic Integration in Education Project* is in the name. USAID and the Macedonian Centre for Civic Education named the project 'interethnic integration' (rather than 'ethnic integration') to emphasise the reciprocity and symmetry of initiatives.[280] Indeed, even the name of the *Strategy for Integrated Education* retains a negative connotation. Zenkolli recalls that at the recent opening of a Nansen school, the mayor insisted that 'the *strategy for integrated education* will not be implemented in my municipality'.[281] Thus, it is unlikely that the disparate initiatives loosely linked to the *Strategy for Integrated Education* will translate into mainstream policies in the current political climate.[282]

Moreover, Lazarevska points out that in Macedonia, debates over education and society in general focus on 'integration' rather than on 'inclusion'. As a result, she argues that the onus for change falls on minorities, absolving the most numerous ethnolinguistic groups of any responsibility.[283] With increasing sociopolitical polarisation of ethnic Albanian and ethnic Macedonian communities into parallel and mutually exclusive realms, smaller communities fear they 'will cease to matter' and will 'just get assimilated'.[284] As in the past, in the context of inter-group tensions, schools emerge as both potential instruments for assimilation and as channels for resistance. For example, when ethnic Albanians were appointed as principals in two Turkish-language primary schools in Vrapciste and Centar Zhupa, Turkish parents viewed the appointments as signals of Albanian intent to assimilate their children. Boycotts and violent protests erupted.[285]

Ultimately, Cupi is justified in arguing that Macedonia's ethnic communities value the protection and thriving of their distinctive languages and identities above shared schools.[286] In contrast to results of public polls in Lebanon and Northern Ireland, many citizens in Macedonia openly admit they would not 'send their children to schools where another group is the majority'.[287] Local political commitment to the promotion of intergroup contact through education also remains questionable. Local politicians often present the *Strategy for Integrated Education* as an initiative driven by foreign donors and passively accepted by the Macedonian government.[288] OSCE consultant Schenker admits that 'I ended up doing the bulk of the work' as the 'interest in participation [of the Ministry of Education working group] was not so fantastic'.[289] He also recalls that the strategy was adopted by the Education Ministry partly because of 'huge pressure, international pressure' on ethnic Albanian politicians.[290] However, as Zenkolli argues, the most successful initiatives for mixed education give parents, local communities and local authorities ownership and a voice in the design of projects.[291]

7.4.4 Permanent Coexistence

The Ohrid Agreement reframed the Macedonian state to ensure the proportional representation of its people in its political and non-political institutions. The new political context helped achieve extensive community rights, but, as an officer in an international mission reflects, 'the safeguarding of rights has become an excuse to separate'.[292]

A generalised culture of silence and unwillingness to articulate the roots of Macedonia's conflict may explain some of the difficulties in formulating context-appropriate education policies to aid inter-group relations. However, Sabani explains that, despite 'political commitment' to quality education and interethnic contact, 'the investment is really going' towards increasing access to compulsory education.[293] Like their Lebanese counterparts, Macedonia's political leaders have largely employed the education system to gain leverage within their own ethnopolitical communities.[294]

The evolving structure of Macedonia's education system epitomises a wider process of communal pillarisation. Local politicians and policymakers often nostalgically mention Macedonia's long past of coexistence as their preferred model for a peaceful future.[295] In fact, Macedonia's pre-Yugoslav past, according to Vetterlein, was marked by 'the notion of permanent coexistence', the peaceful cohabitation of different groups in the state with minimal interactions.[296] Similarly, in consociational Macedonia, knowledge of each other's languages is dwindling, sources of common identification are rare and the physical and psychological distance between members of different ethnic communities is increasing. In this context, the curricula and structures of compulsory education both reflect and contribute to cementing mutually exclusive ethnic, linguistic and political communities.

7.5 Conclusion

In 2005, Gallagher pondered the fact that in Northern Ireland 'the outworkings of the peace process may have legitimised difference to the extent that [they] left little space for the articulation of any discourse of a common good'.[297] The same reflection applies to Lebanon and Macedonia.

The Taif and Belfast Agreements mapped the establishment of state control over private schools and the expansion of integrated education, while the Macedonian *Strategy for Integrated Education* aimed to encourage contact among children of different ethnolinguistic backgrounds. These three documents implicitly endorsed the position that separate schools affiliated with communities perpetuate conflict by conveying externally bound, fixed and mutually exclusive communal identities. Thus, they favoured sustained and meaningful inter-group contact in schools, and implied that by helping reduce prejudices, political extremism and fear of different others, contact could contribute to the success of the three peace processes.

However, political commitment to improving public schools in Lebanon, expanding integrated schools in Northern Ireland and implementing the *Strategy for Integrated Education* in Macedonia has been fickle at best. This may be due to the numerous constraints on the formulation and implementation of successful initiatives for mixed education in deeply divided societies. This chapter shows that initiatives for mixed schooling are successful when they have consistent institutional support (both political and financial), are tailored to local demands and conditions, and impact symmetrically on local communities. To appeal to parents and teachers, they should also provide academic benefits for participants, such as an improved quality of education (as in Macedonia's Nansen schools or in Lebanon's private international schools), more curricular choice (as with *shared education* in Northern Ireland) or better facilities and personnel (as in Macedonia's Mozaik kindergartens). Finally, reforms that promote mixed schooling need to accommodate both demands for group equality and aspirations for better inter-communal relationships.

Consociational governments in Lebanon, Northern Ireland and Macedonia may also have neglected the promotion of common schools because, as Farry explains, 'any issues that challenge the model on which our political parties are founded are the ones around which we have most difficulty finding agreement'.[298] Research in Northern Ireland has established that mixed schooling does not affect religious, national or ethnic self-definition but impacts social attitudes and political orientation. Thus, common schools challenge the foundations of political parties and the integrity of their constituencies in deeply divided societies. This chapter confirms that, rather than challenging the political system, schools in Lebanon, Northern Ireland and Macedonia reproduce the basic building blocks of political consociations: mutually exclusive confessional, ethnic, national and political communities. Thus, education systems evolve into 'consociational' institutions: they accommodate a plurality of (equally funded) separate schools rather than encouraging the creation of plural common schools.

Lijphart argues that autonomous schools are an expression of communal autonomy in consociations and that 'the voluntary self-segregation that [these] schools entail is acceptable as long as the option of multicultural and multiethnic education is also made available and provided that all schools are treated equally'.[299] Indeed, local communities generally treasure their separate institutions and present them as channels for social mobility and equality. The Albanian community in Macedonia and the Shia community in Lebanon would probably agree with the CCMS that separate schools are part of their 'collective determination to establish ourselves securely as equal citizens'.[300] Despite their integrationist rhetoric, successive shared governments in Lebanon, Northern Ireland and Macedonia have endorsed and legitimised this argument. Thus, Northern Ireland and Macedonia fund equally and fully their separate schools while Lebanon subsidises the private sector indirectly (through grants and subsidies) and directly (through private free schools). Separate schools allow for the exercise of patronage (in Lebanon and Macedonia), and for populist politics, including the politicisation of educational debates to the point of stalemate (as with debates over the 11-plus test and ESA in Northern Ireland). Thus, they help crystallise the boundaries between the ethnic and confessional communities that participated in conflict and now share political power. By legitimising their political elites and consolidating mutually exclusive constituencies, they contribute to the short-term operation of consociational politics.

However, this chapter also shows that the zero-sum politics of education policy often threatens the survival of unaffiliated institutions, such as multilingual schools in Macedonia and state schools in Lebanon. Even when they are equally funded by the state, separate schools are deeply different, and rarely equal. For example, pupils in Macedonian-language schools, Lebanese private schools and Catholic maintained schools in Northern Ireland have access to a better quality of education than their peers in Albanian-language schools, Lebanese state schools and state-controlled schools in Northern Ireland. In the long term, this is likely to have a negative impact on their employment opportunities, and to foster feelings of relative deprivation, which can destabilise peace processes.

Notes

1. Joanne Hughes, 'Are Separate Schools Divisive? A Case Study from Northern Ireland,' *British Educational Research Journal* 37, no. 5 (2011): 829.
2. Amy Gutmann, 'Unity and Diversity,' in Banks (ed.), *Diversity and Citizenship Education*, 86.
3. Ibid., 87.
4. Ibid., 88.
5. Tony Gallagher, 'Desegregation and Resegregation,' in Bekerman and McGlynn (eds.), *Addressing Ethnic Conflict*, 17; Gutmann, 'Unity and Diversity,' in Banks (ed.), *Diversity and Citizenship Education*, 88.
6. Gallagher, 'Desegregation and Resegregation,' in Bekerman and McGlynn (eds.), *Addressing Ethnic Conflict*, 17.
7. O'Leary, 'Foreword,' in Kerr *Imposing Power-Sharing*, 142.
8. Gallagher, *Education*, 149–150; Banks, 'Preface,' in Banks (ed.), *Diversity and Citizenship Education*, xix; Banks, 'Democratic Citizenship Education,' in Banks (ed.), *Diversity and Citizenship Education*, 9.
9. Skutnabb-Kangas, 'Language Rights', Cummins (ed.), *Encyclopedia of Language and Education Volume 5*, 128.
10. Walter C. Parker, 'Diversity, Globalisation and Democratic Education,' in Banks (ed.), *Diversity and Citizenship Education*, 434.
11. Hughes, 'Are Separate Schools Divisive?,' 831; Gallagher, *Education*, 125.
12. Ibid.; Hughes, 'Are Separate Schools Divisive?,' 831; B.K. Lambkin, *Opposite Religions Still?*, 195.
13. Claire McGlynn, 'Challenges,' in Bekerman and McGlynn (eds.), *Addressing Ethnic Conflict*, 86; Hughes, 'Are Separate Schools Divisive?,' 829.
14. Claire McGlynn, 'Negotiating Cultural Difference in Divided Societies. An Analysis of Approaches to Integrated Education in Northern Ireland,' in McGlynn et al. (eds.), *Peace Education*, 11.

15. Ibid.; Hughes, 'Are Separate Schools Divisive?,' 842.
16. Ibid., 844.
17. Shepherd Johnson, 'Moving from Piecemeal,' in Bekerman and McGlynn (eds.), *Addressing Ethnic Conflict*, 22; Ulf Hansson, Una O'Connor Bones, and John McCord, *Integrated Education: A Review of Policy and Research Evidence* (Belfast: Integrated Education Fund, 2013), 53. Hughes, 'Are Separate Schools Divisive?,' 839. Hansson et al., *Integrated Education*, 53.
18. Interview with Tony Gallagher (Pro-Vice Chancellor, Queen's University Belfast), Belfast, 26/02/2013.
19. Ulf Hansson, Una O'Connor Bones, and John McCord, *Integrated Education: A Review of Policy and Research Evidence* (Belfast: Integrated Education Fund, 2013), 53; Lambkin, *Opposite Religions Still?*, 30.
20. Qtd. in Thomas F. Pettigrew and Linda Tropp, *When Groups Meet: The Dynamics of Intergroup Contact* (New York: Psychology Press, 2011): 8.
21. Gallagher, *Education*, 125.
22. Joanne Hughes and Caitlin Donnelly, 'Is the Policy Sufficient? An Exploration of Integrated Education in Northern Ireland and Bilingual/Binational Education in Israel,' in Bekerman and McGlynn (eds.), *Addressing Ethnic Conflict*, 131.
23. Ulrike Niens and Ed Cairns, 'Conflict, Contact and Education in Northern Ireland,' *Theory into Practice* 44, no. 4 (2005): 338, 341; Gallagher, *Education*, 25–26.
24. Stefania Paolini et al., 'Effects of Direct and Indirect Cross-Group Friendships on Judgments of Catholics and Protestants in Northern Ireland: The Mediating Role of an Anxiety-Reduction Mechanism,' *Personality and Social Psychology Bulletin* 30, no. 6 (2004): 771.
25. Hughes, 'Are Separate Schools Divisive?,' 845; Interview with Caitlin Donnelly (Expert on Faith Schools and Inter-Group Relations, Queen's University Belfast), Belfast, 4/03/2013; Arlow Interview.
26. Paolini et al., 'Effects of Direct and Indirect Cross-Group Friendships,' 771.
27. Interview with Joane Hughes (Expert on Education in Divided Societies and Chair of the School of Education, Queen's University Belfast), Belfast, 20/02/2013.
28. McGlynn, 'Challenges,' in Bekerman and McGlynn (eds.), *Addressing Ethnic Conflict*, 78; McGlynn et al., 'Moving out of Conflict', 153; Niens and Cairns, 'Conflict, Contact and Education,' 340; Hansson et al., *Integrated Education*, 54; Paolini et al., 'Effects of Direct and Indirect Cross-Group Friendships,' 783; Hughes Interview.

29. McGlynn et al., 'Moving out of Conflict,' 154; Interview with Expert of Religious Education and Citizenship Education, Belfast, 19/02/2013; Hansson et al., *Integrated Education*, 55.
30. McGlynn, 'Challenges,' in Bekerman and McGlynn (eds.), *Addressing Ethnic Conflict*, 78; Niens and Cairns, 'Conflict, Contact and Education,' 340; McGlynn et al., 'Moving out of Conflict,' 153–154.
31. Hansson et al., *Integrated Education*, 54; Expert of Religious Education and Citizenship Education Interview; McGlynn et al., 'Moving out of Conflict,' 155.
32. Ross, 'Peace Education,' in Salomon and Cairns (eds.), *Handbook on Peace Education*, 130.
33. Paolini et al., 'Effects of Direct and Indirect Cross-Group Friendships,' 770, 772.
34. Jan Germen Janmaat, *Classroom Diversity and its Relation to Tolerance, Trust and Participation in England, Sweden and Germany* (London: Centre for Learning and Life Chances in Knowledge Economies and Societies, 2010): 34–36.
35. Katherine Torney, 'How Integrated Are Schools Where You Live?,' *The Detail TV*, 23/11/2012; Hughes Interview.
36. Donnelly Interview.
37. Ibid.
38. Connolly and Maginn, *Sectarianism*.
39. Hughes Interview.
40. Taush et al., 'The Social Psychology of Intergroup Relations,' in Salomon and Cairns (eds.), *Handbook on Peace Education*, 80.
41. 'Peter Robinson Calls for End to School Segregation,' *Belfast Telegraph*, 16/10/2010.
42. Bashshour Interview; Bashshour, 'Chances for Conflict Regulation,' in Hanf (ed.), *The Political Function of Education*, 181.
43. Nemer Frayha, 'Developing Curriculum,' in Tawil and Harley (eds.), *Education, Conflict and Social Cohesion*, 173; Qabbani Interview.
44. Part III, Section F, Art. 1 and 3, *Taif Agreement*.
45. Abouchedid et al., 'The Limitations of Inter-Group Learning'.
46. Bashshour Interview.
47. Interview with Wafa Kotob (Senior Education Advisor UNICEF), Beirut, 9/07/2012.
48. Moreno Interview.
49. Telephone Interview with Juan Manuel Moreno (Team Leader, World Bank Education Development Project), 13/06/2012. The World Bank, *Public Spending on Education Total (% of GDP)*, http://data.worldbank.org/indicator/SE.XPD.TOTL.GD.ZS
50. Moreno Interview.

51. Baumann, 'The 'New Contractor Bourgeoisie',' in Knudsen and Kerr (eds.), *Lebanon after the Cedar Revolution*, 131.
52. Interview with Senior USAID Official, Beirut, 2/07/2012.
53. Daw Interview; Moreno Interview.
54. Public school principal, qtd. in Joceleyne Zablit, 'Lebanon's Public Schools Students Face Uphill Battle,' *AFP*, 8/10/2011; Kotob Interview.
55. Interview with Nada Mneimneh (Director, Education Sector Development Secretariat, Ministry of Education), Beirut, 4/07/2012.
56. Senior USAID Official Interview.
57. Ibid.; Kotob Interview.
58. Ibid.
59. Senior USAID Official Interview.
60. Moreno Interview; Qabbani Interview.
61. Bashshour Interview.
62. Al-Khatib Interview.
63. Interview with Adnan El-Amine (Lebanese Association for Educational Studies Director and Curriculum Specialist), Beirut, 13/07/2012.
64. United Nations Development Programme, *Education and Citizenship*, 35–36.
65. Mneimneh Interview; Shuayb, 'Education', in Choueiri (ed.), *Breaking the Cycle*, 191.
66. Daw Interview.
67. Senior Officer, CERD, Interview.
68. Ali Khalife, 'La Place De La Religion À L'école ' *Confluences Méditerranée* 56, (2006), 154.
69. Ibid.
70. Reuven Erlich and Yoram Kahati, 'Hezbollah as a Case Study of the Battle for Hearts and Minds', Intelligence and Terrorism Information Centre at the Israel Intelligence Heritage & Commemoration Centre http://www.terrorism-info.org.il/data/pdf/PDF_07_030_2.pdf
71. Kathleen Fincham, 'Nationalist Narratives', 5; Al-Khatib Interview.
72. Shuayb, 'Education', in Choueiri (ed.), *Breaking the Cycle*, 183, 167.
73. Qabbani Interview.
74. El-Amine Interview.
75. Mneimneh Interview.
76. Ministry of Education and Higher Education, *Le Développement*, 7; El-Amine Interview.
77. Moreno Interview; Akar Interview.
78. Ibid.
79. Chartouni Interview.
80. El-Amine Interview; Bashshour Interview; Kotob Interview.

81. United Nations Development Programme, *Lebanon Human Development*, 27; Kotob Interview.
82. Yahya Interview.
83. Ibid.
84. Moreno Interview; Bashshour Interview.
85. Moreno Interview; Jim Quilty, 'Separate Learning'.
86. Only 17 independent schools according to the Department of Education Northern Ireland, *Independent Schools List*, http://www.deni.gov.uk/index/schools-and-infrastructure-2/schools-management/10-types_of_school-nischools_pg/schools_-_types_of_school-independent-schools.htm
87. Gallagher Interview.
88. Hughes, 'Are Separate Schools Divisive?,' 845.
89. O'Duibh Interview.
90. Bell Interview; Interview with Senior Officer, Belfast Education and Library Board, Belfast, 26/02/2013.
91. Hughes Interview; Caitlin Donnelly, 'In Pursuit of School Ethos,' *British Journal of Educational Studies* 48, no. 2 (2000), 144; Donnelly Interview.
92. McGlynn, 'Negotiating Cultural Difference,' in in McGlynn et al. (eds.), *Peace Education*, 12; McGlynn et al., 'Moving out of Conflict,' 152.
93. Torney, 'How Integrated'.
94. Kinahan Interview; Interview with Sam Fitzsimmons (Communications Director, Integrated Education Fund), Belfast, 4/03/2013; Interview with Stephen Farry (Alliance MLA and Minister for Employment and Learning), Belfast, 25/02/2013; Telephone Interview with Expert of Primary Religious Education, 25/03/2013.
95. Priscilla Chadwick, *Schools of Reconciliation*, 134; Arlow Interview.
96. Torney, 'How Integrated'; Hansson et al., *Integrated Education*, 28
97. Ibid., 9, 15, 56–57.
98. Ibid.
99. Qtd. in Lindsay Fergus, 'Northern Ireland Schools 'Must Cooperate or Face Closure',' *Belfast Telegraph*, 11/01/2012.
100. Tony Gallagher, 'Balancing Difference', 436.
101. Hansson et al., *Integrated Education*, 31–41.
102. Hansson et al., *Integrated Education*, 5.
103. Ibid., 11. Equality, interdependence, inclusivity and celebration of other cultures according to McGlynn, 'Challenges,' in Bekerman and McGlynn (eds.), *Addressing Ethnic Conflict*, 83; Interview with Baroness May Blood (President, Integrated Education Fund), London, 19/03/2013; Fitzsimmons Interview; Donnelly, 'In Pursuit of School Ethos,' 146; Mcilwaine Interview; Hughes and Donnelly, 'Is the Policy Sufficient?' in

Bekerman and McGlynn (eds.), *Addressing Ethnic Conflict*, 122; Interview with John McCallister (Independent MLA), Belfast, 25/02/2013.
104. Hansson et al., *Integrated Education*, 5.
105. Ibid.
106. Paul Connolly, Dawn Purvis, and PJ O'Grady, *Advancing Shared Education. Report of the Ministerial Advisory Group* (Belfast, 2013), xx.
107. Blood Interview; Mcilwaine Interview; Valerie Morgan and Grace Fraser, 'When Does 'Good News' Become 'Bad News'?,' 372–375.
108. Blood Interview.
109. Hansson et al., *Integrated Education*, 3.
110. Fitzsimmons Interview; Blood Interview.
111. Hansson et al., *Integrated Education*, 3; Fitzsimmons Interview.
112. Hansson et al., *Integrated Education*, 44–47; Department of Education Northern Ireland, *Towards a Culture of Tolerance. Integrating Education* (Belfast: Department of Education Northern Ireland, 1998): 8; Claire McGlynn, 'Integrated and Faith-Based Schooling in Northern Ireland,' *The Irish Journal of Education* 36, (2005): 52; McGlynn et al., 'Moving out of Conflict,' 152.
113. Donnelly Interview; Gallagher Interview; Bell Interview; Senior Officer (Education and Skills Authority) Interview.
114. McDevitt Interview.
115. Fionnuala O'Connor, *A Shared Childhood, the Story of the Integrated Schools in Northern Ireland* (Belfast: Blackstaff Press, 2002): 64; Interview with Eimear Bush (Programme Manager, Special European Union Programmes Body), Belfast, 20/02/2013.
116. McDevitt Interview.
117. Murphy Interview. The St Columbanus College in Bangor is generally mentioned as an example of a Catholic maintained school where out of 597 pupils only 256 had a Catholic background in 2012. Torney, 'How Integrated'.
118. Personal Communication with Ex-Principal in a Catholic Maintained School, 21/02/2013. In fact, research proves most schools" emphasis on parity of esteem and on ecumenical Christianity, see: McGlynn, 'Negotiating Cultural Difference,' in in McGlynn et al. (eds.), *Peace Education*, 20; Chadwick, *Schools of Reconciliation*, 166; O'Connor, *A Shared Childhood*, 98.
119. Hansson et al., *Integrated Education*, 9, 50.
120. McGlynn et al., 'Moving out of Conflict,' 155; McGlynn, 'Challenges,' in Bekerman and McGlynn (eds.), *Addressing Ethnic Conflict*, 78.
121. McGlynn et al., 'Moving out of Conflict,' 154; Hansson et al., *Integrated Education*, 50.
122. Farry Interview; Blood Interview.

123. 'Peter Robinson Calls for End to School Segregation,' *Belfast Telegraph*, 16/10/2010.
124. Storey Interview; Hughes and Donnelly, 'Is the Policy Sufficient?,' in Bekerman and McGlynn (eds.), *Addressing Ethnic Conflict*, 131; O'Connor, *A Shared Childhood*, 68, 70.
125. Storey Interview.
126. Interview with Kathryn Torney (Journalist, the Detail Tv), Belfast, 18/02/2013.
127. O'Connor, *A Shared Childhood*, 168.
128. Blood Interview; Mcilwaine Interview.
129. Ibid.
130. Ibid.; Mcdevitt Interview.
131. Department of Education Northern Ireland, *Northern Ireland Summary Data*, http://www.deni.gov.uk/index/facts-and-figures-new/education-statistics/32_statistics_and_research-numbersofschoolsandpupils_pg/32_statistics_and_research-northernirelandsummarydata_pg.htm
132. Nolan, *Northern Ireland Peace Monitoring Report*, 96.
133. Murphy Interview.
134. Hughes and Donnelly, 'Is the Policy Sufficient?,' in Bekerman and McGlynn (eds.), *Addressing Ethnic Conflict*, 131.
135. McGlynn, 'Challenges,' in Bekerman and McGlynn (eds.), *Addressing Ethnic Conflict*, 81.
136. McGlynn, 'Negotiating Cultural Difference,' in in McGlynn et al. (eds.), *Peace Education*, 20.
137. Hughes and Donnelly, 'Is the Policy Sufficient?,' in Bekerman and McGlynn (eds.), *Addressing Ethnic Conflict*, 129.
138. Murphy Interview; Senior Officer, Belfast Education and Library Board, Interview.
139. Hughes Interview; Gallagher Interview; Blood Interview; McGlynn et al., 'Moving out of Conflict,' 154; McGlynn, 'Challenges,' in Bekerman and McGlynn (eds.), *Addressing Ethnic Conflict*, 78; Hansson et al., *Integrated Education*, 9; Paolini et al., 'Effects of Direct and Indirect Cross-Group Friendships.'
140. Ibid., 153; McGlynn, 'Challenges,' in Bekerman and McGlynn (eds.), *Addressing Ethnic Conflict*, 78; McGlynn et al., 'Moving out of Conflict,' 154.
141. Blood Interview; Hansson et al., *Integrated Education*, 9; McGlynn et al., 'Moving out of Conflict,' 154,156; McGlynn, 'Challenges,' in Bekerman and McGlynn (eds.), *Addressing Ethnic Conflict*, 78; Hughes Interview.
142. Paolini et al., 'Effects of Direct and Indirect Cross-Group Friendships.'
143. Gallagher Interview.
144. Ibid.

145. McDevitt Interview.
146. Murphy Interview.
147. Interview with Senior Education Advisor, Council for Catholic Maintained Schools, Belfast, 18/02/2013.
148. Hughes Interview.
149. Torney, 'How Integrated'.
150. Fraser Agnew, qtd. in Colm Heatley, *Interface: Flashpoints in Northern Ireland* (Belfast: Lagan Books, 2004).
151. Ibid.
152. Connolly et al., *Advancing Shared Education*, xiii.
153. Donnelly Interview.
154. Gallagher Interview.
155. McGlynn et al., 'Moving out of Conflict,' 157; Hughes Interview.
156. Hughes Interview.
157. Gallagher Interview. Purdy et al., 'Primary Languages,' 153.
158. Donnelly Interview; Interview with Chris Hazzard (Sinn Féin MLA and Member of the Education Committee), Belfast, 18/09/2013; Connolly et al., *Advancing Shared Education*, xvii; Hansson et al., *Integrated Education*, 17; Hughes Interview.
159. Connolly et al., *Advancing Shared Education*, xviii; Gallagher Interview.
160. Hansson et al., *Integrated Education*, 28; Murphy Interview; Gallagher Interview.
161. Murphy Interview; Senior Officer (Education and Skills Authority) Interview.
162. Ibid.
163. Connolly et al., *Advancing Shared Education*, xvii; Bell Interview; Mcilwaine Interview.
164. Gallagher Interview; Bell Interview; Interview with a Senior Officer, Council for Catholic Maintained Schools, Belfast, 18/02/2013.
165. McDevitt Interview.
166. Gallagher Interview.
167. Senior Officer, Belfast Education and Library Board, Interview; Murphy Interview.
168. Ibid.
169. Ibid.
170. Hughes, 'Are Separate Schools Divisive?,' 845–846.
171. Ibid.
172. Torney Interview; Farry Interview.
173. Mcilwaine Interview; Donnelly Interview.
174. Connolly et al., *Advancing Shared Education*, xxi.
175. Mcilwaine Interview; Gallagher Interview.
176. Hansson et al., *Integrated Education*, 25; Bell Interview.

177. Hansson et al., *Integrated Education*, 46.
178. Storey Interview.
179. Fitzsimmons Interview; Hansson et al., *Integrated Education*, 18.
180. Bell Interview; Hughes Interview; Hansson et al., *Integrated Education*, 19–22.
181. Fitzsimmons Interview.
182. Hansson et al., *Integrated Education*, 6.
183. Connolly et al., *Advancing Shared Education*, xvii.
184. Gallagher Interview; Expert of Religious Education and Citizenship Education Interview.
185. Hughes Interview.
186. Gallagher Interview.
187. Ibid.
188. Gallagher Interview; Mcilwaine Interview.
189. McCallister Interview.
190. Senior Officer (Education and Skills Authority) Interview.
191. Kinahan Interview; Gallagher Interview; Senior Officer (Education and Skills Authority) Interview; Blood Interview.
192. Interview with Chris Hazzard (Sinn Féin MLA and Member of the Education Committee), Belfast, 18/09/2013; Kinahan Interview; Storey Interview; Blood Interview; Farry Interview; Fitzsimmons Interview; Senior Officer (Education and Skills Authority) Interview; Hansson et al., *Integrated Education*, 4.
193. Mcilwaine Interview; Senior Officer, Belfast Education and Library Board, Interview.
194. Kinahan Interview.
195. Lindsay Fergus, 'ESA: £17m Down the Drain as Death Knell Signalled for Single Education Body,' *Belfast Telegraph*, 10/04/2014.
196. Kinahan Interview.
197. Chris Hazzard, 'Governors Board Association Support for ESA Welcome' http://www.sinnfein.ie/contents/28964; Personal Communication with Chris Hazzard (Sinn Féin MLA and Education Spokesperson), 14/04/2014.
198. 'The Controversial Education and Skills Authority: Stormont Fails to Deliver Again,' *Belfast Telegraph*, 10/04/2014.
199. Kinahan Interview; McDevitt Interview; McCallister Interview.
200. Senior Officer (Education and Skills Authority) Interview.
201. Hughes, 'Are Separate Schools Divisive?,' 847.
202. Murphy Interview; Farry Interview; McCallister Interview.
203. Hansson et al., *Integrated Education*, 66; Torney Interview; Gallagher, 'Balancing Difference,' 439.
204. Connolly et al., *Advancing Shared Education*, xxi.

205. Hazzard Interview.
206. Ibid; Bell Interview.
207. Bishop Donal McKeown, qtd. in 'Cardinal Brady Accuses Catholic Schools of Getting Pupils by 'Stealth',' *BBC*, 13/02/2012; McDevitt Interview; 'The Controversial Education and Skills Authority: Stormont Fails to Deliver Again,' *Belfast Telegraph*, 10/04/2014.
208. McDevitt Interview.
209. Ibid.
210. Officer in an International Mission Interview.
211. Sabani Interview.
212. Ministry of Education and Science, *National Programme for the Development of Education in the Republic of Macedonia 2005–2015*, 21; Sabani Interview; Aisling Lyon, *Decentralisation and the Delivery of Primary and Secondary Education* (Skopje: Centre for Research and Policymaking, 2011), 9.
213. Ministry of Education and Science, *National Programme*, 23; Officer in an International Delegation Interview; Sabani Interview; Lyon, *Decentralisation*, 18–21.
214. Interview with Officer, World Bank, Skopje, 15/09/2012; Interview with Emilja Tudjarovska (Scholar and Activist), Skopje, 13/09/2012; Grodzanovska Interview; Officer in an International Mission Interview.
215. Vetterlein, 'The Influence of the Ohrid Framework Agreement', 15; Ministry of Education and Science, *Steps Towards Integrated Education*, 13.
216. Grodzanovska Interview; Vetterlein, 'The Influence of the Ohrid Framework Agreement,' 15.
217. Officer in an International Delegation Interview.
218. Sabani Interview; Lyon, *Decentralisation*, 26–27; Officer in an International Delegation Interview.
219. Lyon, *Decentralisation*, 28.
220. Ibid.
221. Officer in an International Mission Interview.
222. Ibid.
223. Vetterlein, 'The Influence of the Ohrid Framework Agreement', 16.
224. Deralla Interview; Officer in an International Mission Interview.
225. Ali Cupi Interview; Sabani Interview.
226. Officer in an International Delegation Interview.
227. Sabani Interview.
228. Officer in an International Delegation Interview; Sabani Interview.
229. Ibid.; United Nations International Children's Emergency Fund, *Study on Multiculturalism and Inter-Ethnic Relations in Education* (Skopje: UNICEF Country Office, 2009), 7.

230. Ministry of Education and Science, *Steps Towards Integrated Education*, 5; Zenkolli Interview; Hani Interview; Mickovska Interview; Sabani Interview; see Chap. 6.
231. 'The Segregation Solution,' *Transitions Online*, 26/05/2003; Vetterlein, 'The Influence of the Ohrid Framework Agreement', 17.
232. Zenkolli Interview; Ali Cupi Interview.
233. Vetterlein, 'The Influence of the Ohrid Framework Agreement', 17.
234. Mickovska Interview.
235. Ministry of Education and Science, *Steps Towards Integrated Education*, 6.
236. Sabani Interview; United Nations International Children's Emergency Fund, *Study on Multiculturalism*, 7.
237. Hughes Interview.
238. Organisation for Security and Co-operation in Europe Spillover Mission to Skopje, *Age, Contact, Perceptions*, 20.
239. Ana Tomovska, 'Social Context and Contact Hypothesis. Perceptions and Experiences of a Contact Program for Ten- to Eleven-Year-Old Children in the Republic of Macedonia,' in McGlynn et al. (eds.), *Peace Education*, 98.
240. Mickovska Interview.
241. Arshinkovska Interview.
242. Ibid.
243. Interview with Rada Arshinkovska (Physics Teacher and Member of IEARN), Skopje, 17/09/2012.
244. Grodzanovska Interview.
245. Deralla Interview.
246. Officer in an International Donor Interview; Arshinkovska Interview; Ali Cupi Interview; Organisation for Security and Co-operation in Europe Spillover Mission to Skopje, *Age, Contact, Perceptions*, 20; Officer, Ministry of Education and Science, Interview; Deralla Interview; Lyon, *Decentralisation*, 40.
247. Zenkolli Interview; Officer in an International Mission Interview.
248. Officer in an International Mission Interview; Interview with Officer in an International Donor.
249. Ibid.
250. Sabani mentioned two schools in Kumanovo.
251. Officer in an International Mission Interview.
252. This is because they are often prevented from enrolling in schools serving different catchment areas according to Recep Ali Cupi.
253. Ljubica Dimishkovska-Grozdanovska, 'A Poor Report Card for Macedonia's Schools,' *Transitions Online*, 12 /01/2012.
254. Ali Cupi Interview; Officer in an International Delegation Interview.
255. Tomovska, 'Social Context', in McGlynn et al. (eds.), *Peace Education*, 98.

256. Officer in an International Donor Interview; Arshinkovska Interview; Mickovska Interview.
257. Ibid.
258. Officer in an International Mission Interview; Ali Cupi Interview.
259. Officer in an International Donor Interview.
260. 'The Segregation Solution,' *Transitions Online*, 26/05/2003.
261. Officer, Ministry of Education and Science, Interview; Officer in an International Mission Interview; Officer in an International Donor Interview.
262. Vetterlein, 'The Influence of the Ohrid Framework Agreement', 16; Lyon, *Decentralisation*, 33.
263. United Nations International Children's Emergency Fund, *Study on Multiculturalism*, 21.
264. Officer in an International Mission Interview.
265. Ministry of Education and Science, *Steps Towards Integrated Education*, 17; Schenker Interview; Officer in an International Donor Interview; Officer, Ministry of Education and Science, Interview.
266. Schenker Interview.
267. Ministry of Education and Science, *Steps Towards Integrated Education*, 11.
268. Ibid. 18; Schenker Interview.
269. Ibid.; Ministry of Education and Science, *Steps Towards Integrated Education*, 17.
270. Sabani Interview.
271. Schenker Interview.
272. Ibid.
273. Zenkolli Interview; see also Chap. 6.
274. Lazarevska Interview.
275. Sabani Interview.
276. United States Agency for International Development, *Interethnic Integration in Education Project* , http://www.usaid.gov/macedonia/fact-sheets/interethnic-integration-education-project
277. Georgieva Interview; USAID, 'Interethnic Integration'.
278. Ibid.; Officer in an International Donor Interview.
279. Schenker Interview.
280. Officer in an International Donor Interview.
281. Zenkolli Interview.
282. Interview with Senior Officer, Ministry of Education and Science, Skopje, 19/09/2012.
283. Lazarevska Interview.
284. Ali Cupi Interview; Officer in an International Mission Interview.

285. Nazif Mandaci, 'Turks of Macedonia', 17; Ronny Myhrvold, *Former Yugoslav Republic of Macedonia*, 29.
286. Ali Cupi Interview.
287. United Nations Development Programme, *People Centered Analysis Report*.
288. Zenkolli Interview; Officer, Ministry of Education and Science Interview; Hughes Interview; Officer in an International Delegation Interview; Novkovski Interview.
289. Schenker Interview.
290. Ibid.
291. Zenkolli Interview.
292. Officer in an International Mission Interview. Also argued by Loreta Georgieva.
293. Sabani Interview.
294. Officer in an International Mission Interview; Interview with Albanian Historian.
295. Novkovski Interview; Officer, Ministry of Education and Science, Interview.
296. Vetterlein, 'The Influence of the Ohrid Framework Agreement', 4.
297. Gallagher, 'Balancing Difference,' 431.
298. Farry Interview.
299. Lijphart, *Thinking About Democracy*, 70.
300. Murphy Interview; For the Shia, see: Catherine Le Thomas, *Les Écoles Chiites Au Liban* (Paris: Karthala, 2012).

CHAPTER 8

Conclusion: Separate to Unite

The Taif, Belfast and Ohrid Agreements established consociational power-sharing to regulate three violent conflicts in Lebanon, Northern Ireland and Macedonia. To further long-term peace-building and reconciliation, these agreements also mapped reforms of compulsory education. Specifically, they prescribed reforms in history education, citizenship education and languages of instruction, and recommended changes to the overall structure of the three education systems.

This study has compared these reforms and traced subsequent debates over their implementation, focusing on approaches to history education, citizenship education, languages and attempts to encourage mixing between children of different backgrounds in school. It confirms that the education systems of Lebanon, Northern Ireland and Macedonia differ because of 'deep-seated historical traditions now institutionalised in structures, practices and institutional cultures'.[1] However, this study also shows that, regardless of local historical traditions and the contents of the peace agreements, debates over education policy in the three consociations converge.

In consociational Lebanon, Northern Ireland and Macedonia, education systems navigate between the Scylla of parity of esteem and the Charybdis of overarching pluralism. On the one hand, schools are expected to promote unity and social cohesion among citizens belonging to different ethnic, confessional, linguistic and national communities. On the other hand, they are expected to further reconciliation by reflecting, acknowledging and valuing the specific narratives of each community. In this delicate balancing act, education policy adopts and reproduces consociational models and expedients. For example, Macedonia transposes proportional representation into the contents of the history curriculum and its policies for mother tongue education. By granting more linguistic rights to children belonging to the largest communities, schools reproduce the power hierarchies between different ethnic groups in the state. Similarly, Northern Ireland's education reforms are founded on the principle of parity of esteem for the Catholic/Nationalist and Protestant/Unionist traditions. The history curricula adopt a multiperspective approach, and language policies help construct the Irish language and the Ulster-Scots vernacular as parallel legitimate markers of communal identity. Finally, in the three societies, the consociational principle of communal autonomy legitimises the existence of separate schools catering only to certain communities. This explains why Lebanese governments consistently protect private education; why integrated education remains a small, self-contained sector in Northern Ireland; and why the overcrowding of Macedonia's secondary schools has been solved through 'ethnic shifts' and buildings.

This study set out to determine whether the Taif, Belfast and Ohrid Agreements, and the new patterns of power they institutionalised, fundamentally altered the political function of education in Lebanon, Northern Ireland and Macedonia. It shows that the political function of education in the three consociations remains remarkably similar to that of education during conflict. Through their manifest and hidden curricula, schools reflect and reproduce the basic building blocks of a consociation: mutually exclusive ethnic, religious and national communities that participated in conflict and currently share political power.

This reveals a lack of consensus over the end of conflict. Perhaps this is not surprising, given that consociations are premised on the management, rather than on the resolution, of civil wars. Continuing debates over the past, the meaning of citizenship, markers of national identity, security, and the future of the state hinder the formulation and implementation of a consistent education policy. Thus, debates over schools generally echo wider political struggles rather than reflecting purely educational concerns. This is apparent from the 'ethnicisation' of educational debates, resulting in Northern Ireland's controversies over ESA and the 11-plus test, in Lebanon's stalemate over the history curriculum, and in Macedonia's disputes over the teaching of the official state language in schools.

This study also shows that consociations generate consociational education systems, which accommodate a plurality of separate narratives and institutions associated with different communities, rather than promoting overarching contents and plural common schools. Chapter 7 explained that separate schools help consolidate separate political communities and constituencies in consociations. Similarly, Chaps. 4, 5 and 6 demonstrated that certain school curricula and pedagogical approaches can help legitimise communal elites, discourage student participation in transformative political life, and even hamper inter-group dialogue by depriving children of a common language. The consolidation of mutually exclusive constituencies overlapping with local ethnic, confessional and national communities does not hamper the short-term operation of power-sharing. Indeed, Lijphart views 'the segmental isolation resulting from separate political and social organisations as a method [rather] than as a precondition of consociational democracy'.[2] Moving beyond the focus of consociational research on 'political (executive and legislative) issues',[3] this study suggests that non-political institutions can contribute to political stability in deeply divided societies. In particular, through their manifest and hidden curricula, consociational education systems convey certain core values and practices, which may help create a culture of power-sharing. The production and reproduction of this culture through schools, facilitates the short-term operation and stability of consociational politics and the re-establishment of power-sharing after violent conflicts.

This study opens a debate on constructive approaches to the reform of consociational education systems to aid transition out of conflict. It shows that too often 'society itches and schools get scratched'.[4] The failure of the Taif Agreement's ambitious integrationist initiatives confirms that education reform cannot be expected to change societies. Still, the case of Northern Ireland suggests that appropriate policies can make schools flexible enough to accommodate and even encourage social change. However, this study also demonstrates that three overarching factors constrain the formulation and implementation of education reforms in consociations. First, reforms succeed only when they promote values congruent with those of the political system: they need to accommodate group equality while fostering overarching identities. Second, education reforms face insurmountable opposition when they do not impact symmetrically on all the major ethnic, religious and linguistic communities. Third, reforms with explicit social aims generate more resistance than open-ended initiatives, which, while perhaps furthering skills conducive to reconciliation, do not prescribe specific societal outcomes. Thus, schools in consociations are unlikely to contribute to social cohesion by fostering integration. The destiny of both the Lebanese history curriculum and the Macedonian *Strategy for Integrated Education* confirms that the top-down integration of schools and imposition of unified narratives may hamper, rather than further, reconciliation and transition out of conflict.

Herein lies the paradox of education in deeply divided societies. Consociational education systems are unlikely to foster unity through a state-promoted narrative and common schools. Rather, they tend to accommodate separate institutions and mutually exclusive identity-forming narratives. Thus, social cohesion and peace in consociational education systems can only be furthered by, as Gallagher puts it, 'leaving those boundaries in place but making them less important, making them porous'.[5] For example, multiperspective curricula for history and active approaches to citizenship education can help expose students to different narratives and encourage them to think critically about the conflict. Similarly, additive bilingualism in all schools can ensure that citizens belonging to different ethnic or national groups retain a common language of communication. Curricular approaches to reconciliation need to be accompanied by sustained and positive contact between children belonging to different backgrounds. Where mixed schools are not possible, context-specific initiatives such as *shared education* can provide both academic benefits and opportunities for contact.

These curricular and structural initiatives do not challenge communal rights to separate schools or the equal legitimacy of different narratives of identity, but they are examples of how education reform can make schools flexible enough to accommodate social change. Moreover, additional overarching identities can emerge when children are exposed to multiple identity-forming narratives and when they have friends from a variety of confessional, ethnic and national backgrounds. Thus, well-managed consociational education systems can nurture forms of collective identification across communal lines. Plural, overarching identities should not be thought of as displacing or replacing communal allegiances. Rather, they can help qualify and 'hyphenate' individual belonging: this will make it harder to mobilise identities for violent conflict.

Finally, this study confirms that consociation per se is not incompatible with initiatives for the long-term transition out of conflict. The Taif, Belfast and Ohrid Agreements provided for (albeit temporary) political stability and absence of violence: these are essential in order to formulate and implement education reforms aimed at reconciliation. For example, *shared education* would not be possible without security and a modicum of inter-communal trust. Similarly, multiperspective curricula require a minimum level of legitimacy for all the identity-forming narratives of the major local communities. However, at times of instability, schools in both corporate and liberal consociations tend to convey mutually exclusive identity-forming narratives and to further the physical separation of children of different backgrounds. Internal political instability and negative external pressures also transform schools into precious instruments of patronage (as in Lebanon and Macedonia).

This comparative analysis of education reform in Lebanon, Northern Ireland and Macedonia suggests that consociational education systems, while fostering short-term political stability, can also contribute to the long-term vulnerability of power-sharing. Schools can encourage prejudice and fear through their curricula, pedagogical approaches and separate structures. Macedonia's 'smaller communities' also warn that consociational education systems may entrench the rights of certain politically assertive ethnic groups, while paving the way for the assimilation of others. Last but not least, paraphrasing the landmark decision in *Brown v. Board of Education*, separate facilities are often perceived as unequal by different communities in deeply divided societies.[6] In particular, when combined with unequal employment opportunities, separate schooling can stimulate collective frustration and feelings of relative deprivation, facilitating a relapse into conflict. Thus, this study shows that reforms in compulsory education have contributed more to maintaining the differences underpinning violent inter-group conflict, than to promoting long-term reconciliation in Lebanon, Northern Ireland and Macedonia.

Notes

1. Green, *Education*, 178.
2. Lijphart, *Democracy*, 89.
3. McGarry and O'Leary, *The Northern Ireland Conflict*, 13.
4. Hughes Interview.
5. Gallagher Interview.
6. Luther A. Huston, 'High Court Bans School Segregation. 9-to-0 Decision Grants Time to Comply ' *New York Times*, 18/05/1954.

Bibliography

Interviews and Personal Communication

Lebanon
Abu Assali, Mounir (Lebanese Academic and Former Director of the Centre for Educational Research and Development, 1994–1999), Telephone interview, 6/09/2012.
Akar, Bassel (Lebanese Academic and Civic Education Specialist), Beirut, 28/06/2012.
Al-Khatib, Walid (Director, UNRWA Field Education Office), Beirut, 3/07/2012.
Awad, Elie (Project Manager, Youth for Tolerance), Beirut, 20/06/2012.
Bashshour, Munir (American University of Beirut), Beirut, 18/06/2012.
Chartouni, Charles (Lebanese Academic and Political Analyst), Beirut, 6/07/2012.
Daw, Anwar (Progressive Socialist Party Member, Member of the Advisory Committee on History Books), Beirut, 10/07/2012.
El-Amine, Adnan (Lebanese Association for Educational Studies Director and Curriculum Specialist), Beirut, 22/06/2012.
El-Amine, Adnan (Lebanese Association for Educational Studies Director and Curriculum Specialist), Beirut, 13/07/2012.
Frayha, Nemer (Lebanese Academic and Former Director of the Centre for Educational Research and Development, 1999–2001), Beirut, 19/06/2012.
Frayha, Nemer (Lebanese Academic and Former Director of the Centre for Educational Research and Development, 1999–2001), Beirut, 26/06/2012.

Kotob, Wafa (Senior Education Advisor UNICEF), Beirut, 9/07/2012.
Mneimneh, Nada (Director, Education Sector Development Secretariat, Ministry of Education), Beirut, 4/07/2012.
Moreno, Juan Manuel (Team Leader, World Bank Education Development Project), Phone interview, 13/06/2012.
Murad, Abd-Al-Rahim (Lebanese Politician and Former Education Minister), Beirut, 27/06/2012.
Qabbani, Khaled (Lebanese Jurist and Former Education Minister, 2005–2008), Beirut, 17/07/2012.
Yahya, Maha (ESCWA Regional Advisor and Editor of the 2008 UNDP Human Development Report), Beirut, 3/07/2012.
Yakinthou, Christalla (Consultant at International Centre for Transitional Justice), Beirut, 21/06/2012.

Anonymous

Senior Officer, Centre for Educational Research and Development, Beirut, 27/06/2012.
Senior USAID Official, Beirut, 2/07/2012.

Northern Ireland
Arlow, Michael (Director, the Spirit of Enniskillen Trust and Former Curriculum Developer for Local and Global Citizenship), Belfast, 22/02/2013.
Bell, Andrew (Community Relations Coordinator, Department of Education Northern Ireland), Bangor, 26/02/2013.
Blood, May (President, Integrated Education Fund), London, 19/03/2013.
Bush, Eimear (Programme Manager, Special European Union Programmes Body), Belfast, 20/02/2013.
Donnelly, Caitlin (Expert on Faith Schools and Inter-Group Relations, Queen's University Belfast), Belfast, 4/03/2013.
Farry, Stephen (Alliance MLA and Minister for Employment and Learning), Belfast, 25/02/2013.
Fitzsimmons, Sam (Communications Director, Integrated Education Fund), Belfast, 4/03/2013.
Gallagher, Tony (Pro-Vice Chancellor, Queen's University Belfast), Belfast, 26/02/2013.
Hanna, Richard (Chief Executive, Council for Curriculum, Examination and Assessment and Expert on History Curriculum), Belfast, 19/02/2013.
Hazzard, Chris (Sinn Féin MLA and Member of the Education Committee), Belfast, 18/09/2013.
Hazzard, Chris (Sinn Féin MLA and Education Spokesperson), Personal Communication, 14/04/2014.

Hughes, Joanne (Expert on Education in Divided Societies and Chair of the School of Education, Queen's University Belfast), Belfast, 20/02/2013.
Kinahan, Danny (Ulster Unionist Party MLA and Member of the Education Committee), Stormont, 19/09/2013.
McCallister, John (Independent MLA), Belfast, 25/02/2013.
McDevitt, Conall (Social Democratic and Labour Party MLA and Former Member of the Education Committee), Belfast, 1/03/2013.
McIlwaine, Paula (Professional Development Officer, Northern Ireland Council for Integrated Education), Belfast, 21/02/2013.
Murphy, Terry (Head of Education Standards, Council for Catholic Maintained Schools), Holywood, 19/02/2013.
O'Duibh, Micheal (Chief Executive, Council for Irish-medium Schools), Phone interview, 5/03/2013.
O'Duibh, Micheal (Chief Executive, Council for Irish-Medium Education), Personal Correspondence, 2/10/2013.
Storey, Mervyn (Democratic Unionist Party MLA, Chair of Education Committee), Stormont, 27/02/2013.
Torney, Kathryn (Journalist, the Detail TV), Belfast, 18/02/2013.

Anonymous

Expert of Post-Primary Religious Education, Telephone interview, 8/03/2013.
Expert of Primary Religious Education, Telephone interview, 25/03/2013.
Expert of Religious Education and Citizenship Education, Belfast, 19/02/2013.
Ex-Principal in a Catholic Maintained School, Personal communication, 21/02/2013.
Officer (Ulster-Scots Agency), Belfast, 20/02/2013.
Officer (Statistics and Research Branch, Department of Education Northern Ireland), Personal correspondence, 22/05/2014.
Project Manager (Teaching Divided Histories, Nerve Centre, Derry/Londonderry), Phone interview, 10/04/2013.
Senior Education Advisor, Council for Catholic Maintained Schools, Belfast, 18/02/2013.
Senior Officer, Belfast Education and Library Board, Belfast, 26/02/2013.
Senior Officer, Council for Catholic Maintained Schools, Belfast, 18/02/2013.
Senior Officer (Education and Skills Authority), Telephone Interview, 13/03/2013.

Macedonia

Arshinkovska, Rada (Physics Teacher and Member of IEARN), Skopje, 17/09/2012.
Cupi, Recep Ali (Director of the Directorate for the Development and Promotion of the Languages of the Nationalities), Skopje, 19/09/2012.

Deralla, Xabir (President of Civil – Centre for Freedom), Skopje, 18/09/2012.
Georgieva, Loreta (Executive Director, Macedonian Civic Education Centre), Skopje, 11/09/2012.
Grodzanovska, Ljubica (Journalist, Transitions Online, Edno Magazine), Skopje, 9/09/2012.
Hani, Albert (Executive Director Training Centre for Management of Conflicts, Deputy Country Director Forum ZFD Skopje), Skopje, 13/09/2012.
Lazarevska, Spomenka (Education Program Director, Foundation Open Society Macedonia), Skopje, 17/09/2012.
Mickovska, Ana (Policy Analyst, Centre for Research and Policymaking), Skopje, 10/09/2012.
Mladenovski, Mire (President of the History Teachers' Association of Macedonia), Skopje, 13/09/2012.
Novkovski, Nenad (Academic and Former Minister of Education 1998–2002), Skopje, 11/09/2012.
Petrovski, Boban (Macedonian Historian and Professor, Saints Cyril and Methodius University), Skopje, 19/09/2012.
Sabani, Nora (Education for Development Specialist, UNICEF), Skopje, 18/09/2012.
Schenker, Harald (Independent Consultant and Drafter of the Strategy for Integrated Education), Skopje, 12/09/2012.
Tudjarovska, Emilja (Scholar and Activist), Skopje, 13/09/2012.
Veteroska, Silvana (Head of Sector for Professional Development, Bureau for Development of Education), Skopje, 14/09/2012.
Zenkolli, Veton (Project Manager, Nansen Dialogue Centre), Skopje, 12/09/2012.

ANONYMOUS
Albanian Historian, Skopje, 14/09/2012.
Coordinator, Ministry of Education, Skopje, 19/09/2012.
Officer, International Delegation, Skopje, 11/09/2012.
Officer, International Donor, Skopje, 14/09/2012.
Officer, International Mission, Skopje, 10/09/2012.
Officer, Ministry of Education and Science, Skopje, 18/09/2012.
Officer, World Bank, Skopje, 15/09/2012.
Senior Officer, Ministry of Education and Science, Skopje, 19/09/2012.

News Media

Cardinal Brady Accuses Catholic Schools of Getting Pupils by 'Stealth'. *BBC*, 13/02/2012.
Dnevik: Action for Eliminating Macedoanian Classes in Albanian Municipalities Continues. *Focus Information Agency*, 21/09/2012.

Macedonia Awaits Results of Schoolbook Revision. *Balkan Insight*, 23/02/2011.
Mikati: History Curriculum No Place for Narrow Interests. *The Daily Star*, 28/02/2012.
Million Syrian Refugees Registered in Lebanon – UN. *BBC*. http://www.bbc.co.uk/news/world-middle-east-26864485. Last accessed 14/12/2014.
Peter Robinson Calls for End to School Segregation. *Belfast Telegraph*, 16/10/2010.
The Controversial Education and Skills Authority: Stormont Fails to Deliver Again. *Belfast Telegraph*, 10/04/2014.
The Segregation Solution. *Transitions Online*, 26/05/2003.
Ahadzi-Zafirova, Zaklina. Macedonia's textbook Trauma. *Transitions Online*, 30/11/2011.
Dérenset, Jean Arnault, and Laurent Geslin. The nationalist movement rewriting Macedonia's history. *Le Temps*, 13/08/2012.
Dimishkovska-Grozdanovska, Ljubica. A poor report card for Macedonia's schools. *Transitions Online*, 12/01/2012.
Fattah, Hassan M. Lebanon's history textbooks sidestep its Civil War, *New York Times*, 10/01/2007.
Fergus, Lindsay. Northern Ireland schools 'Must cooperate or face closure'. *Belfast Telegraph*, 11/01/2012.
Fergus, Lindsay. Esa: £17m down the drain as death knell signalled for single education body. *Belfast Telegraph*, 10/04/2014.
Grncarovska, Tamara. Ambassador Herrero interview in *Utrinski Vasnik*. Learning of the Language should not bring these divisions. http://www.osce.org/skopje/67529?download=true. Last accessed 21/04/2014.
Huston, Luther A. High Court bans school segregation. 9-to-0 decision grants time to comply. *New York Times*, 18/05/1954.
Karajkov, Risto. Roma in Macedonia: A decade of inclusion?. *Osservatorio Balcani e Caucaso*, 16/05/2005.
Kollock, Paige. Lebanese children learn abbreviated national history. *Voice of America*, 11/11/2012.
Krauthamer, Ky. Reconciling differences in Macedonian classrooms. *Transitions Online*, 3/09/2012.
Lamb, Franklin. Why did Palestinian refugees come to Lebanon? *Eurasia Review*, 6/02/2012.
Maktabi, Rima. Lebanon's missing history: Why school books ignore the past. *CNN*, 8/06/2012.
Marusic, Sinisa-Jakov. Macedonia Court annuls controversial classes. *Balkan Insight*, 15/07/2010.
Marusic, Sinisa-Jakov. Macedonia 'Very surprised' by OSCE letter. *Balkan Insight* 28/01/2010.
Meguerditchian, Van. History curriculum revision sparks controversy. *The Daily Star*, 31/01/2012.

Meredith, Robbie. School children 'Could study Ulster-Scots for Gcse'. *BBC News*, 25/07/2012.
Perry, Duncan M. Republic of Macedonia: On the road to stability – or destruction? *Transitions Online*, 25/08/1995.
Quilty, Jim. Separate learning. Learned separatedness. *The Daily Star*, 19/02/2007.
Schmidt, Fabian. Ethnic Albanians: Balancing the power triangle. *Transitions Online*, 26/05/1995.
Schmidt, Fabian. Macedonia: From national consensus to pluralism. *Transitions Online*, 29/03/1995.
Sikimic, Simona. Debate over history curriculum reignites. *The Daily Star*, 30/04/2011.
Torney, Katherine. How integrated are schools where you live?. *The Detail TV*, 23/11/2012.
Vaknin, Sam. The education of Macedonia. Interview with Ljubica Grozdanovska of Bid consulting, 2007. http://www.globalpolitician.com/default.asp?23540-macedonia/. Last accessed 20/05/2013.
Zablit, Joceleyne. Lebanon's public schools students face Uphill battle. *AFP*, 8/10/2011.
Zhelev, Veselin. Skopje's attitude to neighbours causes worry: Bulgaria's EU ambassador. *Focus Information Agency*, 30/04/2013.

Official Documents and Reports

Bureau for the Development of Education of the Republic of Macedonia. 2008a. *Curriculum: Civic education*. Skopje: Ministry of Education and Science.
Bureau for the Development of Education of the Republic of Macedonia. 2008b. *Curriculum: Life-skills based education*. Skopje: Ministry of Education and Science.
Central Administration of Statistics. 2008. *Education*. Beirut: Central Administration of Statistics.
Central Administration of Statistics. 2010. *State statistical yearbook*. Beirut: Central Administration of Statistics.
Centre for Educational Research and Development. Approach to citizenship and civic education. http://www.crdp.org/CRDP/all%20curriculum/Civic%20Education/Civic%20Education%20Curriculum%20_ar.htm. Accessed 15 Aug 2013.
Centre for Educational Research and Development. 1997. *Civic education curriculum*. Beirut: CERD.
Court Orders Department of Education to reconsider its transport policy for Irish-medium secondary school. Summary of Judgment. 25/10/2011. http://www.courtsni.gov.uk/en-GB/Judicial%20Decisions/SummaryJudgments/

Documents/Summary%20of%20judgment%20-%20In%20re%20Colma%20 McKee/j_sj_RE_Colm_McKee_251011.html. Accessed 22 Apr 2014.

Connolly, Paul, Dawn Purvis, and P.J. O'Grady. 2013. *Advancing shared education. Report of the ministerial advisory group*. Belfast: DENI.

Council for Curriculum Examination and Assessment. Northern Ireland curriculum. http://www.nicurriculum.org.uk/. Accessed 22 Apr 2014.

Council for Curriculum Examination and Assessment. Progression framework: The world around us – history. Key stages 1–2. http://www.nicurriculum.org.uk/docs/key_stages_1_and_2/areas_of_learning/the_world_around_us/WAUGridHistory.pdf. Accessed 22 Apr 2014.

Council for Curriculum Examination and Assessment. Environment and society: History. Minimum statutory content key stage 3. http://www.nicurriculum.org.uk/docs/key_stage_3/areas_of_learning/statutory_requirements/ks3_history.pdf. Accessed 22 Apr 2014.

Council for Curriculum Examination and Assessment. 2012. *CCEA GCSE specification in history*. Belfast: Council for Curriculum Examination and Assessment.

Department of Education Northern Ireland. 1998. *Towards a culture of tolerance. Integrating education*. Belfast: Department of Education Northern Ireland.

Department of Education Northern Ireland. Northern Ireland summary data. s-new/education-statistics/32_statistics_and_research-numbersofschoolsandpupils_pg/32_statistics_and_research-northernirelandsummarydata_pg.htm. Accessed 22 Apr 2014.

Document of National Accord. 4/11/1989. http://www.al-bab.com/arab/docs/lebanon/taif.htm. Accessed 22 Apr 2014.

Economic and Social Commission for Western Asia. 2009. *Unpacking the dynamics of communal tensions: A focus group analysis of perceptions among youth in Lebanon*. New York: United Nations.

Framework Agreement. 13/08/2001. https://peaceaccords.nd.edu/site_media/media/accords/Macedonia_framework_agreement.pdf. Accessed 22 Apr 2014.

French Mandate for Syria and the Lebanon. 1923. *The American Journal of International Law* 17(3). 177–182.

Human Rights Council. 2009. *Report of the special rapporteur on freedom of religion or belief, Asma Jahangir. Mission to the former Yugoslav Republic of Macedonia*. Geneva: United Nations General Assembly.

Independent Strategic Review of Education. 2006. *Schools for the future: Funding, strategy, sharing*. Belfast: Department of Education Northern Ireland.

International Bureau of Education. 1946. *Annuaire International de L'Education et de L'Einsegnement*. Geneva: UNESCO.

International Bureau of Education. 1949. *International yearbook of education*. Geneva: UNESCO.

International Bureau of Education. 1951. *International yearbook of education*. Geneva: UNESCO.

International Bureau of Education. 1952. *International yearbook of education.* Geneva: UNESCO.
International Bureau of Education. 1953. *International yearbook of education.* Geneva: UNESCO.
International Bureau of Education. 1957. *International yearbook of education.* Geneva: UNESCO.
International Bureau of Education. 1959. *International yearbook of education.* Geneva: UNESCO.
International Bureau of Education. 1995. *Différenciation Intergroupes En Milieu Scolaire. Discussion Métodologique Et Analyse Comparative Dans Dix Pays.* Geneva: UNESCO.
International Bureau of Education. 2007. *World data on education*, 6th ed. Geneva: UNESCO.
International Bureau of Education. 2011. *World data on education, seventh edition 2010/2011.* Geneva: UNESCO.
Joint Council for Qualifications. 2012. *Provisional GCSE (Full Course) results – June 2012 (Northern Ireland only).* Belfast: Council for the Curriculum, Examinations and Assessment.
Lebanon-Syria Treaty of Cooperation. 20/05/1991. http://www.jewishvirtuallibrary.org/jsource/arabs/LebSyrCoop.html. Accessed 22 Apr 2014.
Lord Melchett. 1977. Secretary of state: Integrated education (3 June 1977). Memorandum by Lord Melchett, Minister of state at the Northern Ireland Office to the Secretary of State for Northern Ireland. PRONI CENT/1/10/3.
McAllister, J. 1979. *Integration in the education service.* PRONI CENT/1/9/1.
Ministry of Education and Higher Education. Achievements: 2010. https://www.google.co.uk/search?q=Ministry+of+Education+and+Higher+Education%2C+Achievements%3A+2010&oq=Ministry+of+Education+and+Higher+Education%2C+Achievements%3A+2010&aqs=chrome..69i57.164j0j4&sourceid=chrome&es_sm=91&ie=UTF-8. Accessed 22 Apr 2014.
Ministry of Education and Science. Interethnic integration in education. http://www.mon.gov.mk/index.php/component/content/article/1112. Accessed 4 Aug 2013.
Ministry of Education and Science. 2004. *National programme for the development of education in the Republic of Macedonia 2005–2015.* Skopje: Ministry of Education and Science.
Ministry of Education and Science. 2010a. *Manual for the prevention and protection against discrimination in the educational system in the republic of Macedonia.* Skopje: Ministry of Education and Science.
Ministry of Education and Science. 2010b. *Steps towards integrated education.* Skopje: Ministry of Education and Science.
Ministry of Education and Science. 2013. *Plan of activities of the donor organisations in the area of inter-ethnic education for 2012.* Skopje: Ministry of Education and Science.

Ministry of National Education and Arts. 1981. *Report of the Lebanese delegation to the 38th session of the international conference on education.* Beirut: Ministry of National Education and Arts.

Nolan, Paul. 2014. *Northern Ireland peace monitoring report number three.* Belfast: Community Relations Council.

Northern Ireland (St Andrews Agreement) Act 2006. 22/11/2006. http://www.legislation.gov.uk/ukpga/2006/53/contents/enacted. Accessed 22 Apr 2014.

Northern Ireland Statistics & Research Agency. Census 2011. http://www.nisra.gov.uk/Census/2011Census.html. Accessed 22 Apr 2014.

Office of the First Minister and Deputy First Minister. 2005. *A shared future. Policy and strategic framework for good relations in Northern Ireland.* Belfast: Office of the First Minister and Deputy First Minister.

Organisation for Security and Co-operation in Europe Spillover Mission to Skopje. 2010. *Age, contact, perceptions: How schools shape relations between ethnicities.* Skopje: OSCE.

Pitt-Brooke, J. 1976. Note for the record: Shared schools (30 July 1976). Meeting between R. Moyle, Minister of state at the Northern Ireland Office, with Cardinal Conway, Catholic Primate of Ireland. PRONI ED/32/B/1/11/1.

State Statistical Office. 2002. *Census of population, households and dwellings 2002. Book X: Total population according to ethnic affiliation, mother-tongue and religion.* Skopje: State Statistical Office.

State Statistical Office. 2006. *Statistical yearbook.* Skopje: State Statistical Office.

State Statistical Office. 2008. *Statistical yearbook.* Skopje: State Statistical Office.

State Statistical Office. 2013a. *Primary, lower secondary and upper secondary schools at the end of the school year, 2011/2012.* Skopje: State Statistical Office.

State Statistical Office. 2013b. *Statistical yearbook.* Skopje: State Statistical Office.

The agreement reached in the multi-party negotiations. Belfast. 10/04/1998. http://www.britishirishcouncil.org/about/agreement-reached-multi-party-negotiations. Accessed 22 Apr 2014.

The education reform (Northern Ireland) order 1989. 19/12/1989. http://www.legislation.gov.uk/nisi/1989/2406/contents/made. Accessed 10 May 2014.

The Lebanese constitution, Promulgated May 23, 1926 with its amendments. 1995. http://www.presidency.gov.lb/English/LebaneseSystem/Documents/Lebanese%20Constitution.pdf. Accessed 22 Apr 2014.

United Nations Development Programme. 2008a. *Education and citizenship. Analysis of survey results of 9th grade students in Lebanon.* Beirut: UNDP.

United Nations Development Programme. 2008b. *People centered analysis report.* Skopje: UNDP.

United Nations Development Programme. 2009. *Lebanon human development report: Toward a citizen's state, 2008–2009.* Beirut: UNDP.

United Nations Economic and Social Council. 2003. *The right to education. Report submitted by Katarina Tomasevski, special Rapporteur, in accordance* with commission resolution 2002/23. *Mission to the United Kingdom (Northern Ireland) 24 November–1 December 2002.* Geneva: United Nations.

United Nations Educational Scientific and Cultural Organisation. 2011. *Education for all global monitoring report 2011. The hidden crisis: Armed conflict and education.* Paris: UNESCO.

United Nations International Children's Emergency Fund. 2009a. *Child-focused public expenditure review.* Skopje: UNICEF Country Office.

United Nations International Children's Emergency Fund. 2009b. *Study on multiculturalism and inter-ethnic relations in education.* Skopje: UNICEF Country Office.

Yaacoub, Najwa, and Lara Badre. 2012. *Education in Lebanon.* Beirut: Central Administration of Statistics.

Secondary Sources

Abouchedid, Kamal, and Ramzi Nasser. 2000. The state of history teaching in private-run confessional schools in Lebanon: Implications for national integration. *Mediterranean Journal of Educational Studies* 5(2): 57–82.

Abouchedid, K., R. Nasser, and J. Van Blommestein. 2002. The limitations of inter-group learning in confessional school systems: The case of Lebanon. *Arab Studies Quarterly* 24(4): 61–82.

Akar, Bassel. 2006. Teacher reflections on the challenges of teaching citizenship education in Lebanon: A qualitative pilot study. *Reflecting Education* 2(2): 48–63.

Akar, Bassel. 2007. Citizenship education in Lebanon: An introduction into students' concepts and learning experiences. *Educate* 7(2): 2–18.

Akar, Bassel. 2009. Exploring the challenges and practices of citizenship education in national and civic education grades ten and eleven in Lebanon. *Compare* 39(5).

Akenson, Donald Harman. 1973. *Education and enmity, the control of schooling in Northern Ireland 1920–1950.* Newton Abbot: David and Charles.

Arlow, Michael. 2000. *The challenges of social inclusion in Northern Ireland: Citizenship and life skills.* Geneva: IBE.

Babuna, Aydin. 2000. The Albanians of Kosovo and Macedonia: Ethnic identity superseding religion. *Nationalities Papers* 28(1).

Bahous, Rima. 2011. Multilingual educational trends and practices in Lebanon: A case study. *International Review of Education* 57: 737–749.

Banks, James A. (ed.). 2007. *Diversity and citizenship education. Global perspectives.* San Francisco: Jossey-Bass.

Barakat, Halim (ed.). 1988. *Toward a viable Lebanon.* London: Croom Helm.

Barany, Zoltan, and Robert G. Moser (eds.). 2005. *Ethnic politics after communism*. London: Cornell University Press.

Bar-Tal, Daniel. 2001. Why does fear override hope in societies engulfed by intractable conflict, as it does in the Israeli society? *Political Psychology* 22(3): 601–627.

Barton, Keith C. 2001a. A sociocultural perspective on children's understanding of historical change: Comparative findings from Northern Ireland and the United States. *American Educational Research Journal* 38(4): 881–913.

Barton, Keith C. 2001b. History education and national identity in Northern Ireland and the United States: Differing priorities. *Theory into Practice* 40(1): 48–54.

Barton, Keith, and Alan McCully. 2005. History, identity and the school curriculum in Northern Ireland: An empirical study of secondary students' ideas and perspectives. *Journal of Curriculum Studies* 37(1): 85–116.

Bashshour, Mounir. 1966. Higher education and political development in Syria and Lebanon. *Comparative Education Review* 10(3): 451–461.

Batt, Judy (ed.). 2008. *Is there an Albanian question?* Paris: European Union Institute for Security Studies.

Bekerman, Zvi, and Claire McGlynn (eds.). 2007. *Addressing ethnic conflict through peace education*. London: Palgrave.

Bell, John, Ulf Hansson, and Nick McCaffery. 2010. *The troubles aren't history yet. Young people's understanding of the past*. Belfast: Community Relations Council.

Bieber, Florian. 2000. Bosnia-Herzegovina and Lebanon: Historical lessons of two multireligious states. *Third World Quarterly* 21(2): 269–281.

Bizri, Fida. 2013. Linguistic green lines in Lebanon. *Mediterranean Politics* 18(3): 444–459.

Bokovoy, Melissa K., Jill A. Irvine, and Carol S. Lilly (eds.). 1997. *State-society relations in Yugoslavia, 1945–1992*. New York: St Martin's Press.

Bourdieu, Pierre, and Jean-Claude Passeron. 1990. *Reproduction in education, society and culture*. London: Sage.

Briza, Jan. 2000. *Minority rights in Yugoslavia*. London: Minority Rights Group.

Brown, Graham K. 2011. The influence of education on violent conflict and peace: Inequality, opportunity and the management of diversity. *Prospects* 41(2): 191–204.

Brunnbauer, Ulf. 2002. The implementation of the Ohrid agreement: Ethnic Macedonian resentments. *Journal on Ethnopolitics and Minority Issues in Europe* 1: 2–24.

Buchenau, Klaus. 2005. 'What went wrong? Church–state relations in socialist Yugoslavia. *Nationalities Papers: The Journal of Nationalism and Ethnicity* 33(4): 547–567.

Byram, Michael. 2008. *From foreign language education to education for intercultural citizenship. Essays and reflections*. Toronto: Multilingual Matters.

Camargo Abello, Marina. 1997. Are the seeds of violence sown in schools? *Prospects* XXVII(3): 447–465.
Carta, Alessia, Carla Podda, and Claudia Secci. 2012. Cittadinanza Democratica in Construzione. Lettura Dei Rapporti Di 'Esclusione/Inclusione' in Macedonia. *Ricerche di Pedagogia e Didattica* 7(1): 1–13.
Chadwick, Priscilla. 1994. *Schools of reconciliation. Issues in joint Roman Catholic-Anglican education.* London: Cassell.
Chapman, Arthur, Lukas Perikleous, Christalla Yakinthou, and Rana Zincir Celal. 2011. *Thinking historically about missing persons: A guide for teachers.* Cyprus: International Centre for Transitional Justice.
Chartouni, Charles. 1993. *Conflict resolution in Lebanon. Myth and reality.* Beirut: Foundation for Human Rights.
Chehabi, E.H. (ed.). 2006. *Distant relations: Iran and Lebanon in the last 500 years.* London: IB Tauris.
Choueiri, Youssef (ed.). 2007. *Breaking the cycle. Civil wars in Lebanon.* London: Stacey International.
Chung, Fay. 1999. Education: A key to power and a tool for change – a practitioner's perspective. *Current Issues in Comparative Education* 2(1).
Cole, Elizabeth A. (ed.). 2007. *Teaching the violent past. History education and reconciliation.* Plymouth: Rowman & Littlefield.
Cole, Elizabeth A., and Judy Barsalou. 2006. *Unite or divide? The challenges of teaching history in societies emerging from violent conflict.* Washington, DC: United States Institute of Peace.
Colwill, Ian, and Carmel Gallagher. 2007. Developing a curriculum for the twenty-first century: The experiences of England and Northern Ireland. *Prospects* 37: 411–425.
Connolly, Paul, and Julie Healy. 2004. *Children and the conflict in Northern Ireland: The experiences and perspectives of 3–11 years olds.* Belfast: OFMDFM Research Branch.
Connolly, Paul, and Paul Maginn. 1999. *Sectarianism, children and community relations in Northern Ireland.* Coleraine: University of Ulster.
Connolly, Paul, Alan Smith, and Berni Kelly. 2002. *Too young to notice? The cultural and political awareness of 3–6 years olds in Northern Ireland.* Belfast: Northern Ireland Community Relations Council.
Cordell, Karl, and Stefan Wolff (eds.). 2010. *Routledge handbook of ethnic conflict.* London: Routledge.
Coulter, Colin, and Michael Muray (eds.). 2008. *Northern Ireland after the troubles, a society in transition.* Manchester: Manchester University Press.
Cummins, Jim (ed.). 2008. *Encyclopedia of Language and education volume 5. Bilingual education.* Philadelphia: Springer.
Cummins, Jim, and David Corson (eds.). 1998. *Encyclopedia of Language and education volume 5. Bilingual education.* London: Kulwer Academic Publishers.

Darby, John P. 1974. Divisiveness of education in Northern Ireland. *Equity & Excellence in Education* 12(1): 3–11.
Darby, John. 1976. *Conflict in Northern Ireland: The development of a polarised community*. Dublin: Gill and Macmillan.
Darby, John. 1978. Northern Ireland: Bonds and breaks in education. *British Journal of Educational Studies* 26(3): 215–223.
Daskalovski, Zhidas. 2002. Language and identity: The Ohrid framework agreement and liberal notions of citizenship and nationality in Macedonia. *Journal on Ethnopolitics and Minority Issues in Europe* 1: pp. 2–32.
Davies, Lynn. 2004. *Education and conflict: Complexity and chaos*. London: Routledge : pp. 7–34.
Davies, Lynn. 2005. Teaching about conflict through citizenship education. *International Journal of Citizenship and Teacher Education* 1(2).
Dean, Jacqueline. 2002. History and citizenship: Concepts and practice. *Educational Evaluation and Policy Analysis* 3(13): 9–16.
Dekmejian, R. Hrair. 1975. *Patterns of political leadership: Lebanon, Israel, Egypt*. Albany: State University of New York Press.
Den Heyer, Kent. 2003. Between every 'now' and 'then': A role for the study of historical agency in history and citizenship education. *Theory and Research in Social Education* 31(4): 411–434.
Diab, Rula L. 2006. University students' beliefs about learning English and French in Lebanon. *System* 34: 80–96.
Donkova, Maria. 2000. Teaching history differently: A lesson from the Balkans. *History: Beyond the Battlefield. UNESCO Sources* 120: 8–9.
Donnelly, Caitlin. 2000. In pursuit of school ethos. *British Journal of Educational Studies* 48(2): 134–154.
Duffy, Terence. 2000. Peace education in a divided society: Creating a culture of peace in Northern Ireland. *Prospects* XXX(1): 15–29.
Dunn, Seamus. 1986. The role of education in the Northern Ireland conflict. *Oxford Review of Education* 12(3): 233–242.
Dunn, Seamus (ed.). 1995. *Facets of the conflict in Northern Ireland*. London: St Martin's Press.
Dunn, Seamus, and Valerie Morgan. 1999. 'A fraught path': Education as a basis for developing improved community relations in Northern Ireland. *Oxford Review of Education* 25(1/2): 141–153.
Dupuy, Kendra E. 2008. Education in peace agreements, 1989–2005. *Conflict resolution quarterly* 26(2): 149–166.
Easton, David. 1969. *Children in the political system*. New York: McGraw-Hill Book Company.
elKhazen, Farid. 2000. *The breakdown of the state in Lebanon, 1967–1976*. London: IB Tauris Publishers.

Elliott, Marianne (ed.). 2007. *The long road to peace in Northern Ireland.* Liverpool: Liverpool University Press.

Engström, Jenny. 2002. Multi-ethnicity or bi-nationalism? The framework agreement and the future of the Macedonian state. *Journal of Ethnopolitics and Minority Issues in Europe* 1: 2–21.

Eurydice. 2000. *Foreign language teaching in schools in Europe.* Brussels: Euridyce.

Ewart, Shirley, and Dirk Schubotz. 2004. *Voices behind the statistics. Young people's views of sectarianism in Northern Ireland.* Belfast: National Children's Bureau.

Faour, Muhammad. 2007. Religion, demography, and politics in Lebanon. *Middle Eastern Studies* 43(6): 909–921.

Faour, Muhammad, and Marwan Muasher. 2011. *Education for citizenship in the Arab world. Key to the future.* Washington, DC: Carnegie Endowment.

Fincham, Kathleen. 2012. Nationalist narratives, boundaries and social inclusion/exclusion in Palestinian camps in South Lebanon. *Compare* 42(2): 1–22.

Finlay, Andrew. 2006. Anthropology misapplied? The culture concept and the peace process in Ireland. *Anthropology in Action* 13(1–2): 1–10.

Finlay, Andrew. 2008. The persistence of the 'old' idea of culture and the peace process in Ireland. *Critique of Anthropology* 28: 279–291.

Finlay, Andrew. 2010. *Governing ethnic conflict. Consociation, identity and the price of peace.* London: Routledge.

Fischer, Karin. 2011. University historians and their role in the development of a 'shared' history in Northern Ireland schools 1960s–1980s: An illustration of the ambiguous social function of historians. *History of Education* 40(2): 241–253.

Fontana, Giuditta. 2015. Religious education after conflicts: Promoting social cohesion or entrenching plurality? *Compare.* October 2015. http://www.tandfonline.com/doi/full/10.1080/03057925.2015.1099422

Foundation Open Society Macedonia. 2010. *Analysis of the implementation of Roma language and culture as an elective subject.* FOSIM: Skopje.

Fowkes, Ben. 2002. *Ethnicity and ethnic conflict in the post-Communist world.* London: Palgrave.

Frayha, Nemer. 2003. Education and social cohesion in Lebanon. *Prospects* XXXIII(1): 77–88.

Gallagher, Tony. 2004. *Education in divided societies.* Basingstoke: Palgrave Macmillan.

Gallagher, Tony. 2005. Balancing difference and the common good: Lessons from a post-conflict society. *Compare* 35(4): 429–442.

Gasanabo, Jean-Damascène. 2006. *Fostering peaceful co-existence through analysis and revision of history curricula and textbooks in Southeast Europe, preliminary stocktaking report.* Geneva: UNESCO.

Georgeoff, John. 1966a. Nationalism in the history textbooks of Yugoslavia and Bulgaria. *Comparative Education Review* 10(3): 442–450.

Georgeoff, John. 1966b. Social studies in Yugoslav elementary schools. *The Elementary School Journal* 66(8): 432–437.
Georgeoff, Peter John. 1982. *The educational system of Yugoslavia.* Washington, DC: National Institute of Education.
Ghait, Ghazi M., and Kassim A. Shaaban. 1996. Language-in-education policy and planning: The case of Lebanon. *Mediterranean Journal of Educational Studies* 1(2): 95–105.
Gilmour, David. 1983. *Lebanon, the fractured country.* Oxford: Martin Robertson.
Green, Andy. 1997. *Education, globalisation and the nation state.* London: Macmillan.
Green, Andy, and John Preston. 2001. Education and social cohesion: Recentering the debate. *Peabody Journal of Education* 76(3/4): 247–284.
Green, Andy, P. Preston, and R. Sabates. 2003. *Education, equality and social cohesion: A distributional model.* London: Institute of Education.
Green, Andy, John Preston, and Jan Germen Janmaat. 2006. *Education, equality and social cohesion.* London: Palgrave.
Green, Andy, Germen Janmaat, and Christine Han. 2009. *Regimes of social cohesion.* London: Centre for Learning and Life Chances in Knowledge Economies and Societies.
Hanf, Theodor. 1994. *Coexistence in Wartime Lebanon. Decline of a state and rise of a nation.* London: IB Tauris.
Hanf, Theodor (ed.). 1999. *Dealing with difference. Religion, ethnicity and politics: Comparing cases and concepts.* Baden-Baden: Nomos.
Hanf, Theodor. 2007. *E Pluribus Unum? Lebanese opinions and attitudes on coexistence.* Byblos: UNESCO.
Hanf, Theodor (ed.). 2011. *The political function of education in deeply divided countries.* Baden-Baden: Nomos.
Hanf, Theodor, and Karim El Mufti (eds.). 2013. *Policies and politics of teaching religion.* Baden-Baden: Nomos.
Hanf, Theodor, and Nawaf Salam (eds.). 2003. *Lebanon in Limbo. Postwar society and state in an uncertain regional environment.* Baden-Baden: Nomos.
Hansson, Ulf, Una O'Connor Bones, and John McCord. 2013. *Integrated education: A review of policy and research evidence.* Belfast: Integrated Education Fund.
Harik, Judith. 1994. *The public and social services of the Lebanese militias.* Oxford: Centre for Lebanese Studies.
Heatley, Colm. 2004. *Interface: Flashpoints in Northern Ireland.* Belfast: Lagan Books.
Hewstone, Miles, Nicole Taush, Joanne Hughes, and Ed Cairns. 2008. *Can contact promote better relations? Evidence from mixed and segregated areas of Belfast.* Belfast: OFMDFMNI.
Hogg, Michael H., Deborah J. Terry, and Catherine M. White. 1995. A tale of two theories: A critical comparison of identity theory with social identity theory. *Social Psychology Quarterly* 58(4): 255–269.

Hooge, Marc, and Britt Wilkenfeld. 2008. The stability of political attitudes and behaviors across adolescence and early adulthood: A comparison of survey data on adolescents and young adults in eight countries. *Journal of Youth and Adolescence* 37: 155–167.

Hornberger, Nancy H. (ed.). 2008. *Encyclopedia of language and education volume 8. Language socialisation*. Philadelphia: Springer.

Huddy, Leonie. 2001. From social to political identity: A critical examination of social identity theory. *Political Psychology* 22(1): 127–156.

Huddy, Leonie. 2004. Contrasting theoretical approaches to intergroup relations. *Political Psychology* 25(6): 947–967.

Hudson, Michael C. 1969. Democracy and social mobilization in Lebanese politics. *Comparative Politics* 1(2): 254–263.

Hudson, Michael C. 1999. Lebanon after taif. Another reform opportunity lost?. *Arab Studies Quarterly* 21(1): 27–40.

Hughes, Joanne. 2011. Are separate schools divisive? A case study from Northern Ireland. *British Educational Research Journal* 37(5): 829–850.

International Crisis Group. 2000. *Macedonia's ethnic Albanians: Bridging the Gulf*. Brussels: International Crisis Group.

International Crisis Group. 2001a. *Macedonia: The last chance for peace*. Brussels: International Crisis Group.

International Crisis Group. 2001b. *The Macedonian question: Reform or rebellion*. Brussels: International Crisis Group.

International Crisis Group. 2004. *Macedonia: Make or break*. Brussels: International Crisis Group.

International Crisis Group. 2008. *Lebanon: Hizbollah's weapons turn inward*. Brussels: International Crisis Group.

Janmaat, Jan Germen. 2010. *Classroom diversity and its relation to tolerance, trust and participation in England, Sweden and Germany*. London: Centre for Learning and Life Chances in Knowledge Economies and Societies.

Kerr, David. 1999. Citizenship education in the curriculum. An international review. *The School Field* X(3/4): 5–32.

Kerr, Michael. 2005. *Imposing power-sharing: Conflict and coexistence in Northern Ireland and Lebanon*. Dublin: Irish Academic Press.

Kerr, David, and Cliff O'Neill (eds.). 1995. *Professional preparation and professional development in a climate of change*. Lancaster: University College of St Martin.

Khalife, Ali. 2006. La Place De La Religion À L'école. *Confluences Méditerranée* 56: 145–160.

Knudsen, Are, and Michael Kerr (eds.). 2013. *Lebanon after the cedar revolution*. London: Hurst.

Koppa, Maria-Eleni. 2001. Ethnic Albanians in the former Yugoslav republic of Macedonia: Between nationality and citizenship. *Nationalism and Ethnic Politics* 7(4): 37–65.

Koulouri, Christina (ed.). 2002. *Clio in the Balkans. The politics of history education*. Thessaloniki: Centre for Democracy and Reconciliation in SouthEast Europe.
Krasniqi, Gëzim. 2011. The 'Forbidden fruit': Islam and the politics of identity in Kosovo and Macedonia. *Southeast European and Black Sea Studies* 11(2): 191–207.
Labaki, Boutros. 1988. *Education Et Mobilite Sociale Dans La Societe Multicommunautaire Du Liban*. Larnara: Materialen zu Gesellschaft und Bildung in multikulturellen Gesellschaften.
Lambkin, B.K. 1996. *Opposite religions still? Interpreting Northern Ireland after the conflict*. Aldershot: Avebury.
Lampe, John R. 1996. *Yugoslavia as history: Twice there was a country*. Cambridge: Cambridge University Press.
Larkin, Craig. 2010. Beyond the war? The Lebanese postmemory experience. *International Journal of Middle Eastern Studies* 42: 615–635.
Le Thomas, Catherine. 2012. *Les Écoles Chiites Au Liban*. Paris: Karthala.
Levinson, David. 1998. *Ethnic groups worldwide. A ready reference handbook*. Phoenix: Oryx Press.
Lijphart, Arend. 1975. The Northern Ireland problem: Cases, theories, and solutions. *British Journal of Political Science* 5(1): 83–106.
Lijphart, Arend. 1977. *Democracy in plural societies*. London: Yale University Press.
Lijphart, Arend. 1996. The framework document on Northern Ireland and the theory of power-sharing. *Government and Opposition* 31(3): 267–274.
Lijphart, Arend. 2008. *Thinking about democracy. Power sharing and majority rule in theory and practice*. London: Routledge.
Loughlin, John, John Kincaid, and Wilfried Swenden. 2013. *Routledge handbook on regionalism and federalism*. London: Routledge.
Low-Beer, Ann. 1999. Report. Seminar on 'the reform of history teaching: Curriculum, textbook and teacher training,' Mavrovo, the former Yugoslav republic of Macedonia, 19–21 October 1999. Strasbourg: Council of Europe.
Lyon, Aisling. 2011. *Decentralisation and the delivery of primary and secondary education*. Skopje: Centre for Research and Policymaking.
Mac Giolla Chríost, Diarmait. 2005. *The Irish language in Ireland. From Goídel to globalisation*. London: Routledge.
Magill, Claire, Alan Smith, and Brandon Hamber. 2009. *The role of education in reconciliation. The perspectives of children and young people in Bosnia Herzegovina and Northern Ireland*. Londonderry: INCORE.
Makdisi, Ussama. 1996. Reconstructing the nation-state: The modernity of sectarianism in Lebanon. *Middle East Report* 200; 23–26, 30.
Mandaci, Nazif. 2007. Turks of Macedonia: The travails of the "smaller" minority. *Journal of Muslim Minority Affairs* 27(1): 5–23.

Marthoz, Jean-Paul. 2000. The hidden history of Latin America. *History: Beyond the Battlefield. UNESCO Sources* 120: 7–8.

Martin-Jones, Marilyn, and Anne-Marie de Mejia. 2008. *Encyclopedia of language and education volume 3. Discourse and education.* Philadelphia: Springer.

Massialas, Byron G. 1975. Some propositions about the role of school in the formation of political behaviour and political attitudes of students: Cross-national perspectives. *Comparative Education Review* 19(1): 169–176.

May, Stephen, and Hornberger Nancy H. (eds.). 2008. *Encyclopedia of language and education volume 1. Language policy and political issues in education.* Philadelphia: Springer.

McCrudden, Christopher, and Brendan O'Leary. 2013. *Courts and consociations. Human rights versus power-sharing.* Oxford: Oxford University Press.

McCully, Alan, Keith C. Barton, and Margaret Conway. 2003a. History education and national identity in Northern Ireland. *International Journal of Historical Learning, Teaching and Research* 3(1): 31–43.

McCully, Alan, Brendan Hartop, and Keith Barton. 2003b. *Teaching history in societies emerging from conflict.* Coleraine: University of Ulster.

McDermott, Philip. 2011. 'Irish isn't spoken here?' Language policy and planning in Ireland. *English Today* 27(2): 25–31.

McGarry, John (ed.). 2001. *Northern Ireland and the divided world. Post-agreement Northern Ireland in comparative perspective.* Oxford: Oxford University Press.

McGarry, John, and Brendan O'Leary. 2004. *The Northern Ireland conflict. Consociational engagements.* Oxford: Oxford University Press.

McGarry, John, and Brendan O'Leary. 2006a. Consociational theory, Northern Ireland's conflict, and its agreement. Part 1: What consociationalists can learn from Northern Ireland. *Government and Opposition* 44(1): 43–63.

McGarry, John, and Brendan O'Leary. 2006b. Consociational theory, Northern Ireland's conflict, and its agreement part 2. What critics of consociation can learn from Northern Ireland. *Government and Opposition* 41(2): 249–277.

McGarry, John, and Brendan O'Leary. 2007. Iraq's constitution of 2005: Liberal consociation as political prescription. *International Journal of Constitutional Law* 5(4).

McGlynn, Claire. 2005. Integrated and faith-based schooling in Northern Ireland. *The Irish Journal of Education* 36: 49–62.

McGlynn, Claire, Ulrike Niens, Ed Cairns, and Miles Hewstone. 2004. Moving out of conflict: The contribution of integrated schools in Northern Ireland to identity, attitudes, forgiveness and reconciliation. *Journal of Peace Education* 1(2): 147–163.

McGlynn, Claire, Michalinos Zembylas, and Zvi Bekerman. 2009. *Peace education in conflict and post-conflict societies. Comparative perspectives.* London: Palgrave.

McMonagle, Sarah. 2010. Deliberating the Irish Language in Northern Ireland: From conflict to multiculturalism? *Journal of Multilingual and Multicultural Development* 31(3): 253–270.

Menken, Kate, and Ofelia Garcia (eds.). 2010. *Negotiating language policies in schools*. London: Routledge.

Minority Rights Group International. 1994. *Education rights and minorities*. London: Manchester Free Press.

Morgan, Valerie, and Grace Fraser. 1999. When does 'good news' become 'bad news?' Relationships between government and the integrated schools in Northern Ireland. *British Journal of Educational Studies* 47(4): 364–379.

Morgan, Valerie, Seamus Dunn, Ed Cairns, and Grace Fraser. 1992. *Breaking the mould: The roles of parents and teachers in the integrated schools in Northern Ireland*. Coleraine: University of Ulster.

Mulholland, Marc. 2000. Assimilation versus segregation: Unionist strategy in the 1960s. *Twentieth Century British History* 11: 284–307.

Murray, Dominic. 1985. *Worlds apart: Segregated schools in Northern Ireland*. Belfast: Appletree Press.

Myhrvold, Ronny. 2005. *Former Yugoslav Republic of Macedonia: Education as a political phenomenon*. Nordem report. Oslo: Norwegian Centre for Human Rights.

Nagle, John, and Mary-Alice Clancy. 2010. *Shared society or benign apartheid? Understanding peace-building in divided societies*. London: Palgrave.

Neofotistos, Vasiliki P. 2004. Beyond stereotypes: Violence and the porousness of ethnic boundaries in the republic of Macedonia. *History and Anthropology* 15(1): 1–36.

Niens, Ulrike, and Ed Cairns. 2005. Conflict, contact and education in Northern Ireland. *Theory into Practice* 44(4): 337–344.

Niens, Ulrike, and Marie-Hélène Chastenay. 2008. Educating for peace? Citizenship education in Quebec and Northern Ireland. *Comparative Education Review* 52(4): 519–540.

Niens, Ulrike, and Lorraine McIlrath. 2010. Understandings of citizenship education in Northern Ireland and the republic of Ireland: public discourses among stakeholders in the public and private sectors. *Education, Citizenship and Social Justice* 73(5): 73–87.

Niens, Ulrike, and Jacqueline Reilly. 2010. *The global bimension: School approaches, teaching and learning in Northern Ireland*. Belfast: DfID.

Noel, S. (ed.). 2005. *From power sharing to democracy*. Quebec: McGill University Press.

Oakes, Penelope. 2002. Psychological groups and political psychology: A response to Huddy's 'critical examination of social identity theory. *Political Psychology* 23(4): 809–824.

O Caoimhghin, Croidheáin. 2006. *Language from below. The Irish Language, ideology and power in the 20th century*. Oxford: Peter Lang.

O'Connor, Fionnuala. 2002. *A shared childhood, the story of the integrated schools in Northern Ireland*. Belfast: Blackstaff Press.

O'Leary, Brendan, and John McGarry. 1996. *The politics of antagonism: Understanding Northern Ireland*. London: Athlone Press.
Oberschall, Anthony. 2007. *Conflict and peace building in divided societies*. London: Routledge.
Olson, David, and Nancy Torrance. 1996. *The handbook of education and human development*. Oxford: Blackwell Publishers.
Osler, Audrey, and Hugh Starkey. 2006. Education for democratic citizenship: A review of research, policy and practice 1995–2005. *Research Papers in Education* 21(4): 433–466.
Ouane, Adama (ed.). 2003. *Towards a multilingual culture of education*. Hamburg: UNESCO Institute for Education.
Oulton, Christopher, Vanessa Day, Justin Dillon, and Marcus Grace. 2004. Controversial issues: Teachers' attitudes and practices in the context of citizenship education. *Oxford Review of Education* 30(4): 489–507.
Paolini, Stefania, Miles Hewstone, Ed Cairns, and Alberto Voci. 2004. Effects of direct and indirect cross-group friendships on judgments of Catholics and protestants in Northern Ireland: The mediating role of an anxiety-reduction mechanism. *Personality and Social Psychology Bulletin* 30(6): 770–786.
Peatling, Gary K. 2004. *The failure of the Northern Ireland peace process*. Dublin: Irish Academic Press.
Pettigrew, Thomas F., and Linda Tropp. 2011. *When groups meet: The dynamics of intergroup contact*. New York: Psychology Press.
Phillips, John. 2004. *Macedonia. Warlords and rebels in the Balkans*. London: Yale University Press.
Phillips, Robert, Paul Goalen, Alan McCully, and Sydney Wood. 1999. Four histories, one nation? History teaching, nationhood and a British identity. *Compare* 29(2): 153–169.
Poulton, Hugh. 1995. *Who are the Macedonians?* London: Hurst.
Price, Glanville (ed.). 2000. *Languages in Britain & Ireland*. Malden: Blackwell.
Purdy, Noel, Laurence Siberry, and George Beale. 2010. Primary languages in Northern Ireland: Too little, too late? *The Language Learning Journal* 38(2): 149–158.
Quercia, Paolo. 2004. Bordeline religion: The role of Churches in Balkan nation building. *CeMiSS Quarterly* II(1): 21–33.
Ramet, Sabrina P. 2002. *Balkan Babel. The bisintegration of Yugoslavia from the death of Tito to the fall of Milošević*. Boulder: Westview Press.
Ripiloski, Sasho. 2011. *Conflict in Macedonia. Exploring a paradox in the former Yugoslavia*. London: First Forum Press.
Risteska, Marja, and Zhidas Daskalovski (eds.). 2011. *One decade after the Ohrid agreement: Lessons (to Be) learned from the Macedonian experience*. Skopje: Centre for Research and Policymaking.
Rossos, Andrew. 2008. *Macedonia and the Macedonians, a history*. Stanford: Hoover Institution Press.

Rothschild, Donald, and Philip Roeder (eds.). 2005. *Sustainable peace: Power and democracy after civil wars*. Ithaca: Cornell University Press.
Roudometof, Victor. 2002. *Collective memory, national identity and ethnic conflict*. Westport: Praeger.
Rubin, Mark, and Miles Hewstone. 2004. Social identity, system justification, and social dominance: Commentary on Reicher, Jost et al., and Sidanius et al. *Political Psychology* 25(6): 823–844.
Russell, Raymond. 2013. *Census 2011: Key statistics at Northern Ireland and LGD level*. Belfast: Northern Ireland Assembly Research and Information Service.
Salamé, Ghassane. 1986. *Lebanon's injured identities. Who represents whom during a civil war?* Oxford: Centre for Lebanese Studies.
Salamey, Imad. 2014. *The government and politics of Lebanon*. London: Routledge.
Salamey, Imad, and Rhys Payne. 2008. Parliamentary consociationalism in Lebanon: Equal citizenry vs quoted confessionalism. *The Journal of Legislative Studies* 14(4): 451–473.
Salem, Paul. 1998. Framing post-war Lebanon: Perspectives on the constitution and the structure of power. *Mediterranean Politics* 3(1).
Salibi, Kamal. 1988. *A house of many mansions: The history of Lebanon reconsidered*. London: I.B. Tauris & Co.
Salomon, Gavriel, and Edward Cairns (eds.). 2009. *Handbook on peace education*. New York: Psychology Press.
Sawsan, Abdulrahim, and Marwan Khawaja. 2011. The cost of being Palestinian in Lebanon. *Journal of Ethnic and Migration Studies* 37(1): 151–166.
Sears, A., and I. Wright. 2004. *Challenges and prospects for Canadian social studies*. Vancouver: Pacific Educational Press.
Seixas, Peter. 1993. Historical understanding among adolescents in a multicultural setting. *Curriculum Enquiry* 23(3): 301–327.
Shoup, Paul. 1968. *Communism and the Yugoslav national question*. London: Columbia University Press.
Shuayb, Maha (ed.). 2012. *Rethinking education for social cohesion. International case studies*. New York: Palgrave Macmillan.
Sidiropoulos, Elizabeth. 1999. Minority protection in the former Yugoslav republic of Macedonia: Will it preserve the state? *Cambridge Review of International Affairs* 12(2): 139–152.
Simpson, Kirk, and Peter Daly. 2004. Politics and education in Northern Ireland – an analytical history. *Irish Studies Review* 12(2): 163–174.
Simpson, George Eaton, and J. Milton Yinger. 1985. *Racial and cultural minorities: An analysis of prejudice and discrimination*. London: Plenum.
Sinclair, Margaret. 2004. *Learning to live together: Building skills, values and attitudes for the twenty-first century*. Paris: UNESCO IBE.
Smith, Anthony D. 1999. *The ethnic origins of nations*. Oxford: Blackwell.

Smith, Alan. 2001. Religious segregation and the emergence of integrated schools in Northern Ireland. *Oxford Review of Education* 27(4): 559–575.
Smith, Alan. 2003. Citizenship education in Northern Ireland: Beyond national identity? *Cambridge Journal of Education* 33(1): 15–32.
Smith, Alan. 2005. Education in the twenty-first century: Conflict reconstruction and reconciliation. *Compare* 35(4): 373–391.
Smith, Alan. 2010. *The influence of education on conflict and peace building.* Background paper prepared for the education for all global monitoring report 2011. Paris: UNESCO.
Smith, Alan, and Alan Robinson. 1997. *Education for mutual understanding: The initial statutory years.* Belfast: University of Ulster. Centre for the Study of Conflict.
Smith, Richard, and Philip Wexler (eds.). 1995. *After postmodernism: Education, politics and identity.* London: The Falmer Press.
Stewart, Frances. 2009. *Religion versus ethnicity as a source of mobilisation: Are there differences?* Britghton: Microcon.
Stojanovska, Vera, and Biljana Krsteska-Papic. 2010. Multicultural component in elementary education in the republic of Macedonia. *Practice and Theory in Systems of Education* 5(1): 27–38.
Tajfel, Henri (ed.). 2010. *Social identity and intergroup relations.* Cambridge: Cambridge University Press.
Tankersley, Dawn. 2011. Bombs or bilingual programmes? Dual-language immersion, transformative education and community building in Macedonia. *International Journal of Bilingual Education and Bilingualism* 4(2): 107–124.
Tawil, Sobhi, and Alexandra Harley (eds.). 2004. *Education, conflict and social cohesion.* Geneva: International Bureau of Education.
Taylor, Rupert. 2006. The Belfast agreement and the politics of consociationalism: A critique. *The Political Quarterly* 77(2): 217–226.
Taylor, Rupert (ed.). 2009. *Consociational theory: McGarry and O'Leary and the Northern Ireland conflict.* London: Routledge.
Tonge, Jonathan. 2004. *The new Northern Irish politics?* New York: Palgrave.
Tonge, Jonathan, and Jocelyn Evans. 2002. Party members and the Good Friday agreement in Northern Ireland. *Irish Political Studies* 17(2): 59–73.
Traboulsi, Fawwaz. 2007. *A history of modern Lebanon.* London: Pluto press.
Trajkovski, Ilo. 2003. The place and the role of civic education in the republic of Macedonia. *Journal of Social Science Education* 2: 1–7.
van der Leeuw-Roord, Joke. 2012. *A key to unlock the past. History education in Macedonia: An analysis of today, suggestions for the future.* Skopje: EuroClio.
Varshney, Ashutosh. 2003. *Ethnic conflict and civic life: Hindus and Muslims in India.* London: Yale University Press.

Vik, Ingrid. 2001. *Divided communities: A study of inter-ethnic relations and minority rights in Macedonia*. Oslo: The Norwegian Helsinki Committee.
Whimster, Sam (ed.). 2007. *The essential Weber: A reader*. New York: Routledge.
Wilmer, Franke. 2002. *The social construction of man, the state and war: Identity, conflict and violence in former Yugoslavia*. New York: Routledge.
Wolff, Stefan, and Christalla Yakinthou (eds.). 2012. *Conflict management in divided societies. Theories and practice*. London: Routledge.
Wylie, Ken. 2004. Citizenship identity and social inclusion: Lessons from Northern Ireland. *European Journal of Education* 39(2): 237–248.
Zajda, Joseph (ed.). 2010. In *Globalisation, ideology and education policy reforms*. Newyork:Springer.http://link.springer.com/book/10.1007%2F978-90-481-3524-0. Accessed 22 Apr 2014.
Zajda, Joseph, and Holger Daun (eds.). 2009. In *Global values education*. New York: Springer. http://www.springer.com/education+%26+language/book/978-90-481-2509-8. Accessed 22 Apr 2014.
Zajda, Joseph, and Macleans A. Geo-JaJa (eds.). 2010. In *The politics of education reforms*. New York: Springer. http://www.springer.com/education+%26+language/book/978-90-481-3217-1. Accessed 22 Apr 2014.
Ziadeh, Anna. 2006. *Sectarianism and intercommunal nation-building in Lebanon*. London: Hurst.

Conference and Research Papers

Bahous, Jocelyne. 1999. What language should a Lebanese child learn first? Paper presented at the conference on *Multilingualism and Multiculturalism in Lebanon*. Beirut, 3/12/1999.
Bashshour, Munir. 2005. History teaching and history textbooks in Lebanon. Paper presented at the conference on *Learning about the Other and Teaching for Tolerance in Muslim Majority Societies*. Istanbul: Centre for Values Education, 10/11/2005.
Comisso, Ellen. 2005. Now that the fighting in the Balkans is over, did we learn anything? A retrospective analysis of Yugoslavia's dissolution. Paper presented at the conference on *East European Studies*. Woodrow Wilson International Centre for Scholars, 20/04/2005.
Gallagher, Tony. 2002. Results of the consultation on the burns report. Paper presented to the Graduate School of Education, Queen's University Belfast, 6/12/2002.
Makdisi, Samir, and Richard Sadaka. 2003. The Lebanese civil war. Paper presented at the *Yale-World Bank Workshop on 'Case Studies on the Economics and Politics of Civil War,' April 13–14, 2002*. Yale University.
Petrova-Gjorgjeva, Emilija. 2010. Democratic society and moral education. Paper presented at the *World Conference on Educational Sciences*. Istanbul, Turkey, 6/05/2010.

Smith, Alan. 1999. Education and the peace process in Northern Ireland. Paper presented at the *Annual Conference of the American Education Research Association*. Montreal.

Terc, Mandy. 2006. Iconisation and linguistic ideologies in Lebanon's Makassed schools. *Unpublished research paper*. American University of Beirut.

Vetterlein, Merle. 2006. The influence of the Ohrid framework agreement on the educational policy of the republic of Macedonia. Paper presented at the *8th Annual Kokkalis Graduate Student Workshop*. Cambridge, 2–3/02/2006.

Voss, Christian. 2004. The Macedonian standard language: Tito-Yugoslav experiment or symbol for 'Great Macedonian' ethnic inclusion? Paper presented at the conference on *Language and the Future of Europe: Ideologies, Policies and Practices*. University of Southampton.

Wolff, Stefan. 2011. Liberal consociationalism in theory and practice: Power sharing and territorial self-governance. Unpublished research paper, http://www.stefanwolff.com/files/LibConTalkPaper.pdf. Accessed 24 Apr 2014.

Web Pages

Department of Education Northern Ireland. Independent schools list. http://www.deni.gov.uk/index/schools-and-infrastructure-2/schools-management/10-types_of_school-nischools_pg/schools_-_types_of_school-independent-schools.htm. Accessed 12 June 2014.

Department of Education Northern Ireland. Timeline on the development of transfer policy. http://www.deni.gov.uk/index/schools-and-infrastructure-2/admission-and-transport/6-post-primary-transfer-and-wider-reform.htm. Accessed 30 May 2014.

Dorrington, Eric M. 2010. Lebanese historical memory and the perception of national identity through school textbooks. Http://Www.Scribd.Com/Doc/27022561/Lebanese-Historical-Memory-and-the-Perception-of-National-Identity-through-School-Textbooks. Accessed 24 Apr 2014.

Erlich, Reuven, and Yoram Kahati. Hezbollah as a case study of the battle for hearts and minds. Intelligence and terrorism information centre at the Israel intelligence heritage & commemoration centre. http://www.terrorism-info.org.il/data/pdf/PDF_07_030_2.pdf. Accessed 24 Apr 2014.

Hazzard, Chris. Governors board association support for Esa welcome. http://www.sinnfein.ie/contents/28964. Accessed 15 Apr 2014.

Moukahal, Rehab. Values and experience. Lebanese association for educational studies. http://www.laes.org/_publications.php?lang=en&id=13. Accessed 24 Apr 2014.

Nansen Dialogue Centre. Nansen model for integrated education. http://www.nansen-dialogue.net/index.php?option=com_content&view=article&id=475&Itemid=549. Accessed 12 Oct 2013.

State Statistical Office. MakStat database. http://makstat.stat.gov.mk/pxweb-2007bazi/Dialog/Saveshow.asp. Accessed 27 May 2014.

Sutton, Malcolm. An index of deaths from the conflict in Ireland. CAIN web service. http://cain.ulst.ac.uk/sutton/tables/Status_Summary.html. Accessed 20 Feb 2014.

United Nations International Children's Emergency Fund. At a glance: Lebanon. http://www.unicef.org/infobycountry/lebanon_statistics.html. Accessed 22 May 2014.

United States Agency for International Development. Interethnic integration in education project. http://www.usaid.gov/macedonia/fact-sheets/interethnic-integration-education-project. Accessed 3 Dec 2013.

The World Bank. Population (total). http://data.worldbank.org/indicator/SP.POP.TOTL. Accessed 27 May 2014.

The World Bank. Public spending on education total (% of GDP). http://data.worldbank.org/indicator/SE.XPD.TOTL.GD.ZS. Accessed 11 Jun 2014.

The World Bank. School enrolment, primary (percentage net). http://data.worldbank.org/indicator/SE.PRM.NENR?page=2. Accessed 6 Dec 2014.

Index

A
Abouchedid, Kamal, 69, 134
Abu Assali, Munir, 128, 129, 134, 163, 164
Accra, Adonis, 165, 166
Akar, Bassel, 135, 164, 166, 181
Akenson, Donald, 77
Albanian Language. *See* Language Teaching
Anderson, Benedict, 194
Arabic. *See* Language Teaching
Arab-Israeli conflict, 68
Arab Spring, 10, 76
Area Planning. *See* Northern Ireland
Arlow, Michael, 168–71, 173

B
Barsalou, Judy, 127
Bar-Tal, Daniel, 44
Barton, Keith, 124, 137, 140
Bashshour, Mounir, 129, 134, 232, 233, 245
Bell, John, 78, 125, 139

Beydoun, Ahmad, 38, 135
Bilingual Education. *See* Language Teaching
Bizri, Fida, 199, 201
Bourdieu, Pierre, 41, 49

C
Chartouni, Charles, 199
Chehab, Fouad, 69
Citizenship, 2, 3, 12, 14, 15, 46, 68, 70, 75, 77, 87, 99, 104, 105, 107, 159–81, 199, 218, 228, 229, 236, 279, 280, 282
Citizenship education
  approaches, 161, 162, 167
  Lebanon, 159, 162–8, 181
  Macedonia, 175–81
  Northern Ireland, 168–75
  political function, 159–65, 167–9, 171–3, 175, 178, 180, 181
Civic education. *See* Citizenship education
Cole, Elizabeth, 127

Community Relations, Equality and
    Diversity Policy. *See* Citizenship
    education
Conflict
    conflict resolution, 4, 17, 30–9, 45,
        48, 163, 164, 173, 179, 231
    ethnic, 2, 9, 28, 29, 43, 103, 104,
        259
    psychological components, 30, 45
    transformation, 17, 146 (*See also*
        (reconciliation)
Connolly, Paul, 6, 48, 49
Consociation, 1–4, 10–18, 23–50, 61,
        62, 66, 67, 69, 71, 74–7, 86, 87,
        89, 90, 96, 102–5, 107, 123,
        133, 135, 145–7, 159, 165, 178,
        180, 181, 193, 194, 201, 208,
        209, 211, 215–17, 227, 228,
        236–8, 252, 253, 256, 263–5,
        279–83. *See also* power-sharing
    characteristics, 25, 31, 48, 166, 230
    consociational education systems, 3,
        4, 15, 16, 18, 48, 227, 228,
        281–3
Contact Hypothesis, 15, 38, 230
    (*See also* separation)
    critics, 36–8
    factors facilitating establishment, 33
    paradox, 36, 162, 282
Coulter, Colin, 37
Council for Irish-Medium Education
    (CNaG). *See* Language Teaching
Craig, James, 80, 202
Cultural, 4, 10, 28, 30, 31, 33, 37,
        40, 41, 46, 47, 63, 64, 68, 69,
        73, 74, 82, 90, 91, 93–6, 103,
        104, 124, 130, 161, 169, 172,
        173, 175, 177, 181, 195,
        197–200, 202, 203, 205, 206,
        209, 215, 217, 228, 229, 236,
        248, 253
Cupi, Recep, 214, 262

Curriculum
    citizenship education (*See*
        Citizenship education)
    History Education (*See* history)
    languages (*See* Language Teaching)

D
Darby, John, 79
Davies, Lynn, 46, 48, 49, 180
Decentralisation, 11, 35, 96, 103,
        212, 254–6. *See also* Macedonia
Democratic Unionist Party, 86
Demography
    Lebanon, 4–6, 8
    Macedonia, 4, 5, 8, 9
    Northern Ireland, 4–8
Diab, Rula, 198
Directorate for Development and
        Promotion of Education in the
        Languages of the Communities,
        213, 214
Divided societies, 1, 3, 8, 17, 18,
        23–50, 89, 107, 124–7, 146,
        147, 159–62, 181, 193–7, 212,
        216–218, 227–32, 246, 264,
        265, 281–3
Donnelly, Caitlin, 231
Dupuy, Kendra, 44

E
Easton, David, 42, 43, 49
Education
    autonomy, 10, 13, 33, 94
    citizenship education (*See*
        Citizenship education)
    consociational education systems, 3,
        4, 15, 16, 18, 48, 227, 228,
        281–3
    contribution to conflict, 13, 17, 44
    contribution to reconciliation, 246

curriculum, 75, 85, 168, 176–8
education reform, 2, 3, 11, 12, 14,
  15, 61, 68, 87, 104, 107;
  Belfast Agreement, 37, 78, 87;
  Ohrid Agreement, 1, 2, 10, 11,
  123, 141, 143, 176, 208; Taif
  Agreement, 1, 11, 62, 87
history education (*See* History
  Education)
language (*See* Language Teaching)
mass education, 40
political function, 1, 2, 3, 12, 14,
  16, 46, 50, 77, 78, 87, 96,
  105, 206, 217, 227, 238, 280
separate schools, 15, 16, 33, 44, 45,
  47, 48, 78, 80, 81, 95, 107,
  227–30, 240, 242, 243, 249,
  250, 258, 264–6, 280–2 (*See
  also* separation)
shared education, 4, 39, 139, 242,
  248–51, 253, 260, 264, 282,
  283 (*See also* Northern Ireland)
structure (*See* separation)
Education and Skills Authority, 88,
  252
Education for Mutual Understanding.
  See Citizenship education
El-Amine, Adnan, 165–7, 236, 237
English Language. *See* Language
  Teaching
Entitlement Framework, 88, 249

F
Federal People's Republic of
  Yugoslavia
  1974 constitution, 96
  Monarchy, 34, 90–2
Finlay, Andrew, 37, 38
Former Yugoslav Republic of
  Macedonia. *See* Macedonia
Frayha, Nemer, 128–2, 164, 168

French Language. *See* Language
  Teaching
Future party, 76

G
Gallagher, Tony, 45, 229, 264, 282
Gellner, Ernest, 194
Green, Andy, 40

H
Hanf, Theodor, 9, 38, 43, 63
Harik, Judith, 72
Hariri, Rafic, 76, 236
Healey, Julie, 48
Hewstone, Miles, 38
History Education
  approaches, 125, 126, 136, 279
  conditions for reform, 126
  contribution to conflict, 133
  Lebanon, 5, 12, 46, 62–77,
    127–36, 146, 147, 162–8
  Macedonia, 5, 12, 46, 89–105,
    140–6, 147, 175–80
  Northern Ireland, 5, 12, 14, 46,
    77–89, 136–40, 146, 147,
    168–75
  political function, 123, 125, 126, 147
  textbooks, 11, 14, 46, 75
Hizbollah, 72, 74, 76, 135, 163, 237,
  733
Hobsbawm, Eric, 194
Höpken, Wolfgang, 93, 96, 97, 126,
  146
Hudson, Michael, 75
Hughes, Joanne, 24, 229, 230

I
Identity
  ethnic, 2

Identity (*cont.*)
  internalisation, 25, 29, 43
  marker, 4, 24, 25, 29, 61, 62, 69, 78, 86, 99, 106, 218
  reformulation, 30, 99
  saliency, 25–7, 37
Immersion Education. *See* Language Teaching
Integration, 11, 17, 30, 35, 36, 39, 47, 67, 79, 84, 87, 168, 175, 212, 213, 229, 242, 243, 245, 246, 248, 259, 261, 262, 265, 281, 282
  approaches, 30, 35
Interethnic Integration in Education Project, 261, 262
Irish Language. *See* Language Teaching
Irish-medium Education. *See* Language Teaching

J
Janmaat, Germ, 231
Jordanovski, Nikola, 140
Jumblatt, Walid, 127, 133

K
Kataeb, 133
Kerr, David, 160
Kerr, Michael, v, 34
Kitson, Alison, 136
Knudsen, Are, 76

L
Language Teaching
  approaches, 196, 197, 206, 246, 255
  contribution to conflict, 261
  immersion education, 205
  Lebanon, 193, 194, 197–202, 207, 216–8
  Macedonia, 193, 194, 207–18
  Northern Ireland, 193, 194, 202–7, 216–18
  political function, 193–9, 202, 204, 206, 207, 213–18
Lebanese Forces, 133
Lebanon
  civil war; 1975–1989 civil war, 6, 130, 133, 198; 1958 war, 69
  confessional political system, 6, 63, 65 (*See also* power-sharing)
  curriculum; citizenship education, 3, 12, 14–15, 68, 75, 104, 107, 165, 229; history education, 12, 14, 46, 123, 127–36, 146–7; language teaching, 201–2
  history, 127–36
  identities, 14
  Mandate, 62–5, 69, 134
  National Pact, 10, 34, 65–9, 73, 74
  Taif Agreement, 1, 11, 32, 74, 129, 162, 163, 165, 232, 281 (*See also* Peace Agreement)
Leenders, Wiel, 160
Lijphart, Arend, 31–4, 38, 47, 265, 281
Local and Global Citizenship. *See* Citizenship education
Lynn, Robert, 79, 180

M
Macedonia
  2001 conflict, 11, 28, 102, 105, 208, 254
  curriculum; citizenship education, 107, 175–80; history education, 12, 140–6; language teaching, 196, 201, 202, 218, 259

decentralisation, 96–8, 254–6 (*See also* Decentralisation)
education funding, 11, 32, 95, 99, 107, 177
history, 3, 11, 14, 46, 143
identities, 14, 15, 32, 91, 106, 181, 262
Ohrid Agreement, 10, 11, 14, 34, 44, 48, 102–4, 123, 141, 232, 280
separation, 10, 15, 38, 254–64
Strategy for Integrated Education, 14, 178–9, 213, 214, 216, 259–64, 282
Macedonian Language. *See* Language Teaching
Magill, Clare, 48, 139, 140
McCrudden, Christopher, 3, 9, 36
McCully, Alan, 124, 126, 137
McGarry, John, 11, 31, 33, 34, 36, 87
McGuinness, Martin, 88, 170, 204
McIvor, Basil, 83
Messara, Antoine, 134
Methodology, 199
Mother Tongue. *See* Language Teaching
Mozaik kindergartens. *See* Macedonia
Murad, Abd-al-Rahim, 131, 132

N

Nansen schools. *See* Macedonia
Nasser, Ramzi, 69, 134
Nationalism, 25, 27, 62, 66, 67, 69, 71–3, 81, 89, 92–4, 97, 99, 101, 124, 160, 164, 175, 194, 207
Niens, Ulrike, 174
Northern Ireland
  Belfast Agreement, 1, 15, 78, 86–8, 168 (*See also* Peace Agreement)
  controlled schools, 79–81, 136, 174, 239, 245
  curriculum; citizenship education, 3, 46, 104, 107, 168–75, 177–81; Education for Mutual Understanding, 84, 169; history education, 12, 46, 107, 136–40, 146, 147, 279; language teaching, 218
  history, 14, 138
  identities, 6
  integrated schools, 174, 231, 242, 244, 248, 264
  Irish-medium schools, 203, 239
  maintained schools, 79, 81, 83, 84, 86, 136, 203, 240
  11-plus test, 88, 170, 239, 252, 265, 280
  separation, 10, 174, 227–9
  shared education, 4, 39, 251, 260, 264
  shared schools, 83, 262
  Sunningdale Agreement, 10, 83
  Troubles, 9, 28, 78, 82–6, 136, 146, 203
Northern Ireland Council for Integrated Education, 242

O

O'Duibh, Micheal, 204–6
O'Leary, Brendan, 3, 9, 11, 31, 33–6, 87
Organisation for Security and Cooperation in Europe, 178, 213, 257
Osler, Audrey, 160

P

Palestine Liberation Organisation (PLO), 70, 71
Palestinian refugees, 70

Peace Agreement
  Belfast Agreement, 1, 2, 10, 11, 14, 35, 44, 107
  Ohrid Agreement, 1, 10, 11, 14, 34, 35, 44, 107, 279
  Taif Agreement, 1, 11, 32, 35, 46, 48, 62, 74, 75, 77, 86, 87, 128–30, 141, 162, 163, 165, 168, 199, 202, 232, 233, 236, 238, 281
Personal Development and Mutual Understanding. *See* Citizenship education
Petrova-Gjorjeva, Emilija, 176, 177
power-sharing
  autonomy, 1, 10, 11, 31
  centripetal, 37
  complex, 35, 39
  corporate, 10, 11
  executive power-sharing, 1, 10, 31
  liberal, 10, 11
  proportionality, 1
  veto, 1, 10, 31
Prejudice, 16, 48, 49, 83, 98, 138, 139, 169, 172, 177, 178, 229–31, 247, 249, 264, 283

R
Reconciliation, 4, 11, 12, 15–17, 30, 36, 38, 39, 44, 85, 89, 107, 123, 125–8, 134, 135, 140, 146, 147, 169, 172, 173, 179, 227, 230, 231, 240, 246, 254, 279–83
Reilly, Jacqueline, 174
Robinson, Peter, 169, 245, 246
Roma, 8, 62, 80, 100, 143, 177, 193, 212, 214–18, 258, 259. *See also* Language Teaching

S
Sabani, Nora, 177, 254, 255, 261, 263
Salibi, Kamal, 67, 147

Segregation, 33, 38, 47, 84, 196, 211, 216, 217, 228, 229, 251, 257, 265
Seixas, Peter, 124, 125, 137
Separation
  approaches, 246, 255, 283
  contribution to conflict, 17
  contribution to reconciliation, 16, 38, 127, 227, 230, 231, 240, 246, 254
  Lebanon, 10, 17, 38, 104, 227, 228, 232–8, 245, 248, 260
  Macedonia, 10, 15, 17, 38, 178, 216, 227, 228, 230, 232, 254–64
  Northern Ireland, 10, 38, 45, 104, 227–32, 238–51, 260
  political function, 2, 227, 238
Serbian. *See* Language Teaching
Shaaban, Kassim A., 199
shared education, 4, 39, 139, 242, 248–51, 253, 260, 264, 282, 283. *See also* Northern Ireland
Shirlow, Peter, 37
Shuayb, Maha, 161, 162, 164, 167, 237
Sinn Féin, 86, 170, 248, 252, 253
Skuttnabb-Kangas, Tove, 195
Smith, Alan, 24, 47, 86, 169, 180, 181
Social Cohesion, 43, 48, 49, 69, 104, 125, 126, 128, 147, 159, 162, 164, 165, 168, 171, 172, 174, 227, 229, 231, 234, 236, 240, 279, 282
Social Identity Theory, 25–7
Socialisation, 13, 40–2, 48, 75, 89, 106, 125, 128, 147, 161, 180, 194
Starkey, Hugh, 160
Stereotypes, 24, 26, 29, 40, 41, 98, 197, 210, 229

Strategy for Integrated Education. *See* Macedonia
Subject, 16, 17, 45, 46, 67, 68, 70, 73, 86, 90, 93, 99, 107, 129, 137, 138, 142, 161–3, 167, 168, 171–4, 176–9, 194, 196, 198–201, 205, 211, 213–16, 261. *See also* curriculum
national subject, 16, 45–8, 70, 73, 93, 99, 107, 177, 194, 199–201
Syria, 10, 35, 62–4, 66, 74–6, 132, 135

T
Tajfel, Henri, 25, 27
Tawil, Sobhi, 161
Territorial Autonomy, 11, 67, 93, 103, 175. *See also* Decentralisation
Todorov, Nikola, 213, 214
Turkish Language. *See* Language Teaching
Turner, John, 25

U
Ulster-Scots. *See* Language Teaching
United Nations Children's Emergency Fund, 179, 257

V
Varshney, Ashutosh, 38
Veugelers, Helene, 160
Vlach. *See* Language Teaching

W
Wylie, Ken, 168, 169

Y
Yugoslavia, 89–98, 105, 106, 141, 175, 208

Z
Zenkolli, Veton, 211, 257, 262, 263

The manufacturer's authorised representative in the EU is Springer Nature Customer Service Centre GmbH, Europaplatz 3, 69115 Heidelberg, Germany. If you have any concerns regarding our products, please contact ProductSafety@springernature.com

Printed and bound by CPI Group (UK) Ltd, Croydon, CR0 4YY

23/03/2026

02076662-0011